PROSTITUTION AND EIGHTEENTH-CENTURY
CULTURE: SEX, COMMERCE AND MORALITY

The Body, Gender and Culture

Series Editor: Lynn Botelho

Titles in this Series

1 Courtly Indian Women in Late Imperial India
Angma Dey Jhala

2 Paracelsus's Theory of Embodiment: Conception and Gestation in Early Modern Europe
Amy Eisen Cislo

3 The Prostitute's Body: Rewriting Prostitution in Victorian Britain
Nina Attwood

4 Old Age and Disease in Early Modern Medicine
Daniel Schäfer

5 The Life of Madame Necker: Sin, Redemption and the Parisian Salon
Sonja Boon

6 Stays and Body Image in London: The Staymaking Trade, 1680–1810
Lynn Sorge-English

Forthcoming Titles

The Aboriginal Male in the Enlightenment World
Shino Konishi

Blake, Gender and Culture
Helen Bruder and Tristanne Connolly (eds)

Sex, Identity and Hermaphrodites in Iberia, 1500–1800
Richard Cleminson and Francisco Vázquez García

PROSTITUTION AND EIGHTEENTH-CENTURY CULTURE: SEX, COMMERCE AND MORALITY

EDITED BY

Ann Lewis and Markman Ellis

LONDON AND NEW YORK

First published 2012 by Pickering & Chatto (Publishers) Limited

Published 2016 by Routledge
2 Park Square, Milton Park, Abingdon, Oxon OX14 4RN
711 Third Avenue, New York, NY 10017, USA

Routledge is an imprint of the Taylor & Francis Group, an informa business

© Taylor & Francis 2012
© Ann Lewis and Markman Ellis 2012

All rights reserved, including those of translation into foreign languages. No part of this book may be reprinted or reproduced or utilised in any form or by any electronic, mechanical, or other means, now known or hereafter invented, including photocopying and recording, or in any information storage or retrieval system, without permission in writing from the publishers.

Notice:
Product or corporate names may be trademarks or registered trademarks, and are used only for identification and explanation without intent to infringe.

BRITISH LIBRARY CATALOGUING IN PUBLICATION DATA

Prostitution and eighteenth-century culture: sex, commerce and morality. – (The body, gender and culture)
1. Prostitution in literature. 2. Prostitutes in literature. 3. English literature – 18th century – History and criticism.
I. Series II. Lewis, Ann Marie. III. Ellis, Markman.
820.9'3538-dc22

ISBN-13: 978-1-84893-134-3 (hbk)

Typeset by Pickering & Chatto (Publishers) Limited

CONTENTS

Acknowledgements   vii
List of Contributors   ix
List of Figures and Tables   xiii

Introduction: Venal Bodies – Prostitutes and Eighteenth-Century Culture
  – *Markman Ellis and Ann Lewis*   1
Part I: (Auto)Biographical and Classificatory Fictions: Madams,
  Courtesans, Whores
  1 Classifying the Prostitute in Eighteenth-Century France – *Ann Lewis*   17
  2 In Her Own Words: An Eighteenth-Century Madam Tells Her Story
    – *Kathryn Norberg*   33
  3 'All the World Knows Her Storie': Aphra Behn and the Duchess
    of Mazarin – *Claudine van Hensbergen*   45
  4 Marie Petit's *Persian Adventure* (1705–8): The Eastward Travels of a
    French 'Concubine' – *Katherine MacDonald*   59
  5 'A First-Rate Whore': Prostitution and Empowerment in the Early
    Eighteenth Century – *Lena Olsson*   71
Part II: Visibility and Theatricality: Fiction, Image and Performance
  6 Prostitutes and Erotic Performances in Eighteenth-Century Paris
    – *Thomas Wynn*   87
  7 Visible Prostitutes: Mandeville, Hogarth and 'A Harlot's Progress'
    – *Charlotte Grant*   99
  8 The Narrative Sources of *Candide*'s Paquette – *Edward Langille*   115
  9 The Prostitute as Neo-Manager: Sade's *Juliette* and the New Spirit
    of Capitalism – *Olivier Delers*   127
Part III: The Magdalen House: Marriage, Motherhood, Social Reintegration
  10 Figuring the London Magdalen House: Mercantilist Hospital,
    Sentimental Asylum or Proto-Evangelical Penitentiary?
    – *Mary Peace*   141
  11 Mothers and Others: Sexuality and Maternity in *The Histories of Some
    of The Penitents in the Magdalen-House* (1760) – *Jennie Batchelor*   157

Part IV: Wider Perspectives: Constructing the Prostitute in Social History
   12 Making a Living by 'Indecency': Life Stories of Prostitutes in Christiania, Norway – *Johanne Bergkvist*   171
   13 Male Prostitution and the Emergence of the Modern Sexual System: Eighteenth-Century London – *Randolph Trumbach*   185

Notes   203
Index   241

ACKNOWLEDGEMENTS

This project began life, under another title, at Queen Mary University of London, at the inaugural meeting of the Centre for Eighteenth-Century Studies. The editors would like to thank their departments for their support of the project: the Department of English at Queen Mary University of London, the Department of European Cultures and Languages and School of Arts at Birkbeck, University of London. We would also like to thank the Leverhulme Trust, which made much of the work on the initial conference possible (through the Early Career Fellowship awarded to Ann Lewis). Many people have graciously given time and advice in bringing this project to completion, not least the speakers and audience at the 'Venal Bodies' conference at the Institute of Germanic and Romance Studies at the School of Advanced Studies of the University of London. The editors would particularly like to thank: Rebecca Beasley, Andrew Block, Emma Clery, Megan Hiatt and little Leo Joseph Block, who arrived just in time to enliven the proofs of this volume.

LIST OF CONTRIBUTORS

Jennie Batchelor is Reader in Eighteenth-Century Studies at the University of Kent. She has published widely on prostitution, material culture and women's writing in the long eighteenth century. Her most recent monograph is *Women's Work: Labour, Gender, Authorship, 1750–1830* (2010). With Megan Hiatt, she is editor of *The Histories of Some of the Penitents in the Magdalen-House* (2007). She is currently working on a book about women's magazines of the Romantic era, provisionally titled *Guilty and Other Pleasures*.

Johanne Bergkvist has an MA in history from the University of Oslo (2008), where she specialized in social history and marginalized groups. She works in the historical section of Oslo City Archives, and is currently working on a documentation project of the Norwegian Romany people.

Olivier Delers is Assistant Professor of French at the University of Richmond in Richmond, Virginia. He has published articles on Crébillon *fils*, Graffigny, Diderot, and Sade and is currently working on a book project titled *The Other Rise of the Novel: Reading Economic Behavior in Eighteenth-Century French Fiction*.

Markman Ellis is Professor of Eighteenth-Century Studies in the Department of English at Queen Mary University of London. He is the author of *The Politics of Sensibility* (1996), *The History of Gothic Fiction* (2000) and *The Coffee House* (2004).

Charlotte Grant has taught in Cambridge and London and writes on literature and visual culture in eighteenth-century Britain, and on contemporary art. She co-edited *Women, Writing and the Public Sphere, 1700–1830* (2001), and *Imagined Interiors: Representing the Domestic Interior Since the Renaissance* (2006) She has also published on eighteenth-century women poets, literature and the domestic interior, and womens' involvement in the Society of Arts.

Claudine van Hensbergen completed her doctoral thesis, 'The Courtesan's Narrative in English Literary Culture, 1660–1730' at the University of Oxford in 2010. She teaches English literature of the seventeenth and eighteenth centuries, and has published articles on both the eighteenth-century letter and Aphra Behn in addition to co-editing a special issue of the journal 'Eighteenth-Century Life'. She is currently a postdoctoral research assistant on a collaborative project between the University of York and Tate Britain, 'Court, Country, City: British Art, 1660–1735'.

Edward Langille is Professor of French at St. Francis Xavier University, Nova Scotia, Canada. He has recently published *Candide, second partie* (1760) and *Candide en Dannemarc* (1764); as well as a series of articles in which he identifies the sources of Voltaire's *Candide*, most notably, Fielding's *Tom Jones*, through the 1750 French translation of that work known as *L'Enfant trouvé*.

Ann Lewis is Lecturer in French at Birkbeck, University of London. Her research interests include the topic of sensibility, theories of reception and reader-response, and word-and-image relations in eighteenth-century French literature and culture. Her book *Sensibility, Reading and Illustration: Spectacles and Signs in Graffigny, Marivaux and Rousseau* was published by Legenda in July 2009, and her current book project, started during the tenure of her Leverhulme Early Career Fellowship, focuses on the representation of the figure of the prostitute in eighteenth-century France, adopting an interdisciplinary perspective.

Katherine MacDonald is Senior Lecturer in the Department of French at University College London. She is the author of *Biography in Early Modern France 1540–1630: Forms and Functions* (2007), as well as of articles on various topics in sixteenth and seventeenth-century French literature and cultural history. She is currently working on a scholarly biography of the French traveller Marie Petit (1673–172?), which sets her journey to Persia and back in the context of Franco-Persian diplomatic and commercial relations in the early eighteenth century.

Kathryn Norberg, Professor of History, teaches women's history and social history in the History and Women's Studies Departments of the University of California, Los Angeles. Between 2000 and 2005 she was co-editor of *Signs: Journal of Women in Society and Culture,* one of the oldest and more prestigious journals of academic feminism. Recent publications include *Furnishing the Eighteenth Century: What Furniture Can Tell Us about the European and American Past*, co-edited with Dena Goodman (2007) and 'Salon as Stage: Courtesan/Actresses and their Homes in Eighteenth-Century Paris', in *Architectural Space in Eighteenth-Century Europe*, edited by Denise Amy Baxter and Meredith Miller (2010). In progress is a manuscript entitled *Prostitution in Seventeenth-Century France,* which deals with mercenary sex in Paris and the provinces from approximately 1622 to 1730, and a book based upon the journal of the brothel madam Dhosmont analysed in this volume's article

Lena Olsson is a researcher in English Literature at Lund University, Sweden. She wrote her PhD thesis on John Cleland's *Memoirs of a Woman of Pleasure* and is the editor of Cleland's abridged *Fanny Hill* and the anonymous *The Genuine History of* [...] *Sally Salisbury* (2004). Other publications include an article in Patsy S. Fowler and Alan Jackson, *Launching Fanny Hill: Essays on the Novel and Its Influences* (2003). She is at present working on a study of the whore biography genre.

Mary Peace is Senior Lecturer in Eighteenth-Century Studies in the English Department at Sheffield Hallam University. She is director of the Hallam Corvey Project (http://extra.shu.ac.uk/corvey/), and editor of the *Corvey Women Writers on the Web* journal. Her research interests include the figure of the prostitute in eighteenth-century sentimental literature and its relationship to the paradoxical development of sentimental discourse over the century, and Romantic-era writing by women.

Randolph Trumbach is Professor of History, Baruch College and the Graduate Center, City University of New York. Trumbach studies the eighteenth-century origins of the modern western culture of the last three hundred years, concentrating on the family, sexuality, and religion. He has published *The Rise of the Egalitarian Family: Aristocratic Kinship and Domestic Relations in Eighteenth-Century England* (1978) and *Sex and the Gender Revolution, Vol. 1: Heterosexuality and the Third Gender in Enlightenment London* (1998). *Vol. 2: The Origins of Modern Homosexuality*, is forthcoming and will summarize and revise his twenty published papers on the subject. He is currently engaged in research on books of devotion in seventeenth and eighteenth-century England.

Thomas Wynn is Senior Lecturer in French at Durham University. He is a specialist in eighteenth-century theatre and libertine writings, and has published on Sade, Voltaire and erotic theatre. His current research interests include authorship, violence and metatheatre.

LIST OF FIGURES AND TABLES

Figure 3.1: Jacob-Ferdinand Voet, *Hortense Mancini, Duchess of Mazarin*
   (*c.* 1670)   52
Figure 7.1: William Hogarth, *A Harlot's Progress, Plate 1* (1732)   101
Figure 8.1: Henry Fielding, trans. Pierre Antoine de La Place, *Histoire de
   Tom Jones, ou l'enfant trouvé* (London [Paris]: chez Jean Nourse, 1750)   117

Table 1.1: Rétif de la Bretonne's taxonomies of prostitution in two editions
   of *Le Pornographe*   25

INTRODUCTION: VENAL BODIES – PROSTITUTES AND EIGHTEENTH-CENTURY CULTURE

Markman Ellis and Ann Lewis

Prostitutes, and prostitution, were notoriously visible in eighteenth-century European culture, a visibility that was amply reflected in political and cultural discourses. Commonly understood as an index of the moral temperature of society, the perceived increase in prostitution in the major cities of Europe offered its own conclusions. Moral reformers, who considered prostitutes a 'common nuisance', were numerous. In London, the Rev. William Dodd, writing in the *Public Ledger* in 1760, discovered in prostitution a telling sign of public vice:

> Impudence no longer courts the shade. Let any man walk up a certain street leading from the Strand, and he will see numbers of unhappy prostitutes in the broad daylight, plying their miserable trade! Cannot this be prevented? – If not, where is decency? If it can, where are our magistrates? They are not ignorant of these things.[1]

Pierre Jean Grosley, a French academician, in his *A Tour to London* (1772), reported that in 1765, prostitutes, or 'Women of the Town', as he called them,

> were more numerous than at Paris, and have more liberty and effrontery than at Rome itself. About night-fall they range themselves in a file in the foot-paths of all the great streets, in companies of five or six, most of them dressed very genteelly. The low-taverns serve them as a retreat, to receive their gallants in: in those houses there is always a room set apart for this purpose. Whole rows of them accost passengers in the broad day-light; and above all, foreigners.[2]

Similar observations were made in France, where moral indignation was sometimes combined with a lucid awareness of the prostitute's plight. Louis-Sébastien Mercier observed in his *Tableau de Paris* (1781–8) that:

> the scandal of *filles publiques* is taken too far in the capital. Contempt for good morals ought not to be so visible, so flagrant. Modesty, and public decency should be respected more. How can an honest but poor paterfamilias hope to preserve his young daughter innocent and intact when she reaches the age of the passions, when

she sees an elegantly dressed prostitute attacking men, parading her vice before them, ostentatious in her debauchery, and even, protected by the laws, benefiting from her unbridled emancipation. ... And what inspires a truly profound horror, is the fact that if prostitution were suddenly to stop, twenty thousand *filles* would die of penury, the employment of this unfortunate sex being inadequate here to provide her with food, or maintain her.[3]

In both London and Paris, in provincial cities in both France and England, and even more broadly in Europe, the public visibility of prostitution, whether in the street or in the enclosed spaces of the theatre, tavern and brothel, ensured that prostitution was central to moral debate on sexual behaviour in the period.

Prostitution can be defined as sexual activity undertaken for money or some other remuneration. Its precise meaning is hard to pin down in this period, whether in moral, legal or practical terms, and problems of definition are interrogated throughout this volume: for example through the examination of explicit attempts at classification on the part of French writers (Lewis), the contested notion of the 'venal woman' in the court case of a French courtesan-diplomat (MacDonald) or the use of other terms such as 'vagrancy' and 'indecency' to suggest prostitution within Norwegian court records (Bergkvist). Nonetheless, the visible prevalence of prostitution suggests that some general notion of sex work was widely understood across society. The scandal of prostitution in eighteenth-century culture was exactly its visibility in urban spaces: especially noticed in the prostitutes' distinct and particular modes of public interaction. The scene of prostitution – vulgar, sexual, deviant, boundary-crossing – undermined or contravened the established ideology of gender that championed a chaste and domestic femininity, both in England and France. As a result, prostitutes were the focus of intense debate in competing reformist discourses arguing for the regulation of public cultures of the street.

Tony Henderson's study of the lived experience of prostitution in mid-eighteenth-century London, derived from close analysis of the lowest levels of court and judicial records, show that women arrested for offences related to prostitution were most often born into poverty, undereducated, associated with textile and fashion trades, and had been born in London and the provinces. For most, prostitution was not the sole source of their income, but took its place alongside respectable employment, reception of charity and petty crime. These findings correspond closely to the situation in France, according to Erica-Marie Benabou's survey of different types of prostitution in eighteenth-century Paris, largely based on police records.[4] In London, most did not work in brothels, but solicited on the street: they were more numerous where customers were more numerous, such as around the docks, and in centers of entertainment, such as the West End and Covent Garden. As Henderson concludes:

> Prostitutes were not therefore geographically separated from the mass of the city's population. Nor were they separated socially. They walked the same streets, drank at the same public houses and gin-shops, frequented the same parks, and in many cases lived in the same houses as Londoners of most, if not all, social classes.[5]

However prostitution is defined, it was always more than an act of mercenary sex. The event of prostitution in the eighteenth century was an extended performance, not simply confined to the act of fornication itself: as the written literary and polemic evidence suggests, it had its own spatial and temporal frame. In this sense, prostitution may be said to have a sexual dimension, and an economic one, but also a social one, and was constituted as the sum of all the parts of this performance. Analysis of prostitution needs to pay attention to all these parts. In the case of 'public' prostitution, the performance often began in the street, when the client encountered the prostitute ('the pick-up'). The prostitute was herself already acting up, performing being a prostitute in the street: loud, vulgar, impolite, breaching established habits of manners by accosting male clients as they walked past. Prostitution in the space of the street was occasioned with a clamor and gendered boundary-crossing not met elsewhere (except perhaps the theatre). It is here that the prostitution event performance begins. In this performance, the prostitute acts out 'being-a-prostitute': in doing this she (and although it was normally she, it was not always) contravenes and subverts all the approved modes of behavior of normative gender roles for women: passive politeness, public invisibility, sexual submissiveness, social domesticity, linguistic refinement. While the gendered discourse on manners inscribed certain forms of behavior as polite, domestic and feminine, the prostitute acted out of this expectation. It is this sense that sustains the heroic reading of the prostitute as a wild woman, a rebel against repressive social orthodoxy. In addition, in the prostitution event, the client acts out 'being-a-client', a situation with its own repertoire of received narratives: the duped country-man, the tempted drunk, the defrauded innocent, the wastrel libertine, the frustrated virgin. Received narratives of prostitution were in this way relentlessly recycled by popular culture, and repurposed in high culture, in novels, plays and visual culture. In their structuring of the cultural imaginary, such narrative stereotypes were fed back into real-life behaviour and perceptions of reality, as is shown in this volume by Kathryn Norberg's analysis of the use of libertine narrative conventions in the autobiography of a Parisian brothel madam of the mid-eighteenth century. The prostitution performance continues on various stages: diversely, a back room of a public house or coffee-house, a dark corner of an alleyway or street, under a bridge, in a carriage, or in the self-consciously staged environment of a brothel, bagnio or hummum, or in their own lodgings nearby. Each stage of the performance has at its centre an act of sexual activity ('the sex'), which is polymorphous in its variety, and diversely imagined as climactic, deflationary or violent. It continues until the sex act reaches its denouement or conclusion, whatever that may be, but ends not with this sexual activity, but with the commercial transaction, 'the pay-off', in which money is exchanged for services rendered at the agreed rate of remuneration, or at least, the contracted event is somehow concluded and the transaction closed. And even after this point, the performance continues with the departure (variously dramatized as escape, criminal despoliation, anticlimax) and reflection (in the case of such a one as Boswell, occasioning a prolonged period of moral self-examination, recrimination and excoriation). In considering prostitution in the eighteenth century, the essays in this book examine many diverse aspects of its performance.[6]

A key aspect of the representation of the prostitution performance is the narrative position: answering the question, who is speaking? As Vivien Jones argues, one of the ethical difficulties of approaching the topic of eighteenth-century prostitution is precisely the fact that we rarely have access to the authentic voices of prostitutes.[7] More often, the life of the prostitute is constructed from records made by authorities in the exercise of their judicial and charitable powers: police records, watch charge books, charity accounts, court records. Discourse on prostitution is also commonly found in the voice of the moralist or reformer, who writes about prostitution as an object of political or religious concern. Detailed first-person accounts of prostitution written by sex-workers themselves in this period are not common, if indeed there were ever any. Norberg's study of Marie-Madeleine Dossemont, in this collection, offers an unusual and therefore highly significant account of the life and business practices of a brothelkeeper in mid-eighteenth-century Paris, derived from her own accounts of her brothel made in reports to police. Of the first-person voice of the client there are the private diaries of William Byrd and James Boswell, which provide revealingly detailed accounts of what men thought they were doing in the performance of prostitution.[8] But although the voice of the prostitute is largely missing from the historical record, there are numerous instances in which the voice of the prostitute or client is imitated and imagined. Numerous eighteenth-century writers found creative potential in the narrative of prostitution. Some of these literary accounts indeed offer themselves in the voice of the prostitute: the subgenre of the prostitute or whore biography is a good example. Such texts, modelled on the criminal biography, provide supposedly first-person accounts of the life story of a single-named prostitute or courtesan (following the term criminal biography, they have sometimes been called 'whore biographies').[9] In France, a similar but purely fictional genre of 'romans-mémoires des filles du monde' existed, recently defined and analysed in an important study by Mathilde Cortey.[10] In this volume, Lena Olsson examines the group of texts narrating the life of a celebrated prostitute Sarah Prydden, better known under her assumed name Sally Salisbury. Literary representations of women sex workers also proliferated in the eighteenth century in, for example, novels such as Defoe's *Moll Flanders* (1722) and Cleland's *Memoirs of a Woman of Pleasure* (1749), and they feature in a large proportion of canonical French novels, with varying degrees of centrality to the narrative. As Laura Rosenthal has recently argued, the discourse on prostitution also reflects on, and extends to include, such apparently moral or virtuous novels as Richardson's *Pamela* (1740) and *Clarissa* (1748–9).[11] This is also true of the French tradition, where we see several important episodes involving prostitutes in Rousseau's *La Nouvelle Héloïse* (1761) for example. And, as attested and explored in the recent work of Kathryn Norberg, Valérie van Crugten-André, and Patrick Wald Lasowski, among others, prostitutes were also central to libertine and erotic fiction.[12]

By the mid-century, in England at least, the topic of prostitution had become a matter of public concern – that is to say, not merely as an issue of public order (in which calls for the suppression or regulation of prostitution had a long history), but also one of humanitarian concern. Proposals for the reform of prostitution, whether utopian or practical, located the debate on mercenary sexuality within wider topics in social philosophy, on female education, on the morality of commerce, on marriage, and on slavery. As the research of Coward and Benabou has shown, schemes of a commensurate nature were also imagined in France in this period.[13] As a visible sign of the sexualized female body, the prostitute was also a point of convergence for debates on the feminization of culture.

Venal Bodies: What Is Prostitution in the Eighteenth Century?

Adam Smith does not have much to say about prostitution in *The Wealth of Nations*, and what he does say, is actually addressed to the topic of opera-singers and actresses. He notes that women who possess the 'very agreeable and beautiful talents' used in these employments must be paid a considerable amount in order to overcome the stigma attached to the work, the stigma of what he calls 'publick *prostitution*'.

> The pecuniary recompence, therefore, of those who exercise them in this manner, must be sufficient, not only to pay for the time, labour, and expence of acquiring the talents, but for the discredit which attends the employment of them as the means of subsistence.[14]

Reading these lines in Smith, the feminist philosopher Martha Nussbaum suggests that one of the unique aspects of prostitution is the social stigma attached to it, both now and in the early modern period.[15] This stigma is manifested in a number of overlapping social formations, many of which, especially disease, violence and poverty, are distinctly immiserating in the daily life of the sex worker. The force of stigma is also felt in and through language: through the extraordinary linguistic fluidity of the terms for prostitution. Prostitution is intensely metaphorized: none of the terms for this activity frequently in use in the eighteenth century – prostitute, harlot, strumpet, whore; *catin, putain, raccrocheuse* – are free from a distinct moral shading. Although the term 'sex-worker' was not used in the eighteenth century, it has been adopted in many of the essays in the present volume as a way to obviate the habitual stigma of the terms prevalent in the period. Although anachronistic, the term 'sex work', and 'sex worker', encompasses a wider variety of sexually related services and activities, including prostitution, but also (in this period) brothelkeeping, courtesans, mistress keeping, and concubinage – just as in the modern era sex-work research has expanded to cope with new varieties of sex labour (lap-dancing, phone sex, sex shop assistants).[16]

Discourse on prostitution is complex and braided by conflicting language and nuance because prostitution itself was understood in a variety of conflicting and overlapping ways as a social problem, a criminal activity, a moral state and a commercial activity. This complexity and fluidity can be traced in the language that was used to describe sex workers. Johnson's *Dictionary of the English Language*, first published in 1755, gives some evidence of this peculiar fluidity. Johnson traces the etymology of the verb 'to prostitute' to the Latin *prostituo*, defining it as 'to sell to wickedness; to expose to crimes for a reward. It is commonly used of women sold to whoredom by others or themselves', quoting *Leviticus* (xix, 29), 'Do not prostitute thy daughter, to cause her to be a whore'. As a noun Johnson defined the term 'prostitute' as firstly 'a hireling; a mercenary; one who is set to sale'; and secondly as 'a publick strumpet', and prostitution, first, 'the act of setting to sale; the state of being set to sale' and second 'The life of a publick strumpet'. In Johnson's opinion, prostitution is firstly a commercial notion, and secondly a quality of moral stigma. This is revealed further in the other terms Johnson recognizes for this employment: whore, harlot and strumpet. The word '*whore*' Johnson traces to a Saxon root: '*Whore*. 1. A woman who converses unlawfully with men; a fornicatress; an adultress; a strumpet. 2. A prostitute; a woman who receives men for money'. The term 'whore' thereafter figures in a range of definitions of vulgar slang: '*Laced mutton*. An old word for a whore'; 'to *lecher*. To whore'; '*Miss*. ... A strumpet; a concubine; a whore; a prostitute'; '*Mistress*. ... A whore; a concubine'; '*Punk*. A whore; a common prostitute; a strumpet'; '*Riggish*. ... Wanton; whorish'; '*Strumpet*. A whore; a prostitute'.[17]

A similar pattern can be determined in the French context, where the language used to describe and define 'prostitutes' carries a heavy ideological freight. The definition for 'prostituer, prostitution' in Diderot's *Encyclopédie* uses morally charged vocabulary to evoke this activity, whose sexual and mercenary nature are outlined first, before a metaphorical sense is suggested (in terms of writers and philosophers prostituting their pens):

> terme relatif à la débauche vénérienne. Une prostituée est celle qui s'abandonne à la lubricité de l'homme par quelque motif vil & mercenaire.[18]

In the highly colourful range of French terms for different types of prostitute identified and categorized by Rétif de la Bretonne and Louis-Sébastien Mercier in the last decades of the eighteenth century (see Table 1.1 in the present volume), not only the names but also the descriptive language used to define them are far from morally neutral, and frequently highly pejorative. Rétif describes 'les gouines', for example, as 'sales et dégoûtantes' (dirty and disgusting), while Mercier talks of those near the bottom of his scale of prostitutes as 'brutes' and 'hideuses créatures'. The pejorative associations of a number of the terms they use are also suggested in corresponding dictionary definitions of the period. The 'Dictionnaire de l'Académie française' (1798), for example, defines 'gouine' as a a term of abuse, used by the 'popular classes': 'terme d'injure, qui se dit d'une coureuse, d'une femme de mauvaise vie ... il est populaire', and its definition of 'barboteuse' is similar: 'Raccrocheuse. Terme d'injure et de mépris, en parlant d'une femme de mauvaise vie, qui sollicite les hommes dans la rue ... Il est familier et même populaire'. In his *Dictionnaire libertin*, Wald Lasowski cites Furetière's definition of 'putain', which interestingly evokes both a sense of the social stigma associated with prostitution, and its implications in terms of social class: 'Terme barbare. La haine qu'on a contre ce nom l'a décrédité chez les honnêtes gens, et il n'est plus en usage que chez le peuple, quand il veut dire une injure atroce' (A barbarous term. The disgust that this term inspires has discredited it in honest company, and only common people use it, when they wish to give a dreadful insult).[19]

The stigma associated with prostitution need not be stated to be self-evident in eighteenth-century discourse. Mary Wollstonecraft, who one may suppose was inclined to support benevolent treatment of women in distress whenever and wherever she found them, reckoned the life of the prostitute the lowest in society. In *A Vindication of the Rights of Woman* (1792) she considered the 'pernicious effects which arise from the unnatural distinctions established in society' by the force of gender. The poverty of the education open to women, she noted, meant they were given few options in commerce that would allow them a secure livelihood.

> Business of various kinds, they might likewise pursue, if they were educated in a more orderly manner, which might save many from common and legal *prostitution*. Women would not then marry for a support, as men accept of places under government, and neglect the implied duties; nor would an attempt to earn their own subsistence, a most laudable one! sink them almost to the level of those poor abandoned creatures who live by *prostitution*. For are not milliners and mantua-makers reckoned the next class?[20]

In her mingling of the language of strata with the opprobrium of moral stigma, Wollstonecraft accepts and confirms the stigmatized social exclusion of prostitutes.

As this suggests, the language of prostitution is especially ideological: lexical choice is embedded in complicated sets of social and moral attitudes. What follows is an attempt to map a broad sweep of the eighteenth-century discourse on prostitution (mercenary sex), using the British context as a case study.. This map is in part horizontal, extending from the wilder shores of puritan moral discourse through the libertine to the sentimental. But it is also broadly, and complicatedly, historical, tracing an important shift in the language, discourse and culture of prostitution in the eighteenth century, noticing the emergence of a new understanding of the mercenary sex worker as a state of reduced agency, a form of slavery, to which amelioration, if not emancipation, might be appropriate. Adam Smith again: in his *Lectures on Jurisprudence*, Smith further considers the state of slave concubines in the West Indian colonies (women slaves taken as wives by plantation owners). These women, he argues, exist in a state of prostitution, as they are not free to leave their 'marriage', and yet may be discharged by their master at his will. Smith's understanding of prostitution as a form of wage slavery reinforces the stigma associated with the term, but also indicates that this stigmatized existence is itself a social scandal, as morally troubling to a civilized and commercial society as slavery itself.

The dominant understanding of the stigma of prostitution at the beginning of the eighteenth century, in the British world, can be seen in the actions and discourse of Protestant social reform movements. These movements trace their origin to Puritan campaigns against urban vice: during the English Republic in the 1650s, for example, the Rump parliament had, in the Adultery Act of May 1650, passed legislation against prostitution, which specified that 'prostitutes and brothel-keepers were to be whipped, branded and imprisoned for a first offence, and to suffer the death penalty following any subsequent conviction'.[21] But the legislation was not widely enforced, and lapsed with the Restoration in 1660. The religious climate for moral reform returned after the accession to the throne of William III in 1689. In London especially, but also in many provincial towns, societies for the reformation of manners were established, lasting for almost five decades. The reformation of manners campaigners agitated against many forms of vice in the late seventeenth century, especially swearing and cursing, Sabbath breaking, drunkenness and gambling. The offence they prosecuted most frequently was 'lewd and disorderly practices': that is prostitutes and, to a much lesser extent, their clients. Robert Shoemaker argues that the 'vast majority' of those prosecuted for 'lewd and disorderly practices' were women; recent research has found some evidence that their male clients were also targeted.[22] As prostitution did not contravene any specific law in England, the societies for the reformation of manners had to use common law arguments to bring private prosecutions against fellow citizens they personally brought before the magistrates. In this sense, their own arguments, in the texts produced by the societies, provide an important commentary of contemporary moral debate on prostitution. In their view, prostitution was sinful inasmuch as it was fornication outside marriage, and as such, it constituted a breach of the peace, as defined in common law. A guide first prepared for the society in 1698 ('An Abstract of the Penal-Laws against Immorality and Prophaneness') described all the 'Lewd' and 'Disorderly Practices' that could be prosecuted. Prostitution itself was not criminalized by any legislation, but prostitutes could be prosecuted, as 'Adultery, &c, and all Acts of Bawdry, are Breaches of the Peace'. The guidebook advised that 'If a Constable, &c., has Notice that a Woman is in Adultery, &c. with a Man, or that a Man and a Woman of evil Fame is gone to a suspected House', then 'He may take Help with him, and if he find them so, he may carry them to Prison, or to a Justice, to be Bound over, and Prosecuted'. The guide also cited the legislation used to prosecute bawdy houses, resorters to and frequenters of bawdy houses, and common whoremasters. Those prostitutes and their clients found guilty of being 'Idlers that refuse to work', disorderly persons or wandering rogues could be committed to the House of Correction, where they could face punishment by whipping or banishment to their place of birth.[23] In order to promote their cause, the societies even printed blank warrants to be issued to offenders, and specimens of the language to be used in the 'informations' to be given to the magistrates.[24] Societies prosecuted large numbers of offenders: an official report of their activity for 1720 stated that they had prosecuted 1,189 persons for 'Lewd and Disorderly Practices'. Describing the effects of their efforts for in the early decades of the eighteenth century, the report commented:

> Great numbers of Baudy-Houses, and other disorderly Houses, have been suppressed and shut up, and the Streets were very much purged from the wretched Tribe of *Night-walking Prostitutes*, and the most *detestable Sodomites*. Many young Men, taken with lewd Women, have, by their being brought to timely Shame and Punishment, have been discouraged and turned ... from following such sinful Courses.[25]

As the report suggests, the prostitutes (lewd women) are the agents of the corruption, seducing young men from the path of virtue.

To most historians, the reformation of manners campaigners articulated ideas about prostitution located within a discourse about adultery and sin of considerable historical longevity. Faramerz Dabhoiwala notes that campaigns against illicit sex were a 'commonplace of medieval, Tudor, and early Stuart policies',[26] but also notes that these campaigns found their work increasingly difficult as the eighteenth century passed. Despite high-profile support from bishops and reformers, successive attempts to pass legislation against prostitution and brothelkeeping failed. Despite the vocal criticism of public vice, and the specific focus on urban prostitution, there was a considerable body of assent to, and toleration of, prostitution and brothelkeeping in the period. Bernard Mandeville (1670–

1733), with his usual complicated irony, proposed in his mock-treatise *A Modest Defence of Public Stews* (1724) that the aim of the reformers – the suppression of street prostitution – could be achieved more efficiently by the establishment of state-controlled brothels. These 'publick stews', he argued with suspiciously rational logic, would provide safe and clean working conditions for prostitutes, so lessening the ruinous effects of venereal disease and illegitimate children, as well as providing the service at a cheaper rate to clients.[27]

To some extent, Mandeville shared in the modernizing discourse of libertinism. James Grantham Turner, focusing on the Stuart to Restoration period, shows how libertine representational strategies in British literature and visual culture borrowed freely from Italian renaissance pornography, itself explicitly recalling the classical tradition.[28] Libertine discourse was in this sense self-consciously modern and European, linked to the empirical method of the new science and defiantly anti-clerical and republican in its politics. Libertine writing about sex championed the pursuit of erotic pleasure as a core activity of life (hedonistic, epicurean). Restoration and early eighteenth-century libertine representations of the prostitute, such as *The Wandering Whore* (1660), *The London Bawd* (1711) and *Satan's Harvest Home* (1749) depict prostitution within scandalous sexual practices (such as sodomy or coprophagia), developing narratives of cuckoldry and adultery, and of prostitutes using their trade to criminal ends by defrauding or thieving from clients.[29] The common whore or wanton woman in the libertine verses of Rochester, such as 'A Ramble in St James's Park', and Philip Gould's 'Love Given O're', is not only promiscuous, but also unchaste and without virtue, depicted as a rapacious female monster, criminal, raving, diseased and alcoholic.[30] In libertine literature, the demi-monde of prostitution has disruptive potential enough to be represented as completely depraved and outside society.

Yet if libertine discourse was self-consciously modern and revolutionary, libertine representation of prostitution also shared many of the same tropes as the discourse of religious campaigners of the period: that the prostitute was a body to be enjoyed and used, that her status was irretrievable and essentially disposable, that she was monstrously sexualized, consumed by lust, corruption and disease. Libertine discourse, more interested in consensual than mercenary fornication, encouraged a view of the prostitute as a lusty enthusiast rendered monstrous, diseased and criminal by her activities. By exploding the coy language of orthodox religious discourse, the libertine liberated himself to enjoy polymorphous sexual encounters; but as he did so, his actions reincarcerated the prostitute in the prison house of misogyny. Even in the polite 'pornotopia'[31] of Cleland's *Memoirs of a Woman of Pleasure*, in which both the prostitute's sex work is clean, safe, healthy and pleasurable, and the language of the novel abjures sexual vulgarity, the echo of the lustful libertine whore can be seen. Although Cleland depicts his heroine Fanny Hill as a sex worker who finds her self and prosperity through prostitution, libertine literature was not liberationist.

Historiography of Prostitution

In recent decades, a consensus has emerged in the Anglophone historiographical tradition, that the eighteenth century witnessed profound changes in the representation of prostitution. The period is a transitional moment that operates as a hinge between the pre-modern and modern worlds of sexuality. The historically enduring account of the prostitute in the early modern period sees her as an agent of corruption, a libertine seducer of men and a fornicating sinful adulteress, inhabiting a violent world of excessive consumption, insatiable desire, criminal behaviour and bestial depravity. In the course of the eighteenth century, although the legacy of the sinful prostitute remains apparent, a new, sentimental, construction of the prostitute emerges, transforming the prostitute from a criminal to a victim, from an agent of sin to an object of compassion. In the battles over the meaning and representation of prostitution, as Laura Rosenthal has argued in *Infamous Commerce* (2006), in the eighteenth century 'prostitution took on its modern form'. The key to this transformation is the new language of commerce and sensibility, central to the eighteenth-century gendered transformation of manners identified by historians and critics such as Nancy Armstrong, G. J. Barker-Benfield, and Randolph Trumbach.[32] In this view, a polite and civilized commercial society established a new ideal of domestic femininity as a model for the polite reformation of manners. As Emma Clery has argued, this places the construction of femininity at the centre of the properly philosophical debates over the nature of the commercial impetus in eighteenth century capitalism.[33] In his novels, for example, Richardson provided a powerful emblem of women as the embodiment of virtue and agent of moral reform. The case of the prostitute, a woman with a different kind of interaction with commerce and virtue, provides a telling test case for the articulation of this new discourse on femininity.

The 'modern' or 'new' prostitute was articulated in the discourse of sensibility, although of course sympathy for the plight of prostitutes can be traced back to the early eighteenth century, in for example *The Spectator*. In the sentimental mode, prostitutes could be represented as objects of passive distress, and as such, appropriate objects of benevolent concern and reformation.[34] This reconceptualization took place against concerted opposition: the prostitute remained a recalcitrant object of benevolence for numerous reasons, not least historically enduring discursive formations, and most obviously, their real-life resistance to polite culture. Research in recent decades has argued that in the mid-century, the prostitute is redrawn as an object of pity, as a victim of a corrupting seducer, and as such as an unwilling subject of the underworld of brothels, streetwalking and disease.

The single most spectacular sign of the re-evaluation of the construction of the prostitute in eighteenth-century England was the establishment of the Magdalen Hospital in London in 1758, the subject of two essays in this volume. This was an innovative institution: a charitable foundation established to provide a reformative refuge for distressed women who were either prostitutes or who had no recourse except prostitution. As an early anonymous defender of the charity suggested, the work of the Magdalen Hospital began with a revolutionary shift in attitudes to the prostitute: 'Tho' the profession of a prostitute is the most despicable and hateful that the imagination can form; yet the individuals are frequently worthy objects of compassion'.[35] The properly philosophical aspect of the hospital, explored in their foundational debates, promotional literature, and in creative responses, was its reorganization of the narrative of prostitution, which in their mind no longer ended in poverty, disease and death, but was reimagined with a new conclusion, that saw the reformed prostitute pass though the hospital's self-incarceration to achieve, in the status of the Magdalen, a form of penitence and reformation, so that she might finally be restored to passive domestic servitude in the world of the virtuous. Rescripting the narrative of prostitution translated the prostitute from aggressive moral criminal to innocent victim, and as such, an appropriate object of compassion and benevolence.

Historical analysis of prostitution in eighteenth-century France has in recent decades made a similar transition, and is increasingly studied through surviving archival evidence, rather than on the impressionistic commentary of contemporaries. An important set of studies by Erica-Marie Benabou, Colin Jones and Alain Corbin made use of archival evidence from police and court records to establish both official and unofficial attitudes to prostitution.[36] Benabou suggests that the regulation of prostitution began in Paris in the eighteenth century, with the consequence that it became more institutionalized and more professional, leaving more and more detailed records in the archive. Colin Jones's doctoral research in the 1970s used archival records to reconstruct the regulatory regime and official attitudes to prostitution in Montpellier, in Languedoc, between the mid-seventeenth century and the fall of the Ancien Régime.[37] He begins by noting the alarm felt at the rise of prostitution in the late seventeenth century: and argues this is caused by a rise in poverty and the collapse of systems for the relief of poverty after the Revocation of the Edict of Nantes in 1685. He notes a series of government measures in the 1680s that were aimed at tighter regulation and repression of 'female sexual deviancy': (i) legislation passed between 1684 and 1687 that tackled the problem of prostitutes following the army; (ii) royal ordinances in 1684 that gave the heads of well-born families new powers to detain children, especially young women, who had disgraced or dishonoured their families; (iii) the establishment of specialist correctional institutions within the *hôpitaux généraux* for the detention and correction of public prostitutes, along with other 'crimes of poverty', such as pauperism, begging, vagrancy, foundlings, gypsies and lunatics.

Jones examines in some detail the foundation in 1692 of a specific institution in Montpellier, created within the *hôpitaux généraux*, for the reception of 'girls and women of scandalous and notoriously debauched life'.[38] The Bon Pasteur ('Good Shepherd') was supported by the wealthy elite in the city, and served as a house of correction until the Revolution. The institution was supported by wider networks of volunteer policing, which were arguably analogous to the societies for the reformation of manners campaigns in London. The regime of the Bon Pasteur included spiritual instruction, and was aimed at restoring the reformed prostitute to productive labour (analogous to the ideals if not the practice of the Magdalen Hospital). Jones describes the hospital as lying clearly within 'the main-stream of Counter-Reformation thinking about charity'.[39] By the end of the eighteenth century, however, the charitable impetus that had maintained the institution was waning, and it was increasingly forced to support itself from the forced labour of its inmates working in basic textile trades.[40] This was reflected in the institutions' attitudes to its inmates, which increasingly understood prostitutes as criminals whose reintegration into society was not to be achieved by moral reform but punitive confinement.[41] The more punitive regime also encouraged more sustained and invasive policing by the authorities, and in this way, more extensive records of prostitution. Among these records are extensive evidence that in the mid-century, police inspectors tolerated and protected the operation of a significant number of brothels, although only those which were well ordered and frequented by polite clientele. As Norberg's essay in this volume testifies, police records systematically noted the habits, appearance, social status and sexual activities of the clientele, and of the sex workers employed there.[42]

Benabou provides a broader survey of police practices and policies in her study of prostitution – initially examining the changing legal framework relating to prostitution throughout the eighteenth century, and then reconstructing the more pragmatic structures of policing and surveillance (*la police des mœurs*). She includes a series of case studies based on archival evidence surrounding specific individuals and their collaborations and interactions, including several important players within the police hierarchy (for example, lieutenant général Sartine, specialist police inspectors Meusnier and Marais); various well-known procuresses (for example, La Gourdan); and a number of individual prostitutes of different types. Her work consistently brings out the arbitrariness of the justice meted out to prostitutes, and in particular the one-sided nature of the punishment of 'vice' – that is, the systematic punishment of venal women rather than their clients. She also explores the ways in which the policing of prostitution was periodically used as a weapon against elements of the clergy.

While examinations of the institutional contexts of repression – police, hospitals, prisons – forms an important facet of historical writing on the topic of prostitution in eighteenth-century France,[43] another important/critical strand is the cultural-historical investigation of how prostitutes and prostitution became a key trope in political debates and controversies in the years preceding the revolution. The works of Sara Maza on scandalous court cases; Pamela Cheek on actresses and 'public women'; Robert Darnton on the publishing trade and 'philosophical sex'; and Chantal Thomas on pamphlet representations of Marie Antoinette,[44] amongst others, have foregrounded the ways in which the figure of the prostitute was increasingly used polemically – as a vehicle for the critique of aristocratic lifestyles, or for devastating attacks on specific individuals, especially women perceived as wielding too much power (Madame de Pompadour, Madame du Barry, Marie Antoinette). The representation of the prostitute as a monstrous seductress, an emancipated woman riven by insatiable desires, in a range of different discourses and media, thus brings together powerful cocktail of assumptions and prejudices regarding class and gender, whose consequences were played out at the highest levels of politics. Unlike the historiographical tradition associated with British culture, then, historical writing focusing on prostitution in the French context seems not to have produced a clear overarching narrative regarding the emergence or increasing dominance of the sentimental construction of the prostitute as victim over the course of the century. While such forms of representation were undoubtedly important in France too,[45] the prostitute as dangerous libertine remained as dominant a figure as her sentimental counterpart.

Prostitution in Eighteenth-Century Culture

The chapters in this book traverse historical, cultural and literary studies. As they do so, they remind us of what might be called the 'reality deficit' in many eighteenth-century representations of prostitution. Prostitution was throughout the eighteenth century a significant cause for concern by authorities and regulators, who read in the visibility of prostitution, for example, important evidence of the city's corruption. Responses to prostitution by moral campaigners and representations of prostitution by literary writers and visual artists reinforced the scandal occasioned by the sex work of prostitutes, whether street whores or noble courtesans. Yet despite the significance of prostitution in eighteenth-century writing, both polemic and imaginary, there is little evidence that it made much difference to the lives of the prostitutes themselves. Tim Hitchcock suggests that 'there is very little necessary relationship between the way sex, sexuality and in this case prostitution worked and the intellectual and social discourses constructed around them'.[46] In everyday life, there was significant toleration for, and acceptance of, the presence of prostitutes in the streets, even if their sex work was demonized and stigmatized in almost all official discourse.

The book is organized into four major sections. The first brings together four articles exploring the textual constructions of four 'venal' women who were real historical figures: from the French adventuress Marie Petit and the aristocratic Duchess de Mazarin, to the middle-class brothel-owner Mme Dossement, and working-class whore Sally Salisbury. These articles, which focus on various forms of memoirs, biographies and other textual fragments, explore how some of these women chose to present themselves, through forms of self-fashioning that consciously (or unconsciously) relate to existing literary models, or created them. Others left no voice of their own. Their appropriation by others – telling and reworking their stories, sometimes ostensibly from their own perspective – for a variety of purposes, similarly points to the complexities of textual mediation, and the agendas at stake in these elaborate reinscriptions. In each case, the question of these women's 'venal' status, and the meaning of this designation, is affirmed, contested and debated. This problem of definition is also explored in the article which opens the section, which examines a series of classificatory schema by which different types of venal women are brought together in texts by Rétif de la Bretonne and Louis-Sébastien Mercier, suggesting that at the end of the eighteenth century, the notion of the 'prostitute' could be used as an overarching category despite the elusiveness of this term. The relationship between Rétif's and Mercier's hierarchies of prostitutes and questions of social rank and class that are discussed here, provides a useful counterpoint to the narratives of and by such different classes of venal women examined in the following articles.

The second section of the book brings together articles dealing with texts and images that were more explicitly fictional, mainly in the French context. The theatricality of the prostitute's art and her dangerous visibility – her appearance before the public eye – are explored through the analysis of a range of media. The literal elision between actress and prostitute is examined and problematized in relation to erotic plays written for the private theatre of the notorious actress Sophie Arnould, while the question of visual pleasure is explored in relation to perhaps the most iconic of eighteenth-century images of the prostitute: William Hogarth's *A Harlot's Progress*. Two further articles explore literary 'figures' of the prostitute: the intertextual links between Voltaire's Paquette in *Candide* and various French and English antecedents are traced out, to suggest the originality of Voltaire's rewriting, while Sade's Juliette is reread in the light of recent theoretical work on capitalist 'neo-managers': each of these articles, in different ways, bringing out, or embodying, a rereading produced by the confrontation of different cultures.

The third section considers further the theme of seduction and prostitution in sentimental discourse on prostitutes, especially that aroused by the debate on a public charity for the relief of distressed prostitutes. In this section, the two articles by Jennie Batchelor and Mary Peace, focus on texts and debates engendered by the Magdalen Hospital in London in the 1750s and 1760s, the most significant example of the sentimental reorganization of discourse on prostitution. Each article brings out the way in which discourse on prostitution is inseparable from (and indeed, despite its apparent marginality, comes to figure) wider debates on marriage, motherhood and the possibility of redemption and social reintegration following sexual misconduct.

The book's final section opens out some wider perspectives. Both articles are written from a social-historical perspective, and each interrogates a range of juridical sources. In the first, Johanne Bergkvist develops a particular case study using eighteenth-century police records for Christiania (Oslo), the capital city of Norway, exploring the changing attitudes to work and poverty in the civic authorities' response to prostitutes. Randolph Trumbach offers a groundbreaking study of the history of the male prostitute in England in this period. As Trumbach's article reminds us, prostitution was also practiced by men, not only as clients willing to pay for sexual encounters, but also as practitioners, willing to engage in sexual acts, such as sodomy, for money. His article thus reminds researchers that the habitual use of the feminine pronoun for the prostitute, and the masculine for the client, is hasty: early modern prostitution is more complicated than that.

These four sections, individually and together, interrogate and articulate the highly contested fictions of the 'venal body', in all their heterogeneity. This diversity (the juxtaposition of representations of prostitutes in different discourses, different national contexts, and at different moments of the eighteenth century), allows us to complicate traditional historical schemas – both at the level of individual cases, and of national grand narratives – for example, concerning the eighteenth-century reformist discourse and its transforming of the prostitute from a vicious and sexualized criminal into a reluctant victim of commercial depravity. After all, the life of a prostitute on the streets of London or Paris in the late eighteenth century was no better than at the beginning. Discourse was distant from everyday life. The essays in this book recognize the recalcitrant particularity of the world of the prostitute, and the complicated, sophisticated, and elastic discourses that scripted their production as objects of debate and creativity.

1 CLASSIFYING THE PROSTITUTE IN EIGHTEENTH-CENTURY FRANCE

Ann Lewis

The figure of the prostitute is common in the canonical literary texts of eighteenth-century France, as well as proliferating in a host of lesser known sentimental, libertine and pornographic novels. In fact, it is difficult to think of any novels of the period (at least those written by men) that do not include them in some form or other. However, compared to the large field of criticism dealing with the prostitute in nineteenth-century French literature and culture (or in the eighteenth-century English context), there is relatively little criticism relating to the eighteenth-century French field. This reticence may at least in part be due to the problems encountered when trying to define the category 'prostitute' itself. The first part of this article will explore various facets of this defining ambiguity, and I will then turn to two French writers from the late eighteenth century, Louis-Sébastien Mercier and Nicolas-Edme Rétif de la Bretonne, who explicitly set out and categorize different types of venal women, through a series of shifting classificatory schema.

This article will examine the unstable and at times contradictory ways in which these different sets of categories are defined and ordered, with a particular focus on the mediation of a series of anxieties relating to the structure of society more generally. It is striking that both Rétif's and Mercier's taxonomies of prostitution take the form of hierarchies, in which the different 'classes' or categories are described in terms similar to those of different types of social rank – the terminology of 'rang', 'classe' and 'condition' being used in both cases. Of course, the notion of 'class' in Ancien Régime society (as opposed to that, for example, of orders) has long been contested in historiographical writing on the period preceding the revolution, particularly in reaction to the oversimplified postulation of a so-called 'rise of the bourgeoisie' (a recent refutation of this putative 'rise', for example, is Sarah Maza's polemical book on the *Myth of the French Bourgeoisie*).[1] Nonetheless, a close inspection of Rétif's and Mercier's texts sheds interesting light both on the construction of social categories and those of varying classes of prostitutes. The mapping of one onto the other – both in the delineating of boundaries, and their blurring and collapse – is particularly revealing of certain ambiguities and anxieties at the heart of the eighteenth-century social imaginary.

Defining the Prostitute

For various reasons, defining the category we recognize as 'prostitute' is highly problematic, and it immediately raises the possibility of an anachronistic projection backwards. Was the term used at all in eighteenth-century France, and if so, did it mean the same as what we understand by it today? The 1762 *Dictionnaire de l'Académie française* entry for 'prostituée', for example, simply mentions 'femme ou fille abandonnée à l'impudicité'. In the same dictionary, a 'catin' is described as a 'une personne de mauvaise vie'. These descriptions evoke immorality and sexual incontinence but not necessarily our modern understanding of the 'prostitute' as a 'person, typically a woman, who engages in sexual activity for payment' (the definition in the *New OED*). The potential conflation of the 'prostitute' with any woman transgressing the eighteenth-century norms of legitimate sexuality (for example, marriage) is visible in many texts of the period.

Erica-Marie Benabou's *La Prostitution et la police des mœurs au dix-huitième siècle*, which remains the most comprehensive social-historical account of the topic, specifically draws attention to the difficulties in pinning down legal definitions of the crime of prostitution, noting that 'l'aspect "mercenaire" n'y apparaît nullement au cœur du délit' ('its mercenary aspect was by no means a defining feature of the offence'),[2] instead, it was scandal and visible indecency which constituted the crime. In this respect, a distinction might be drawn between 'public' prostitution (for example, involving visible soliciting on the streets), and 'private' arrangements (kept mistresses, courtesans, etc., conducted discreetly behind closed doors) which might not be considered as falling within the category of 'prostitution' at all. The *Encyclopédie* article for 'courtisane', for example, states: 'on appelle ainsi une femme livrée à la débauche publique, surtout lorsqu'elle exerce ce métier honteux avec une sorte d'agrément et de décence, et qu'elle sait donner au libertinage l'attrait que la prostitution lui ôte presque toujours' ('this is the name for a woman given over to public debauchery, especially when she exercises this shameful trade with a kind of charm and decency, and knows how to make *libertinage* appealing in a way that prostitution cannot').[3] This definition both aligns the courtesan and prostitute in the exercise of the 'shameful trade' of 'public debauchery', but at the same time invokes 'prostitution' as a separate category.

Benabou's study, which provides a detailed survey of the practice of prostitution also draws attention to the fact that, in many cases, women engaged in occasional part-time sex work ('des soupers', 'des partis-de-plaisir' to use the terminology of the period), rather than being full-time professional prostitutes. Women from the lower social classes who had a *métier* (such as filles de boutique, marchandes de modes, coiffeuses) would identify more closely with this *métier* than with a category or identity 'prostitute', although terms such as 'fille du monde', 'du monde', were often used by the women themselves to evoke their availability and venal status. In fact, how frequently the term 'prostituée' itself was used in different eighteenth-century contexts would be worth investigating further, and it is perhaps significant that Mathilde Cortey opts for the terms 'courtisanes' and 'filles du monde' in her recent study of the subgenre of memoir novels narrated by fictional characters of this type.[4] It is worth noting, however, that both Rétif and Mercier do use the terms 'prostitution' and 'prostituée' frequently, in addition to a large number of other less specific epithets such as 'malheureuses', 'créatures' and 'filles publiques', and the multiple categories examined in the sections below.[5]

These more general reservations concerning the understanding of what we call 'prostitution' in an eighteenth-century context make Rétif's and Mercier's attempts to pin down a series of definitions – and their grappling with some of these issues at a very particular moment of the eighteenth century – all the more revealing. Before examining the ways in which both writers evoke and construct elaborate hierarchies of prostitutes, it is worth noting that there is no attempt in the present article to gauge how far these constructions mapped on to the social realities of prostitution (although they purport to describe them).[6] The aim is to explore what they might tell us about the social and sexual anxieties of these particular writers, and what they therefore also tell us about the social imaginary of the period.

Other Orders for Exploring the 'Spectrum' of 'Prostitutes'

It is also worth noting that Mercier and Rétif were not alone in exploring the broad spectrum of and connections between different levels of prostitution. Such classifications can also be found in a range of British texts,[7] but different principles of ordering can also be found in various other genres and contexts. Many novels of the period (including, for example, Rétif's own *La Paysanne pervertie*) also dramatize the rapid ascent and descent of a central character through the ranks of prostitution, thus exploring a similar range of categories in a different way – often from a fictional first-person perspective in which the psychological effects of such mobility are evoked.[8]

The multiple publications in both England and France in the genre of *Harris's Covent-Garden Ladies* or *Les Demoiselles de Paris* also provide us with various types of lists of prostitutes.[9] These almanacs, 'guides' and *dictionnaires* generally comprise a list of 'stage names', addresses, prices, physical attributes and erotic specialities, and sometimes related anecdotes and stories – thus providing a succession of individual (presumably largely fictionalized) portraits in serial form (although several names are recognizably those of famous actresses). The entries are sometimes listed in alphabetical order by name (for example in the *Nouvelle Liste des plus jolies femmes publiques de Paris*, 1801), and sometimes according to geographic location (the *Liste complète des plus belles femmes publiques et des plus saines du Palais de Paris* evokes a series of dwellings in Palais-Royal in turn, and their inhabitants), but sometimes there is no discernable order structuring the list of names and descriptions at all. The lists rarely provide overarching categories or groupings by 'type' – the ladies enumerated come under generic headings such as 'nymphes', 'demoiselles', 'courtisanes' in the titles of such publications. (An exception is *Les Bordels de Paris*, 1790, which provides the following categories: 'Bordel de négresses', 'bordel des pucelles', 'bordel des élégantes', 'bordel des bourgeoises', 'bordel des grisettes et marchandes', 'bordel des provinciales', 'bordel des paillardes'.) Generally speaking though, the order of exposition in these lists seems to correspond more to an erotic-aesthetic principle based on stimulating the reader's pleasure and amusement through wit, variety and piquancy, and structured to provide entertainment and distraction, rather than a more systematic arrangement according to price or type.

The narrative potential inherent in Rétif's and Mercier's taxonomies, suggestive of the clichés of fictional narrative of the period, will be touched on in the following analysis, while the 'pleasure' principle of the almanacs may also be perceived at some level in the exuberant inventiveness of Rétif's classifications. And although there is no scope to explore the relationship between these different genres more fully in this context, it is useful to compare the structuring principles of Rétif's and Mercier's taxonomical enterprises in the context of these other models of order/disorder.

Mercier's Classification of the Prostitute in the *Tableau de Paris* (1781–8)[10]

Louis-Sébastien Mercier and Nicolas-Edme Rétif de la Bretonne were writing in the decades before the revolution, and their texts have been the object of fascination both for historians and literary scholars, given their desire to observe and provide various kinds of documentary account of the society and social values of their time (as well as a series of utopian projects for their reform). Critics have been particularly struck by their focus on everyday life, and evocation of social groups from across the whole social spectrum, using a range of innovative literary forms.[11] The two writers knew each other personally, and Mercier's *Tableau de Paris*, makes several references to Rétif's writings on prostitution.[12] In fact, there are very few texts in Rétif's vast literary output that do not feature and discuss prostitutes; in reference to his project for the reform of prostitution, *Le Pornographe*, a contemporary writer sarcastically remarked on his obsessive interest in this field, or his 'érudition en matière de prostitution' ('erudite knowledge on the subject of prostitution').[13]

What is most immediately striking about Rétif's and Mercier's respective taxonomies of the prostitute is that, while they draw attention to the large variety of different types of women and activities that could be encompassed within this 'métier' (whether practised publically or in private, as amateurs or professionals), they nonetheless clearly suggest that it could be perceived as an overarching category at this stage of the eighteenth century. In the *Tableau de Paris* Mercier imagines a painter representing: 'le gradin symbolique, où seraient [représentées] toutes les femmes qui font trafic à Paris de leurs charmes' ('Matrones', Chapter 542) ('the symbolic spectrum of all the women who traffick their charms in Paris').[14] He insists repeatedly on the sameness of the activity from the highest class of courtesan to the lowest streetwalker. And the identifying characteristic of this métier is *venality*:[15]

> Il y a de la différence dans les noms ... mais le métier n'est-il pas le même? ('St, St, St', Chapter 964)
> (The names are different ... but surely the métier is the same.)

> Quelle hiérarchie dans le même métier! Que de distinctions, de nuances, de noms divers, et ce pour exprimer néanmoins une seule et même chose ... Cent mille livres par an, ou une pièce d'argent ou de monnaie pour un quart d'heure, causent ces dénominations qui ne marquent que les échelles du vice ou de la profonde indigence. ('Courtisanes', Chapter 239)
> (What a hierarchy within the same métier! What distinctions, nuances and diverse titles, and all this to express what is but the exact same thing. One hundred thousand livres a year, or a silver coin or small change for a quarter of an hour, this is what defines the categories which mark only the different grades of vice or of extreme poverty.)

In the article 'Matrones' ('Madams') (Chapter 542), Mercier also provides a detailed outline of the different classes of the imaginary 'gradin symbolique', whose hierarchical structure is suggested in visual terms through a series of adjectives and adverbs evoking each category's position: 'au sommet', 'immédiatement au-dessous', 'au milieu', and so forth.

> Au sommet, l'on verrait ces femmes ambitieuses et altières, qui ne couchent en joue que les hommes en place et les financiers. Elles sont froides, elles calculent en politiques ce que peuvent leur rendre les faiblesses des Grands.
>   Immédiatement au-dessous d'elles se verraient les filles d'Opéra, les danseuses, les actrices, moitié tendres, moitié intéressées, et qui commencent à placer le sentiment où l'on ne l'avait pas encore vu.
>   Ensuite les bourgeoises demi-décentes, recevant l'ami de la maison, et le plus souvent du consentement du mari: espèce dangereuse et perfide, qui voile et pare l'adultère de couleurs trompeuses, et qui usurpe l'estime dont elle est indigne.
>   Au milieu de cet amphithéâtre figurerait la race innombrable des gouvernantes ou servantes-maîtresses, cohorte mélangée.
>   La base en s'élargissant offrirait les grisettes, les marchandes de modes, les monteuses de bonnets, les ouvrières en linge, les filles qui ont leur chambre, et qu'une nuance sépare des courtisanes. Elles ont moins d'art, aiment le plaisir, s'y livrent, ne ravissent point les heures précieuses destinées aux devoirs de votre état. On les nourrit, on les divertit, et elles sont contentes, paisibles. Si elles se permettent un amant à la suite de l'entreteneur, voilà ou se borne leur tromperie.
>   L'œil en descendant saisirait les phalanges désordonnées des filles publiques, qui garnissent impudemment les fenêtres, les portes, qui étalent leurs charmes lascifs dans les promenades publiques. On les loue comme les carrosses de remise, à tant par heure. Elles seraient pêle-mêle confondues avec les danseuses, chanteuses et actrices des Boulevards.
>   Le dernier gradin plongeant dans la fange montrerait les hideuses créatures du *Port au Blé*, de la rue *du Poirier*, de la rue *Planche-Mybray*; et le peintre, pour ne pas trop blesser les règles délicates du goût, n'en ferait saillir que la tête. Ici le vice a perdu son attrait, et le frisson qui court dans les veines dit que la débauche sait se punir elle-même.

(At the top of the ladder you see the ambitious and haughty women, who aim always at the highest; nothing less than a financier will serve their turn. They have no passions, but only calculating brains to note a weakness and turn it to their own account.

Below these come the opera-girls, dancers, actresses, neither wholly venal nor altogether disinterested, who bring a trifle of sentiment into their relations with men.

Then there are the half-honest wives, the women whose 'friends' come to their houses, often as not with the husband's connivance; these are dangerous and worthless creatures who set out adultery in pleasant colours, and lay claim to a social respect which they have forfeited by their conduct.

And lastly, we must reckon another immense class; servants who are something closer to their masters; housekeeper-mistresses; there are plenty of these, and they are the most mixed lot of all.

The base of the pyramid rests upon what may be called the amateurs; milliners, dressmakers, sewing-girls, women who rent their own room and whom a nuance separates from the rank of courtesans. These have made no special study of the art of love, but they accept what pleasure comes their way, take pains to please, and are conscientious in the performance of their duties. You take them occasionally to a play, or stand them a supper, and they ask no more; perhaps now and then they permit themselves a variant upon the official lover, but otherwise they are honest, decent girls.

The eye travelling down this structure of disorder rests uncomfortably upon the great mass of common prostitutes, leaning in doorways, leering from windows, and otherwise displaying their lascivious charms in public places. These may be hired like hackney carriages at so much an hour; among their number you find singers, dancers and actresses from the smaller theatres or the shows on the boulevards.

Now come those horrors, buried too vilely deep for the casual eye to discover; the hideous women of the Pont-au-Bled, and the Rue du Poirier, or the Rue Planche-Mibray. The painter who sets these in his composition will do well to show nothing but their heads, which are awful enough. Vice loses, in these places, even the semblance of allure, and soon, dreadfully, brings its own punishment.)[16]

The different classes are evoked in terms of their own and their clients' social class and wealth (the 'courtisane' at the summit, the 'demi-décentes bourgeoises' in the middle, and 'grisettes', 'filles publiques', and 'hideuses créatures' at the bottom), in terms of their other 'métier' or status (as performers, wives, servants, or shop girls), and also in moral terms (the degree of 'sentiment', 'art', or 'tromperie' defining their relationship with their clients, and their relative degree of mercenary ambition). 'Grisettes', for example, are described as being 'susceptibles d'attachement', and as 'plus décentes et réservées' than the 'filles entretenues' and 'filles d'opéra', between which they are positioned. The 'filles de l'opéra' are qualified as 'moitié tendres, moitié intéressées' ('half venal, half tender'). Interestingly, the highest class – 'courtisanes' – in their cold and ambitious calculation seem to be evoked as the most morally (if not medically) corrupt. In Chapter 240, they are compared with 'filles entretenues' who are of a lower class in terms of wealth and status, but morally superior: 'au-dessous des courtisanes par le rang, elles sont moins dépravées' ('below *courtisanes* in terms of rank, they are less depraved'). In this respect, the translation of the overall schema in Popkin's *Panorama of Paris* as 'the various degrees of women's degradation in Paris'[17] is oversimplified, as it overlooks the ways in which the structure sets up an inverse relationship between certain moral qualities (the capacity for authentic feeling, a certain degree of 'decency'/discretion), and the hierarchy of social class and wealth. This is consistent with the discussion of the same categories in other chapters. 'Filles publiques' ('common prostitutes'), for example, are described in Chapter 238 as 'malheureuses victimes de l'indigence ou de l'abandon de leurs parents, rarement déterminées par un tempérament fougueux' ('unhappy victims of extreme poverty or abandoned by their parents, rarely motivated by a libidinous temperament') – thus less culpable in moral terms for their behaviour, and later in the same chapter Mercier suggests that 'une *fille publique* est plus près de devenir honnête femme que *la femme galante*' ('a common prostitute is closer to becoming an honest woman than a *femme galante*'). The archetypal figures of prostitute as 'predator' and as 'victim' are thus both present within the schema, but attributed to different ends of the scale.

As the previous paragraph suggests, in addition to the 'gradin symbolique' outlined in the 'Matrones' chapter, Mercier also provides descriptions of various categories in a series of further chapters, many of which follow each other in quick succession, for example: 'Filles d'Opéra' (234), 'Le nom que vous voudrez' (236), 'filles publiques' (238), 'courtisanes' (239), 'filles entretenues' (240) , 'les demoiselles' (247). This arrangement suggests their associative relation to each other, as do a series of cross-references within each article to other categories, which serve to 'position' them relationally within a broader classificatory structure – although their sequence in chapters does not correspond to this order.[18]

In fact, the categories' exact places within the hierarchy seem not to be consistent when these different chapters are compared ('filles entretenues' are variously described as being between 'above' 'courtisanes' or 'below' them (in Chapters 239 and 240), and they are not explicitly named in the 'gradin symbolique' in Chapter 542 (at all). Likewise, 'grisettes' are described as being in between the 'filles entretenues' and 'filles d'Opéra' in Chapter 247, while they are near the bottom of the scale in Chapter 542. Rather than the precise position, what seems to matter is that each category should be seen as related to others, that is, to have a place within the structure. This might be related to Mercier's broader project in the *Tableau*, by which he seeks to juxtapose and contrast different classes in order to build up an overall picture, as described in the preface: 'J'ai fait des recherches dans toutes les classes de citoyens, et n'ai pas dédaigné les objets les plus éloignés de l'orgueilleuse opulence, afin de mieux établir par ces oppositions la physionomie morale de cette gigantesque capitale'[19] ('I have studied every class of citizen, and I have not forgotten those farthest removed from haughty opulence. These contrasts allow one to better define this gigantic capital's moral physiognomy').[20] In this respect, it is less a question of establishing a static system, than providing a dynamic set of terms/oppositions, which each shed light on each other, and suggesting a provisional sketch rather than a finished work of art.

The instability of the structure can also be seen at another level, in the potential for movement between the ranks, which is suggested at various points in several of the chapters enumerated above – for example, when Mercier notes that the distance between the diamond-clad courtesan and the impoverished streetwalker selling themselves for a fortune or a pittance is largely down to caprice and fate and perhaps a little art (Chapter 239), or in his observation that 'grisettes' are capable of attachment and, like 'filles entretenues', may choose to marry in the end (Chapter 247). But this narrative potential is brought out most explicitly outside the description of the classes themselves, in the paragraphs following the 'esquisse' of the 'gradin symbolique', where this dynamic instability is set in motion:

> Il est des métamorphoses très surprenantes parmi ces femmes, et qui les font tout à coup changer de place sur le haut gradin pyramidal. Elles montent et descendent, selon que le hasard leur amène des entreteneurs plus ou moins riches. Le caprice, l'engouement, des rapports inconnus font que la petite fille dédaignée la veille et qu'on ne regardait pas, est préférée à toutes ses compagnes ...
>
> L'autre retombe dans l'indigence, après avoir mené un train, et devient dans son abaissement le partage du laquais qui la servait six mois auparavant.
>
> Qui pourra deviner les causes de ces vicissitudes? ...
>
> Une fille d'Opéra qui vient de décéder laisse un mobilier immense, une somme d'argent considérable. Avait-elle plus de beauté et d'esprit qu'une autre? Non: sortie de la plus basse classe du peuple, elle eut pour elle les faveurs de ce destin inconcevable, qui dans ce monde élève, abaisse, maintient, renverse ministres et catins. (Chapter 542, 'Matrones')
>
> (The changes to be observed in the hierarchy are amazing. Up or down the women go, and take precedence or lose it, according to whether chance accords them protectors with more money or less. It is all pure luck; an infatuation, rightly bestowed, may mean that some little person is lifted to the skies overnight, and leads the mode, who before was never heard of ...
>
> Another, having outlived her moment, falls back into poverty and throws in her lot with the lackey who wore her livery six months before.
>
> And the causes of the spectacular vicissitudes? Who can tell? ...
>
> Another who has just died, an opera-girl, left quantities of furniture and a good round sum in cash. Was she more lovely, wittier than her peers? Not she; she came from the lowest stratum of the people, but luck was on her side; luck, that can pull ministers down from their chairs of state, or keep a prostitute in favour.)[21]

Mercier expresses amazement and perplexity at the rapidity and extremity of such upward/downward mobility, which undermines any notion of an essential, fixed order (which might have been suggested by the structure of the 'gradin symbolique'). His repeated diagnosis of the arbitrariness of such movement (based on chance, luck, the whim of clients, rather than any inherent qualities such as talent, wit, beauty, skill or the social origins of the woman concerned) suggests an extreme – and paradigmatic – example of the vagaries of the wheel of fortune, especially in the comparison of the prostitute's fortune to that of ministers of state. The threatening aspect of such social mobility where embodied by the prostitute's trajectory is relatively understated in Mercier's account, but invoked more forcefully by Rétif, both within his taxonomies in *Le Pornographe*, and his narratives of urban corruption (such as *Le Paysan perverti/La Paysanne pervertie*). I will return to Mercier later in the argument, but we can now turn to Rétif's taxonomies of prostitutes to see how they compare with Mercier's *esquisse*.

Rétif's Taxonomies in *Le Pornographe* (1769, 1775)[22]

In his 1769 project for the reform of prostitution and the setting up of official brothels that he calls 'parthénions', Rétif provides a list of twelve categories of prostitutes, each with its own name. It is within the series of supplementary notes appended to the epistolary exchange containing the main argument, and more specifically, within the historical account of varying forms of prostitution in different periods throughout history, and in different cultures (the list of categories refers to eighteenth-century France, following descriptions of prostitutes in other European countries). So it is a list which is already within a broader relativizing structure, which serves to bring out the range of different possible attitudes towards this activity, as well as its different forms. Rétif's twelve 'classes' were then reworked into a series of sixteen in the second edition of the text written in 1774 and published in 1775[23] – suggesting both his continuing interest in this form of classification, and perhaps a slight overenthusiasm for refining and reinventing the different categories (in line with his more general propensity to rewrite and republish different versions of his own texts). But the second version also suggests some more fundamental shifts, as we will see. A fuller version of Table 1.1 is accessible at http://www.bbk.ac.uk/european/downloads/al_classifying_the_prostitute_appendix.pdf.

Table 1.1 Rétif de la Bretonne's taxonomies of prostitution in two editions of *Le Pornographe*.

Rétif, 1st edition of *Le Pornographe* (1769), pp. 171–7 in the Fayard edition (1985).	Rétif, 2nd edition of *Le Pornographe* (Nourse, Gosse junior and Pinet, 1775), pp. 313–21.
1. *Les filles entretenues par un seul*	(I) Les Courtisanes
2. *Les filles publiques par* état	1. *Les filles entretenues par un seul*
3. *Les demi-entretenues*	2. *Les filles galantes*
4. *Les filles de moyenne vertu*	3. *Les actrices*
5. *Les courtisanes*	4. *Les petites-bourgeoises*
6. *Les femmes du monde*	5. *Les concubines*
7. *Les demoiselles ... chez les mamans*	(II) Les prostituées communes, ou
8. *Les raccrochantes, mises sur* le bon ton	putains proprement dits
9. *Les boucaneuses*	6. *Les filles a parties*
10. *Les raccrocheuses*	7. *Les chauvesouris de vénus*
11. *Les gouines*	8. *Les filles-de-modes*
12. *Les barboteuses*	9. *Les femmes du monde*
	10. *Les débutantes*
	11. *Les boucaneuses*
	12. *Les araignées de cythère*
	13. *Les raccrocheuses*
	14. *Les gourgandines*
	15. *Les gouines*
	16. *Les barboteuses*

In the 1775 version of the taxonomy, several categories have been rebranded, although they retain similar descriptions (les 'demies-entretenues' become 'concubines', for example). Sometimes elements of the commentaries have simply been transferred from one category to another (for example, comments relating to the 'raccrochante' (no. 8 in version 1) are very similar to those relating to the 'araignée de Cythère' (no. 12 in version 2). The number of categories has been amplified by the inclusion of several entirely new ones, such as: 'les chauvesouris de Vénus' and 'les gourgandines' (the latter of which, like 'barboteuses', 'gouines' and 'raccrocheuses' can be found in dictionaries of this period and are not simply Rétif's own linguistic inventions).[24] Both versions of the taxonomy are cross-referred to a series of Greek and Latin terms, whose function is presumably to suggest the categories' 'authenticity' as types through a kind of scholarly apparatus, and to put them in a wider cultural context (although the Latin and Greek terms used seem at times to be somewhat arbitrarily switched around).[25]

In the 1775 version of the classification, the most significant modification is Rétif's introduction of an additional second order division between two major categories ('deux grandes classes'): 'Les courtisanes' and 'les prostituées communes, ou putains proprement dits' (elsewhere, this second category is given as 'les prostituées communes, ou filles absolument publiques'). The difference between two main classes of the second edition is not given an explicit formulation, other than the titles themselves (which suggest that the difference is largely bound up with how 'public' the women are). This idea is, however, developed through a couple of quotations in the paragraphs preceding the list, which suggest various types of distinction, relating to availability on the one hand, and skill on the other:

> a) 'On voit à nos promenades et autres endroits publics (dit M. de Saintfoix), deux sortes de Prêtresses de Vénus: les Filles entretenues, & celles qui n'ayant pas encore l'avantage de l'être, ne refusent aucune offrande'[26]
>
> (You can see, on the promenades and in other public places (according to M. de Saintfoix), two types of Priestess of Venus: women who are kept, and those who, not yet having this advantage, cannot refuse any offer)
>
> b) 'Une courtisane qui s'enrichit aux dépens d'un Sot, emploie mille souplesses, mille artifices, qui supposent en elle de grands talens', dit un penseur'.[27]
>
> (A courtesan who enriches herself at the expense of a fool, employs a thousand subtleties, and a thousand artifices, which presumes great talents on her part', says a thinker.)

The second class 'ne refusent aucune offrande' – they are more 'public' both in their visibility and in that they cannot refuse a customer, and thus do not know their clientele (designated earlier on in class terms as 'du bas-étage' ('of the lowest order')). The 'courtisane' class, on the other hand, is described as employing 'mille souplesses, mille artifices ... qui supposent en elles de grands talens':

greater skill, and consequently, more control over their destiny, and over clients. Rétif further implicitly separates the two in his remark that it is only prostitutes in the 'Courtisane' category who sometimes marry and leave the profession if it procures them 'une fortune & un rang' ('a fortune and rank'), while noting that those from the 'les prostituées communes', are rarely tempted to marry and return to 'honesty', since they could only aspire to the lowest classes; and even if they do marry, 'on les voit bientôt retomber bientôt dans la débauche' ('they very soon fall back into debauchery'): thus establishing a subset of women who are irredeemably 'lost' to society, and may never escape their status as prostitute.[28] Lastly, Rétif remarks on the 'tricks' played by each of the five categories of the courtesan class on their 'dupes' (in the first version of the taxonomy, a similar point was made regarding the first three classes) – so the arts of dissimulation, artifice and seduction are a particular feature of this class. Interestingly then, whereas Mercier invoked luck as the key factor in women's ascent and descent through the hierarchy, Rétif seems to attribute their position in the courtesan class as a function of a certain degree of talent and skill (which is also cause of their ultimate descent through the ranks – when their charms diminish).

In both versions of this taxonomy, Rétif's description of each category provides details of the different types of prostitutes' typical living conditions: whether they work in their own lodgings, in a brothel or on the street; whether they work part-time/seasonally or full-time; the different numbers and types of clients they might see and how these clients are solicited (by themselves, or by an intermediary); whether they display their status as a prostitute when in public; and price. He also incorporates details of the relative age, charms, cleanliness and dangers of disease attending their respective personae – his evaluative perspective is sometimes uncomfortably close to that of the client, and this slippage from detached observer to potential client is also apparent in Mercier's occasional use of the personal pronouns 'on' and 'vous' – in particular his description of 'grisettes'.[29]

The descending order of the hierarchy seems to be broadly related to price, and to the quality of their clientele: dukes and financiers are mentioned in relation to actresses, 'les libertins d'une fortune bornée' ('libertines with limited resources') in relation to 'les filles de modes' (no. 8 version 2), and unmarried artisans, builders and water-carriers in relation to 'les barboteuses' (no. 16). The relative degree of promiscuity or availability of the prostitute also appears to determine their positioning to some extent: while those in the courtesan class may dupe their clients, they nonetheless exercise some control over who they take on (with a relatively limited number of lovers); women who only sell themselves occasionally or on a part-time basis to supplement their income come next (whether 'les filles à parties', 'les chauvesouris de Vénus', or 'les filles de moyenne vertu'); and these are broadly followed by those who work in various types of brothel, or their own quarters; but there is a shift from those who have some capacity for limiting access to them ('les femmes du monde', 'les débutantes'), to those who are 'au premier venu' ('les boucaneuses' onward, with a couple of exceptions). This schema of degradation can also be seen in the trajectory written into the description of the 'fille entretenue par un seul':

> C'est par elle qu'ordinairement commence la corruption; une jeune fille qui s'est procuré le nécessaire au prix de ses faveurs, trouve cette route si aisée qu'elle ne veut plus en suivre d'autre. Mais les apas, comme les fleurs, se flétrissent en les palpant; l'Entreteneur s'éloigne; il faut se mettre à un taux plus bas; les besoins se sont accrus par l'habitude; on prend deux amants au lieu d'un, puis trois, quatre, enfin on s'abandonne au public.[30]
>
> (It is with her we see the onset of corruption; a young girl has procured herself the necessary by selling her favours and finds this path so easy to follow that she no longer wishes to try another. But charms, like flowers, wither when they are handled – her keeper leaves her; she has to lower her price; her needs have multiplied through habit and she takes two lovers instead of one, then three, four and ultimately, she abandons herself to the public.)

The language used to describe the various levels becomes increasingly pejorative: 'gouines' are described as 'monstres', as 'sales' and 'dégoûtantes' (no. 15), 'barboteuses' as 'viles, laides' and 'crapuleuses' (no. 16), but several categories emphasize the way in which prostitutes can be seen as victims who are exploited (e.g. 'les filles de moyenne vertu' in version 1, 'les chauvesouris de Vénus' and 'les boucaneuses' in version 2), and the expression of disgust does not always exclude that of pity. As with Mercier's hierarchies, Rétif is able to reconcile the notion that prostitutes may be victims, as well as predators (who are capable of ruining their clients' health and fortune), within the same sliding scale.

Blurring the Boundaries

In the present context, there is no scope to analyse the shifts entailed by Rétif's reconfiguring of his classificatory schema fully. But what is particularly striking is the way in which both he and Mercier come back to the question of classes and hierarchy, each providing more than one version. This suggests not only their preoccupation with the subject, and with providing a more adequate definition for the 'prostitute', but also perhaps the attempt to more clearly separate the whole range of venal from honest women – in their constituting of them as an identifiable overarching class (notwithstanding the later distinction between 'courtisane' and 'prostituée').

Mercier's frequent insistence that the practised eye can always tell the difference between the venal and the honest woman reasserts this distinction, and also corresponds to his repeated claim that prostitution is one and the same métier, at whatever level it is practised. Mercier's chapter on Palais-Royal is interesting in its clear privileging of experience over theory in the ability to make such judgements:

Là sont les filles, les courtisanes, les duchesses et les honnêtes femmes; et personne ne s'y trompe ... Or, je soutiens que M. Lavater aurait peine à distinguer une femme de condition d'une fille entretenue; et le moindre clerc de procureur, ... sans avoir tant médité sur cet objet, en saurait plus que lui ('Palais-Royal', Chapter 162)

(There we find whores, courtesans, duchesses and honest women; and no one mistakes one for the other ... Now I maintain that Monsieur Lavater would find it difficult to distinguish between a woman of quality and a kept mistress; and the slightest clerk ... without having meditated so much on this subject, would know more than he.)

However, Mercier's insistence on this point, and the drawing up of these taxonomies, which define, order and place the prostitute (notwithstanding their instabilities and ambiguities, to which I will return in a moment), perhaps corresponds to the fact that at this time, in a range of sources, there is increasing commentary and anxiety regarding the visibility of prostitutes and – precisely – the difficulty of distinguishing them from honest women.

Even within Mercier's own 'gradin symbolique' such ambiguities are not absent, and we should note that the most threatening category – that to which danger is ascribed – is the 'bourgeoises demi-décentes', because they are not as they appear to be: 'espèce dangereuse et perfide, qui voile et pare l'adultère de couleurs trompeuses, etc.' ('a dangerous and perfidious type, which masks adultery and presents it in false colours). This class roughly corresponds, in other chapters, to the categories entitled 'Le nom que vous voudrez' (Chapter 236) and 'états indéfinissables' (Chapter 154), whose blurring of the boundaries is evident from their very title. The refusal to name 'Le nom que vous voudrez' results from Mercier's ironic criticism of the social acceptability of such women, who appear in public, and command respect, despite their actual (hidden) venal status: 'la mode autorise que ces femmes se montrent au bal, au Colisée, aux spectacles ... Malheur à qui voudrait en médire' ('Fashion allows these women to show themselves at balls, at the Coliseum, at the theatre ... Woe betide he who wishes to speak ill of her'). And he makes a similar point in relation to the highest grade of 'filles d'opéra', who comport themselves with the airs and graces befitting 'une femme de qualité', and are also treated with respect; while those from the 'états indéfinissables' 'ne veulent voir que la classe où est l'homme qui soutient leur maison' ('wish to see only the class of the man supporting their household'), thus rejecting the less exalted social entourage of their husbands.

Mercier here attempts to neutralize these ambiguities by squarely placing these women within the venal category, despite their apparent 'demi-décence', and society's acceptance of their honesty and social status at face value. In this respect, common prostitutes represent far less of a threat to society, because they do not pretend to be what they are not (either in class terms, or emotional ones):

> Elles se donnent après tout pour ce qu'elles sont; elles ont un vice de moins, l'hypocrisie. Elles ne peuvent causer les ravages qu'une femme libertine et prude occasionne souvent sous les fausses apparences de la modestie et de l'amour. (Chapter 238, 'Filles publiques').
>
> (After all, these women give themselves for what they are: hypocrisy does not enter in the catalogue of their vices. They never can occasion such mischiefs as the prudish woman of pleasure, hanging out the false colours of love and modesty.)

The rhetorical assertion of the impossibility of distinguishing between honest and certain classes of venal women is frequently used by other writers of the period to make a range of types of social and moral critique, bearing the trace of – or at least coinciding with – Rousseau's diatribe against 'public women' in the *Lettre à d'Alembert sur les spectacles*, in which he provocatively conflates the woman who lives her life in the *monde* rather than in the domestic privacy of the home with actresses and thus prostitutes, and suggesting a moral equivalence between their respective lack of *pudeur* and promiscuity.

Three examples of these rhetorical formulations by different authors can therefore serve as a concluding gesture towards some of the ways in which this kind of 'blurring of the boundaries' could be used polemically, to map onto anxieties about social class and the social and/or moral order. The following remarks by Fougeret de Montbrun, who is better known for his prostitute novel *Margot la ravaudeuse* (1750), are from *La Capitale de Gaules ou la Nouvelle Babylone* (1759):

> La pudeur et la modestie, la discrétion et la retenue, qui faisaient autrefois l'ornement du sexe, sont maintenant remplacées par l'effronterie et la licence, et par tout ce qui porte le caractère de la prostitution la plus scandaleuse. Au sacrament près, il n'est pas possible d'apercevoir aucune différence entre ce qu'on appelle une honnête femme et une femme publique ... On se marchande comme un meuble et l'on se livre indifféremment au plus offrant et au dernier enchérisseur'[31]
>
> (Propriety and modesty, discretion and reserve, which used to be the ornament of the fair sex, have now been replaced by effrontery and licentiousness and by all that characterizes the most scandalous form of prostitution. Barely excepting marriage, it is practically impossible to see any difference between an honest woman and a prostitute ... They haggle over their person as if it were a piece of furniture and give themselves indiscriminately, to the best offer and the highest bidder.)

In this quotation, the suggestion that immodesty, 'effronterie', and 'tout ce qui porte le caractère de la prostitution la plus scandaleuse' are visible in the behaviour of women at large collapses the boundary between honest and venal women in order to suggest the corrupt values of society at large.

In *Le Paysan perverti*, Rétif's naive protagonist Edmond makes a similar point, in order to bring out the difficulty of distinguishing moral qualities on the basis of outward appearance, and the pitfalls which such appearances can lead young men into (as well as potentially suggesting, through the slightly ironic tone of his comment, a more fundamental blurring between the two categories – which perhaps cannot be separated with certainty at all):

Dans les commencements que j'étais à Paris, je ne savais pas distinguer les mœurs à la parure; je croyais toutes les femmes honnêtes: après une demi-expérience, je fis tout le contraire et je pris toutes les femmes pour des catins. Il faut un long usage, pour les distinguer sûrement! (Rétif, *Le Paysan perverti*, Letter 107)

(At the beginning when I was in Paris, I didn't know how to tell moral behaviour from their attire; I thought all the women were honest. Following a certain degree of experience, I formed the opposite view and took all women to be whores. It takes a lot of practice to distinguish them with certainty!)

In Godard d'Aucour's dedicatory epistle to Rosalie Duthé (a well-known actress and courtesan) included in the 1776 edition of his *Mémoires Turcs*, we see a variation on the same theme, but here it is the courtesan's behaviour which is the focus of the critique (rather than that of so-called 'honest women'). Here, the author ironically applauds her and her fellow courtesans' triumph: not only are they fully visible in high society rather than staying in the shadows as was previously the case, but they, rather than honest women, now set the tone, and in their ostentation, they eclipse even the most opulent ladies of high society:

Ce n'est qu'avec admiration, Mademoiselle, que j'envisage le haut point de gloire où vous et vos compagnes êtes parvenues ... la douce licence, sous le nom de liberté, a ouvert enfin la carrière à vos vastes désirs; vous triomphez, divines enchanteresses, et vos charmes séducteurs ont changé la face de la France ... Dans ma jeunesse, il faut en convenir, toutes les belles n'étaient pas des vestales, ... mais alors ce que le vulgaire appelle les femmes honnêtes, permettez-moi ce radotage, avaient encore le haut du pavé et donnaient le ton ... Nous avions l'imbécillité de suivre leur char, et contents de vous adorer en secret, nous n'avions pas même l'esprit de nous ruiner avec vous. Ignorant vous-mêmes de l'excellence de votre état, vous n'osiez encore vous risquer au grand jour. Mais aujourd'hui que la commode licence a tiré le rideau qui vous tenait à l'écart, vous éclipsez par votre faste la femme la plus opulente: c'est avoir franchi la barrière à pas de géant.

... Depuis cette heureuse révolution, rien ne vous arrête, plus d'obstacles; l'hymen, tourné en ridicule, ose à peine se montrer; vous paraissez publiquement dans les voitures de vos amants; vous portez leurs livrées, leurs couleurs, souvent les diamants de leurs épouses, et toujours leur aisance ...' (Godard d'Aucour, 'Epître à Mademoiselle D. T. [i.e. Rosalie Duthé]', added in the 1776 edition of *Mémoires turcs*)

(It is with admiration alone, Mademoiselle, that I envisage the peaks of glory which you and your companions have reached ... that sweet licentiousness, given the name of liberty, has finally opened the path to your vast desires. Divine enchantresses, you are triumphant, and your seductive charms have changed the face of France ... In my youth, I admit, not all beautiful women were vestal virgins, ... but at that time what the vulgar call honest women, permit me this rambling thought, still had the high ground and set the tone ... We had the imbecility to follow their lead, and, happy to adore you in secret, we certainly didn't have the thought of ruining ourselves with you. You yourselves were unaware of the excellence of your state, and dared not risk appearing in the light of day. But now that an opportune licentiousness has swept aside the veil that kept you out of sight, in your splendour you eclipse the most opulent woman: this is to breach the boundary by leaps and bounds.

> ... Since this happy revolution, nothing can stop you, there are no more obstacles in your path; marriage is ridiculed and barely dares to show itself; you appear publicly in the carriages of your lovers; you wear their livery, their colours, often their wives' diamonds, and always their comfortable self-assurance

The visibility of the higher echelons of courtesan society is not only damaging because of their seduction of high-ranking men (the corrosive effect on their fortunes is specifically invoked here), nor is it because of the morally corrupting example they set to young girls (a danger that both Mercier and Rétif frequently invoke); but their very public display of high status undermines the function of clothing, and other outward signs of prestige, as a means of reaffirming the social order. Their public appearance in their lover's 'voiture', adoption of his livery, and of his wife's diamonds, specifically subverts the social meaning of such signs.

In their ability to take on the social status of their lover (at least: to adopt the airs and graces, and visible display of wealth that such a status suggests), they embody the spectre of social mobility, further exacerbated by the rapidity with which they ascend and descend the ranks of their profession; an instability that we already saw in Mercier's comments following the *esquisse* of the 'gradin symbolique', and which is written even more explicitly into Rétif's taxonomies, in the frequent reference to how one type leads to another within the descriptive passages following each definition.[32] In this way, the figure of the prostitute, in her embodiment of artifice, 'luxe' and the cult of appearance, represents the threat of social disorder and disintegration of a society's moral compass all at once.

In conclusion, it seems that Rétif's and Mercier's interest in pinning down the various categories of prostitutes, unstable as these very categories are in their shifting terms and porous definitions, may well be an attempt to reverse the dangerous (social) ambiguities noted in the final section. This attempt to neutralize the dangerous confusion and subversion of the social and moral orders is taken even further in the main part of Rétif's *Le Pornographe*, which includes a further list, of how the prostitutes in his ideal official brothel, the 'parthénion', should be classed. This involves an elaborate set of prices and an arrangement within a series of six corridors. The prostitute's position – her location within the *parthénion* – is to depend on her beauty and age: the only criteria invoked. A separate wing is given over to *filles entretenues*. In the *parthénion*, then, prostitutes are classed according to 'verifiable' qualities – their 'natural' qualities – and artifice, deception and *luxe* are banished from the equation. All ambiguity is removed from their status, and their assigned place within the hierarchical structure is clearly defined and controlled. And because the *parthénion* is 'outside' society, the question of social class is also banished from the equation, since prostitutes are no longer in the public eye, and no longer threaten to eclipse honest women, or to seduce young men and young women from their social and moral obligations through their all too ostentatious example of beautiful vice.

2 IN HER OWN WORDS: AN EIGHTEENTH-CENTURY MADAM TELLS HER STORY

Kathryn Norberg

Marie-Madeline Dossement, who lived in Paris from approximately 1748 to 1763, is the subject of this study.[1] Dossement was without accomplishments or distinction, completely obscure during her own lifetime and generally ignored thereafter. She would have remained forgotten and unknown had she not embarked in about 1750 on an unusual career, that of police informer. Every fortnight, she submitted what she called her *feuille* (paper) or *écrit* (writing) to Paris police chief, René Berryer de Ravenoville or, more accurately, to his clerks, who then had it copied onto sheets of white paper loosely bound with blue ribbon. In these pages, now preserved in the Archives de la Bastille at the Arsenal library in Paris, Dossement detailed daily life in her brothel, for she was a 'madame' or brothel mistress.

Despite her intriguing profession, Dossement and her text have not attracted the attention of many historians, professional or amateur.[2] Only Gaston Capon, a *belle époque* bibliophile and connoisseur of dirty books, took an interest in her and included a selection from her 'notebook' in his two volume study, *Les Maisons closes au XVIIIe siècle*, published in 1903. Capon analysed only the first forty-one pages of the journal, stopping in July 1751 because 'this suffices to convey the tone of the institution'.[3] The reports *are* repetitive, with their long lists of clients that Capon has meticulously footnoted. Clearly Capon found the men in Dossement's world more interesting than the woman herself, for he has little or nothing to say about her. 'Une tenacière de bordel' (a brothel manager), he remarks, and leaves it at that, assuming that the (male) reader shares his familiarity with this *belle époque* type and the institution which she ran, the *maison de tolérance*.

Dossement's text can be boring: it consists mainly of names of clients listed by the day and time they entered and exited her brothel. But it also includes digressions and anecdotes which Dossement included (like a good student mindful of the length requirement) to fill out her text. In this padding, Dossement expressed her opinions, attitudes and even personality. This text is unusual, maybe even unique. We have very few writings by early modern sex workers and even fewer that deal with sex work itself.[4] In Dossement's journal we learn about life in a brothel, not from the usual perspective of the courts or the police, but from the position of a sex worker. Elsewhere I have written about the men and women who frequented Dossement's brothel.[5] In this essay, I focus on Dossement herself, on her writing and her view of her world and her place in it, and especially on her conception of prostitutes and prostitution.

The Text

Dossement was not the only madam in eighteenth-century Paris to act as a police informer. At least a dozen women submitted lists of clients to the police and many more provided information on an occasional basis. But Dossement was the only one to address her revelations directly to the man-in-charge, the police chief. Why was she so privileged? She was the daughter of an officer, albeit it very minor one, of the Châtelet court, the very court over which the police chief presided. Her background elevated her above the other madams and bestowed upon her superior, though far from perfect, literacy. But what distinguished her most was her aptitude for informing. Dossement seems to have known instinctively the kinds of information that would interest the police chief: gossip about court figures, instances of insubordination by his inferiors, the inspectors and of course salacious anecdotes concerning the rivals of his patron, Madame de Pompadour. Dossement supplied all these in quantity (her text runs to 500 pages) and meticulous detail. She notes what was said in her brothel, who worked there, how she recruited them, which men frequented the brothel, at what time of day, for how long and how much they paid down to the last penny.[6]

For six years, Dossement recorded her daily activities and thoughts, and as with any lengthy text, Dossement's 'writing' changed over time. She relaxed and permitted herself digressions as her confidence in the police chief's protection grew. She wrote both more (discussing her personal life and expressing her opinions) and less (declining to submit reports when she had nothing of interest to report). Around 1754, she even found a way to make her disclosures work to her benefit. She adopted a strategy of pre-empting potential complaints from disgruntled customers or neighbours and discounting rumors before they even reached the police chief's ears. She also included more anecdotes simply for the pleasure of telling them and allowed herself to describe her own intimate attachments.[7]

We can learn a great deal about Dossement's life and her personality from her chronicle, but the text is still far from perfect. The year 1749 is missing and many pages have suffered such severe water-damage that they are nearly unreadable.[8] The manuscript copy we possess is not written in Dossement's hand, but rather in that of anonymous clerks charged with recopying her poorly spelled and punctuated text. Most important, Dossement's goal was always to please the police, to provide them with the information they valued in return for the protection that allowed her to operate her brothel with near impunity. The appetite of the eighteenth-century police for information was voracious and sometimes inexplicable. But their main goal was to acquire leverage, to possess information that allowed them to blackmail or at least to coerce individuals.[9]

In her notebooks, Dossement tries to provide information of use to the police. Consequently, the police chief though never heard or seen exerts a great deal of influence on the text. He determines to a large degree its contents because Dossement wanted above all else to please him. Berryer is a hard man to know. We know he was born in 1703 and rose quickly from *maître des requêtes*, to Intendant of Poitou and then, in 1748 to the extremely powerful position of *lieutenant général de police* or Parisian police chief.[10] All sources agree that Madame Pompadour was his patron and that his brutal enforcement in 1750 of a law targeting beggars provoked rioting.[11] Otherwise Berryer is a mystery. His correspondence as police chief is decisive, brief and impersonal, the work of a perfect bureaucrat.[12]

Dossement addressed her reports to Berryer (or 'Monseigneur' as she called him) and frequently invoked his name in her text. Consequently, Dossement's reports often read like letters or memoirs and bear a suspicious resemblance in form (if not in content) to a number of salacious novels. The voice of the brothel *madame* is heard in *Le cannevas de la Paris ou mémoires pour servir à l'histoire du Roule* (1750); *Portefeuille de Madame Gourdan* (circa 1780); *Correspondance de Madame Gourdan dite la petite comtesse* (1783) and *Les Serails de Paris* (1802). These texts feature either the memoirs of a madam (*Le Cannevas*) or her letters (*La Portefeuille de Madame Gourdan*) and all were written by men who appropriated the brothel madam's voice in order to titillate and amuse. The formal similarity between these libertine novels and Dossement's text raises the suspicion that Dossement was an example of eighteenth-century 'ventriloquism', another Grub Street hack masquerading as a whore. Was Dossement a real woman or just a literary device?

Madame Dossement's Life

Dossement is in fact a real woman whose life has left traces in parish records, judicial proceedings and financial documents of the period. Marie-Madeleine Dossement was born in the village of Charly in the current department of the Aisne and baptized there in January of 1711.[13] According to a brief autobiography inserted in her notebooks, Dossement's father was a Parisian who trained as a lawyer.[14] Her mother was also from Paris, the daughter of a prosperous grocer. Her parents wanted her 'to marry a merchant or a surgeon but she preferred', Dossement writes, 'the *petit maître* or one who appeared to be a *petit maître*'.[15] The family was not rich. Dossement's father purchased the office of *huissier à cheval* attached to the Châtelet. This office allowed the holder to exercise his profession anywhere in France and Dossement's father moved several years before her birth to Charly-sur-Marne, a village of only 400 souls at that time.[16] The first eleven years of Dossement's life were spent in this tiny, champagne-producing commune. The family was nearly invisible. Examination of the town's parish registers reveals few traces of the Dossement family, and the notarial records do not mention them at all. Madame's father did not stand as godparent to the children of the local nobles or even magistrates. He did attend a few funerals but only those of other *huissiers*. He did not act as a witness at any marriage and buried alone a son who died. A Châtelet *huissier's* job was to deliver summons and decrees, begin the process of foreclosure, and sell furniture and farm machinery at auction in the event of foreclosure. All in all, this was not a job to make one popular or (it seems) a member of the elite.[17]

Around 1721, the Dossements (now a family of one son and three daughters) moved from Charly to Chateau-Thierry.[18] Here, Madame grew, she tells us, 'tall and fierce' ('grande et farouche'). Her parents sent her to a local convent, the Dames de la Congrégation. Madame's father and mother frequented 'Messieurs and Mesdames' of the town. They were, she infers, very *mondain*, that is, fashionable. But the names of the town's great nobles and magistrates do not appear anywhere in her account. Madame mentions (as if they were quite elegant) officers from the *grenier à sel* (the salt tax bureau), a minor noble and a barrister. These middle-level officials made up the 'fine company' frequented by the Dossements.

Around 1726, Madame's mother went to Paris to pursue a lawsuit and took Marie-Madeleine with her. There the fifteen-year old girl went to the opera and visited Versailles. In her autobiography, Madame tells us that she learned to like coaches, fine clothing and Parisian men. Only with regret did she return to Chateau-Thierry. A few years later she managed to travel back to Paris. One of her older sisters had married a grocer there and Marie-Madeleine became her 'little chambermaid'. This role did not suit her at all. She became a sort of companion to an older woman, a friend from Chateau-Thierry. But when the woman returned to Chateau-Thierry, Dossement had to follow her.

Then disaster struck: her father, now quite old, died in 1734.[19] Marie-Madeleine's mother moved to Paris to live near her birth family and her older daughter. Still according to Madame's autobiography, a canon who was a family friend took Marie-Madeleine and her mother under his wing. He visited the house, bought Marie-Madeleine dresses and helped her mother liquidate her husband's office. At this point, the circumstances of the family were dire. Marie-Madeleine and her mother were nearly destitute and had been so for some time. Ten years had passed since the tax (the *paulette*) on the father's office of *huissier* had been paid. The canon's 'gifts' were greatly appreciated but the few suitors who came courting were not. Marie-Madeleine was of marriageable age and several 'bourgeois' presented themselves. But she refused them all because she sensed that [her] 'mother was not able to offer an appropriate dowry which was humiliating' ('je sentais que ma mère n'étoit point en état d'offrir une dot honnête et qui m'humiliait').[20]

Marie-Madeleine was, according to her autobiography, seized with greed, ambition and the desire for more glamorous company. She began to sneak out of the house at night and meet young men. She hired coaches and went to 'fine suppers'. She had 'rendez-vous' with 'gentlemen'. Finally she gave in to libertinism. In a narrative that read as if it was straight out of a novel, Dossement describes her 'fall' and attributes it, like eighteenth-century moralists, to desire for luxury: 'At this time, I slipped and abandoned virtue ... and the reason was that I wanted to buy things ... and had no other way to get money' ('Alors, je lâchay pied à la vertu et la raison qui m'y portoit c'est que je voulois toujours acheter des choses'). But romance was also a part of her life. She fell in love with an artist, the son of the sculptor Tarlet, but he broke her heart. Still, she claimed he was her only true love.[21]

Sometime thereafter, she accompanied her mother to Brittany where, on the 16 February 1743, she married Charles Estienne Bedoy in the St Nicolas parish of Nantes. Bedoy was a widower and a *vérificateur des domaines du roi,* the holder of a venal office and a lower-level official in the management of royal properties. All the witnesses save Dossement's mother were local merchants. In her notebooks, Dossement says little about her husband. She does not even mention his given name. Later, in financial documents, she describes him as a 'bourgeois de Paris' who 'lived off his investments' ('un bourgeois qui vit de son bien'). At 32 years of age, Dossement was finally married, but the relationship soured fast though why we do not know. Dossement says nothing about the collapse of her marriage but the split was definitive. Dossement fled 'with some merchandise' to London. There she remained for only six months because she found the English 'badly dressed and vulgar' ('mal vêtus et grossier'). Perhaps it was in London that she first embarked on a career as a *fille à la mode*.

She quickly returned to Paris. Dossement says nothing about this period in her autobiography. Perhaps the police chief was familiar with her first steps in the world of venal sex. By 1747, she was already the head of a fully operational brothel located in the Louvre on the rue Jean Saint Denis. In 1748, she moved to the nearby rue des Deux Portes and began writing her police reports. In April 1752 she signed a lease on a house located in the rue Saint Fiacre just south of the boulevards and north of the Porte Saint Martin, in what is today the Sentier quarter. There, Dossement lived in some comfort. When a gang of youths broke in and ransacked her house in 1753, Dossement reported the incident to her local police commissioner and stated that three large mirrors in gilt frames, the painted silk hangings on her bed, brocade upholstered chairs and silver candlesticks had been damaged or stolen. Dossement's three-bedroom apartment was well but not lavishly furnished. It was not that different from the homes of the wealthy merchants and officials who lived in Paris.[22]

Madame Dossement's Opinions

Though her background was more modest than aristocratic, Dossement was at pains to claim some distinguished antecedents. She boasts of a grandfather who was a physician to Queen Marie Thérèse, a cousin who was a prioress at an abbey in the Charonne and her brother-in-law whose great-uncle was the poet La Fontaine.[23] Clearly she wanted to impress the police chief but she was also ambivalent about her own origins, rooted as there were in the milieu of prosperous merchants and lower-level officials. After all, as a young woman she had discouraged the marriage proposals of the merchants who came calling and sought instead clandestine rendezvous with 'gentleman'.

Dossement was not an aristocrat, but she was a snob. Court connections and lofty titles dazzled her. In 1752, Monsieur Curys, a steady client, asked her to bring some girls to a party thrown by the Duc de Richelieu. Dossement describes the evening in loving detail. The Duke was positively charming, sitting next to the procuress, complimenting her and admiring her girls. She carefully enumerates the other men at the party, noting who spoke in private with the famous Duke and for how long and what decorations each man wore. It was a glimpse of the high life, of aristocratic libertinism.[24]

If Dossement carefully observed the social hierarchy that evening, she had no comment on the sex. In fact, Madame never writes about sex directly. Whether this is a concession to the police chief's sensibilities or a deep-seated modesty is hard to say. Or maybe sex was just too ordinary to Dossement to merit description. In any event, Dossement never describes what a client does with a girl. 'He came, had supper, went to bed and left at nine': this is all she has to say about a trick. She does not blink an eye when a Swedish client requested the tallest girls in Paris.[25] Nor is she particularly surprised by clients who insist on twelve-year-old girls. 'The connoisseurs of virginity', she observes 'are not particularly numerous but they pay well'.[26] Kinky preferences or erotic performances do not appear to have occurred in the Dossement brothel. No whips or chains, no erotic *ombres chinoises*, not even dancing enlivened the quiet atmosphere. The place seems rather dull but maybe Dossement took pains to describe it that way. Or maybe discretion was the institution's primary offering.

At 44, Madame herself, it seems, rarely serviced the clientele. Every other female in the brothel (including the domestics) did, but the girls were generally no more than 20 years of age, much younger than Dossement herself. Still, Madame had what she described as a last 'adventure'. In 1754, she began a liaison with a younger doctor, a certain Million whom the girls dubbed Monsieur de St Blême in honor of his pallor. He was not a dashing character. But he incarnated the qualities that Madame most respected and appreciated: order, consistency, prudence and predictability. 'He comes on Thursday and Sunday', she writes, 'and because he is concerned about his health makes only one sacrifice' ('Il ne vient que les jeudis et dimanches et ne fait qu'un seul sacrifice parce qu'il soigne sa santé'). 'He is as regular', she says, 'as a clock' ('Il est reglé comme du papier à musique').[27]

Many of Dossement's clients were anything but regular when it came to paying. Her chronicle is filled with examples of men who tried to evade payment or failed to reimburse her for expenses or loans made at short term. But she was not greedy. When in her absence, a wealthy client absconded with a girl and most of the wardrobe, Madame had loaned her, she was not upset but found the pair and struck a bargain with the client.[28] Small losses – the supper that was not paid for, or the carriage fees ignored – she accepted philosophically, to retain a prestigious client or preserve an image of wealth.

Rumors circulated that she was very wealthy. For her clients, Dossement cultivated the notion that she was rich: 'I try to appear more comfortable than I am because men bargain for girls as they would bargain for oranges in a fruit market, and the less poor one appears, the more they offer'.[29] A veneer of wealth served Dossement, but not when it came to the police chief. She was careful to quash such gossip in the pages of her journal. 'It is said that I am rich', Dossement wrote, 'but I just pawned my earrings for 5 louis' ('On pense que je suis riche, pourtant je viens de mettre en gage pour cinq louis mes boucles d'oreille'). 'Fate', she tells the police chief, 'has not meant for me to make money in this profession'.[30] Does she protest too much?

Dossement was probably quite comfortable because she (like other brothel madams) loaned money. A heretofore unknown or at least underappreciated aspect of eighteenth-century French brothels is that they functioned as primitive banks. Most madams probably operated on a very small scale. But Dossement was more successful: she extended credit, exchanged bills of exchange, liquidated annuities and when really large sums were needed suggested other individuals (usually women) who could handle the transaction. All of the regular brothel clients were in debt to her. The more successful *filles à la mode* came to her to sell jewels or liquidate the annuities that their boyfriends bestowed on them. Most transactions were relatively small: only longstanding clients or friends were advanced more than 800 livres. When she did loan, she weighed the risks and benefits carefully. Should she advance money to Tarlet? As if thinking out loud, she weighed the risks:

> I had dinner with Monsieur Tarlet tonight and he promised to pay me a *rente* of 2,000 livres which he has owed me for a long time. He will pay me when he inherits from his mother. And because I know him for a reliable man, I will advance him 1,500 livres and then he will guarantee me a lifetime annuity based on his property and income. He must have 6,000 to 7,000 livres of income annually. He does not gamble anymore. He has calmed down and he does not spend much money which makes me think that this is a good business deal.[31]

With her earnings, Madame invested wisely and conservatively, setting aside money for her old age. In the 1760s, she began purchasing government annuities, a strategy followed by many single and widowed women.[32] In 1762, she bought 2,000 livres worth of government-issued annuities. She continued to save for her old age: in 1765 and again in 1770 she purchased government annuities. Then she disappears, perhaps because she was dead or because at her age – fifty-nine years – annuities were no longer a profitable investment.

Dossement was conservative in business, but also, it seems, in politics. The police were particularly interested in criticisms of the king, his ministers or his mistresses, so when such comments were made at Dossement's table, she gleefully reported them. She was always careful to condemn these propositions and even scold those who had made them. 'One should not complain about the ministers', she admonished a client, 'but rather approve everything that the government does'.[33] When several clients got drunk and sang slanderous songs about 'court women', Dossement informed Berryer and then remarked 'I find that Croisil and Aubry lack the prudence, respect and discretion one should have for the great (les Grands) especially their Prince and the Court'.[34] Was Dossement genuinely obedient or just protecting herself? It is hard to tell.

Dossement did have one subversive attitude: she hated priests. 'I do not like priests' she remarked at several points in her journal and she certainly did not see the cream of the clergy in her brothel. 'I hate the men of the church', she confided 'because they make of religion a kind of job which procures for them a livelihood and the means of diverting themselves but at bottom they have less devotion and more intemperance than ordinary people. I admit that the least devout are often the most intelligent because they know enough to excuse their beliefs'.[35] Dossement may have acquired her anti-clericalism early in life, but it is more likely that she began to hate priests once she became a *fille à la mode*. Priests were the whores' traditional enemy because they frequently denounced them to the police.

Madame Dossement Writes about Sex Work

Dossement did not hesitate to complain to the police chief about the hazards and heartbreaks of brothel life. She criticizes, for example, the desultory treatment for syphilis doled out at the state-run Bicêtre hospital. Many of Dossement's girls returned from the Bicêtre as sick as they had entered. Dossement blamed the treatment's lack of effectiveness on the laziness of the staff who did not enforce the hospital regimen. 'Monseigneur', she told Berryer, 'if you could only redouble your charitable concern for these poor girls and order that a dependable and sufficiently mature person be entrusted with the maintenance of discipline and the dispensing of medical treatment, then the girls might be cured'.[36]

Dossement also did not hesitate to criticize the policing of prostitution. In May 1751, she suggested that the police outlaw not prostitutes but the bands of young men that persecuted them. 'Monseigneur', she writes:

> you cannot imagine, how much scandal these young men cause in a neighborhood ... If young men were forced to act differently people would not know about many of the gallant women in Paris, whom you are now obliged to arrest and punish, so that it would be as if there were no girls or women suspected of prostitution in Paris.[37]

Girls (*les filles*): this is how Dossement always referred to prostitutes when she does not call them by name. She never adopted the derogatory expressions used by the police to define and denigrate prostitutes. *Putain, raccrocheuse, pierreuse, garce* – the inspectors used these labels to distinguish between and fix different levels of prostitutes. Dossement appears to have resisted such labels as she did the inspectors' snide remarks about the girls' looks ('she is slightly hunchbacked' or 'misshapen') or intelligence ('very dull' or 'not lively').[38] Nor did she laugh about the venereal diseases that the girls inevitably caught. Dossement could say negative things about the women who worked in her brothel. 'A girl with a conscience', she wrote, 'is as rare as a phoenix' and she was particularly hard on girls who stole from her.[39] But she also expressed fondness for some of her long-term employees and conceived of each girl as an individual, attributing her virtues and weaknesses to her character and not to her prostitution.

Did Dossement consider her sex a key element in her destiny? Dossement was certainly no feminist. How could she be? Nor did she engage in serious thought about the status of women. But she did believe that women were at a disadvantage in this world while men were 'the most conniving creatures alive'.[40] Marriage she condemned. When one of her clients offered to marry her because she was rich, Dossement refused: 'Even if it were true that I am rich, I wouldn't marry because I prefer to keep my independence.'[41] Generally, Dossement saw men (perhaps even Berryer?) as a constant menace. 'One must always be on guard', she said. 'One must be careful not to be duped.' Repeatedly in her reports, Dossement voices her fear of 'being tricked'. Her clients wore disguises, they gave her false names, and one of her most loyal clients borrowed money from her only to weasel out of payment later. Her only ambition in life, Dossement claimed, was to avoid being duped.

Dossement was rarely tricked, for she was extremely clever and perceptive, two qualities a successful madam – and informer – needed. Clients regularly gave false names and addresses when they visited her brothel. Madame was not fooled and noted very frequently in her report that she had yet to learn a client's true identity or address. For a while, she employed a small boy who followed the clients when they left the brothel in order to ascertain where they lived. Such information enhanced her reports, but also provided her with leverage if she needed to coerce a client into paying. Dossement was almost always in control and she managed to handle even the most difficult situations. She could dissuade drunken soldiers from knocking down her door or calm enraged clients by persuasive argument alone. Sangfroid was one of her most salient characteristics.

Dossement is a far cry from the pleasure-seeking, ever-agreeable madams of libertine fiction. With her roots in lower officialdom and her disinterest in sex, she bears little resemblance to fiction's Madame Pâris or Mother Brown. Dossement was not the illegitimate daughter of a bishop or a lusty sex fiend. The real eighteenth-century procuress was much tamer than her fictional equivalents and so too was her brothel. Dossement's house was quiet, discrete and not in the least kinky. Madame's clients did not come to her door 'openly and in joy' (to cite Rossiaud on medieval clients).[42] They came in secret, wearing disguises, and bearing false names. Inhibition, not orgies, seems to have been the norm.

Feminist scholarship has portrayed the prostitute as either a powerful sexual rebel (in response to the prostitutes' rights movement of the 1970s) or, more recently, as a hapless victim (as a result of the current interest in the trafficking of women).[43] Dossement never thought of herself as either empowered or victimized as a result of her profession. Neither would anyone familiar with her notebook. Though she complained of bad luck, Dossement was an independent woman, and most likely a wealthy one. She was usually in control in interactions with her clients and did not hesitate to bar her door to a quarter of the men who sought entry. On the other hand, she was keenly aware of her vulnerability. She feared, it is important to note, not prostitution per se or male lust in general, but rather the authorities, the police. What Madame Dossement feared was not disease, violence or dehumanization, but arrest.

One night in November of 1751 revealed the extent of her vulnerability and terror. A minor procuress named Miller had been arrested for corrupting a twelve-year-old girl. Corrupting a minor (*macquerellage*) was a serious crime, whose penalty was public whipping, branding and banishment. Only a year earlier a procuress had suffered just this fate, so Dossement's worries were far from unjustified.[44] Dossement was peripherally involved and feared that she might be arrested as several other madams already had been. When she learned of the arrests, she 'had a terrible fright', and fled her home in the middle of the night. She sought shelter at the other end of Paris, on rue du Four in the Faubourg

Saint Germain des Près but not before switching carriages twice to avoid being followed. 'Imagine my terror', she tells the police chief. The next day she threw herself on the mercy of a police commissioner who was a friend. In the end, she was neither subpoenaed nor arrested.

Dossement would continue to evade arrest in the years that followed. She prospered on rue Saint Fiacre: her business grew to include at least one additional apartment near the Louvre. She continued to receive many men and provide girls to some of the wealthiest men in Paris. Then on 7 October 1757 the reports suddenly stop. Police chief Berryer had been promoted to minister of the Navy and his departure created a rupture in the flow of reports from the brothel madams and other spies. Did Dossement vanish? Thanks to the records of her notary LeLoere, and his successor Girault we know that she continued to purchase annuities up to 1770.[45] At this point, she vanishes leaving us to wonder if she took the early retirement for which she longed, moved away from Paris or (most likely) died.

3 'ALL THE WORLD KNOWS HER STORIE': APHRA BEHN AND THE DUCHESS OF MAZARIN

Claudine van Hensbergen

In December 1675, Hortense Mancini, Duchess of Mazarin (1646–99), rode into London on horseback disguised in male clothing (*en cavalier*). The event did not go unnoticed. A record in the *Calendar of State Papers* contains an account of a coffee house conversation that took place between a pair of Frenchmen and several 'coffists' detailing Mazarin's arrival:

1st Coffist.	Pray tell us, if you know, what news the late notable express brought.
Frenchmen.	We know not of any.
1st Coffist.	Have you not heard of the courier arrived three days since with a retinue that marked him for a man of great quality?
2nd Coffist.	I saw him and his attendants alight from their post horses, terribly weather-beaten, having rid in the late storms.
1st Frenchman.	I now understand. Was it not in Bedford Street, Covent Garden?
1st Coffist.	Yes.
1st Frenchman.	Then I will tell you that the person you saw was indeed an extraordinary courier and one of great quality.
2nd Frenchman.	In truth it was not a courier, but a very illustrious 'courreuse'.
1st Frenchman.	The courier you saw alight, booted and spurred, covered with a great coat and still more covered with mud was the fair Duchess of Mazarin herself.
2nd Frenchman.	It was in very truth that new Queen of the Amazons, who is so come from beyond the mountains, to conceive a martial race by your Alexander.
4th Coffist.	She could not have taken a better way of recommending herself, both for vigour and soundness, than by riding astride, booted and spurred, 500 miles on a post horse in the depth of winter.[1]

The 2nd Frenchman's prediction was to prove accurate. Mazarin soon became a mistress to Charles II, the English 'Alexander', adopting the role alongside contemporaries including Barbara Villiers, Countess of Castlemaine and Duchess of Cleveland, Nell Gwyn, and Louise Kerouelle, Duchess of Portsmouth. Mazarin's arrival in London – an act first recounted in a conversation and subsequently recorded as a text – is one of numerous examples of a contemporary fascination in the figure of the courtesan in England from the Restoration onwards. Courtesans, Sonya Wynne notes, occupied a space combining 'luxury, eroticism and power', while the 'association of pleasure and power' they embodied 'exercise[d] a powerful hold on the public imagination'.[2]

Since the late fifteenth century, when the term *cortegiana* was coined in Italy to describe the mistresses of courtiers, the courtesan was understood both as producer and subject of the Arts.[3] Courtesans were whores, yet unlike their sister prostitutes they were defined by their association with the space of the court and through their engagement with the artistic sphere.[4] Courtesans are artful in two senses of the word: they engage with the arts – as artist and muse – to promote notions of their own worth; and in doing so, they employ artful behaviour to ensure their success. The courtesan's success depends upon her visibility, unlike the common prostitute or streetwalker whose public invisibility conceals the sexual transgressions of men. Courtesans like Mazarin made that transgression public, and were consequently celebrated or condemned by their contemporaries. In this essay I will examine how the courtesan's trade is not concerned solely with sexual-economic exchanges, but also with cultural exchanges for various types of profit. Mazarin gained influence through her sexual liaisons with powerful men, yet she was also sold and marketed through various mediums including portraits and printed texts.[5] Significantly, the Duchess engaged with the arts directly, staging her body, character and story for the public in a way that mirrored the way she staged it as a courtesan to her intimate circle. This public staging brought Mazarin a cultural and social profit that can be measured, in part, by her influence on other artists of the period including the contemporary English writer, Aphra Behn (1640–89).[6] In this essay I focus on the connection between Behn and Mazarin, understanding the latter to be an important influence on Behn's professional output, especially in the representation of the multiple courtesan figures found in Behn's oeuvre. I begin by outlining the public attention Mazarin courted through the medium of print, before examining the textual allusions to the Duchess we can trace in Behn's work. This process suggests how the circulation of a series of printed 'stories' about Mazarin – some of them produced by herself – played a formative role in both the wider circulation of stories about courtesans, and the development of early prose fiction in the period.

The Memoires of the Dutchess Mazarin (1676)

By the time of her arrival in London in 1675 Mazarin's personal circumstances had undergone a series of developments so fantastical that her life had, in effect, become a story, reported and read through a public lens. Some of the works written about Mazarin, both prior to and following her arrival in England, were of Mazarin's own production or involved her directly, while others, such as newspaper reports and satirical poetry, were produced to condemn her and the adulterous activities she was known to perform.[7] Taken together, all these works shaped her publicly perceived identity, creating a living narrative more culturally influential than her private person. Indeed, Mazarin recognized the valency of what we might term 'celebrity' – how her perceived persona could be crafted and sold to the public to her own advantage. In this way, she sought to practice a different form of venality – presenting herself as an alluring woman to not just one client, but also to hundreds of potential readers. Mazarin achieved this, in large part, by writing a memoir the year before her arrival in England, *Mémoires D.M.L.D.M.*[8] This text was subsequently translated into English by Peter Porter as *The Memoires of the Dutchess Mazarine*, available from the booksellers of London from February 1676.[9]

Mazarin's story was certainly unique. Born of Italian blood, the young Hortense was raised in the French Court during the ascendancy of her uncle, Cardinal Mazarin. The Cardinal rejected a number of marital propositions made for Hortense's hand by Charles Stuart (then in exile), Charles Emmanuel, Duke of Savoy, and Charles IV, Duke of Lorraine. In 1661, Hortense was married to Charles de la Porte, Duc de la Meilleraye. The couple were given the Mazarin dukedom and made the Cardinal's joint heirs. Despite their social status and financial prospects, the Mazarin marriage was not to be a happy one. The Duke subjected his wife to an array of despotic and repressive orders, confining her within the Palais Mazarin and the convents of Chelles and Saint-Marie de la Bastille. In her memoirs, Mazarin recalls how her husband restricted her access to her friends and those who empathized with her:

> He has often made me travel two hundred Leagues when I was big with Child, and very near my time; my Relations and Friends were apprehensive of the Dangers to which he Exposed my Health .... What would they say, if they had known that I could not once speak to any of my Domesticks but they were turned away the next day? That I could not receive two Visits successively from any one man but he was presently forbid the House; and if I shewed more kindness for any of my Maids more than for the rest, she was immediately taken away from me. If I called for my Coach, and he thought it not convenient to let me go abroad, he would laughing forbid the Coach to be made ready .... He would be content that I should see none in the world but himself.[10]

Stretched to the limits of marital obedience, the Duchess fled into exile in 1668, first to Italy and next to Savoy, taking up residence at the Chateau Chambéry in 1672. Here, Mazarin was protected by the influence of her former suitor (and reported lover) the Duke of Savoy, and was financially assisted by a pension granted her by Louis XIV.[11] Savoy's death in 1675 made it necessary to leave Chambéry for a new home, and Mazarin arrived in London in December 1675, seeking the protection of another former suitor, Charles II. She was to remain resident here until her death in November 1699.

While Mazarin's public relation of her story in *The Memoires* broke with traditional codes of femininity, her need to promote that story was part of a strategy to find support in a patriarchal world in which public opinion held increasing influence. In light of the drama of Mazarin's early life and marriage, it is unsurprising that the first English edition of *The Memoires* proved popular, with a second impression printed before the end of the year. In *The Memoires*, Mazarin's first-person narration of her own story enables her to forge a unique, intimate relationship with her reader. She stages herself as a fiction that speaks to the desires of her reader, just as the courtesan stages herself as a lover who speaks to the desires of her client. Mazarin composed *The Memoires* to prioritize the reader's enjoyment of the text over the need to present a complete record detailing her marital disharmony: 'If I did not apprehend to tyre your Patience, I could tell you a thousand such little malitious tricks which he playd me, without any manner of necessity, out of the meer pleasure he took to torment me'.[12] Here we see an example of how the success of the work, like the success of the professional courtesan, relied on its favourable reception by clients, or readers.[13] As a courtesan and a writer, Mazarin understood how the arts of both professions could be put to similar effect, and in *The Memoires* she adopts a series of narrative voices from conservative adult to playful ingénue. In *The Memoires* we also find evidence of Mazarin's conscious staging of herself as the heroine of a novel, as she employs the language and stylistic devices of early prose fiction:

> This Adventure made us go to lodge at the Intendant's house, and from thence, some few days after-wards to *Aix*, where we stayed a month, and whither Madam *de Grignan* was so Charitable, as to send us some Shifts, adding, *That we travelled like True Roman Heroines, with abundance of Jewels, but no clean Linnen*.[14]

Porter, the work's English translator, here translates the French word 'Roman' in terms of geographical provenance rather than through its other meaning as 'novel' or 'story'. This obscures the direct association made between the adventuress, Mazarin, with the heroines of novels and romances. This is an association Mazarin has encouraged from the outset of *The Memoires*, comparing her life story to those found in prose fictions: 'if what I am going to acquaint you with, seem to savour much of the *Romance*, impute it rather to my Destiny, than to my Inclination'.[15]

The fictional potential of Mazarin's story had been recognized in France before the publication of her memoirs. Marie-Catherine Desjardins de Villedieu published her *Mémoires de la Vie de Henriette-Sylvie de Molière* in six parts between 1671 and 1674.[16] Elizabeth Goldsmith and Sarah Nelson have noted how Mazarin and her sister Marie, young aristocrats on the run from their husbands, provided influential models for Desjardin's heroine, Sylvie:

> Between 1671 and 1674, Hortense's friend Madame de Villedieu published her fictional *Mémoires de la vie de Henriette-Sylvie de Moilère*, in which the protagonist (whose initials happen to be H. M., as Elizabeth Goldsmith has observed), repeatedly jumps the walls of convents and takes off on picaresque adventures disguised as a man, just as Hortense and Marie were doing in real life (with their progress being reported and commented upon every step of the way by the gazettes and individual letter writers).[17]

The printed works influenced by Mazarin's story, including Desjardin's novel and the Duchess's own memoirs, belong to a larger cultural narrative about Mazarin that we might term a 'living narrative', formed through those works printed and circulated about Mazarin during her lifetime, with Mazarin's memoirs placing a parallel version of herself – a textual one – into public circulation. As an early autobiographical account, *The Memoires* presented a unique opportunity for readers to buy knowledge, and in this way ownership, of an aristocratic and sexually promiscuous woman. The intimacy between Mazarin and her reader, encouraged through the Duchess's use of her first-person voice, is enhanced by the paratextual materials added to *The Memoires*, including César Vischard de Saint-Réal's letter which provides a sensory description of Mazarin's attractive physical appearance and unique character: 'The Colour of her Eyes has no name … when she looks stedfastly up-on any one, which she rarely does, they think she pierces their very Souls, and sees into the very bottom of their Hearts'.[18] These paratextual materials position Mazarin's own voice and perspective alongside other voices' descriptions of her life and character, negotiating the scandalous implications of the work and pleading for Mazarin's status as a woman whose distressing circumstances should be voiced to the world.

Mazarin and Behn: Personal Connections

In October 1688 an English work was published that engaged directly with Mazarin's living narrative. Aphra Behn's prose novella, *The Fair Vow-Breaker, or The History of the Nun* was licensed for print bearing a dedication to the Duchess:

> Madam, when I survey the whole toor of ladies at court, which was adorned by you, who appeared there with a grace and majesty peculiar to your great self only, mixed with an irresistible air of sweetness, generosity, and wit, I was impatient for an opportunity to tell Your Grace how infinitely one of your own sex adored you.[19]

The dedication establishes a link between Behn, England's first professional woman writer, and Mazarin. Janet Todd has noted that there is no evidence that Behn and the Duchess knew one another personally, supported by the fact that this 'intense dedication was speculatively written'.[20] However, Behn would have been aware of Mazarin and her story for more than a decade in this, the thirteenth, year of Mazarin's residence in London. Todd does suggest that Behn may have intended to dedicate an earlier work to Mazarin, such as her play *The Feign'd Curtezans* (1679), had not the political climate of the Popish Plot and Exclusion Crisis made an association with a foreign and Catholic mistress potentially damaging.[21]

While Behn's 1688 dedication to Mazarin appears to be written from a distant admirer, the women did share common acquaintances. Maureen Duffy has explored the social links of Behn's circle, noting Sir Thomas Gower's importance to her career. Duffy describes Gower as the 'keystone to her [Behn's] life'; through Gower, Behn was to claim an association with the Grenville family, Earls of Bath, leading, in all likelihood, to her friendship with the contemporary writers Edmund Waller, John Wilmot, Earl of Rochester and George Grenville, Lord Lansdowne.[22] The latter men all knew Mazarin well, providing, at the least, an indirect link between Behn and the Duchess.[23] Duffy suggests that Behn's '[p]ermission for the dedication [to Mazarin in *The History of the Nun*] was probably brought about by the combination of George Grenville, St Evremond and her acquaintance with Waller who had been a great friend and frequent visitor to the duchess'.[24]

The dedication to Mazarin came in the final months of Behn's life. However, Mazarin's influence upon Behn's writing can be glimpsed in her earlier work, suggesting a longer held interest in the Duchess. Indeed, I wish to suggest that Behn recognized the cultural and literary valency of Mazarin's living narrative, engaging with it throughout her professional career as she turned elements of Mazarin's character and story to her own profit as a writer. In this essay I will elucidate a number of textual allusions to a Mazarin 'narrative' in Behn's work, in which the Duchess may be seen to serve as a model for some of the literary characters and stories that Behn wrote. I focus first on the literary interest provoked by Mazarin's living narrative in London, before identifying a number of textual connections to Mazarin present in Behn's work.

Mazarin and Behn: Textual Traces?

Behn has long been discussed in relation to the perceived association of acts of writing and prostitution during the period in which she lived and worked.[25] As the first professional woman writer in England, it was inevitable that Behn should encounter such an association, abandoning the traditional space of woman in the domestic sphere to participate, so successfully, in the male-dominated literary marketplace. Behn was certainly interested in the figure of the courtesan, a woman who sells herself as a symbol of unique artistry and sexual allure. Courtesan characters feature in a number of Behn's plays including *The Rover* (1677), *The Feign'd Curtezans* (1679), *The Revenge* (1680) and *The Second Part of the Rover* (1681). In addition to creating dramatic courtesan characters, Behn was to display an interest in living courtesans, dedicating *The Feign'd Curtezans* to Nell Gwyn, and later *The History of the Nun* to Mazarin. Behn was also to explore the relationship between fictional and living courtesans in her novel in three volumes, *Love-Letters between a Nobleman and His Sister* (1684–7).[26] Finally, Behn's interest in living courtesans is shown by the copying of numerous poems about such women, including Mazarin, into her commonplace book during the most prolific years of her career.[27]

During the 1670s and 80s, the period during which Behn's oeuvre was composed, Mazarin provided a prominent public example of a living courtesan. As a professional writer, Behn must have been aware of Mazarin's memoirs from the time of their publication in London, if not earlier, with the French original. Behn was a fluent French translator and the influence of French *novelles* on her prose writing is clear.[28] Certainly, Mazarin's story was in circulation in England in its original French text prior to the Duchess's arrival on English shores, evident from the 3rd Coffist's words in the report recorded in the *Calendar of State Papers*:

> 3rd Coffist. I have heard this matter variously discoursed of already. Some say, that the nation, already too sensible of the amorous excesses of their Prince, may be more inflamed by such an accession of great expense that way as this appears likely to prove. Besides, her great beauty, quality and adroitness, of which there is so great a character in print, seem to furnish occasion for apprehending a greater power in her over the King, if once he come to love her, than any other of his mistresses have had.[29]

The coffist's claim that he has 'heard this matter variously discoursed of already' suggests that the coffee house conversation recorded here post-dates public awareness of Mazarin's arrival in London. The entry's purpose is to further, and not to initiate, a 'discourse' that is already being publicly disseminated. The coffist emphasizes Mazarin's 'beauty, quality and adroitness', of which he states 'there is so great a character in print'. The coffist here refers to Mazarin's memoirs, printed earlier that year in France with his knowledge of this work demonstrating the international interest that Mazarin had generated as a 'character'. Indeed on her arrival in London, Mazarin rapidly provoked a widespread literary interest. For example, the resentment of Charles II's *maîtresse en titre*, the Duchess of Portsmouth, was famously sparked by Mazarin's temporary usurpation of this role, leading to an intense competition between the mistresses at court captured in Waller's poem, 'The Triple Combat' (*c*.1677), a work satirizing the public obsession with the Portsmouth-Mazarin rivalry. Also that year a flurry of tragic drama was produced, taking as its subject the influence of rival mistresses on national concerns.[30] The classical settings and plots of these plays by John Dryden, Nathaniel Lee and Charles Sedley, reflected Mazarin's previous self-association with Cleopatra; the Duchess had posed as Cleopatra with the pearl for the Flemish artist Ferdinand Voet sometime around 1670 (see Figure 3.1). The allusion to Cleopatra – Egypt's Queen, Antony's mistress and rival to Octavia – was a fitting one to draw, and Mazarin was later to invoke the parallel again in a poem of her own printed in 1680.[31]

Figure 3.1: Jacob-Ferdinand Voet, *Hortense Mancini, Duchess of Mazarin* (c. 1670), Althorp House, Northampton; reproduced with permission of Althorp House.

The Rover (1677)

English public interest in Mazarin must have gathered pace quickly as within just a year of her arrival in London John Evelyn was making reference to 'the famous beauty & errant lady the Dutchesse of Mazarine (all the world knows her storie)'.[32] Contemporary professional writers interested in transgressive female characters, such as Aphra Behn, found in Mazarin a living example to draw on for inspiration. Behn was the second most prolific playwright of the period, second only to Dryden, and it is inconceivable that she would have been unaware of the dramatic interest in royal mistresses, including Mazarin, displayed in the tragic drama of 1677. Indeed, Behn actively took advantage of the public fascination with the figure of the courtesan, that same year reworking Thomas Killigrew's earlier play, *Thomaso*, into *The Rover*.[33] In *The Rover*, Behn made the Neapolitan courtesan, Angellica Bianca, a more central figure than in Killigrew's play. In Behn's hands, Angellica also becomes a more sympathetic character – a beautiful courtesan undone by her love for the rakish Willmore. Behn was to return to this empathetic portrayal of the courtesan in her subsequent drama, placing her at odds with other contemporary dramatists who tended to present courtesans as avaricious and lascivious women.

In *The Rover* Behn displays an impressive familiarity with the behaviour and customs of Italian courtesan culture. Angellica's first stage entrance is a socially encoded public display on a Neapolitan balcony:

> *Enter two bravos [Biskey and Sebastian] and hang up a great picture of Angellica's against the balcony, and two little ones at each side of the door ...*
> *Willmore gazes on the picture ...*
> *[Willmore] turns from the picture ...*
> *Enter Angellica and Moretta in the balcony, and draw a silk curtain.*[34]

The significance of visual imagery is apparent in Behn's stage directions. Angellica's picture – the sign of her trade – is hung out to draw attention to the availability of her body. This availability is, however, very limited. As a courtesan, Angellica only consents to sexual liaisons with men who can afford to pay her the sum of a thousand pounds a month (a sum the character of Frederick describes as equal to 'a portion for the Infanta').[35] Behn's brief stage directions encode Angellica's status. Her curtain is 'silk', aligning her with a market of exotic, luxury goods. The courtesan's position in this scene, first above and out of reach of the other characters, and subsequently obscured behind the silk curtain, suggests her physical presence yet social and sexual unavailability.

There is no evidence that Behn travelled to Italy, and she must have drawn on contemporary texts and accounts to create the setting and characters for plays like *The Rover*. One such source for Angellica's entrance in the play may be found in a curious episode recollected by Mazarin in *The Memoires*:

> One day as I was at the Window, she [Mazarin's aunt] commanded me very roughly to get me from thence, *That it was not the custome at Rome to stand looking out at Windows*. Another time as I stood at it, she sent me her Ghostly Father to tell me *That she would cause me to be haled from it by force*.[36]

The vigour of Mazarin's aunt's rebuke, coupled with the implication that standing by windows defies socially acceptable aristocratic codes of female behaviour, suggests that Mazarin's stance carries a specific association. This is, as Angellica's display in *The Rover* suggests, an association with the figure of the courtesan.[37] In *The Memoires*, the potentially damning nature of Mazarin's association with the courtesan is enforced by a description of how Mazarin's aunt, on finding her niece at the window a second time, threatens to have her 'Ghostly Father' hale her niece from it 'by force'. The need for clerical intervention suggests the sinful associations of Mazarin's pose as both her reputation and soul are placed at risk.[38] Read in light of *The Rover*, this otherwise mystifying description of Mazarin's behaviour during a visit to Rome associates her with courtesan culture, and raises the question of whether Behn would have perceived this connection, potentially drawing on Mazarin's recently published memoirs as a source for Angellica's characters and actions in her play.

Love-Letters between a Nobleman and His Sister (1684–7)

Behn certainly recognized the potential of living women to serve as models for literary characters and stories. In 1684 the first installment was printed of her three-volumed novel, *Love-Letters between a Nobleman and His Sister*. The work, like Desjardin's fictional novel of the 1670s, was based upon the story of a living woman, Lady Henrietta Berkeley (1664–1706). Where Desjardins had turned to Mazarin and her sister, Marie, for inspiration, Behn capitalized on a contemporary English scandal. In 1682 Henrietta Berkeley's affair with her sister's husband, Ford Grey, Earl of Tankerville, was discovered. A chain of high profile events ensued, including a court trial brought by her father, Lord Berkeley, against his son-in-law in November of that year. At the trial it was discovered that Henrietta had been married to Grey's servant, making her father's legal claims to her redundant. Grey was embroiled in scandal again the following year, with his involvement in The Rye House Plot of 1683 leading to his exile on the Continent, where he was joined by Henrietta.

In writing *Love-Letters*, Behn employed reports of Berkeley's life and adventures to create her own narrative charting the progress of a young aristocratic woman, Silvia. Behn's protagonist runs away to the Continent with her sister's husband, breaking with social codes and expectations to lead a life of adventure and sexual freedom, culminating in her career as a courtesan. In writing her novel, Behn must have realized that Berkeley's transgressive acts had a contemporary precursor in Mazarin's own. Indeed, the way the narrative of *Love-letters* functions mirrors Mazarin's memoirs, with Silvia learning 'the tricks of the professional woman writer of amatory fiction, generating fictions around the figure of the courtesan while appearing to reveal it'.[39] Behn, like Mazarin, is attentive to the reader's reception of the work, providing and withholding information in order to maintain the reader's interest. Behn surely had the examples of Desjardin's *Mémoires de la Vie* and Mazarin's *Memoires* in mind when writing *Love-Letters*, with both these works providing examples of how the printed adventures of living women could be turned to literary profit. Behn may have read Desjardin's novel in its original six-volume printing, and if not, the work's translation into English in two parts between 1672 and 1677 cannot have escaped her notice.[40] *Love-letters* draws on the same style of early prose memoir and scandal fiction writing found in Desjardins fictional novel and Mazarin's memoirs. Behn even appears to have drawn a direct association between *Love-Letters* and Desjardin's earlier novel, taking the name of her own protagonist, Silvia, from the postfix attached to Desjardin's heroine, Henriette-Sylvie (also conveniently the namesake of Henrietta Berkeley).

In *Love-Letters* Behn employs other devices used in Desjardin's earlier novel, and by Mazarin in her memoirs and life, with Silvia dressing *en cavalier* to incite Octavio's desire, encouraging in him 'a secret hope she was not what she seem'd, but of that Sex whereof she discovered so many softnesses and beauties'.[41] Silvia's dress, like Behn's language, suggests the importance of curiosity to Silvia's seduction of Octavio: 'at last he became a confirm'd slave to the *lovely unknown*; and yet that which was *more strange* she captivated the Men no less than the Women'.[42] *Love-letters* here mirrors Mazarin's style of writing and dress in *The Memoires*:

> My Train Consisted of a maid *I* had but six months, called *Nannon*, dressed in mans Apparel, as *I* was... We were almost every where known to be Women; and *Nanon* still through forgetfulness called me Madam; whether for this Reason, or that my Face gave some Cause of suspition; the People watched us through the Keyhole, when we had shut our selves in, and saw our long Tresses, which as soon as we were at liberty we untied, because they were very troublesome to us under our Perriwigs.[43]

Mazarin's disguise, foreshadowing that related in the coffeehouse entry in the *Calendar for State Papers*, here creates a 'suspition' that she is, in truth, a woman. Like Silvia, her disguise does not allow her to pass unnoticed as a man, but makes her of increased interest to others because she incites their curiosity. Mazarin was not the only prominent contemporary woman to dress *en cavalier* who could have provided a model for Behn's Silvia. Queen Christina of Sweden, a woman Mazarin solicited for assistance during her flight from her husband, also adopted such dress. However, Behn's biographer Maureen Duffy has noted the immediacy of Mazarin's continued example in England:

> art was fed by life in the person of Hortense Mancini wandering about Europe in men's clothes ... Art fed life, I suspect, when she went out in St. James's Park in the mornings to practise swordsmanship with Jane Middleton or one of the other ladies of the court.[44]

The History of the Nun (1688)

The year after the publication of the final instalment of *Love-Letters*, *The History of the Nun* was printed bearing its dedication 'To the most illustrious princess, the Duchess of Mazarine'.[45] Here, Mazarin's influence on Behn's work is directly evident, with Behn writing that her debt 'Madam, can only be expressed by my pen, which would be infinitely honoured in being permitted to celebrate your great name forever, and perpetually to serve where it has so great an inclination'.[46] While these words may be read as the verbose flattery of a writer desperate to gain patronage, the sincerity of the dedication is suggested, perhaps, in the detail of Behn's admiration:

> Madam, when I survey the whole toor of ladies at court, which was adorned by you, who appeared there with a grace and majesty peculiar to your great self only, mixed with an irresistible air of sweetness, generosity, and wit, I was impatient for an opportunity to tell Your Grace how infinitely one of your own sex adored you, and that, among all the numerous conquest Your Grace has made over the hearts of men, Your Grace had not subdued a more entire slave; I assure you, Madam, there is neither compliment, nor poetry in this humble declaration, but a truth which has cost me a great deal of inquietude, for that fortune has not set me in such a station as might justify my presence to the honour and satisfaction of being ever near Your Grace, to view eternally that lovely person and hear that surprising wit ... to hear you speak and to look upon your beauty? A beauty that is heightened, if possible, with an air of negligence in dress wholly charming, as if your beauty disdained those little arts of your sex which nicety alone is their greatest charm.[47]

If Behn had not met Mazarin personally, the thirty-one-page letter printed alongside *The Memoires* provided an external perspective of the Duchess that Behn may have used as a model to describe Mazarin in her dedication.[48] This would suggest that Behn had read the letter to *The Memoires* closely, or had a copy at hand. Critics have commented on the homoerotic nature of Behn's dedication to *The History of the Nun*, reading it alongside Behn's pastoral poetry of these years as evidence of the writer's bisexuality. However, there are other elements stressed in the dedication that provide a more plausible explanation for the bequest; not least, that due to Mazarin's unfortunate marriage and residence in convents, the story related in *The History of the Nun* was an apt one to dedicate to her.

The History of the Nun tells the story of the beautiful and devout Isabella who breaks her convent vows through her secret marriage to Henault. Upon her husband's reported death on the battlefield, Isabella remarries an earlier suitor, Villenoys. Henault returns years later and, following the discovery of her bigamy, Isabella smothers the unsuspecting Henault in his sleep, later telling Villenoys that Henault has died of shock. Villenoys plans to dispose of the body by throwing it off a bridge and thereby avoid public scandal. Isabella fears that her second husband may discover her murderous act and therefore sews Villenoys's collar to the sack containing Henault's body, and Isabella's two husbands fall to a shared death. The double murder is soon exposed, and Isabella is publicly beheaded, dying a beautiful death. Critics have suggested that in light of Isabella's actions, Behn's dedication of *The History of the Nun* to Mazarin is entirely confusing, as at the story's conclusion it is unclear whether Isabella should be considered a tragic heroine or villainess. Jacqueline Pearson has attempted to navigate this problem, noting that the

> dedication, with its convincing respect for Mancini, gives a different slant to a tale ostensibly about broken vows, suggesting that subjection to the church or to a husband need not necessarily be a virtue and that what the world calls female guilt may be understood in completely different ways.[49]

Pearson's reading of the dedication is testament to the fictional potential of Mazarin's character and story. For Mazarin provided a unique example of how to understand society in completely new ways. As Saint-Réal notes in his aforementioned letter in *The Memoires*, '[s]ome other Women have don the same things that she does : But she does them another way.'[50]

In addition to her many roles as adventuress and aristocrat, courtesan and disenfranchised wife, Mazarin embodied the spectrum of female qualities that Behn most admired. Behn's heroines are women of 'wit', 'beauty' and 'charm' who break with social convention to navigate their own path through the world. Mazarin provided the most visible living example of this type of woman throughout the two decades of Behn's literary career. As a professional writer in a competitive literary marketplace, Behn traded on aspects of Mazarin's public character and narrative, and although the full extent of Mazarin's influence on Behn's work is impossible to fully ascertain, the glimpses that we can discover in Behn's work show the Duchess to be more important to Behn's oeuvre than previously acknowledged.

Mazarin's success, like that of any courtesan, depended on her ability to create the correct effect on those around her. She transferred this skill to her writing, seeking out a wider clientele of readers with *The Memoires* from whom to profit. In this work, and in the many others stories circulated about her life, Mazarin provided contemporaries like Behn with a unique and accessible female narrative of direct relevance to the day. Writers continued to engage with Mazarin's narrative following her death in 1699, her potential as a textual model diversifying yet further as she came to inspire works as varied as contract theory and gambling histories.[51] In light of this legacy, Mazarin's wider and more complex cultural significance within her own age has been obscured, her story rewritten for later generations as an example either of disobedient wife or wanton mistress.

By recovering the ways in which Mazarin became subject to a process of textual venality in her lifetime – her story and character sold by herself, and by other writers – it is possible to perceive her wider importance to literary and cultural history. Mazarin provides an example of how contemporary women, even those tainted with the brush of 'whore', could actively participate in the ways in which their stories and characters were publicly presented. This, in turn, suggests the wider influence of living courtesans in the period, whose names and stories were directly and indirectly alluded to in printed texts of all kinds, including plays, poems, amatory novellas, pamphlets and early novels. The remarkable concentration of writings about courtesans provides a useful vantage point for thinking about the courtesan's place in English cultural history, posing yet a bigger question: why exactly was the courtesan so popular a figure in culture of the period, and what was it that she offered to readers and consumers of the age beyond sexual gratification?[52] In this brief essay I have discussed just one courtesan example, Mazarin, and only a handful of the ways in which she provides new perspectives on the output of one specific writer, Behn. In doing so, I have shown that the equation between venality and the figure of the whore is not simply always one of sexual exchange, but also of cultural exchange. And in this latter category we find new ways of thinking about female agency and profit, and the myriad ways in which the two could be conceived and function in the period.

4 MARIE PETIT'S *PERSIAN ADVENTURE* (1705–8): THE EASTWARD TRAVELS OF A FRENCH 'CONCUBINE'

Katherine MacDonald

In early February 1709, Marie Petit, aged about 35, entered the Hôpital du Refuge, a prison for 'wayward and disorderly women', including prostitutes, in Marseille.[1] She would regain her freedom only in 1713, after several times the normal period of incarceration imposed on local women for sexual misconduct. But Petit was no ordinary prostitute, if she was one at all. The city councillors had escorted Petit to the Refuge upon her disembarkation from a royal frigate, *L'Entreprenant*, just arrived from Constantinople. A former manager of a gambling establishment in Paris, Petit had spent the previous four years travelling by sea and overland between France and Persia, initially in the company of Jean-Baptiste Fabre, a bankrupt Marseille businessman and Louis XIV's extraordinary ambassador to Shah Sultan Husayn. Petit's story thus presents us with a fascinating historiographical problem: as an independent or masterless woman, she managed to travel widely and have various adventures, but nonetheless, her travels and adventures were registered by her enemies at home as sexual adventurism and troped as prostitution.

Upon Fabre's death under mysterious circumstaces in the Persian provincial capital Erivan in June 1706, Petit took over as unofficial ambassador, passing herself off as a French princess. Charles de Ferriol, the French resident ambassador at Constantinople, alarmed by reports of Petit's scandalous conduct, had dispatched his undersecretary Pierre-Victor Michel to Persia to ensure her swift return to France by whatever means.[2] Michel ultimately obtained his credentials as Louis XIV's official ambassador and completed the mission.

Thus it was that, about nine months after Petit's incarceration, the very same royal vessel, *L'Entreprenant*, docked in Marseille once more, in early September 1709. Off her gangplank stepped Michel, who could triumphantly declare his audience with Sultan Husayn to have been a resounding success. Clutched to Michel's chest was the hard-won fruit of his arduous eighteen-month diplomatic mission: the first capitulation treaty between France and Persia granting protection rights to the Christian missions and facilities for trade.[3] Michel hoped to be rewarded generously for his services to the crown upon presentation of his precious document at Versailles, whither he duly hastened.[4]

Petit's story survives in several forms: her letters from prison to Jérôme Pontchartrain, Secretary of State for the navy and the colonies; letters exchanged between Ferriol and Michel and ministers at Versailles concerning her scandalous behaviour; and Michel's own manuscript account of his journey to Persia.[5] There are also documents from legal proceedings against Petit for licentious conduct and from a lawsuit Petit brought against Michel for promissory notes totalling 12,000 livres allegedly owed her by Fabre, a debt which Michel had assumed in his effort to persuade Petit to return to France.[6] Petit's own narrative of events has, however, regrettably been lost.[7]

In this essay, I shall explore various ways in which Petit undertook to manage her reputation as an honourable woman acting in the service of the French crown, initially during her stay in Persia, and later on her return to France. She did this despite her enemies' self-interested efforts to paint her as a greedy whore, and to embroil her in the workings of a justice system that was anything but transparent and fair. I shall first consider a serious diplomatic incident which illustrates Petit's struggle to assert herself as the legitimate heir to the Persian mission after Fabre's death. Next, I shall examine the circumstances of Petit's imprisonment in the Marseille Refuge, and her self-representation in her letter-writing campaign to Pontchartrain as she endeavoured to obtain justice. Finally, I shall discuss Petit's failed attempt to publicize her own version of her journey to Persia by engaging a successful novelist to edit her memoirs.

A Diplomatic Incident: Competing Interpretations

Both Petit's and Michel's lawyers, in their 'Mémoires d'instruction' for their trials and Michel, in his memoir, describe a dramatic confrontation between the French and the Persians in Erivan triggered by an apparent fit of pique on Petit's part.[8] I would suggest that Petit's performance during these tense moments reveals both her diplomatic skills and her bid to present herself as the salvation of the French mission. According to Michel, this episode, which occurred before his arrival in Persia, confirmed Petit's licentiousness. In his memoir, he alleged that Petit had consoled herself for Fabre's death by taking a Persian lover.[9] Since the Persian provincial governor was too old, Petit settled upon the son of his superintendent. This man, believing himself to be the lover of the envoy of the princesses of France, gave himself entirely to her. At the same time, Petit enjoyed the protection of the governor, who also nursed a great passion for her. Michel insinuates that Petit had deliberately fanned the flames of this passion during her visits to the governor's harem. Having secured the support of the two most powerful men in Erivan, Michel claimed that Petit lorded it over everyone in the French retinue threatening them with beatings and imprisonment if they should do anything to displease her.

One day, when the French were all seated at table, a servant called Justiniani served fruit from a basket to Fabre's nephew. After he had taken his choice, he ordered Justiniani to remove the basket. Petit objected and a violent struggle ensued during the course of which she threw an orange at Justiniani's head. The matter escalated and soon the French were exchanging insults. Michel tells us that Justiniani called Petit a whore ('putain') before pulling a dagger on her. When the governor, enamoured as he was of Petit, heard of the insult to his beloved, he had Justiniani jailed, but Fabre's nephew and an Armenian helper liberated him.

The governor did not take kindly to the freeing of Justiniani, and after asking the French three times for his return, sent 500 armed troops to storm the house where they were staying. According to Michel, in the mêlée that ensued, the Persians fired fifty shots while the French only fired two shots in self-defence. Unfortunately, these shots killed two Persian soldiers, and the governor threw all the French, including the Armenians accompanying them, into jail. Petit's lawyer describes how she secured the immediate release of all the French prisoners except Justiniani and the Jesuit father Mosnier first by using 4,000 livres in bribes and second by her impassioned plea on their behalf.[10] The governor refused to release Mosnier, however, despite Petit's falling to her hands and knees to beg for his pardon. When she realized that the governor was resolute in his decision to execute the Jesuit, she rose majestically to her feet, declaring that she was prepared to follow Mosnier to the gallows to die alongside him. At this point, the governor revoked Mosnier's death sentence, but beheaded two Armenians in retribution for the two Persian soldiers killed by the French. Justiniani died from his treatment in captivity.

In Michel's memoir, he notes that this incident was Petit's way of ensuring that she got rid of three men who could identify her as Fabre's concubine.[11] However, as Petit's lawyer's account makes clear, it also speaks to her skills as a negotiator who was able to rescue the French from their predicament.[12] Even her enemy Michel grudgingly acknowledges her ability to make the governor do what she wanted.[13] She was a deft manipulator of appearances, and she knew that a seemingly minor slight from a servant could have dire consequences for her prestige.

Despite Petit's masterful performance in Erivan, her reign at the head of the French mission effectively ended with Michel's arrival in Persia. When Michel showed Petit the letter from Ferriol containing royal orders that she return to France, her lawyer asserted that she obeyed as soon as she could.[14] Unbeknown to Petit, however, upon her eventual arrival in Marseille some eighteen months later, she would be served with a 'lettre de cachet': a royal arrest warrant to imprison her until further notice.[15] 'Lettres de cachet' allowed the authorities – or private individuals who sent a *placet* (request letter) to the police – to bypass the courts and imprison an individual for an unlimited period with no explanation. Petit would not have known who obtained the 'lettre de cachet' served upon her, or on what grounds.[16]

Petit's Imprisonment in the Refuge

Petit's place of confinement, the Refuge, was a women's prison founded by a confraternity in 1640. At its outset, it was a religious institution established to reform problem women whose behaviour, and in particular whose sexual conduct, did not meet social expectations. Families concerned about scandal caused by adulterous wives or promiscuous daughters could, for a maintenance fee, protect their reputations by having these women confined to the Refuge, usually for one year. There, the women resided alongside nuns and novices who served as models of correct behaviour. Most importantly, as far as their families were concerned, the women were out of view of the local gossips. However, by the time Petit entered the Refuge, it was expanding to accommodate other inmates – generally prostitutes – sentenced there by municipal, provincial or royal officials. The Refuge was thus in transition from a convent with a spiritually reforming agenda to something more closely resembling a modern prison, where detainees were punished by confinement.[17] Indeed, because of the harshness of its conditions, the prison became known as 'la Galère' – the equivalent, for women, of being sent to the royal galleys in the same city. During her first year, Petit herself would refer to her experience in prison up to that moment as 'neuf mois de gallere' (nine months on the galleys).[18]

We are fortunate in possessing numerous documents to help us piece together the history of the prison. These papers cover the four years of Petit's incarceration and include a fairly complete set of the minutes of the weekly meetings of its twelve rectors.[19] In 1688, the rectors had expanded the building of the Refuge so that they could separate the women found to be truly penitent from the 'incorrigibles'.[20] Just under a decade later, the prison governors made further renovations which suggest an increasingly hardline stance with regard to the women under their guard. The minutes of the weekly meeting for 19 May 1697 show that an area adjoining the kitchen was to be designated as 'a place of separation' for the 'incorrigible girls'.[21] Eight chains with manacles were to be attached to its wall. It was a part of the Refuge which unfortunately would soon play a role in Petit's story.

Even for a docile prisoner who followed all the rules, conditions in the Refuge were harsh. Despite the 1688 building expansion, the prison was chronically overcrowded. Food was also in short supply. The fees paid by families to house their problem women hardly covered their maintenance. 1709, the year of Petit's arrival, was a particularly trying one for the Refuge. Dubbed the 'Great Frost', the winter of 1709 had devastated crops across Europe. Major rivers, including the Seine, the Garonne and the Rhône, froze. Fruit and nut-bearing trees and vines were killed off. The birds and small game that many people depended on for food died from starvation. The situation was so dire that a delegation of the Paris *parlement* asked for a dispensation from the fasting requirements of Lent because of the scarcity of vegetables and fish.[22] In Marseille, the temperature dipped to as low as −17°C in January. Two months after Petit entered the Refuge, on 7 April 1709, crowds of starving people gathered outside of the Marseille 'Hôtel de Ville' and forced the governor to open the army granaries.[23] That same month, the baker who usually supplied the prison ran out of wheat and was unable to provision the Refuge with bread.[24]

Under these extreme circumstances, believing herself to be wrongfully imprisoned in an institution meant to punish prostitutes, in early April 1709 Petit wrote to both Louis XIV and minister Pontchartrain in Versailles to defend her reputation as a woman of honour and to obtain justice through the legal system.[25] The handwriting in the letters matches Petit's signature, so it would appear that she wrote them herself. The hand is legible, but hardly elegant. The spelling is largely phonetic, there are frequent grammatical errors (usually arising from the phonetic spelling), and there is often no obvious break between sentences. It is the work of a semi-literate author. Yet the tone of the letter to Pontchartrain, even in the conventional opening and closing formulae of supplication, is hardly subservient.

In its opening sentence, Petit does humbly beg Pontchartrain's pardon for writing to him without a prior introduction. At the same time, though, she styled herself 'l'héroïne de Perse' that Ferriol had spoken about in his letters to Pontchartrain. At one stroke, she both accords herself a glorious title and reveals her knowledge of Ferriol's correspondence about her with Pontchartrain. There can be no question of plotting behind her back. Perhaps disingenuously, she makes no mention of the venomous nature of Ferriol's comments about her.[26] It is enough that she has been a topic of official diplomatic correspondence. The carefully calculated arguments Petit advances in support of her case here and in subsequent letters reveal her to be well informed about the legal system and about what she needed to say to get the minister's attention. Petit ensured that her plea would be heard by addressing not only Louis XIV, but also Pontchartrain, the countersignatory of her 'lettre de cachet'. The king might have other, more pressing matters to deal with; Pontchartrain was more likely to attend to her case. Her letter to Pontchartrain is also more detailed than the pro forma missive to the king.

Petit first interested Pontchartrain in her case by referring to secret letters for Louis XIV from a foreign prince which she had in her possession. In exchange for handing over these letters, Petit hoped that Pontchartrain would put in a good word for her with the king, by whose will she was theoretically being detained in the Refuge. Halfway through the letter, Petit suggested that she had been wrongfully imprisoned following an abuse of a 'lettre de cachet' by the dead ambassador Fabre's heirs and some other unspecified personal enemies. She wrote of her conviction that the king knew nothing of her situation, implying that if he did, he would certainly never have granted the arrest warrant. Specifically, Petit denied her enemies' charges that following Fabre's death in Erivan, she had stolen his property, thus despoiling the family inheritance. Petit denied this and, as evidence of her innocence, she pointed out that her dress is that of a humble respectable woman, not one who has used her ill-gotten gains to dress herself above her station.[27]

Unfortunately for Petit, this first letter to Pontchartrain did not result in her release from the Refuge. However, by July 1709, legal proceedings had at last commenced. It is not impossible that her letter was what got the wheels of justice in motion after over half a year in prison without any official investigation into her case. Petit was escorted from the Refuge to the Marseille 'cour de requêtes' on several occasions over the next two months to give evidence, and she took the opportunity to launch a countersuit against Michel for the debt of 12,000 livres she claimed he had personally undertaken to pay her after Fabre's death.

On 6 July 1709, the day after her first court appearance, Petit instigated a prison riot which was later discussed by the rectors at their weekly meeting.[28] Her wilful behaviour on this occasion resembles that of the episode of the orange in Erivan. Although escapes were fairly common – around 157 women broke free during the Refuge's history – Petit's uprising was the first collective revolt.[29] Petit conducted herself as a charismatic leader who was not prepared to suffer injustice meekly. According to the meeting minutes, it began when Petit lashed out at the gatekeeper, demanding that she hand over the keys to her. When the gatekeeper refused, Petit vituperated the nearby nuns.

The rector in charge deemed the situation threatening enough to justify calling for the police. When the officers arrived, Petit became even more insolent. She jumped on one of them and tore off his cravat, yelling that she did not recognize the authority of the prison guards or of the police. When Petit called out to her fellow inmates 'A moy, filles, a moy!' ('Follow me, girls, follow me!'), this sparked a full-scale riot and soon the Refuge was in total chaos. Petit boasted she would free all the prisoners before escaping herself. Somehow the authorities stopped the disorder before any prisoner escaped. The minutes give the names of five women who played a conspicuous role in the riot. These women were given an exemplary punishment by being chained as 'incorrigibles' until further notice.

They were to receive one bread roll per day, and if they complained, they were to be whipped. Despite the fact that she led the revolt, Petit's name is omitted from the list of women to be punished. The meeting minutes for the week of 15 September 1709 reveal that Petit's conditions of imprisonment did not permit the rectors to administer any additional punishments, a situation which they clearly found frustrating.[30]

Following the riot, the rectors attempted to persuade Marseille intendant Jean-Louis Habert de Fargis de Montmort to find alternate accommodation for Petit pending the outcome of her trial. However, Montmort dismissed their request. The Refuge experienced a summer of discontent in which Petit repeatedly disrupted the daily life of the prison with impunity, even going so far as to hit the recently appointed Mother Superior. Both Petit's desperation to escape and her persistent efforts to make herself so unpopular an inmate that she might be transferred to another institution show her concern that a prolonged stay in the Refuge, whatever the initial grounds for it, would result in her being identified as a prostitute by association.[31]

Moreover, having failed to escape the prison, in the course of her interrogation sessions at the 'cour des requêtes', she had become aware that the charges against her were for capital offenses. Proclaiming her innocence became a matter of life and death. At the end of September, Petit therefore resumed her correspondence with Pontchartrain, beginning a letter-writing campaign which would continue at the rate of one or two letters per month until February 1710.

These letters are strikingly different to the first letter Petit wrote to Pontchartrain, in that the handwriting is no longer the scrawl of a semi-literate person. Since the signature remains unchanged, it seems likely that Petit employed a secretary to write for her in an elegant hand. If she wanted to get attention from the minister, she needed her letter to look the part. Assuming Petit hired an amanuensis, was this person's role restricted to taking dictation, or did her secretary also make suggestions for what she should write? There are a few instances in the letters where Petit refers to herself in the third person as 'Marie Petit', which could indicate that someone else actually composed the letters after an initial conversation.

In her letter dated 27 September 1709, Petit reminded Pontchartrain that she had now been in the Refuge for almost eight months.[32] It was high time that her case be judged. Montmort had completed the inventory of her effects two months previously. Petit had undergone numerous interrogations over the course of which, she told Pontchartrain, she discovered to her horror the nature of the crimes she was accused of committing. The first accusation was that of the murder by poisoning of Jean-Baptiste Fabre. The motivation for such a heinous crime: to get back the 12,000 livres she had lent to him to fund his journey to Persia. Petit also discovered that there were three further charges against her. She was charged with apostasy and of wishing to become Muslim. She was charged with prostitution in foreign lands. Finally, she was charged with having tried to assassinate Michel.

Petit wrote to Pontchartrain that she was certain he would have received the transcript of her interrogations. If he would only read her defence, Petit was sure Pontchartrain would be convinced of her innocence. Still, Petit made clear that she did not expect Pontchartrain to free her immediately upon reading the transcripts of her interrogations. This was a point she would make repeatedly over the course of the correspondence: 'je ne demande point de grâce [mais] Justice' ('I am not asking for a pardon, but rather justice.').[33] She rejected the potentially capricious favour of ministerial grace to demand 'Justice [qui] doit estre pour tout le monde' ('Justice, which must be for everyone').[34] Rather than begging for the minister's pardon, all she asked was that he appoint whichever official he deemed fit to judge her case according to due process. Her arguments, then, rest on the imperative that justice be upheld and the legal procedures respected. For one accused of being a source of social disorder, Petit here emerges as a surprising defender of the legal system, at least rhetorically.

In October's letter, Petit repeated her demand that her case be judged as soon as possible.[35] She was tired of enduring the harsh conditions in the Refuge. Whereas in her previous letter, she had contented herself with refuting the charges laid upon her by Michel, in the present missive she went further and made counter-accusations against the man she described as her 'capital enemy'. She charged him with attempted murder on several occasions: accompanied by his servants, he had entered her lodgings in Tabriz, sword in hand, to attack her. He then set two assassins upon her. Petit claimed that Michel next resorted to poison. It was only with the help of Providence – and the protection of her Persian friends – that Petit had survived. Back in France, Michel would stop at nothing to have Petit hanged on the false charges that he had concocted. Petit closed the letter by again appealing to Pontchartrain's sense of justice: 'Vous estes trop equitable monseigneur pour decider du sort de Marie Petit sur l'esposé que vous fera le sieur Michel' ('Sir, you are too fair to decide Marie Petit's fate based on the report M. Michel will make of it') – he had, after all, a personal interest in her disappearance.

In November, Petit wrote to Pontchartrain that, suffering from kidney stones, she felt herself unable to bear the conditions in the Refuge any longer.[36] At the very least, Petit requested a transfer to another prison. This letter reveals Petit's legal acumen and her confidence in her ability to use legal procedure to win her case. Having previously denied the monstrous crimes imputed to her by Michel, Petit now accused her rival of deliberately trying to have her permanently silenced by his false charges against her. Showing her legal knowledge, Petit argued that Michel could not be a reliable witness against her since he had everything to gain by her demise. If Petit were found guilty of these capital crimes and hanged, Michel would not have to pay her for the promissory note he had signed in his own name. She also questioned the reliability of the other witnesses Michel had put forward, who were all his servants or in his pay. Petit wrote to Pontchartrain that despite her objections, she would not oppose these witnesses as she was legally entitled to do. However, she threatened to prosecute them subsequently as false witnesses.

Petit's main concern in November's letter was to deny all charges of sexual misconduct. She referred to a letter Pontchartrain addressed her (missing), in which he asked her whether she was ashamed of her 'mauvaise vie', not only on her travels but prior to her departure. Petit responded that, despite what her enemies might say, she could never pass for a courtesan. If Pontchartrain were to meet her in person, he would recognize this immediately. Petit further endeavoured to paint a picture of herself as a chaste victim by again mentioning Michel's attack on her in Tabriz. This time, she presented the attack as an attempted rape. When one of Petit's servants informed the governor of Tabriz what had happened, he sent two hundred of his men together with his *kalāntar* ('chief of police') to stop Michel from insulting Petit's honour. Petit also questioned Michel's charge of having been the mistress of the governor of Erivan. This was impossible, she wrote, since she only ever saw the governor in public. Petit used the honours she received at every stage of her stay in Persia to refute the charge of sexual misconduct. A loose woman would not have been accorded the respectful treatment she enjoyed while in Persia. Petit concluded her refutation of the charges of licentious lifestyle with a financial argument. If she had indeed been a courtesan, she would have come back from Persia a wealthy woman, had she come back at all. Petit intimated that she might have stayed in Persia as one of the Shah's wives. Finally, Petit notes that no complaints were made against her in Constantinople or in Smyrna nor indeed aboard ship where there were at least forty young men, for the most part gentlemen 'of quality'.

Petit was aware that she was at a disadvantage to Michel, who had people in Versailles who could speak for him directly to Pontchartrain. All she could do was write. Because of her increasingly poor health, though, Petit could no longer afford to be forbearing. If she did not receive a positive response from the minister after this letter, she would have to ask her family and friends in Versailles to begin a campaign to free her by speaking directly to the king on her behalf.[37] Letter-writing and high-minded allusions to justice could only get a person so far. Ultimately, Petit realized that personal connections were still the most effective means of securing her release from prison.

By early January 1710, Petit had run out of reasoned arguments. Her final two letters have a melodramatic tone as Petit threw herself upon Pontchartrain's mercy.[38] Despite her weakness from the chronic fever caused by her kidney stones, she wrote that she remained just strong enough to write a few lines to

Pontchartrain. Since she despaired of obtaining justice, she begged the minister to hang her anyway, even though she was innocent. At least she would be put out of her misery. Petit also complained that her conditions of confinement in the Refuge were getting worse. She blamed Michel and Fabre's family. They had corrupted the rectors and other Refuge personnel who were now treating Petit 'avec toutes sortes de cruautés' ('with all kinds of cruelty').[39] Petit claimed that Michel and the Fabre family were hoping she would die in captivity, since they were not confident of being able to defeat her legally. They had prevented the treasurer from paying Petit the monthly pension from the king which was part of the terms of her arrest. This pension covered Petit's basic clothing, shoes and any supplements to the Refuge rations. In her final letter to Pontchartrain, dated 10 February, Petit wrote that she had been forced to beg from the other inmates to obtain some broth.[40] Again showing knowledge of legal technicalities, Petit argued that stopping her pension was grounds for her release, since a prisoner without financial support had to be freed.

It is hard to know how Pontchartrain received Petit's letters, since we do not possess his side of the correspondence.[41] The backs of several of Petit's letters are annotated in Pontchartrain's hand with a curt: 'Faire finir absolument' ('Put a stop to this').[42] Pontchartrain had presumably heard enough from Petit. Thus, on 12 February 1710, he nominated Pierre Arnoul (Montmort's successor as intendant) to judge Petit's case at the admiralty court in Marseille. It was a further two years before Arnoul would issue his verdict condemning Petit to one additional year in the Refuge.[43] By the terms of Arnoul's judgement, she was also forced to auction off the goods she brought back with her from Persia before she could finally leave Marseille for Paris.[44] The proceeds of this sale hardly covered her debts to Michel and to the Refuge for her keep over the preceding years.[45]

Penniless and in broken health, Petit returned to Paris hoping to reestablish herself. There are no traces of her in the archives until March 1715, when the Paris chief of police Marc René d'Argenson wrote to Pontchartrain to inform him of Petit's intention to publish the story of her adventures. Petit had asked for d'Argenson's assistance in selecting someone to write them up for her.[46] D'Argenson sought Pontchartrain's approval for his suggestion of Alain-René Lesage, a successful playwright and novelist.[47] Petit's plan to publish corresponded with the arrival in France the previous month of the Persian ambassador, Mehemet Riza Beg, whose visit had created a flurry of interest in the exotic east.[48] By May, Petit had held a personal interview with Lesage and given him her memoirs, which he had agreed to write up for her.[49] However, Pontchartrain had other ideas.[50]

In June 1715, Lesage received a package from Pontchartrain which included Michel's memoirs of the Persian mission. Upon reading them, Lesage thought the better of Petit's commission to rewrite, and presumably add some much-needed literary polish to, her account of her journey. As Lesage wrote in some dismay to the secretary of state for the navy: 'Les papiers qui m'ont été communiqués par votre ordre me jettent dans un embarras' ('The papers I have received on your orders have put me in a most difficult position').[51] In Lesage's letter to Pontchartrain he explains his rejection of Petit's request in a way that was calculated to strengthen his own relations with those in power but which at the same time is ostensibly a matter of literary convention. Lesage refused to put pen to paper to exculpate an enemy of the state because of his sensitivity to the boundaries between history and fiction:

> En suivant ses Mémoires fabuleux je me serais attaché à peindre ses disgrâces d'une manière qui eût intéressé le public pour elle. J'aurais fait valoir jusqu'à ses dérèglements et tourné tout à son profit. C'est ainsi que les historiens trahissent quelquefois la vérité en s'imaginant la faire connaître. (By following her fantastical Memoirs I would have endeavoured to paint a picture of her misfortunes in a way which would have made the public sympathise with her. I would have shown even her excesses in a favourable light and I would have turned everything to her advantage. Thus do historians sometimes betray the truth even as they imagine they are making it known.)

As Lesage wrote to Pontchartrain, reading the competing accounts of the Persian mission put him in a hopeless quandary:

> Les mémoires que Votre Grandeur m'a fait communiquer ... ont renversé toutes mes idées. La plume que je tenais prête à justifier une femme qui me paraissait pouvoir n'être pas si coupable, me tombe des mains, et je ne vois plus qu'une avanturière dont la vie me semble moins digne d'être offerte à la curiosité des hommes que dérobée à leur connaissance. (The memoirs Your Highness sent to me ... have overturned all my thoughts. The pen I was holding ready to justify a woman who, it seemed to me, could not possibly be so guilty, falls from my hand and I now see only an adventuress whose life seems to me to be less worthy of being offered up to a curious public than hidden from their knowledge.)

For Lesage to adopt Petit's perspective on events instead of Michel's would have resulted in him transforming her memoir into a novel: 'J'avais déjà entre les mains une partie des mémoires de la demoiselle Petit ... et je me préparais à faire un ouvrage qui n'aurait guère été conforme aux lettres de M. Michel ... Enfin j'allais composer un roman.' ('I already had in hand part of Mlle Petit's memoirs ... and I was preparing to compose a work that would not have been at all in agreement with M. Michel's letters ... Ultimately, I would be writing a novel.') Telling Pontchartrain what he wanted to hear, Lesage intimated that he found it self-evident that Michel was telling the truth, while Petit was not. Having already agreed to tell Petit's story for her, though, Lesage begged Pontchartrain to help him find an honourable resolution to his dilemma. If Pontchartrain truly wanted to publish a proper history of Petit, Lesage suggested that Michel's memoir might provide the public with 'une histoire dépouillée d'artifice' ('a story stripped of artifice'.) Even so, he warned that such a work could only make for unedifying reading, given the disagreeable nature of the female behaviour described therein.

Michel's manuscript remained unpublished, however. It was not until the end of the nineteenth century that Petit's history would be told again by the archival scholar René de Maulde la Clavière. Maulde la Clavière was largely sympathetic to Petit whom he depicted as a woman with an admirable sense of adventure.[52] Since then, Petit has inspired several works of historical fiction, all of which give her the role of 'héroïne de Perse' she accorded herself in her letters to Pontchartrain and relegate her enemy Michel to the status of arch-villain.[53] Ironically, Lesage's assessment of her story as the stuff of novels has proved to be correct. Despite their favourable presentation of Petit, though, none of these works have considered her attempts to author her own story, first in her letters to Pontchartrain and second by using a celebrated novelist to help her publish her first-person memoirs. In this essay, I hope to have given Petit back her own voice as a woman who struggled to cast off the imputation of venality and who, despite her socially marginal position, was unafraid to take on those at the highest echelons of society.

5 'A FIRST-RATE WHORE': PROSTITUTION AND EMPOWERMENT IN THE EARLY EIGHTEENTH CENTURY

Lena Olsson

Sarah Prydden, better known under her assumed name Sally Salisbury, was one of the most famous prostitutes of the eighteenth century.[1] Born around 1690 as the daughter of a Shrewsbury bricklayer, she worked herself up from the street corners of St Giles to the bedrooms of the nobility; it was said that she had been involved with the then Prince of Wales, the future George II, and that among her keepers were Viscount Bolingbroke, the Earl of Oxford and the Duke of Richmond. She worked for a time for the famous bawd Mother Wisebourn, but most of the time she seems to have been in business for herself, as a kept mistress and lady of pleasure. She apparently amassed a considerable fortune, being able to support a lifestyle that included being waited on by several servants, gambling for high stakes and lavish spending on fashionable clothes and other luxury goods. Late in 1722, however, her notorious temper got the better of her and she stabbed one of her clients, the Hon. John Finch, ostensibly in a quarrel over an opera ticket. Finch survived, and in the ensuing trial Salisbury was convicted of assault but acquitted of premeditation.[2] She was sentenced to a £100 fine and a year in jail, but remained as popular as ever and was frequently visited in Newgate by her old admirers.[3] Three months before her scheduled release in 1724 she died of 'a fever, having been ill of a consumption of a long time'.[4] She was interred in the crypt of St Andrew Holborn, the church where the controversial high-church preacher Henry Sacheverell was rector, and where he himself was buried a few months later, in the crypt alongside Salisbury. Unsurprisingly, a priest and a whore sharing their last resting place was the cause of a good deal of merriment among the town wits.[5]

A trademark feature in many of the stories about Salisbury is her aggressive and uncompromising flaunting of her identity as a whore. Far from being ashamed of it, and refusing to acknowledge the slur in the appellation, Salisbury instead asserts her status and turns it into a badge of honour, 'very frequently' claiming that '*it was always my Ambition to be a First-Rate Whore, and I think,*

I may say, without Vanity, That I am the greatest, and make the most considerable Figure of any in the Three Kingdoms.[6] Identifying with and acting like a whore become strategies of empowerment; traditionally disparaged aspects of the whore persona – for example, avarice, rapaciousness, vulgarity, volubility and lewdness – become advantages, tools with which to successfully negotiate a world increasingly shaped by mercantile values and practices. James Grantham Turner calls the word 'whore' 'a fighting word, a cutting remark', one that 'breaks down the exterior shell of honour and good fame that each citizen needed to maintain her social standing',[7] and while it still has this function in Salisbury's biographies it is also transformed by Salisbury herself: in addition to a weapon wielded *against* the prostitute it becomes a weapon wielded *by* her, a defiant display of the dishonour and infamy which have made possible the creation of her social and economic success.

According to Turner, early-modern cultural productions about illicit sex were informed by two conflicting representations of the prostitute: the courtesan and the whore. In contrast to the 'brutally colloquial *puttana*' (whore), the concept of the courtesan implied 'a refined libertine above mercenary considerations, above the rough subculture of the brothel and the street'.[8] A prostitute with pretentions to a more elevated social status and a better clientele might define herself as a courtesan, but there was a simultaneous and opposing cultural impetus to unmask her and reveal her as a common whore, either in deed or by representation.[9] Well-known and prosperous prostitutes, whose social and financial success was clear from their manner of living, were especially vulnerable to attack from satirists and moralists alike. Turner's study deals with the seventeenth century, but works dealing with prostitution differentiated between high-class prostitutes and common whores throughout the eighteenth century as well, whether expressed as a simple dichotomy or a more elaborate hierarchy.[10] Salisbury, with her town house, clothes, jewels and numerous servants, was perhaps the most prominent embodiment of the successful courtesan in her day, and it is hardly surprising that she became a focus for her culture's ambivalent attitude to prostitutes. At the same time, she differs in interesting ways from the prostitutes in the model presented by Turner. For instance, she is frequently, if not exclusively, shown to identify with the whore, not the courtesan, empowering herself not by distancing herself from the denigrated incarnation of the prostitute but by embracing it, turning its disadvantages into assets, its weaknesses into strengths. But what does it mean to call a successful, culturally prominent prostitute a 'whore', and what happens when that prostitute claims that epithet for herself, rehabilitating it and using it as a means of empowerment? In this article I would like to discuss these issues by reading Salisbury's two main biographies against one another – Charles Walker's *Authentick Memoirs of the Life, Intrigues and Adventures of the Celebrated Sally Salisbury* (1723; henceforth *Authentick*

Memoirs) and the anonymous *The Genuine History of Mrs Sarah Prydden* (1723; henceforth *The Genuine History*).

The production of biographical material was well underway before Salisbury's trial and conviction on 24 April 1723. Already in January, Walker placed two advertisements in *The Post Boy*, asking for biographical material from 'those Gentlemen who can communicate any useful Particulars towards perpetuation [of] the memoir of the eminent Person'.[11] The letters Walker supposedly received in response to these advertisements form the basis and mainstay of *Authentick Memoirs*. In the first chapter of his text, Walker states his rhetorical approach: 'Having been favour'd with the Correspondence of several Gentlemen, since I declared my Intention of writing her [Salisbury's] LIFE, I think my self obliged in Justice to transmit every Paper that I have receiv'd, with the same Freedom it has been communicated'.[12] In addition, Walker 'aver[s], that I have not only done so, but have, as I thought my self obliged to do, submitted the Printed Sheets to the View and Correction of each Correspondent'.[13] After two biographical chapters outlining Salisbury's early life, Walker consequently publishes what is presented as unedited transcriptions, complete with prefatory matter and signatures (altered to protect the anonymity of the writers), of eighteen letters he allegedly received from his correspondents, many of whom claim to be Salisbury's erstwhile clients.[14] Despite these claims, it is difficult to know how authentic, if at all, the quoted letters are. It is entirely possible that Walker at the very least reformulated them somewhat, because there is often an ironic or satiric undertone to them, and it is often the writers of the letters who emerge as targets of this indirect raillery. Also, the narrative style does not vary significantly from letter to letter. Such reformulations do not necessarily have to undermine the ultimate authenticity of the letters; the correspondent 'J.S.', for instance, gives Walker leave to 'put [the contents of his letter] in a proper Stile' in order to 'deserve a place in the Memoirs'.[15] Whether Walker made a contribution to the letters or not, *Authentick Memoirs* can be classified as a compilation of letters with a rudimentary editorial framework consisting of a satiric dedicatory epistle, a short biographical sketch and a brief concluding letter from Walker addressed to the subject of his biography herself.

The Genuine History purports to have been written as a direct reaction to, and refutation of, other biographical works, primarily Walker's text, which is referred to as 'the pretended authentick Memoirs'.[16] The anonymous author several times takes Walker to task, and even quotes directly from his text.[17] Unlike *Authentick Memoirs*, *The Genuine History* is written as a straightforward biographical narrative, with an appendix containing two letters and a description of Salisbury's trial. This work, however, relies as much as Walker's text on information garnered from people supposedly acquainted with Salisbury: it is said to have been written '*at the Desire of certain Noblemen*', and to be built on material forwarded by a man called 'Antony Boles', whose letter to the author is prefaced to the text. According to its own claim, it is a more 'polite' text than the other biographical works, Boles stating as a condition for forwarding his information that the author '*will lay aside that Ribaldry, Obscenity and Billingsgate-Language that appears* [sic] *in others*', claiming in addition that '*those mercenary Scriblers don't so much as pretend to be unprejudiced and impartial, spitting their Venom in every Line*'. Instead, Boles wants Salisbury's '*Follies*' to be '*represented fairly and truly, the better to be a Warning to young People*'.[18] The author likewise promises to 'avoid the unnecessary Flourishes, the ill-natured Language, and the false Reports, that have been published of her ... Confining my self to the Relation of bare Matters of Fact, which I take to be the Duty of an Historian'.[19] Both *Authentick Memoirs* and *The Genuine History* thus advance separate claims to accuracy, the one by publishing supposedly genuine reports, written in their own words by people who knew Salisbury, the other by assuming the role of a historian who relates facts, not fiction, and taking the high moral ground in relation to other texts. Despite these differences, both texts can, to varying extents, be linked to libertine writings: although Walker is clearly the bawdier of the two, they both feature witty puns and double entendres, and they both satirize and ironize over Salisbury, even if they sometimes also appear to valorize her. Both authors thus very clearly have their own agendas, whether this is to defame Salisbury, to defend her, to attack her clients, or simply to make money out of one of the major scandals of the day.

Between them, *Authentick Memoirs* and *The Genuine History* present a number of conflicting representations of prostitution as an exchange between men and women, and of the identity of the prostitute herself. One of these representations is what can be interpreted as Salisbury's own radical reconstruction of the whore as a professional tradesperson who enters into business contracts with her clients on equal terms as an independent operator in the marketplace. In addition, both texts challenge Salisbury's assertive reformulation of the concept of the prostitute, offering three different counter-representations of Salisbury's dealings with her clients and of Salisbury as a prostitute. The first of these is voiced by Salisbury's clients, and is their attempt to counter her representation of prostitution as a business arrangement, instead contending that the relationship between client and prostitute lies outside the marketplace, and is more reminiscent of an emotional bond, such as that between a suitor and his lady or between benefactor and beneficiary. This representation ultimately fails, however, because Salisbury refuses to play her part, instead taking advantage of the men's generosity and victimizing them, ruining them both physically and financially. The second perspective is expressed by Walker, who confirms Salisbury's self-representation as a whore but rejects its empowering potential, instead reaffirming the conventional, opprobrious interpretation of this figure. Walker, in effect, allows Salisbury to damn herself: while revelling in her vitality and drive, her initiative, her outspokenness and her uncompromising frankness, he at the same time directs the reader's attention to her venereal infection, her abusive speech, her callous lack of empathy and, most emphatically, her rapacious, 'money-grubbing' behaviour. In this way, Walker endeavours to unmask Salisbury as a common, if charismatic, lower-class whore. At the same time, from his representation of Salisbury follows a depiction of her clients as emasculated fools, incapable of seeing through Salisbury's obvious whorishness and failing to uphold masculine superiority, allowing her to scold them, beat them and ruin them. It is this satirical ridiculing of the clients that *The Genuine History* attempts to undermine, counteracting it by denying that Salisbury is a whore, and, by extension, that her clients are fools. In this third representation of prostitution and the prostitute, Salisbury is portrayed as more similar to the courtesan than the whore, in that the traits that most suggest her commonness are de-emphasised, and she is instead described as more educated, less prone to violence and shrewish outbursts, less diseased and less interested in money than in the other accounts. Showing her to be more like a courtesan also makes her appear more conventionally feminine – a somewhat softer, more decorous, if still impish and unpredictable, figure whose sexual allure does not intrinsically entail a threat to gender roles and male economic control. This construction restores the clients' masculinity, reinstating them as generous donors and protectors of a spirited and witty woman who, the text implies, is not at all as ungrateful and rapacious as Walker's text suggests.

The Radical Whore

The most interesting of these conflicting representations is arguably Salisbury's own, because of her attempted inversion of one of the most vilified epithets in Western history. The claim that it is Salisbury's own representation may require some defending; after all, she never produced any written texts herself, and it must be remembered that her 'self-representation' is always filtered through the narratives of her two biographers and sometimes through those of her clients as well. Nevertheless, a significant degree of consensus can be said to exist in the two texts concerning her public persona, a contention strengthened by the fact that similar depictions of it appear in both texts, despite their otherwise mutually exclusive counter-representations of Salisbury's identity.[20] Also, Salisbury is in several instances allowed to speak directly to the audience in quoted speech, giving the impression (however illusory) that the text conveys her own voicing of her self-image, a construction which is supported by descriptions of her behaviour towards clients and colleagues alike. Whether or not this is an accurate representation of the historical person Sarah Prydden (or rather, of her public persona, Sally Salisbury), it can be seen as a forceful expression of the potentially empowering role of the whore, rhetorically constructed in the text as being Salisbury's own.

Because of the existence of conflicting representations in the texts, the whorish identity can be read in opposing ways. On the one hand it functions as a condemnation, on the other it is a potentially empowering reformulation of that condemnation, equating prostitution with other service professions, recasting the actions of the prostitute as legitimate business strategies.[21] Acts that from the conventional male perspective testify to Salisbury's mercenary self-interest and grasping rapaciousness become, when viewed from Salisbury's own perspective, commercial common sense and sound business acumen. She is professional and level-headed when trading, never being tempted to confuse business with pleasure and always focusing on the money she can make from potential clients, of whom 'the *Heart* of none ... was valuable to her, but only according as the Purse could keep Time with its Affections'.[22] She is an expert at gauging the state of the market, selecting the men who are most likely to support her 'Extravagance' and afford her the best remuneration for her services: she had, claims Walker's correspondent 'Castalio', 'such a discerning Faculty, that she soon pitch'd upon the most proper Man for her Purpose'.[23] Moreover, she always puts as high a price on her sexual services as possible, as they are the product on which her success as a trader depends. The author of *The Genuine History* complains that she 'seem'd to think, that her Favours were of vastly more Value than Mountains of Gold, or Rocks of Diamonds', something for which he blames 'the surprizing Encouragement given her';[24] he is loath to admit that, like any tradesperson, Salisbury drives up the price of her services for as long as her clients are willing to pay, allowing market pressures to determine the price. If a man has become smitten with or attached to her, she increases her demands, wasting no time making as much money as she can before she loses her precarious hold on him. If not properly reimbursed, she withholds her services completely, even when her clients are some of the most distinguished men in the kingdom: when involved with the Duke of Richmond, she 'receiv'd the Gold, and she receiv'd the Man; and she receiv'd more Gold, and still receiv'd the Man; but when no more Gold was left, she would no more receive the Man'.[25] If a man has no money, she may accept another kind of valuable instead, but there is never any question of her allowing her clients to run up an account. In her dealings with a certain Captain W—x, Salisbury is said to be

> too much what she is and ever will be, to grant him Love Gratis, or *upon Tick*; so that, to ingratiate himself with her, he had been forc'd to promise to bring her some Rich Cull, whom she might *Milk* to good Advantage; and as a Gratification for that Piece of Service she engaged herself to bless him with now and then a *spare Night's* Revelling in her delicious Embraces.[26]

In this unexpected reversal of the customary arrangement between prostitute and client, the client, no longer able to supply the cash the prostitute demands, is forced to provide a service in return for compensation from her, entering into a contractual agreement in which she, by having the authority to decide when the contract has been fulfilled, is clearly in a position of greater power than he.[27]

By adopting the strategies and behaviour of a regular tradesperson, Salisbury manages to shift the balance of power from her customers to herself, attempting to offset the gendered and social power differences that exist between them. That she is able to do this depends to some degree on the gender economy of the eighteenth-century marketplace itself: Bradford Mudge has argued that in early eighteenth-century culture, the very fact that a woman entered into the 'male' marketplace to engage in commercial transactions on equal terms with men would be seen as a challenge to conventional gender structures.[28] Salisbury herself is well aware of the need for a successful whore to trespass conventional gender boundaries: when one of her colleagues has 'made her self, by her good Nature, too Cheap' and ended up in debtor's prison, Salisbury makes it clear that the problem is too much conventional femininity and too little whorish greed.[29] *'Modesty undid this Wench'*, she tells her own client before prevailing on him, using 'the seldom failing Rhetorick of a Harlot', to pay her friend's debts and release her from prison.[30] One of the most valued feminine traits in early-modern culture is thus made to stand in direct opposition to the qualities needed to successfully negotiate the marketplace as a professional tradeswoman: a respectable woman does not have the necessary qualifications, but a whore does.

But Salisbury not only challenges the conventional gender hierarchy through her words, she threatens to overturn it completely by her actions, emasculating men by draining them of money as well as masculine strength and vigour. This is depicted in the texts as an expression of Salisbury's enduring ingratitude and lack of empathy, even as a purposeful act of unkindness which is part and parcel of her regular behaviour towards her clients once they are no longer 'in the midst of Opulence and Wealth'.[31] For instance, when a new admirer wants to help one of her previous clients get out of debtor's prison, she flies into a fit of fury, telling the man that 'if she once gave Ear to the Cries of her *undone Fellows*, as she call'd them, there would be no end; for, says she, *There is scarce a Jayl in Town, but what I have made a Present of a Member or two, nor a quarter of the World, but where I have sent some Stripp'd Lover a Grazing*'.[32] Her customers repeatedly stress their victimization, complaining that they have been ruined by Salisbury, seemingly as incapable of exerting control over their own purses as they are over their sexual desires. 'Caleb Afterwit', one of Walker's correspondents, claims that Salisbury 'reduc'd my Estate ... from Four hundred to Forty Pounds *per Annum*; and my Self, from a Strong-back'd Lusty Fellow ... to a Poor, Sickly, Puny Wretch, fitter for an Hospital than a Mistress'.[33] Such accusations against prostitutes are rather typical of the time, and are linked to traditional ideas about the damaging effect of women's sexuality, especially that of potentially diseased whores, on men's health. Salisbury, however, is also depicted as being capable of emasculating men by assuming traditionally masculine behaviour and psychological qualities. Most particularly, she keeps threatening her clients with violence, sometimes making good on her threats and beating them into submission: a Russian Count who has tried to short-change Salisbury is soundly thrashed for his insolence, and reduced to a 'disabl'd Warrior' who must be rescued from Salisbury's fury by Mother Wisebourn; *The Genuine History* drives home his emasculation by describing how Mother Wisebourn 'threw over the poor ... *Count* an old Gown and Petticoat, and convey'd him safe out of sight, from his too stout *Opponent*, who still flew about, breathing Vengeance, War and Slaughter'.[34] Culminating in the stabbing of John Finch, for which she was subsequently imprisoned, Salisbury is repeatedly shown wielding phallic weapons, for instance when forcing a man to drink to the Pretender's health at sword-point, swearing that 'she'd let out his little Heart's Blood, if he would not drink it full'.[35] She even lays claim to the phallus itself: in a letter appended to *The Genuine History*, a nameless woman relates how Salisbury had been 'well rewarded' by several young ladies for her 'Assistance', which enabled them to 'sit and laugh at all the Sighs, Wishes and Addresses of dying Fellows, who courted a Smile from their fair Faces in vain'.[36] Salisbury's sales pitch undermines male superiority on several levels:

> She told me, That Women had no Occasion for Men ... For there was nothing in the Power of the Fellows, but a Woman could do as well; as keeping a House, managing a Shop, ordering Cookery or Linnen, &c. And as those Things were perform'd by our Sex, as well as by the other, so the same would hold in all other Instances, to which she, by Degrees, descended; and offer'd to go from the Theory to the practick Part, having prepared herself two of three Years before for that Purpose.[37]

As can been seen from this quote, Salisbury is not content with taking over the running of shops and houses but threatens to usurp the male sexual role as well, giving 'young Ladies of gay Fortunes' the ability to stay in control of themselves in courtship situations and enabling them to refuse their suitors, thus undermining men's sexual as well as economic control over women.[38]

In addition to challenging gender and sexual roles, Salisbury's forcefully transgressive behaviour calls the traditional social class structure into question. When the Prince of Wales sends for Salisbury as one of 'three celebrated ladies' to entertain him and two of his friends, Salisbury confidently declares that she is '*good enough for a* Garter, *I am a Who*—', thus putting herself on a par with nobility ('a Garter'), and 'radically collapsing', in Laura Rosenthal's words, 'the difference between her estate and theirs'.[39] Similarly, when the Duke of Richmond becomes irritated with Salisbury for keeping him at a distance, and haughtily reminds her of 'the Advantages of submitting to the Will of a Person of his Dignity', Salisbury answers,

> D—n you, my Lord! Do you think this Yard or two of Ribbon [his Order of the Garter] can bind me to you? The very Foundress of your Order bore no other Title, than what is my Common Name; 'Twas from a Garter slipping from her Leg, which a Mighty King was proud to snatch up, that you derive the Mighty Distance you pretend there is between us.[40]

The traditional signs of social elevation are rejected as currency by Salisbury, and only cash is accepted as valid payment, thus putting a Duke on the same level as any other man who has access to the sum Salisbury requires. The lesson is driven home once more when the Duke runs out of money and Salisbury consequently refuses to 'receive' him, something that makes the Duke 'gall'd and vex'd'.[41] In addition, she treats gentility not as a matter of birth but of money and economic success, viewing it as entirely within the grasp of someone from her own 'low' origins. When a client objects to her having 'rigg'd out' her father in clothes unsuitable for his station, Salisbury retorts that her father is '*as good a Gentleman as you are, and as well, if not better, qualify'd for such a Dress ... My Father is a Gentleman by Profession, a Cadet in the First Regiment of Foot Guards*', adding that '*before I dye I hope to see him a Collonel, if Money can make him one*'.[42] To Salisbury, social advancement is a commodity like any other, and she again uses the potential of the marketplace to offset traditional social and gender hierarchies, in that it has made her, a lower-class woman, capable of wielding the kind of economic power that was normally within reach only of upper-class men.[43]

Victimized Clients

Salisbury's clients, however, strongly reject her presentation of their relationship to her as one between buyer and seller, and instead provide a competing version of how this connection should be viewed. Whereas Salisbury's version stresses her own agency, industriousness and professionalism, and codes the relationship purely as a business transaction, her clients instead construct a fiction that ties her to them not by way of money and economy, but by way of emotional bonds, such as gratitude, loyalty and companionship. 'Castalio', for instance, complains that the stories of Salisbury's volatile temper show 'how fit she is, with all her Charms, to be treated, by any Gentleman, as a Friend, a Mistress, or indeed, a Companion even of his loosest Hours' – clearly the terms he prefers to use.[44] When describing themselves, the men tend to use either the language of romance and courtship, calling themselves her 'suitors', 'lovers', 'admirers' and 'adorers', or they employ terms that suggest a benign paternalism that belies the economic contract underlying their relationship to Salisbury, stressing their own 'generosity' and 'bounty', and calling themselves her 'donors' and 'friends'. Similarly, the men are said to give Salisbury 'presents' and do her 'favours' rather than pay for her services. The use of the word 'favours' is especially interesting in the context. The narrators – clients and biographers alike – tend to conflate the favours done by one friend for another with the conventional euphemism 'favours', which refers to sexual congress and is usually something that a woman bestows on a man, not the other way around; both words normally refer to an exchange that does not involve money or payment, but the second also refers to the very service Salisbury sells. Calling this service a 'favour' again obscures the mercantile nature of the exchange, and it also implies a resistance on the part of the men to view Salisbury's services as currency. Moreover, this usage apparently makes the men feel entitled to unpaid sex on the basis of any 'assistance' they have given Salisbury in the past. 'If she had granted him a Hundred of her Favours, she had receiv'd Thousands at Times from him, and been as fully requited as any Heart, but her's [*sic*], could wish',[45] says one of Walker's correspondents, again stressing the interchangeability between the one type of favour and the other. Instead of a professional who has a right to financial remuneration for a valuable service, the clients thus represent Salisbury as eternally indebted to them,[46] expected to reciprocate by giving them both sex and financial assistance, as well as responding with suitable respect, deference and gratitude.

This attempt to 'elevate' Salisbury and construct a more polite, superficially non-economic relationship is, however, ultimately described as having ended in failure. Salisbury is ungrateful and refractory, and does not recognize what her clients claim to be the advantages of partaking in the refining fiction. Instead, she keeps dragging them back to a 'lower' level, a whorish level, by continually laying bare the money transactions, giving the men the pox, cursing them like a Billingsgate fishwife and using physical violence against them – all indicative of a much lower level of prostitution, a level the men are presumably doing their best to avoid. Despite being given every opportunity to act in a more refined manner, Salisbury is repeatedly shown to be too much of a whore to be able to resist the impulse to act like one. The clients thus ignore, or are unaware of, Salisbury's reinterpretation of the whore identity, and instead see only the traditional, vulgar figure of the common whore. Consequently, they are at a loss to account for the reasons for her refusal to partake in their version of the relationship between prostitute and client. They appear to focus exclusively on their being taken advantage of, and present themselves as victims of this ungrateful and calculating female, ruined gentlemen deserving the readers' sympathy and pity for their unfortunate attraction to a fascinating and beautiful woman who turned out to be nothing but a conventional mercenary whore. For example, one of her clients, whom Salisbury persuaded to wait 'above 2 Hours' for her while she dealt with another customer who had arrived unexpectedly, complains that he was 'Sot enough to stay and be content that whole Night with a *Butter'd-Bunn*, and her dissembling Cant, and was so infatuated afterwards, notwithstanding this, and many other Instances of ill Usage, to continue her Humble Servant; untill I was A Broken Merchant'.[47] Similarly, 'Caleb Afterwit' relates how he, after having kept Salisbury, found his 'Constitution very much impair'd by the *French-Disease*', to such a degree that it was 'beyond the Art of any of the ingenious Sons of *Galen* to master'. Typically, Salisbury, 'tho' she was well acquainted with my present Incapacity' shows no pity: she accuses 'Caleb' of having given the disease to her, and threatens to send him to jail for a debt '*contracted chiefly by her self*', persuading her creditors 'to send Two Bayliffs, who carry'd me to a *Spunging-House* in a very weak Condition'.[48] The anonymous author of *The Genuine History* seems to express the sentiments of her brow-beaten customers when he asks, rhetorically, 'who ever us'd her so well, that she did not sometimes turn foul upon?'[49] All this abuse is depicted as Salisbury's typical requital for male generosity and kindness, although, as will be discussed in the next section, the men are often made to appear naive for having expected anything better from a common prostitute.

Biographers' Dispute: Whore or Courtesan

The conflicting interpretations of Salisbury's persona put forward by Walker and the anonymous author of *The Genuine History* constitute a kind of literary debate. This debate centres on the validity of the clients' representation of their relationship with Salisbury, most especially whether they were right to treat her like a courtesan or whether they were fools for doing so. The crucial point in this debate is Salisbury's identity: is she in reality a whore or is she more like a courtesan? In this, Salisbury's assertive self-representation as a whore is once more rejected, in that Walker uses her radical and empowering reformulation of the whore as evidence that she really is one, again redefined as the derogatory insult the concept traditionally implied. By doing this he simultaneously accomplishes two rhetorical goals: he unmasks Salisbury as a common whore, and he ridicules her clients for their inability to correctly identify her as one, for their insistence in treating her politely and for failing to assert their masculine superiority even when it becomes all too clear what she really is. He thus places the blame for the clients' victimization squarely on their own shoulders, a blame that *The Genuine History* subsequently tries to avoid by questioning Walker's representation both of Salisbury as a whore and, by implication, the clients as deluded, emasculated fools.

Walker's presentation of Salisbury is, however, a little more complex than this suggests, and deserves explicating at greater length. At times, he appears to depict Salisbury in an almost celebratory manner, making the most of her sharp tongue and ready wit, and there is much to recommend Rosenthal's contention that Walker uses Salisbury to '[demystify] both aristocratic ideology *and* certain middle-class claims to a relationship between commerce and manners'.[50] He often allows her to come across as honest, optimistic, assertive and witty, and Walker thus at one level seems to confirm a prostitute identity that successfully makes use of commercial strategies to undermine the conventional condemnation of the whore and instead construct her as a legitimate tradesperson. Whether by design or not, Salisbury's empowering self-representation often shines through: above all, Walker seems to confirm the ability of this identity to challenge traditional hierarchies regarding social class, gender and so on.[51] However, his description of her 'whorish' qualities – whether they are directly related to the marketplace or not – is coded in conventional, if satirical, language that suggests that what he is describing is not Salisbury as an independent tradeswoman but as a traditionally constructed common whore. The text consistently lays stress on the personal qualities that most indicate Salisbury's lower-class whorishness: she is shrewish, vulgar, diseased, violent and ungrateful, and Walker all but obsesses about her mercenary greed, taking every opportunity to emphasize that particular aspect of her character. Walker's narrative may well be said to '[take] pleasure in rather than simply offence at the whore's outrageousness',[52] but at the same time, it also creates a text that functions as one long defamation, a book-length 'Madam, despite your wealth and success you are nothing but a common whore'. That Walker himself was aware of this reading is indicated in the conclusion, addressed directly to 'Mrs. Sally Salisbury', where he claims to have learned that 'your humble Servant, is ... to have the *Severity* of the *Law* inflicted upon him', besides being 'likewise threaten'd with a more *severe Correction* from some *who are to fight very Manfully* under your *Banner*'.[53] He is reasonably referring to the possibility of being sued for defamation by Salisbury, because he ironically declares himself 'at all times ready to defend your *Virtue* in every *Court* of *Justice*, not excluding even *Doctors-Commons* itself'.[54] This reading has special resonance in Walker's text because one of his correspondents has earlier related a story about how Salisbury '*put a Woman into* Doctors-Commons *for calling her* Whore'.[55] Walker's correspondent warns him that he runs the risk of

> being cited in the *Commons*, having your Pockets empty'd by *Spiritual Court* Proctors, and doing *Penance* in a Place, where, in tracing *SALLY*'s Life, I believe you will hardly find she has ever been since her Baptism; for as in writing of her Life I believe it will be impossible for you to avoid giving her a *Title* which more justly belongs to her, than the Name she assumes, so I also believe 'twill be as impossible (considering what a Termagant you have to deal with) to escape the Danger premis'd.[56]

Walker, however, reacts to this good-natured warning by satirizing the writer, just as he satirizes the men who threaten him with a 'more *severe Correction*' for slandering Salisbury.[57] Whether those who advise caution in crossing Salisbury do so in apparent friendship or enmity, Walker draws their masculinity into question, creating the mocking pseudonym 'Tim. Timerous' for his correspondent and ironizing over the men who fight '*Manfully*' under the banners of a whore. Unlike Salisbury's customers, Walker refuses to be either bullied or intimidated by her, or to collude in the gender confusion her assertive and violent behaviour occasions. The solution appears to be to ignore Salisbury and her litigiousness, to dismiss her whorish 'Rhetorick', her rage and her temper tantrums, and instead regard her with the detachment of the nobleman in the final letter in Walker's text, who claims that 'nothing that she [Salisbury] either says or does causes any Admiration in those who know her'.[58] To do anything else makes the men complicit in their own victimization. At the beginning of his narrative, Walker affirms that

> as ... we are indebted to our selves, and to our selves only, for that Extravagance of Power which *They* [women] on all Occasions take the Liberty to exert over *Us* [men], we cannot, upon the strictest Examination, blame the insolent Arrogance of the *haughty Woman*, when we consider the mean Submissions of the *obsequious yielding Man*.[59]

Walker may use the inclusive pronoun 'we', but the text does not appear to satirize men as a group, only men who allow themselves to be intimidated by Salisbury and her whorish wiles. The issue seems to be manhood itself, or rather, the failed manhood represented by Salisbury's clients, incapable as they are of controlling this unruly lower-class female and maintaining conventional gender hierarchies. If Salisbury rallies the power of the marketplace to aid her in her bid for empowerment, the men appear at a loss as to how to counter it, ineffectively allowing her to bully them, 'not [being] courageous enough entirely to refuse' Salisbury's demands for more money, one of them even employing 'all the Money I had receiv'd, and all the Rhetorick I was Master of' to appease her when she throws a temper tantrum, failing to see that the money is all she cares about in the first place.[60] Walker does not accept the clients' representation of themselves as hapless and deluded victims; as men, he seems to suggest, they should have known better than to be misled by the beauty and wit of a woman whose inability to control her own temper continually unmasks her as the common whore she is. According to Walker, the onus for restoring the social and gendered hierarchies rests on the men, and if they fail to do so – in effect, permitting Salisbury to emasculate them – the fault is all their own.

It is this criticism against Salisbury's clients that *The Genuine History* most immediately tries to undermine. It does this by denying Walker's representation of Salisbury as a common whore, showing her instead to be more like a courtesan: more conventionally feminine, more refined, less mercenary and less of a threat to social structures and conventional gender hierarchies alike. This does not mean that her radical reformulation of the whore persona is entirely absent in this text – it is, for instance, in *The Genuine History* that Salisbury monopolizes the Prince of Wales and his two aristocratic friends by frankly declaring herself a whore (quoted above), while her two colleagues are dismissed because they resort to conventional representations of female ruin, such as milliners and farmer's daughters, which deny or obscure their status as prostitutes.[61] However, Salisbury's empowering construction of the whore persona can be said to be muted in this work in comparison to *Authentick Memoirs*, just as the word 'whore' in *The Genuine History* is euphemistically exchanged for '*Who—*'. In presenting Salisbury mainly as a courtesan, *The Genuine History* distances her from a marketplace that gives her the opportunity to assume a position of power over her customers, but which threatens only to degrade them. Thus, by 'defending' her in this manner, *The Genuine History* counteracts Salisbury's attempt to construct a powerful persona for herself. This may seem paradoxical, but *The Genuine History* is arguably more concerned with the representation of Salisbury's clients; it is hardly coincidental that one consequence of socially rehabilitating the prostitute is to make her customers seem more refined and discerning. *The Genuine History* thus rejects the whore identity and improves on Salisbury's social background, the morals of her parents, her motivation for acting in certain ways, specific things she has said and done, and so on. For instance, the author of *The Genuine History* contradicts Walker's report that Salisbury, when young, shelled peas and sold matches, and she is portrayed as being far less violent and less of a termagant, although *The Genuine History* does remark on her tendency to 'turn foul' on her clients.[62] *The Genuine History* only mentions venereal disease once, and no man is said to have been infected by her, unlike in *Authentick Memoirs*, where she is said to have ruined the health of several men. The most interesting thing about *The Genuine History*, however, is that money is rarely mentioned, and when it is, it is more often in connection with gambling than prostitution. More to the point, Salisbury's mercenary nature, on which Walker puts such emphasis, is played down significantly in *The Genuine History*. For instance, *The Genuine History* describes Salisbury as simply angry when the Russian Count tries to defraud her, whereas Walker points out that

> while the poor Count lay sprawling upon the Floor, the Dangerous *Hell-Cat* [Salisbury] had secur'd the five Pieces, and what else she could pick up that was to her liking; for she was not so much blinded with Fury, but that she could discern a convenient Moveable.[63]

The author of *The Genuine History* does mention Salisbury's ingratitude in refusing to lend money to her clients, but suggests that one possible reason may have been that she was short on cash, and that she was not in fact ungrateful at all; once he even straightforwardly rejects this accusation, representing the relationship between her and 'Mr B—s' as one of '*Kindness*' on her part, in that 'her exhausted *Admirer* she generally supply'd with Money, and more than half maintain'd him'.[64] By contrast, Walker depicts Salisbury as too greedy to lend this man any money, which results in his being sent to debtor's prison.[65] Whereas *The Genuine History* can hardly be said to idealize Salisbury, it nevertheless creates an image for her that differs from that of the common and vilified whore, making her more recognizably 'feminine' and thus less of a threat to men and to society around her.

Whether *Authentick Memoirs* or *The Genuine History* can be considered to be more convincing in their argumentation is, however, less interesting than the fact that they, by supporting as well as by denying Salisbury's self-representation as a whore, reject and counteract her attempt to assume a position of power in her professional life. *The Genuine History* reconstructs her as a more polite version of the prostitute, denying the very existence of her transgressive challenge to social and gendered hierarchies; Walker reaffirms the traditional coding of the whore, rejecting Salisbury's reconstruction of it as a legitimate businesswoman. In so doing, he recognizes her transgressive potential, but he codes that transgression as nothing more than a typical violation of conventional social structures and public morality that prostitution has always implied. The various constructions of clients and biographers alike rely on traditional social categories that fit snugly into the hierarchies of the time: patron and supplicant, benefactor and beneficiary, lord and commoner, courtesan and keeper, whore and cully. Salisbury, on the other hand, supports herself on something new and more radical: a contract between equals, between buyer and seller, a relationship in which market forces give her, the seller of a unique, personalized service, the edge over clients who wish to buy what she is offering. The difference between Salisbury's worldview, based as it is on upward social mobility, and that of her clients, which is based on hereditary privilege, is perhaps the reason why her self-representation appears so compelling to twenty-first-century readers despite the passage of almost three centuries. The conflicting opinions of *Authentick Memoirs* and *The Genuine History* may have faded into the historical background, and the cultural significance of the issue they debate has changed over time, but the depiction of the woman over whose identity they disagree stands out in bold relief. Three hundred years later, it is primarily the uncompromising voice of Sally Salisbury that we hear.

6 PROSTITUTES AND EROTIC PERFORMANCES IN EIGHTEENTH-CENTURY PARIS

Thomas Wynn

A commonplace of great persistence in the eighteenth century is that of the actress as prostitute. At a time when writers such as Voltaire, Beaumarchais and even Sade[1] repeated the 'smug assumption'[2] that the theatre is a site moral instruction, this dual figure embodies most acutely the seductive danger posed by the theatre. Pamela Cheek has noted that, whereas in England the actress took on a more respectable status in the eighteenth century, in France 'becoming a star or even a regular actress inscribed in the rolls of a theater remained synonymous with prostitution'.[3] That the prostitute and the actress were coterminous in the public mind is evidenced in the *Etrennes aux grisettes* (*Presents to Girls of Easy Virtue*, 1790), which lists a number of prostitutes and, under the heading of 'actrices', the writer notes: 'Il est de toute justice de les assimiler aux grisettes; cette épithète doit être désormais le synonyme de leur nom' ('It is entirely justifiable to assimilate them with the girls of easy virtue; this epithet must henceforth be the synonym of their name').[4] Patrick Wald Lasowski offers an account for the two professions being synonymous: 'Acteurs, actrices, prostituées: complices dans l'affranchissement des discours et des corps, dans la citoyenneté qui appelle au partage des jouissances, dans l'effronterie – habitée désormais par l'énergie révolutionnaire – de ceux qui sont, avant tout, des hommes et des femmes publiques' ('Actors, actresses, prostitutes: accomplices in the emancipation of speech and the body, in the citizenship which called for pleasures to be shared, in the insolence – now possessed with revolutionary energy – of those who are, above all, public men and women').[5] This chapter accepts Wald Lasowski's emphasis on the public nature of these occupations, but challenges his optimistic sense of revolutionary liberation. Instead I shall argue that the actress and the prostitute provoked anxiety in their contemporaries because they were perceived to circulate in public in an unmanageable, even illegitimate manner.

The key piece of evidence will be François-Thomas-Marie Baculard d'Arnaud's *L'Art de foutre, ou Paris foutant* (*The Art of Fucking, or Paris is Fucking*), a ballet performed by prostitutes in a Parisian brothel in 1741. Featuring nudity, penetration and ejaculation, this work realizes the otherwise abstract commonplace that links the actress and the prostitute. *L'Art de foutre* is an immensely rare work by an author better known for more modest fiction and theatre; his biographer Robert Dawson located a single extant printed copy, printed some six years after the ballet was performed.[6] Held at the Bibliothèque de l'Arsenal, the text is bound with an erotic work similarly set in a bawdy house, the comte de Caylus's comedy *Le Bordel, ou le jean-foutre puni* (*The Brothel or the Chastised Good-for-Nothing*, 1732). By happy irony, this copy appears to owe its survival to the very man who ought to have destroyed it, for it bears the *ex libris* of M. d'Hémery, inspector of the book trade from 1748 to 1753;[7] according to Louis-Sébastien Mercier and Simon-Nicolas-Henri Linguet, both writing in the 1780s, officials responsible for the destruction of condemned works often filched a copy.[8] In addition, the Cushing Library (Texas) holds a manuscript of the work in a collection of transcribed erotic works, and which bears the date 1780, although this is not in Baculard's own hand.[9]

L'Art de foutre is also notable in two other respects: it is the only example of erotic theatre whose performance is vouched for by independent documentation (rather than, say, a play's preface); it is also, as far as we have been able to ascertain, the only erotic play subject to police repression of the most rapid and intense kind. One might assume that these two facts are causally linked, that the embodied obscene performance provoked the authorities to intervene, and thus that the prostitute-as-actress was a target of the police's activities. Yet, as Kathryn Norberg argues in this volume, the police officially condemned prostitution while tolerating the brothel as part of their control of public order. An examination of the police archives allows us to ascertain whether the performing whore was indeed the authorities' main concern, or if a different motivation lay behind their actions.

Scholars including Robert Darnton and Robert Dawson have been instrumental in identifying the authorities' attempts to prevent the publication and circulation of seditious material (including that of a sexually explicit nature) within the public sphere whose 'decisive mark', according to Jürgen Habermas, is 'the published word'.[10] Unlike a private brothel where different bodies come together in paroxysm (Diderot would argue that a similar group effect is operative in a regular theatre, although here spectators laugh and cry rather than orgasm together),[11] the participants in what Habermas calls 'the public sphere of a rational-critical debate in the world of letters'[12] are joined only through disembodied discussion. Open to people irrespective of wealth, rank or occupation, the public sphere is all the more difficult to police due to its diffuse, abstract and proliferating nature, and thus in the eyes of the authorities, pernicious matter might easily fall into the wrong hands.[13] If such assumptions lay behind the suppression of *L'Art de foutre*, then it is the written text rather than the prostitute-as-actress whose illicit circulation within the public realm provokes anxiety.

In the eighteenth century acting and prostitution were considered as being outside of the civic law and excluded from religious practice, such as Christian burial.[14] While there was little in the ecclesiastical tradition that supported the ban on actors receiving the communion (the Church fathers condemned not actors *per se* but 'the cruelties of the amphitheatre or licentious spectacles in pagan temples'),[15] the Paris *Rituel* of 1786, a text detailing religious ceremonies such as administration of the sacraments, states: 'Il faut rejeter de la communion de l'Église les personnes notoirement infâmes, telles que sont les femmes publiques et les Comédiens' ('One must exclude from the communion of the Church such notoriously odious people as prostitutes and actors').[16] Although both this statement and Wald Lasowski's account ignore sexual difference, it should be noted that the convergence of theatrical and sexual performers applies almost exclusively to women. When in the *Lettre à M. D'Alembert* (1758) Rousseau implies that acting is a form of prostitution, he does indeed refer to the male actor: 'Qu'est-ce que la profession du comédien? Un métier par lequel il se donne en représentation pour de l'argent, se soumet à l'ignominie et aux affronts qu'on achète le droit de lui faire, et met publiquement sa personne en vente' ('What is the profession of the actor? It is a trade in which he performs for money, submits himself to the ignominy and affronts that others buy the right to give him, and puts his person publicly on sale').[17] But the only example I have found of a male actor described as a prostitute is Nivelon, a sodomite kept by an English lord.[18] This chapter thus focuses on actresses (dancers as well as dramatic or lyric performers), and women who received money, gifts and financial support for sex.[19] Rather than appeal to some kind of emancipated vision of the two professions, this chapter suggests a number of other institutional and aesthetic reasons for the convergence of the actress with the prostitute.

A common feature in comparisons between the actress and the prostitute is the anxiety rather than the celebration of the public woman. Even secular writers who do not link the two professions outright, nonetheless inherit from Christian orthodoxy the anxiety of the exposed or exhibitionist woman; this is certainly the case with Rousseau.[20] Those texts that do explicitly assimilate prostitution to acting, pinpoint the actress as being a sexually enticing and dangerous woman. For instance Louis Bérenger, who devotes five of his forty-nine propositions for the reform of prostitution to the theatre and actresses, not only decries Audinot's boulevard theatre as a school of bad taste and lubricity which corrupts the common people, but he singles out its actresses for 'ces travestissements indécents, ces costumes *couleur de chair*, qui attirent tant de monde et salissent tant de jeunes imaginations aux fréquentes représentations d'*Azémia* et de l'*Héroïne américaine*' ('those indecent disguises, those *flesh-coloured* costumes, which attract so many people and sully so many young imaginations at the frequent performances of *Azémia* and *The American Heroine*').[21] This misogynistic conflation of the public actress with the public prostitute was a sure way to denigrate a successful, relatively independent woman; the potentially disruptive character is rendered comprehensible, manageable and safe when reconfigured as a whore, a commodity to be owned and traded.

Acting is identified with prostitution at a number of key moments across eighteenth-century theological texts, police reports, reform tracts and narrative fiction. The first reason for this identification might be termed an institutional one. Wages for most actresses were relatively modest, at least until the theatre's increased commercialization from the 1760s onwards,[22] and the supernumeraries at the Opéra earned nothing at all (these women numbered fourteen in 1763–4, and twenty-five a decade later).[23] They had to live on something, and financial support from admirers was one source of income; at least one contemporary recognized that the Opéra should pay its singers and dancers enough so that they would not be in 'la nécessité indispensable de se prostituer' ('the utter necessity to prostitute themselves').[24] The police reports of the period often feature actresses, dancers and singers, and it is clear that some of them received money for their companionship, as is the case with the *demoiselle* Couras, who in 1752 was receiving 400 livres a month as well household expenses from the Swedish Baron de Creutz.[25] The whoring actress is a common figure in eighteenth-century fiction, as well as semi-fictional biographies and anecdotes; indeed it is typical that the actress, whose very craft leads her to straddle reality and fantasy, should appear so frequently in texts that hover between the factual and the imaginary. For example, the heroine (loosely modelled on Mlle Clairon) of Gaillard de la Bataille's *Histoire de la vie et des mœurs de Mademoiselle Cronel dite Frétillon* (*History of the life and morals of Mademoiselle Cronel known as Frétillon*, 1739–40), aims to join the Comédie-Française in order to secure a rich lover, though in fact after an unsuccessful début at the Théâtre-Italien she joins a provincial theatre troupe in Rouen. A similar episode occurs in Chévrier's novel *Le Colporteur* (*The Book Peddler*, 1761), in which attractive but impecunious young women are recommended to join the Opéra or the Opéra-Comique, where they are likely to come into contact with Americans, English, Dutch and even 'pesants Allemands, tous gens ruinables' ('heavy Germans, all ripe for financial ruin').[26] It is in light of the artistic calibre and sexual intentions of the performers that a reform tract, which aims for a wholesale reorganization of the capital, addresses the seemingly minor question of the constitution of the Opéra:

> Qu'il soit fait défense à ce spectacle d'inscrire sur ses registres toute femme ou fille qui ne serait pas réellement actrice, cantatrice ou danseuse. Cette inscription est une véritable injure faite aux artistes de ce théâtre, dont le mérite doit tendre à l'estime du public, comme à son admiration. (It should be forbidden for this theatre to include in its registers any woman or girl who is not really an actress, singer or dancer. Such an inclusion is a true affront to this theatre's artists, whose merit must strive for the public's esteem, as well as its admiration.)[27]

The semi-fictional brochures of brothels and prostitutes that appeared during the Revolution make explicit this link between sexual and theatrical performers, for among the *lingères* and *coiffeuses* are numerous actresses. The *Liste com-*

plète des plus belles femmes publiques et des plus saines du Palais de Paris (1790) includes Henriette Renaud and Adèle from the Louvois and Vaudeville theatres respectively.[28] The *Étrennes aux grisettes* lists, for example, Desgarcins from the Théâtre-Français, Saint-Huberti [sic] from the Opéra, and Tabaraire from the Variétés.[29] An actress's supplementary income might not be entirely for her use, for in the anonymous *Sérails de Paris* (1802), a would-be pimp is recommended to take on an actress or a dancer (even without talent) as a lover, since she will be the ideal bait to rich foreigners, 10 per cent of whose gifts will pass directly to the *souteneur*.[30] Such is the correlation between the professions that the *Nouvelle liste des jolies femmes de Paris* (1808) could state under the heading 'actrices':

> Je n'en nommerai aucune; elles sont si faciles à connaître et à trouver, que les amateurs n'ont pas besoin de mes détails à cet égard; mais je me permettrai d'observer à ces mêmes amateurs, que, s'ils chérissent leur santé, ils prennent de grandes précautions avec ces belles sirènes. (I shall not name a single one; they are so easy to recognize and to find that enthusiasts do not need my information in this regard; but I will allow myself to point out to these same enthusiasts that, if they value their health, they should take great precautions with these beautiful sirens.)[31]

The actress and the prostitute thus appear as seductive, available and dangerous, their venal bodies ready to infect and corrupt the public at large.

This threat of contamination is evidenced in one of Bérenger's propositions for reforming prostitution where he asks that 'bals champêtres' in the outskirts of Paris be banned, for they act as recruiting grounds for procuresses, and it is there that 'les petits acteurs des boulevards vont porter tous les germes de la débauche et de la corruption, d'où elle se répand à la fois dans la ville et dans la campagne' ('the little actors from the boulevards carry all the germs of debauchery and corruption, whence it spreads into the town and the countryside').[32] While the male actor here is the vector of pollution, and thus an undoubtedly pernicious influence, it is the actress who stands as the agent of depravity and who is, in a sense, that pollution, as shown in the anonymous tale *Le Petit-fils d'Hercule* (*Hercules's Grandson*, 1784) in which the hero (a rare example of a heterosexual male prostitute) decides, in his new capacity as governor of the Russian province of Orel, to combat underpopulation by establishing a theatre there. In order to turn the inhabitants' minds towards sexual licence, he brings in a secondment from the Opéra as well as an assortment of travelling actresses and those who played in private theatres in Paris: 'Mes vues se remplirent. Elles ruinèrent des princes et allumèrent dans la ville le désir de la jouissance' ('My ambitions were fulfilled. These women ruined princes and sparked the desire for pleasure in that town').[33] In this respect the actress again resembles the prostitute, who repeatedly appears as a poisoner of men's bodies and therefore of society and future generations.[34]

The performers' status at the Opéra contributed to their perceived venality. This institution was officially part of the royal household, and thus its members, being under the jurisdiction of the *gentilshommes de la chambre du roi*, enjoyed the benefit of immunity from paternal control, even if a minor.[35] For Chévrier, the consequences are all too clear and he writes that opera girls, being no longer subject to paternal authority or to the rigour of the police, can become 'dénaturées et libertines avec impunité' ('perverted and libertine with impunity').[36] Similarly, in Pidansat de Mairobert's *Confession d'une jeune fille* (1784) a provincial girl with a taste for libertinage places herself under the safeguard of the Opéra so that her parents could have no control over her.[37] It is to this legal anomaly that Bérenger refers when he recommends that anyone should be able to claim back his close female relative, even when one of the 'vestales de l'Opéra';[38] and Louis-Sébastien Mercier criticizes this immunity in his *Tableau de Paris*: 'Une fille est enlevée au pouvoir paternel, dès que son pied a touché les planches du théâtre. Une loi particulière rend vaines les lois les plus antiques et les plus solemnelles.' ('A girl is removed from her father's authority as soon as her foot has touched the boards of the stage. A strange law renders invalid the most ancient and solemn laws.')[39] The author draws out the implications of this state of affairs: 'On oublie que ces beautés sont à prix d'or, et qu'elles ont des rivales qui ne sont point *vénales*' (People forget that these beauties cost a fortune, and that they have rivals who are not *venal*').[40]

Given the assimilation of actress with prostitute, the sites of their activities become one and the same. Of great concern to Bérenger are the private boxes within the playhouse; he proposes policing these 'boudoirs', some of which are equipped with beds, and he recommends that their curtains be removed, that they be fully illuminated, and that the 'filles de profession' keep their doors open, all the while supervized by a guard patrolling the corridors, as occurs in Marseille.[41] Even when the actress herself was not depicted as a prostitute, the theatre remained a privileged site of soliciting; novelist Crébillon *fils*, for example, calls the door to the Opéra a market for whores;[42] the anonymous *L'Espion libertin* (*The Libertine Spy*, 1802) depicts the foyer to the Théâtre Montansier as a brothel;[43] and in Pidansat de Mairobert's *L'Espion anglais* (*The English Spy*, 1777–85), the Opéra is decried as a 'réceptacle à l'impudicité, à l'adultère, à la prostitution, à la crapule la plus honteuse; en un mot d'asile à toutes les turpitudes, à tous les vices' ('repository for indecency, adultery, prostitution, the most disgraceful villainy; in a word, a refuge for all depravities, all vices').[44]

As well as such institutional reasons (which make a prostitute of the actress), there is above all an aesthetic or performative rapprochement between the two occupations, in that both deploy a body that is paid to fake emotions for the paying audience's benefit (which makes an actress of the prostitute). With the actress configured as prostitute and vice versa, a public yet marginalized figure is forged that simulates desire so as to stimulate desire in the client, spectator or protector. The fictional *Correspondance de Madame Gourdan* (1783), one of

Paris's most famous madams, features a set of forty 'Instructions for a young girl who in entering the world and who wishes to make her fortune with the charms she has received from nature'. Several of these instructions evoke acting and the theatre, for as well as the recommendation to become a member of the Opéra in order to avoid the police, they suggest that the girl adopt skills that would be useful for an actress:

> IV. Affectez toujours le plus grand plaisir dans l'amoureuse jouissance, quand même vous seriez insensible, afin de faire goûter plus de plaisir à votre entreteneur, en lui faisant croire que vous jouissez aussi ...
>
> XII. Ayez les larmes à commande et les mots de *sentiments*, d'*honneur*, de *perfidie*, de *cruauté*, etc., mais n'employez ces armes qu'avec précaution, afin qu'elles réussissent.
>
> (IV. Always affect the greatest pleasure in amorous ecstasy, even when you feel nothing, in order to make your client taste greater pleasure by making him think you too are in ecstasy ...
>
> XII. Have tears ready at your command as well as the words *feelings*, *honour*, *treachery*, *cruelty* etc. but only ever use these weapons with caution in order that they should hit their mark.)[45]

Thus the prostitute is in command of her gestures and script, in a manner that evokes the advice given to the actor by Diderot in the *Paradoxe sur le comédien* (1773): 'Les cris de douleur sont notés dans son oreille. Les gestes de son désespoir sont de mémoire, et ont été préparés devant une glace ... C'est vous que remportez toutes ces impressions ... Il n'est pas le personnage, il le joue et le joue si bien que vous le prenez pour tel: l'illusion n'est que pour vous; il sait bien lui, qu'il ne l'est pas.' ('The cries of pain are noted in his ear. The gestures of despair are from memory, and have been prepared before a mirror. It is you who takes away these impressions. He is not the character, he performs it and performs it so well that you take him for such; the illusion exists only for you; he knows perfectly well that he is not that character.')[46] Neither actress nor prostitute is subject to the passions she represents; both emotionless women discipline their body in order to stimulate that of the observer. The shared performance practice is evidenced in another of the instructions:

> Jouez bien le sentiment: allez souvent aux Français pour y apprendre à jouer une scène de dépit, de rupture et de raccommodement. Il faut dans l'état de démoiselle entretenue être un peu comédienne. (Perform feelings well: go often to the Comédie-Française to as to learn to play scenes of heartache, rupture and reconciliation. There should be a little bit of the actress in the kept woman.)[47]

We are far from 'l'affranchissement des discours et des corps' (to return to Wald Lasowski's terms); the two women are linked by a controlled performance, by a mediated expression of passion. And so it is not just that the theatre is identified with the brothel, for the comparison may work in the other direction, as the

Nouvelle liste des jolies femmes de Paris demonstrates: 'Voilà, lecteurs, les premiers rôles et les doublures du charmant théâtre de Mde. Deval; vous entendez par théâtre, que je veux dire de la charmante demeure d'une des demi-divinités qui président à vos plaisirs' (Here, readers, are the leading roles and the understudies of Mme Deval's charming theatre; you should understand by theatre, that I mean the charming residence of these semi-divine women who preside over your pleasures').[48] The brothel and the playhouse overlap, such is the expertise of the performers therein.

We have seen that the actress and the prostitute fascinate the public, despite an anxiety that these women might confuse, corrupt and contaminate the unwitting spectator. To neutralize this threat, a host of reform tracts – such as Rétif de la Bretonne's *Le Mimographe* and *Le Pornographe*, as well as texts by Turmeau de La Morandière and Bérenger – recommend that women from both professions be readily identifiable as such by means of coded clothing, and that actresses perform only one appropriate role (thereby minimizing the sense of deceit). It remains to be seen if that same anxiety of public irruption is manifest when these two figures conjoin in one single personage.

Despite the ubiquity of the 'actress-as-prostitute' figure, there is on the contrary very little documented evidence regarding the 'prostitute-as-actress' figure. A not inconsiderable amount of pornographic theatre was written in the eighteenth century, but there is little verifiable trace that this erotic drama was performed.[49] When the period's erotic fiction refers to such plays, it does so in the context not of brothels but of elite private houses,[50] beyond the reach of the authorities; the key example here is Delisle de Sales's *Théâtre d'amour* which was written for the prince d'Hénin and his 'théâtre secret où il n'introduisait que des roués de sa petite cour et des femmes de qualité dignes d'être des courtisanes' ('secret theatre where he invited only the rakes of his little court and women of quality who were worthy of being courtesans').[51] In this respect, Baculard d'Arnaud's obscene ballet *L'Art de foutre, ou Paris foutant* is, as a historian of prostitution remarks, an exceptional episode,[52] for it was performed by prostitutes on 1 January 1741 at the brothel of Madame Lacroix (or Delacroix) on the rue de Clichy in Paris. For want of detailed information, it is as yet impossible to determine the standing of this brothel and its clients, but one may assume that it aspired to some sophistication given the performance of a commissioned ballet.

Baculard's ballet is a parody of the prologue to André Campra and Houdar de La Motte's *L'Europe galante* (1697), transforming such lines as 'Quelle soudaine horreur! et quels terribles bruits! / Ciel! qui peut amener la discorde où je suis?' ('Such sudden horror! And such terrible sounds! / Heavens, what can bring about the discord wherein I find myself?') into 'Quel foutu tintamare! et quel bougre de bruit! / O ciel! un commissaire! Ah! tout mon con frémit' ('What a fucking racket! What a bugger of a noise! / Heavens, a police commissioner. My cunt is all a-tremble").[53] The ballet is a degenerative transformation of the original opera, debasing the divine characters of the original into a bawdyhouse's workers and clients, replete with venereal disease, police corruption and the threat of imprisonment. The work features characters who, although cloaked in vague anonymity, would be recognizable to the audience at Lacroix's brothel. One such character is a certain 'Monsieur D'***, Commissaire',[54] who is bribed by the madam when he tries to cart her and the prostitutes off to the Hôpital. The Cushing manuscript identifies him as 'Monsieur d'Alby'; there was indeed a man by this name who began as *commissaire* at the Châtelet in 1728, and who in 1741 was responsible for the La Grève area.[55] The cast list also features a number of prostitutes:

>Mademoiselle P****, la jeune, *putain*.
>Mademoiselle Le S****, *autre putain*.
>Mademoiselle D********, *troisième putain*.
>Mademoiselle R*******, *quatrième putain*.
>Mademoiselle M*****, *cinquième putain*.
>Mademoiselle L'E******, *sixième putain*.
>Mesdemoiselles A********, R****, & J****, *garces*.[56]

While this code may be indecipherable to a modern audience, it was more legible to an eighteenth-century reader given that someone (Hémery himself?) completed most of the names with the handwritten annotations: 'etit', 'ueur', 'uplessis', 'ousseau', nothing for the next, then 'mpereur', 'ntonia', nothing for the next and finally 'oly'. For the most part the Cushing manuscript confirms these identifications, giving the following names: 'Madl^le Petit la jeune, Madl^le Le Sueur, Madl^le Duplessis, Madl^le Rozette, Madl^le Mouton, Madl^le Angelique, and Mesdl^les L'Empereur, Rabot et Julie'.[57] These prostitutes are called upon to perform unequivocally sexual actions, for as one stage direction indicates:

>Les six putains s'avancent et les six fouteurs; cela forme une scène muette. Deux des fouteurs ne bandent point; deux putains leur mettent la main au vit, et tâchent de rappeler chez eux la nature: des autres fouteurs qui bandent, l'un veut foutre en charrette brisée, l'autre en levrette. (The six whores come forward with the six studs; this forms a silent scene. Two of the studs do not have erections; two whores put their hands on their pricks, and try to revive them; of the other studs who do have erections, one wants to screw in the broken chariot position, another in the doggy position.)[58]

Another stage direction indicates that 'quelques vits même sont déjà dans les cons' ('some pricks are also in the cunts'), the cast form the various sexual positions described by Aretino, and the play ends with widespread debauchery and a general orgasm. Although it is unclear how these acts were realized on stage and to what extent theatrical props might have used instead of relying upon the actors' bodies, this was undoubtedly a sexually explicit performance.

The police soon took an interest in *L'Art de foutre*, but documents relating to the investigation show that they were unconcerned by the representation of the work by prostitutes. The first reference to Baculard's ballet is in a letter dated 21 January 1741 from Maurepas, the *ministre d'état*, to Duval, the *secrétaire de la lieutenance*:

> Je n'ay pris encore qu'une lecture trop rapide de l'imprimé que vous m'avez envoyés pour pouvoir vous mander ce que j'en pense moi même ... Il seroit fort intéressant de découvrir l'autheur et l'imprimeur; la découverte des acteurs seroit plus aisée, mais il y auroit aussi moins de fruit à en attendre et d'ailleurs on doit tout attendre du bénéfice du temps, s'ils ne sont point remplacés. (As yet I have given the printed matter you sent me too fleeting a glimpse to be able to send to you my own thoughts on it ... It would be most interesting to discover the author and the printer; the discovery of the actors would be easier, but there would also be less to be gained from doing so and in any case one should count on the benefits of time for everything, if they are not replaced.)[59]

The ballet does therefore appear to have been staged, since Maurepas writes of 'acteurs'. The prostitutes who performed in the work are, however, of no consequence to him; their identities may come to light at some point, but their discovery and their potential replacement by other women are not pressing concerns. The investigation betrays none of the anxiety over the actress-as-prostitute figure that we have identified in the period's literature. There is no trace of Madame Lacroix in the archives; while several scholars suggest (without proof) that she was arrested, even sent off to America,[60] there is simply no evidence to suggest that the obscene realization of *L'Art de foutre* was of much interest to Maurepas and his colleagues. The claim made on the 1747 edition's title page that the ballet was staged on every holiday of 1741 is thus conceivably true, for Maurepas issues no further commands regarding the performance of the work.

The dossier of police documents regarding *L'Art de foutre* focuses not on those people (principally women) who performed the ballet, but on the three men who wrote, published and distributed it.[61] At the beginning of February the police found thirty copies of the ballet in the possession of a certain Madame Froissart, the domestic servant of a woman named Chauvin. These had apparently been brought to her by a book peddler called Guillaume Dacier,[62] who declared that a man named Auchenon had had the manuscript of the work in his pocket for several days.[63] The investigation revealed that Gabriel Osmont had printed the play. He was sent to the Bastille on 9 February,[64] and Dubut (presumably an *intendant* of some kind) wrote to Maurepas that same day:

> J'ay l'honneur de vous rendre compte qu'en conséquence de vos ordres j'ay aretté et conduit à la bastille le m[r] osmont imprimeur pour avoir *distribué* l'imprimé quy a pour titre l'art de f... qui est des plus obscenes. (I have the honour of informing you that following your orders I have arrested and taken to the Bastille Mr Osmont,

printer, for having *distributed* the printed text titled L'Art de f... which is of the most obscene type.)[65]

An undated document describes Osmont as a printer who '*distribuoit dans le public* un imprimé remply d'obscenités les plus grossieres' ('*distributed in public* a printed book full of the crudest obscenities')[66] and another notes that 'il a imprimé et *distribué* une pièce des vers les plus obscenes' ('he printed and *distributed* a play in the most obscene verse').[67] Freed on 11 March,[68] his imprisonment was, it seems, motivated by the police's concern that obscene material would circulate publicly, beyond their surveillance and control.

Although Baculard d'Arnaud is now better known as the writer of sentimental literature, several documents attest to his authorship of *L'Art de foutre*, variously described as a most licentious play and contrary to decent morals. On 17 February Maurepas identified him as the author of an 'indecent play',[69] and on that same day he was sent to the Bastille for having composed 'une pièce des plus licencieuses ayant pour titre l'art de f...' ('one of the most licentious plays, bearing the title *L'Art de f...*')[70] An undated document indicates that during his detention three packets containing thirty copies of the ballet and various other papers and letters were seized from his residence.[71] At no point in police dossier does Baculard deny authorship of *L'Art de foutre*, although he claimed in the preface to an 1803 edition of *La Mort de Coligny* that it was for having written this tragedy that he merited 'les honneurs de la Bastille'.[72] It is indeed possible that the ballet was used as a pretext by those factions who had been offended by the tragedy, and by those saw in this 'élève de Voltaire'[73] a proxy figure by which to attack the more famous writer.[74] Following his transfer to the Saint Lazare prison on 14 March, he was freed on 18 May. Baculard's imprisonment was not unknown to contemporaries, for the abbé Le Blanc noted on 8 March:

> On a mis à la Bastille pour être de là transféré à St Lazare le nommé *Bacula D'Arnaud* auteur de l'Art de xx & à ce qu'on dit de quelques Couplets satiriques contre la Cour. L'Imprimeur a été mis dans un Cachot & un jeune homme de famille pour en avoir facilité l'impression a été aussi mis à la Bastille. (This *Bacula D'Arnaud* was sent to the Bastille, whence he was transferred to Saint Lazare; he is the author of l'Art de xx and, from what people say, some satirical couplets against the Court. The printer was put in a cell, and a young nobleman was also sent to the Bastille for having helped with the printing.)[75]

This young gentleman is Joseph-Marie-Anne Durey d'Harnoncourt de Morsan; as Le Blanc indicates, he was sent to the Bastille – on 23 February – for paying the ballet's printing costs.[76] Harnoncourt was already known to the police, for on 28 October 1732 the *curé* of St Gervais had written to the *lieutenant général de police* that the nobleman was maintaining a fourteen-year-old girl, whom he saw several times a week and whose rent and other living costs he paid.[77] Baculard and Harnoncourt had been acquainted with each other for several years; the former had written an epistle dated 20 January 1739 in which he apologizes for not visiting his sick friend.[78] When the police searched Harnoncourt's residence, they found several letters from Baculard, who dedicated *L'Art de foutre* to Harnoncourt, recognizable under the 'M. D. D. D. M ...' Harnoncourt was freed on 3 May 1741.

In conclusion, the *Art de foutre* episode reveals that, for all the fascination the actress-whore exerted in eighteenth-century fiction, she was in reality of limited interest to the authorities. While the period's fiction located the danger of the actress and the prostitute in their ability to pass from one realm to another (fact and fantasy, the theatre and the *petite maison*, the street and the boudoir), the police perceived the obscene text's transmission within the public realm to be of far greater importance. The defined and known space of the bawdy house on the rue de Clichy could be observed, whereas the wider public sphere was less amenable to surveillance, and therefore required more attention. The search for and imprisonment of Osmont, Baculard and Harnoncourt indicate that the police were concerned with preventing the circulation of *L'Art de foutre*'s text rather than the continuation of its embodied performance. The authorities' primary aim was not to silence the actresses but to annihilate the text, and they nearly succeeded, for as Dawson notes, 'the minions of the royal censor appear to have been all too successful in destroying every copy of the first edition, and we must rely on the Arsenal's copy, the only one known'.[79] The bodies of Mlles Petit, Sueur and Duplessis were of little consequence to Maurepas and Dubut; they were far more interested in eradicating a seditious text that mocked one of their own men.

7 VISIBLE PROSTITUTES: MANDEVILLE, HOGARTH AND 'A HARLOT'S PROGRESS'

Charlotte Grant

This collection argues that the visibility of prostitutes in eighteenth-century culture, both on the street and in cultural representation, contributed to their moral and political notoriety. This chapter looks at perhaps the most obvious and enduring English example of that visibility, William Hogarth's six-part *A Harlot's Progress* of 1732. Hogarth's harlot has remained a recognizable figure for nearly three centuries. Here I examine the nature of Hogarth's representation of the 'Harlot', arguing that while Hogarth clearly renders the prostitute visible, she is not always straightforwardly legible.

A Harlot's Progress is a dramatic playing out of a key narrative for the period, a defining, and widely recognized pivotal representation, not only of the prostitute in eighteenth-century England, but for visual culture in the period. Any account of *A Harlot's Progress*, as with any examination of Hogarth, has to acknowledge a debt to Ronald Paulson, whose first volume of his three-volume *Hogarth, The 'Modern Moral Subject': 1697–1732* provides an apparently exhaustive account of the references in, and influences on, *A Harlot's Progress*.[1] While Paulson's account traces the genesis of the series in the dense web of meanings and associations it provides and provokes, and emphasizes its topicality, recent critics have questioned the singularity and originality of Hogarth's series. Both Mark Hallett and Sophie Carter see Hogarth working in a tradition of popular prints, and their work has done much to re-place the *Progress* in a richer understanding of early eighteenth-century visual culture, allowing for a subtler reading of the nature of the Harlot's topicality.[2] Carter argues that 'a survey of London's print culture prior to the publication of the Progress suggests that this narrative was already cultural property',[3] while Hallett emphasizes the extent to which

> Hogarth continued to maintain the satirist's traditional critical engagement with, and dependence upon, the representational materials and commercial networks of London's graphic culture, while simultaneously promoting himself as an elevated practitioner of the arts whose work remained independent of those materials and networks, and indeed transcended them.[4]

Following David Solkin and Hallett, recent critics have emphasized Hogarth's place in the burgeoning British art market. By dramatizing the life of a prostitute Hogarth was simultaneously making a moral case, that such low characters and their economic circumstances were worthy of notice and concern, and a claim for a new kind of British art. Traditionally the province of genre painting, Hogarth succeeded in making 'low' characters worthy of consideration as a new and moral kind of history painting, typically regarded as the highest category of painting in the period. As the Tate Gallery commentary puts it, 'Hogarth's modern moral subjects demonstrated his personal crusade to establish modern urban life, including low life as an appropriate subject for high art.'[5]

The representation of Moll Hackabout's seduction into prostitution, from the innocent country girl we see arriving in London in the first plate of the series (see Figure 7.1) through her subsequent career and downward progress towards her death in plate 6, is generally acknowledged to mark a turning point both in British visual culture and in Hogarth's career. The paintings, which Hogarth showed in his house in Covent Garden, attracted so much attention that he engraved them as prints. It was the first series of Hogarth's prints that sold very well, with the prints proving so popular that they were widely copied and pirated. Mark Hallett notes that 'no less than eight pirated versions of *A Harlot's Progress* are mentioned by Hogarth's earliest biographer, many of which appeared in the immediate aftermath of the series' first publication.'[6] Hogarth was instrumental in establishing and manipulating the expanding British art market. He combined a hard-won business sense and a sense of responsibility as a citizen with an understanding of the growing power and social responsibility of the increasingly successful and prosperous professional and middling classes. Hogarth was one of a group of artists and engravers who lobbied Parliament to produce what was effectively the first copyright act. The Engravers' Copyright Act of 25 June 1735, sometimes known as 'Hogarth's Act', gave artists rights over their images for the first time. Moll Hackabout entered the marketplace in more ways than one.

As both painter and engraver of his own images, through the Copyright Act, and the fact that he advertised and sold his own prints, Hogarth established a firm control over his product. Hogarth's *A Harlot's Progress*, like its male counterpart, *The Rake's Progress* (1733–5), which Hogarth engraved after his Act had given him greater control over the sale of prints, is a moral tale, the first of what Hogarth referred to as his 'Modern Moral Subjects', and has been long recognized as a highly influential form.[7] In parallel with the formal experiments of prose writers feeling their way through the possibilities of the novel form in the first half of the eighteenth century, Hogarth is experimenting with a new form, adapting a sequential visual narrative to tell a contemporary tale with a moral message, and he was certainly aware of literary developments while writers were also aware of his prints. Hogarth's Moll owes something to Defoe's *Moll Flanders* (1722) and to the heroines of John Gay's *The Beggar's Opera* (1726) which

Figure 7.1: William Hogarth, *A Harlot's Progress, Plate 1* (1732), lettered with text within image and below 'A Harlots Progress Plate 1./Wm Hogarth invt. pinxt. et sculpt', pressmark: British XVIIIc Mounted Roy; reproduced with permission of The Trustees of the British Museum.

Hogarth painted six versions of between 1728 and 1731. As in the novels of Defoe and Richardson, Fielding and Sterne, Hogarth's morals come in the context of narrative entertainment and various kinds of readerly and imaginative pleasure. Sterne mentions Hogarth, who designed and engraved a frontispiece for the second volume of *Tristram Shandy* in 1760. Fielding's debt to Hogarth has been widely recognised, and the author drew attention to his admiration of Hogarth in his Preface to *Joseph Andrews* (1742). In seeking to define his new genre which he terms the 'comic epic in prose', Fielding claims Hogarth should be seen as more than a burlesque painter, claiming for him a kind of psychological depth. 'He who should call the ingenious Hogarth a burlesque painter', Fielding writes, 'would, in my opinion, do him very little honour: for sure it is much easier, much less the subject of admiration, to paint a man with a nose, or any other feature of a preposterous size, or to expose him in some absurd or monstrous attitude, than to express the affections of men on canvas. It hath been thought a vast commendation of a painter to say his figures seem to breathe; but surely it is a much greater and nobler applause, that they appear to think'.[8] Fielding applauds Hogarth's ability to convey thought, and 'the affections of men', as well as the absurd, and it is this ability which encourages the viewer's sympathy as well as their judgement.

Plate 1 – Moll at the Crossroads

A Harlot's Progress dramatizes a set of key moments in the life cycle of the prostitute. In the first scene we see a young girl, becomingly but modestly dressed, newly arrived from the country. The coach from York, with two other girls seated in it, is visible behind. Her belongings are grouped in the front right hand corner of the image, including a trunk bearing the initials MH, which we later learn stands for Moll Hackabout. She is met neither by the priest on his horse, immediately behind her who ignores her as he reads a letter, not by her 'lofing cosin' for whom she has brought a goose, but by an overdressed madam, covered in beauty spots, who touches her under the chin in an overfamiliar chin-chuck gesture. This figure, identified by contemporaries as a notorious brothelkeeper, stands out against the darker right-hand side of the image, and the heavily highlighted folds of her skirt contrast with the simpler and plainer light fabric of Moll's. The narrative of the innocent country girl who arrives in the capital with the best intentions only to be sucked into a life of prostitution, crime and squalor was well established. One of the likely sources for Hogarth's story was in *The Spectator. Spectator* No. 266 of Friday 4 January 1712 includes a discussion of the prevalence of prostitutes in London. Firstly Steele's Mr Spectator describes seeing a beautiful prostitute in Covent Garden who makes a big impression on him. She has 'as exact Features as I had ever seen, the most agreeable Shape, the finest Neck and Bosom, in a Word, the whole Person of a Woman exquisitely beautiful'. This impression of perfection is complicated by her neediness, and she implicitly presents a moral problem:

> She affected to allure me with a forced Wantonness in her Look and Air; but I saw it checked with Hunger and Cold: Her Eyes were wan and eager, her Dress thin and tawdry, her Mien genteel and childish. This strange Figure gave me much Anguish of Heart.

A few paragraphs later, a description of another girl bears a striking resemblance to Hogarth's Harlot in plate 1. Arriving to pick up belongings sent by coach from the country, Mr Spectator sees 'a most beautiful country-girl who had come up in the same Waggon with my things' being quizzed and examined by 'the most artful Procuress in the Town'. The means by which the procuress gets her to talk is by taking her through the 'Questions and Responses of the Church Catechism'. He concludes: 'This poor Creature's Fate is not far off that of her's whom I spoke of above and it is not to be doubted, but after she has been long enough a Prey to Lust she will be delivered over to Famine'.[9]

The particular figures who prey on Moll were readily identified by contemporaries, including the engraver and antiquary George Vertue. The brothelkeeper was Mother Needham, and the man lurking in the doorway behind her Colonel Charteris, both visible players in the drama of contemporary prostitution. Elizabeth Needham was a well-known bawd, whose house in Park Place, St James's was one of the most exclusive brothels in London. She died in 1731 having been assaulted when she was in the pillory. Charteris, referred to as 'The Rape-Master General of Britain', was a philanderer whose predilection for innocent girls was widely documented. Ronald Paulson gives a persuasive account of quite why Charteris in particular should have attracted Hogarth's attention. As a child Hogarth had suffered when his father had been arrested for bankruptcy following a series of failed business ventures, spending four miserable years living in lodgings attached to the debtor's prison. Charteris had, according to Paulson, been investigated by the House of Commons in 1710–11 for taking advantage of the ruling that allowed debtors to 'escape confinement by enlisting in Her Majesty's armed forces; he took large sums of money from ruined tradesmen to put their names on his roster'.[10] He kept his immoral earnings and escaped with a reprimand while the debtors continued, like Hogarth's father, to languish in prison. In 1728 and 1729 *Fog's Weekly Journal* had described his attempts to rape young servant girls, which resulted in his being sued for assault. A biography of Charteris published in 1730 described him employing a 'noted Procuress to furnish him from time to time with a variety of fresh Country Girls, which were to be hir'd (to prevent any Suspicion) to live with him as Servants'.[11] Finally in February 1730 he was tried for rape at the Old Bailey and convicted following the testimony of one Anne Bond, whom he raped and beat following her being brought to his house under the pretence of being given a place as a servant. Unlike the highwaymen John Dalton and Francis Hackabout, who were convicted at the same time and hanged, Charteris was able to secure his pardon.[12] Hogarth links Moll to all these figures: Dalton's wig box is shown above Moll's bed in plate 3, and in the final plate we learn that Moll's full name is Moll Hackabout, linking her both to Francis, the hanged highwayman, and also to his sister Kate, who was committed to hard labour in August 1730 after being apprehended for keeping a disorderly house by the Magistrate Sir John Gonson (who appears in plate 3 and is discussed below).

Not all critics have seen Moll as an unwitting or unwilling victim of her fate.[13] W. A. Speck argues that Hogarth's harlot, like Defoe's Moll Flanders and Cleland's Fanny Hill, chooses her path (although in both those cases theirs is a severely compromised choice). He sees the first plate as showing Moll Hackabout making a conscious choice between virtue and vice:

> Although the first plate of Hogarth's series is open to other interpretations it makes most sense to me if Moll Hackabout is seen to be making a deliberate choice between the parson and the bawd, i.e. between virtue and vice. Hogarth's view of morality being the autonomous choice of the individual is clear from his other series, *The Rake's Progress* and especially *Industry and Idleness*, while the rest of the *Harlot's Progress* simply does not make sense unless we assume that Moll has quite cold-bloodedly chosen a route which leads to her death from venereal disease.[14]

This view seems to underplay the place of empathy in Hogarth's work, and as Jenny Uglow has noted, Moll's facial expressions are hard to read.[15] I certainly do not see her as making a 'cold-blooded' choice in the first scene; although, as Paulson points out she is clearly placed in the position of Hercules at the crossroads as he chooses between virtue and vice,[16] a key motif for history painting in this period, as has been argued by John Barrell, David Solkin and others.[17] An equally plausible reading emphasizes Moll's initial innocence and subsequent seduction: her powers of choice are surely compromised by the clergyman's error, who, with his back to her, fails to notice Moll's predicament. Instead of noticing what is happening in front of his nose, he is busy reading a letter of preferment, his lack of attention contrasted with Colonel Charteris who watches the scene with eager anticipation from a nearby doorway. We are, I think, given a drama reflecting the ambiguity of feeling towards prostitutes and their fate at this pivotal moment.

Plate 2 – the Lap of Luxury

In the second plate we see Moll as the established mistress of a wealthy Jew. The room in which she receives her employer has all the trappings of luxurious and fashionable society. There are paintings on the walls, a tea table has been laid, a small black servant boy brings the tea kettle, and a mask from a masquerade party rests on a side table. However, the scene is far from polite. Moll kicks over the tea table to provide a distraction as a servant ushers out another, younger, lover. The cups and saucers break on the floor, her keeper looks alarmed, Moll's right breast is on display and the maid carries the young lover's shoes as she hurries him out of the door. The tiny tea cup, the pet monkey, and the black servant boy all reappear in a later painting, *Taste in High Life* of 1742, itself a precursor to the *Marriage a la Mode* series of 1743–5. These images, with their interest in material possessions tie in with contemporary debates about luxury, and key to the luxury debates in England was Bernhard Mandeville's *Fable of the Bees* (1714).[18] The *Fable of the Bees* mentions prostitution, but Mandeville makes the control and regulation of prostitution the subject of his less-often read and rather strange later text: *A Modest Defence of Public Stews* (1724), written, as it teasingly claims on the title page, 'by a Layman'. Produced at the end of a decade of changing attitudes to prostitution, I argue that Hogarth's *Harlot* embodies the ethical and moral issues posed by the prevalence of prostitution in early eighteenth-century London, and evidences some of the conflicting responses to that highly visible problem. Looking at the Mandeville text in some detail casts new light on the ways in which Hogarth's *Harlot* is simultaneously visible but not always easily legible.

Paulson mentions Mandeville's *A Modest Defence*, suggesting in a footnote that 'The *Harlot's Progress* abounds in echoes of Mandeville's *Modest Defence* but also of his *Fable of the Bees*'.[19] Mandeville's *A Modest Defence of Public Stews* takes the theme of its argument from Remark H of *The Fable of the Bees* where Mandeville explores what he sees as the necessary evil of prostitution:

> From what has been said it is manifest, that there is a Necessity of sacrificing one part of Womankind to preserve the other, and prevent a Filthinyss of a more heinous Nature. From whence I think I may justly conclude (what was the seeming Paradox I went about to prove) that Chastity may be supported by Incontinence, and the best of Virtues want the Assistance of the worst of Vices.[20]

In the Dedication to *A Modest Defence* this argument is rendered even more graphic by Mandeville's comparison of women in brothels to the fly-blown meat a butcher will sacrifice to preserve the rest of his stock:

> Observe the Policy of a Modern Butcher, persecuted with a Swarm of Carnivorous Flies; where all his Engines and Fly-Flaps have prov'd ineffectual to defend his Stall against the Greedy Assiduity of those Carnal Insects, he very Judiciously cuts off a Fragment, already blown, which serves to hang up for a Cure; and thus, by Sacrificing a Small Part, already Tainted, and not worth Keeping, he wisely secures the Safety of the Rest.[21]

One way to see Hogarth's harlot, as Paulson has pointed out, is as precisely this kind of sacrifice.[22] Her fate sealed in plate 1, the narrative charts her apparently inevitable fall in the two final plates 5 and 6. It is clear from the strength of language in Mandeville's analogy that, like Hogarth, he accepts that male desire has a defining part to play in the drama of prostitution. In the *Modest Defence*, Mandeville builds on this pragmatism to suggest that, given that whoring is an inevitable vice, its practice should be legalized within state-inspected brothels. Irwin Primer suggests that Mandeville published the *Modest Defence* in 1724 in response to attacks on *The Fable of the Bees*. In 1723 the Grand Jury of Middlesex had charged Mandeville and two others, John Trenchard and Thomas Gordon, with blasphemy, denial of God's providence, and anti-clericalism, with the jurors drawing attention to the fact: 'the very *Stews* themselves have had strained Apologies and forced Encomiums made in their Favour and produced in Print, with Design, we conceive, to debauch the Nation.'[23]

Both Hogarth and Mandeville are working within the discourse on prostitution established and promoted by the Societies for the Reformation of Manners who, in the aftermath of the Restoration, sought to regulate public behaviour across a wide spectrum of social and private behaviours from drunkenness, to swearing, whoring and gambling and even the theatre. The Societies for the Reformation of Manners functioned actively from around 1690 to 1738 during which time they were responsible for over 100,000 prosecutions for moral offences mainly in and around London.[24] Between 1695 and 1707 they published annual lists of those they prosecuted. Prostitutes were stripped to the waist and flogged, often till they bled. In 1708 they prosecuted 1,255 people for 'lewd and disorderly behaviour', but by 1738 they only prosecuted 52.[25] Their activities did little to curb the number of prostitutes working in London, and neither their activities, nor their methods were welcomed by all. Daniel Defoe attacked them in his verse satire 'Reformation of Manners' of 1702, accusing them of mercenary practices open to manipulation:

> The mercenary Scouts in every Street,
> Bring all that have no Money to your Feet,
> And if you lash a Strumpet of the Town,
> She only smarts for want of Half a Crown;
> Your Annual lists of criminals appear,
> But no Sir Harry or Sir Charles is here.[26]

In responding to the challenge to *The Fable of the Bees*, Mandeville provocatively addressed *A Modest Defence* 'To The Gentlemen of the Societies' (that is, the Societies for the Reformation of Manners). The dedication begins:

> Gentlemen, The great Pains and Diligence you have employ'd in the Defence of Modesty and Virtue, give You an undisputed Title to the Address of this Treatise; tho' it

is with the utmost Concern that I find myself under a Necessity of writing it, and that after so much Reforming, there should be any Thing left to say upon the Subject, besides congratulating You upon Your happy Success. It is no small Addition to my Grief to observe, that Your Endeavours to suppress Lewdness, have only serv'd to promote it; and that this *Branch* of Immorality has grown under Your Hands, as if it was *prun'd* instead of being *lopp'd*.[27]

The activities of the Societies for the Reformation of Manners reflect only one aspect of what critics and historians agree were fundamental changes in attitudes towards prostitution during this period. During the 1690s, representations of the whore focused on female desire. The whore was typically represented as a woman whose out-of-control sexual desire led her to prostitution. Money was often seen as a secondary consequence, rather than a primary motivator. The rhetoric of the Societies for the Reformation of Manners addresses both female and male desire. Focusing their attention on the immorality of whoring, they arrested hundreds of streetwalkers. According to Alan Hunt, the conflict between their position and that of Mandeville is symptomatic of the tension between abolitionists and regulationists, a division persisting in today's discourses on prostitution.[28] Alongside this division between these fundamentally different views of how prostitution should be dealt with is an affective change, and it seems to me that Mandeville's texts and Hogarth's *A Harlot's Progess* both hover on the cusp of that change. Speck describes a change in attitudes to prostitution between 1700 and 1800 from seeing prostitutes as 'brazen whores, painted strumpets, totally unregenerate hardened sinners' to 'fit subjects for penitence and salvation, to be rescued from a life of degradation and shame'.[29] However, neither Mandeville nor Hogarth provides a straightforward reading along these lines. Their irony and humour are open to interpretation, and fit the more fluid model proposed by Vivien Jones, who argues for the persistence of a 'satirical trickster tradition' in prostitution narratives, reading 'a series of texts spanning the period from the 1720s to at least the 1780s, texts which cast this binary developmental narrative into doubt'.[30]

Mandeville's address in *The Modest Defence* is both serious and ironic. As in the opening quoted above, horticultural metaphors, stock in trade of seventeenth- and eighteenth-century erotica, proliferate, implying an awareness and acceptance of the erotic, and an acknowledgement that to fail to register the power of desire is both short-sighted and insincere. Mandeville's tone has confused readers, but Jones points to the 1740 reprint of Mandeville 'which attributes the text to "the late Colonel Harry Mordaunt" and suggests that the text is 'written in the persona of a cynical libertine, Sir Harry Mordaunt',[31] and Irwin Primer has recently put forward a convincing case for seeing the *Modest Defence* as a paradoxical encomium.[32] The opening section noted above continues: 'But however your ill Success may grieve, it cannot astonish me: What else could we hope for, from Your persecuting of poor strolling Damsels?' where the readers' sympathy seems to be directed to the objects of the Society's persecution, 'poor' street prostitutes. However, the violence of Mandeville's language does not allow for any simple identification and motivation of sympathy. He continues:

> What else can we hope for from your stopping up those Drains and Sluices we had to let out Lewdness? From Your demolishing those *Horn-works* and *Breast-works* of Modesty? Those Ramparts and Ditches within which the Virtue of our Wives and Daughters lay so conveniently *intrench'd*? ... Or what better could we expect from your Carting of Bawds, than that the Great Leviathan of Leachery, for Want of these Tubs to play with, should, with one Whisk of his Tail, overset the *Vessel* of Modesty? Which, in her best Trim, we know to be somewhat *leaky*, and to have a very unsteady *Helm*.

Primer points out that Mandeville's use of puns allies him with Swift, whose 'A Modest Defence of Punning' had been published in 1716. Hogarth is also a master of the visual pun, and so in the first plate of *A Harlot's Progress*, Moll is associated with the goose she brings for her cousins in Cheapside. She herself proves to be a 'silly goose', or perhaps, in her innocent allowing of Mother Needham's advances, something akin to a sitting duck. For 'goose' the OED also has: 'A foolish person, a simpleton' and 'Winchester goose: a certain venereal disorder (sometimes simply *a goose*); also, a prostitute', all meanings which fit Moll's predicament well. Primer quotes Walter Redfern's remark that 'Puns are a means of circumventing taboos, as are euphemisms, which play a similar hide-and-seek game with the listener/reader'.[33] And Primer's examples, which highlight Mandeville's use of 'conventional military terms applied to the battles of love' such as 'rampart', and the 'incontinent youth' compared to a 'standing army', are consistent with Sterne's pleasure in similar metaphors in *Tristram Shandy* when Toby catalogues his quest for the Widow Wadman's love in similarly euphemistic terms drawn from military language. While Sterne's euphemisms, which describe potential rather than actual events, are consistent with the predominantly sentimental mood of *Tristram Shandy*, Mandeville's analogies are far from sentimental. From one sentence to another in the dedication he moves from seeing the whores pursued and prosecuted by the Societies for the Reformation of Manners as victims to dehumanizing them. They are both the somewhat incongruously pastoral 'poor strolling Damsels', and then 'ramparts' and 'ditches' – a geographical bodily analogy where the bodies of the whores act as barriers to the assault of virtuous women, whose position in society is defined by their relationship to the presumed male readership of the piece: 'our Wives and Daughters'. The pun on landscape and body is a stock identification of much eighteenth-century pornography.[34] Here Mandeville works the analogy with an additional and additionally tasteless pun – the ditches are 'harder to be fill'd up' implying that the whores are either insatiable or physically incapable of being 'fill'd'.

Mandeville's rhetoric may be self-consciously allusive, playfully mimicking the metaphors of pornography but it has, nevertheless, a strong argument. He argues that if attempts to repress desire have the opposite effect, then it would be better to legalize brothels. This would mean that quality control, health care, and the welfare of both sex worker and client could be ensured as well as providing for the inevitable illegitimate children. Mandeville terms his proposal 'publick whoring' and sees it as preferable to risking the greater evils associated with 'private whoring': the potentially violent seduction of more virtuous women, the death of innocent children, and, perhaps above all, the spread of the pox. Like Hogarth, Mandeville clearly liked to tease – why else would the title page conclude 'written by a Layman' with the dedication described above signed off 'Your Fellow-Reformer, and Devoted Servant, Phil-Porney'? But his text is motivated by a pragmatic morality, its tone perhaps best described by Jones, who sees it as an 'inscrutably ironic defence of prostitutes and brothels on the grounds of their social and commercial utility' and argues that 'Mandeville's difficult questions about the beneficial status of commerce and luxury, become, by extension, questions about the status of prostitution itself'.[35]

Plates 3 and 4 – From Drury Lane and Desire to Bridewell

If we accept as authoritative George Vertue's early account of the genesis of the series of images, an early version of plate 3 was the origin of *A Harlot's Progress*. This plate shows Moll, in a state of dishabille, sitting on her bed with a female servant preparing her tea. Prints on the wall show Dr Sacheverell, a controversial clergyman turned politician, and Captain Mackheath, the highwayman hero of Gay's *Beggar's Opera*, and the hatbox above the bed belongs to James Dalton, the highwayman prosecuted by the Magistrate John Gonson. Gonson himself is seen entering Moll's room from a door on the right hand side. So the scene echoes the previous one: where the lover exited, Gonson enters, and where Moll kicked over the tea, here she prepares to enjoy a rather plainer version. It was, according to Vertue, Hogarth's painting of an attractive prostitute in her room in Drury Lane which caught his public's imagination and encouraged him to develop her story. Vertue records that:

> The most remarkable Subject of painting that captivated the Minds of most People persons of all ranks and conditions from the greatest Quality to the meanest was the Story painted and designed by Mr. Hogarth of the Harlots Progress & the prints engravd by him and published.

So *A Harlot's Progress*, as well as being a series which shows persons of all ranks, also appealed to 'all ranks'. Vertue continues:

> Amongst other designs of his in painting he began a small picture of a common harlot, supposed to dwell in drewry lane. just rising about noon out of bed. and at breakfast. a bunter waiting on her. – This whore's desabillé careless and a pretty Countenance & air. – this thought pleasd many, some advisd him to make another. To it as a pair, which he did, then other thoughts encrease'd, & multiplyd by his fruitfull invention. till he made six. different subjects which he painted so naturally, the thoughts, & striking the expressions that it drew everybody to see them – which he proposing to Engrave in six plates to print at, one guinea each sett. he had daily Subscriptions come in, in fifty or a hundred pounds in a Week – there being no day but persons of fashion and Artists came to see these pictures the story of them being related. how this Girl came to Town. how Mother Needham and Col Charters first deluded her, how a Jew kept her how she lived in Drury lane. when she was sent to bridwell by John Gonson Justce and her salivation & death.[36]

Vertue's description emphasizes Hogarth's skilful combination of the generic and the particular. Moll is a 'common harlot' who lives in Drury Lane – the archetypal location for prostitutes, and her 'progress' follows the relentlessly downward spiral typical of the profession from kept woman to 'common harlot' to Bridewell and death. We don't see much evidence of the 'salivation' Vertue mentions (and the pun perhaps suggests his own ambivalence about this outcome), but we do see in some detail the deadly effects of venereal disease and her untimely death. Vertue also names key figures, recognizable by contemporaries. I have already mentioned Mother Needham and Colonel Charteris. The magistrate, John Gonson, first appears here in Plate 3 and again in graffiti on the wall of Bridewell Prison in Plate 4. Gonson was one of the most prominent figures in the Society for the Reformation of Manners and, according to David Dabydeen, a rather controversial figure.[37]

In the first four plates of Moll's progress, she is the object of admiring or desiring glances: in plate 1 from Needham and Charteris, in plate 2 from the lover and the Jew. Here in plates 3 and 4, the nature of that gaze changes – it is the viewer who is most invited to look at Moll in plate 3, while Gonson and his men, appearing from the back of the room, do not have the same view, although Gonson's pose seems to register Moll's appeal, her physical presence giving him pause for thought. In plate 4 she is presented to our sight again, but those observing her from within the image have largely shifted their attention to her possessions – her clothes become the objects of desire in Bridewell. Vertue's description of the original painting behind plate 3 makes clear that viewers appreciated the sensual appeal of Hogarth's Moll. While art historians have, until recently, tended to downplay the erotic appeal of *A Harlot's Progress*, Mark Hallett draws on contemporary responses, both visual and textual, which are frank in their acknowledgement of the seductiveness of Hogarth's representation of Moll in the first half of the series, and argues that the Progress 'opens itself up to [a] doubled reading – as both a moralised *and* an eroticised set of images'.[38]

Desire, illicit or otherwise, is an enduring feature of human existence, and Hogarth makes the desiring gaze central to his aesthetic project. The 2007 Hogarth exhibition at Tate Britain, and its accompanying catalogue, acknowledged the great importance Hogarth placed on variety as a guiding aesthetic principal. Hogarth's aesthetic treatise, *The Analysis of Beauty* (1753) celebrates variety, enshrined in the form of a serpent in a pyramid on its title page. The pyramid, archetypal form of classical painting, rests on a plinth with the word 'variety'. Underneath is a quotation from Book 9 of Milton's *Paradise Lost*:

> So vary'd he, and of his tortuous train
> Curl'd many a wanton wreath, in sight of Eve,
> To lure her eye.[39]

Milton's description here of the serpent's seduction of Eve, which rests on the visual metaphor of the seduction of the eye, underpins *The Analysis of Beauty*'s frankly sexual version of what beauty might mean. Hogarth's model of vision accepts the erotic, the desiring eye, as central to aesthetics. If the serpent, the first seducer on earth, is enshrined in the title page of the *Analysis*, then the body of the woman occupies a central place in the body of the text. Hogarth's model of female beauty is not a prostitute, but the Venus de Medici, who stands at the heart of the Statuary Yard, which forms the central image of plate 1 of the *Analysis of Beauty*. However, Venus, the Goddess of love, her hands simultaneously concealing and revealing her body, is supplanted in the text by Hogarth's appeal to the beauty of the living female form. The central image for the *Analysis* is the human body, which exhibits the qualities of proportion Hogarth singles out as essential to beauty. He writes:

> Observe that part of a beautiful woman where she is perhaps the most beautiful, about the neck and breasts, the smoothness; the softness; the easy and insensible swell; the variety of surface, which is never for the smallest space the same; the deceitful maze, through which the unsteady eye slides giddily, without knowing where to fix, or whither it is carried.[40]

This long sentence, with its idiosyncratic and meandering syntax, registers the pleasure and confusion of the perceiving subject. From the authoritative 'Observe' we are rendered unsteady and passive by the end through the experience of viewing the 'variety of surface', the 'deceitful maze', key terms for Hogarth's theorizing of visual pleasure. He justifies his appeals to antique sculpture, and then characteristically reasserts the primacy of the natural over the artificial, and the triumph of a very sensual, fleshy beauty. 'Neither the ancients, nor the moderns', Hogarth says, have 'ever yet come up to the utmost beauty of nature': 'who but a bigot, even to the antiques, will say that he has not seen faces and necks, hands and arms in living women, that even the Grecian Venus doth but coarsely imitate?'. Then in a coy last sentence, standing on its own as a final paragraph he asks: 'And what sufficient reason can be given why the same may not be said of the rest of the body?'[41]

That word 'bigot' is, I think, a key to Hogarth's motivation in representing Moll Hackabout. Whatever else Hogarth is, he is clearly not a bigot. Instead he lampoons those, who, like Gonson, are blinded to the suffering they cause by the blinkered nature of their vision of the prostitute. Where Gonson saw fornicators whose souls could only be saved, if at all, through enforced labour (as shown in Bridewell in plate 4), Hogarth saw living women whose circumstances rendered them victims of a culture of violence. Prey to sexual predators, greed, both sexual and economic, the corruption of luxury, and the inevitable destruction wrought by sexual diseases, these women deserve pity as well as censure. He is, like Mandeville, a pragmatist, acknowledging desire, incorporating that desire into his model of visual pleasure, and employing the power of affect to effect change.

Hogarth's appeal to the beauty of the female form is eroticized further by the fact that in the *Analysis* he proposes a new way of understanding the process of visualizing objects by imagining objects to be hollow, and to be viewed not from outside, but from within:

> The imagination will naturally enter in to the vacant space within this shell, and there at once, as from a centre, view the whole form within, and mark the opposite corresponding parts so strongly, as to retain the idea of the whole, and make us masters of the meaning of every view of the object, as we walk round it, and view it from without.[42]

This inverts the accepted conception of vision and suggests the penetration of the body of the spectator into the object viewed. So one could argue that his very theorizing of the gaze renders it inherently sexual, and his understanding of the pleasures of vision casts the female body at its centre. Twenty years earlier, the subscription ticket for *A Harlot's Progress* had promised an investigation into the erotic pleasures of aesthetic vision. *Boys Peeping at Nature* (1731) represents nature as a many-breasted female torso without arms but with a disconcertingly lifelike and inscrutable face surrounded by three putti and a faun. Described by Paulson as 'an announcement, a come-on, an elaborate joke, and a statement of theory',[43] the image shows a putto drawing the top half of the sculpture, while another tries to stop a faun from looking under her skirt, and a third has turned away from the figure of Nature as he works on an engraving. This 'statement of theory' came to fruition in *The Analysis of Beauty*, but the examination of the potentially dangerous pleasures of the female body fuels *A Harlot's Progress*.

Plates 5 and 6 – Disease and Death

In the final two plates, Moll retreats from our view. Wrapped in blankets by the fire in plate 5 she is clearly in the last stages of venereal disease, while in the final plate Moll is almost entirely out of sight in her coffin, the drama of life and desire continuing around her: only one of the mourners at her funeral look down at her face, the rest are otherwise occupied. In plate 5 her child plays, unsupervised, by the fire, and himself shows signs of venereal disease. The production of unwanted children was one of Mandeville's concerns in his attempt to control prostitution in the *Modest Defence*, and he was not alone in his concern. One of the very visible products of London's huge population of illicit sex workers was a large number of abandoned children. Unlike Hogarth's Moll who keeps her child at her side until her death (he sits right by the coffin in plate 6), many abandoned their unwanted babies. The plight of these infants, many of whom died on the streets, lead the philanthropist Captain Thomas Coram to campaign for a foundling hospital for London like those in other European cities, and Hogarth was a key figure in his campaign. Like Hogarth, Coram was a tough businessman who had worked hard for his success.[44] His Foundling Hospital received its Royal Charter in 1739 after a long campaign. Hogarth was one of the founding Governors, and made use of it as a public space in which to showcase his own and his contemporaries' paintings. His full-length portrait of Coram from 1740 which he donated to the Hospital makes a brilliant and bravura claim, both for Coram as a figurehead of benevolence, and for Hogarth himself as a painter worthy of comparison with Van Dyck and with his father-in-law, Sir James Thornhill, who had worked on the portrait of Christopher Wren which gave Hogarth one of his models for the pose.[45] Fiercely patriotic, Hogarth made every effort to promote British art over the art of continental Europe, and saw in the Foundling Hospital a meeting of virtuous and moral intent in a new kind of public space and painting as a useful vehicle for public and philanthropic campaigning.

What links Hogarth's *Harlot* and Mandeville's *Modest Defence*, I'd like to suggest, is a knowing humanitarianism combined with a satirical critique of contemporary mores. While Hogarth's vision seems harsh at times, and gleefully incorporates the perverse sexual exploits of his minor protagonists (Colonel Charteris in plate 1 looks like he could be masturbating, while the Priest in plate 6 has his hand up the skirts of the woman next to him, his sexual excitement suggested by the overflowing glass he holds), our sympathy lies with the harlot, hapless victim of circumstances. She may be a silly goose, naive and, in her emulation of her supposed betters, a participant in the dubious pleasures of luxury, but she is not evil. Likewise, Mandeville's playful rhetoric, his adoption of the role of 'Phil-Porney' also entertains, but his object is, like Hogarth, to condemn hypocrisy. It is this championing of affect over precept which, I think, links both these representations of prostitution both to the Foundling Hospital and to the later sentimental motivation behind such initiatives as the Magdalen Hospital.

8 THE NARRATIVE SOURCES OF *CANDIDE*'S PAQUETTE

Edward Langille[1]

Paquette is a minor character in Voltaire's *Candide* who makes just four appearances in the novel, the first as part of the doomed world of Thunder-ten-tronckh, destroyed and then miraculously, if only partially, reconstituted in the novel's final chapter.[2] In Chapter 4, Pangloss wonders aloud whether Paquette is still alive. She is, and her reappearance in Chapter 24 allows the telling of her unhappy life as a prostitute. Paquette then recedes from the forefront of *Candide* and is thereafter referred to only in the third person. In line with the tale's moral purpose, we learn in Chapter 30 that she has abandoned the 'trade' and has taken up embroidery instead!

In 1960, J. H. Broome argued that the character of Paquette was inspired by the eponymous heroine of Fougeret de Monbron's best-known work, the erotic novel *Margot la Ravaudeuse: histoire d'une prostituée* (1750).[3] Broome highlighted a number of verbal and narrative parallels linking Margot's adventures to Paquette's life-story as told in the fifty lines *Candide* devotes to her saga.[4] For instance, he pointed out that Paquette recounts her seduction by a monk; Margot has a similar experience with a Carmelite. Paquette becomes a doctor's mistress, is imprisoned, and freed by a judge. Margot is also imprisoned, and liberated by a *président*. Broome noted that Voltaire would have endorsed Monbron's vigorous denunciation of the social evils associated with prostitution. His main point however was that Monbron's influence on *Candide* flowed chiefly through his *Cosmopolite, ou le Citoyen du monde*, published also in 1750, but that *Margot la Ravaudeuse*, and several other of his lesser satirical works, may have influenced specific episodes in *Candide* as well.

Roughly fifteen years after Broome's article, Manfred Sandmann proposed another source for Paquette: Molly Seagrim, the wayward daughter of the gamekeeper Black George in Henry Fielding's comic masterpiece, the novel *Tom Jones* (1749).[5] Sandmann's case was based on a number of narrative incidents recounted in the first five books of that novel and which are closely paralleled in *Candide*. My research has confirmed Sandmann's view that *Candide* was significantly influenced by *Tom Jones*, but through the mediation of Pierre-Antoine de La Place's 1750 French adaptation of that novel known as *L'Enfant trouvé* (see Figure 8.1).[6] A parallel reading of *Candide* and *L'Enfant trouvé* reveals an astonishing network of verbal, thematic and narrative analogies, which strongly reinforce the thesis that Voltaire's novel owes a great deal to La Place in terms of the characters it portrays, the narrative that binds those characters together, and the language in which the whole is expressed.[7]

These rival theories of Paquette's antecedents both have plausibility and suggest that both sources played a role in Voltaire's creative process. Understanding that process provides an extraordinary glimpse into how the sources of *Candide* cross-fertilized in Voltaire's mind during what we can assume was a long gestation period of note-taking and revision.

Paquette and Molly Seagrim

Readers have always assumed that our first look at the character we come to know as Paquette takes place during Pangloss's outdoor lesson in experimental physics in *Candide*'s opening chapter. Voltaire's text recounts Pangloss's 'experiment' and Cunégonde's voyeuristic response to it.[8] Paquette's presence in the scene seems almost incidental.

> Comme Mlle Cunégonde avait beaucoup de disposition pour les sciences, elle observa, sans souffler, les expériences réitérées dont elle fut témoin; elle vit clairement la raison suffisante du docteur, les effets et les causes, et s'en retourna tout agitée, toute pensive, toute remplie du désir d'être savante, songeant qu'elle pourrait bien être la raison suffisante du jeune Candide, qui pouvait aussi être la sienne.[9]
>
> (Since Miss Cunegonde had an aptitude for the sciences, she observed Pangloss's repeated experiments; she clearly perceived the force of the doctor's reasons, the causes, and the effects; she ran home, her heart aflutter, dreamy, filled with the desire to be learned and hoping that she might well be young Candide's sufficient reason, and he hers.)

The docile 'femme de chambre' with whom Pangloss has his way is described in terms which do not suggests that she is free with her favours. On the contrary, her very docility suggests that Pangloss is the sexual predator and that she, Paquette, is his prey. It comes as a surprise then when some few pages farther we learn that Pangloss has caught the syphilitic pox from the same maid.

> O mon cher Candide! vous avez connu Paquette, cette jolie suivante de notre auguste baronne; j'ai goûté dans ses bras les délices du paradis, qui ont produit ces tourments d'enfer dont vous me voyez dévoré; elle en était infectée, elle en est peut-être morte.[10]
>
> (Oh, my dear Candide! You recall Paquette, that pretty wench who waited on our noble Baroness; in her arms I tasted the delights of paradise, from her I contracted this hellish disease; she was infected and is perhaps dead.)

Figure 8.1: Henry Fielding, trans. Pierre Antoine de La Place, *Histoire de Tom Jones, ou l'enfant trouvé* (London [Paris]: chez Jean Nourse, 1750), opp. p. 189, engr. Hubert Gravelot (1699–1773); reproduced with permission of McMaster University Library.

Or is it the same maid? Pangloss tells us that he contracted the malady from Mme la baronne's 'jolie suivante' named Paquette, rather than the Baronesses's 'femme de chambre' we observed in Chapter 1. A 'suivante' is a lady in waiting, whereas 'une femme de chambre' is a lady's maid.[11] The terms 'femme de chambre' and 'suivante' are not and never have been synonyms. This semantic incongruity can be explained a number of ways. The word 'suivante' as used by Pangloss may indicate that he was unaware of Paquette's status. On the other hand, the 'femme de chambre' we meet in Chapter 1 and Pangloss's Paquette referred to in Chapter 4, may be two distinct individuals. My own view is that the 'femme de chambre' and the 'suivante' are a single character inspired by two models.

If we accept that these two are one and the same, our first sighting of Paquette does indeed take place in Chapter 1. That scene appears to have evolved from two chapters in Book 5 of *L'Enfant trouvé* where Molly Seagrim plays a leading role: a) the philosopher Square's in flagrante exposure in Molly's bedroom, and b) Tom's own outdoor pursuit of the same Molly in a wood. There is certainly strong evidence to suggest that Pangloss's outdoor lesson is based on the scene in *L'Enfant trouvé* where Fielding's model for Pangloss, the philosopher Square, is surprised by Jones with his trousers down in Molly Seagrim's bedroom:

> La situation de nos trois personnages exige un pinceau plus énergique que le mien. Square dans un déshabillé cynique, tapi dans son trou fixant de grands yeux effrayés sur Jones; Moly tremblante et la tête cachée dans ses couvertures. Jones, les bras levés, la bouche ouverte, voulant parler et ne sachant que dire ne présentent qu'une faible esquisse de ce tableau.[12]
>
> (The predicament our three characters were in requires a livelier brush than mine. Imagine Square, trousers down around his knees trying to hide in a corner, and casting pathetic glances toward Jones. And Molly all atrembling, head buried in the covers. And finally Jones, arms raised, open-mouthed as if about to speak, but knowing not what to say. All this, I say, is but the crudest outline of the picture.)

The *brush* La Place refers to was that of the famous Gravelot who illustrated this scene in the 1750 edition. That edition (BV 1341) was owned by Voltaire and can be found today in his library housed in St Petersburg.[13] Voltaire was an admirer of Gravelot's work, and in 1757, he commissioned the engraver to illustrate *La Pucelle* (1762).[14] It is highly likely therefore that Gravelot's depiction of the trousers-down scene made a strong impression on Voltaire and that he adapted it *mutatis mutandis* in *Candide*, ironically conferring the role of *voyeuse* on the ever-curious Cunégonde. As previously suggested, the outdoor feature of the lesson combines this first scene with Tom's summertime tryst with Molly in the woods:

> La soirée était belle; & il [Tom] se promenait seul dans un petit bois, en rêvant aux charmes de sa chère Sophie, lorsque ses réflexions amoureuses furent interrompues par l'apparition d'une femme, qui l'ayant regardé fixement, se sauva dans le plus épais du bois.[15]

(The evening was balmy. Tom, wandering alone in a small wood, was dreaming of his beloved Sophia when suddenly his amorous daydreams were interrupted by the apparition of a woman who, having stared at him, disappeared into a thicket.)

The compression of these two scenes explains the sudden change in climate from Chapter 1 to Chapter 2. Pangloss's romp in the bushes surely must have taken place in warm weather. The text we have just quoted specifically mentions that the evening Tom followed Molly's amorous lead was balmy. Two books farther on Tom is expelled from the Allworthy estate in the dead of winter (Book 7). As for Candide, his fate is decided so quickly that he no sooner falls in love than he is immediately expelled from the 'meilleur des châteaux' and finds himself sleeping rough in a snowstorm: 'il se coucha sans souper au milieu des champs entre deux sillons; la neige tombait à gros flocons'[16] ('he lay down to sleep without supper, in the middle of a field between two furrows; the snow fell in large flakes').

Paquette's debt to Molly Seagrim illustrates Voltaire's selective reading of *L'Enfant trouvé* as well as his need to condense and to transform that sprawling novel into a work of elegant and witty concision. And yet, unlike the docile Paquette, La Place's sixteen-year-old Molly is a lustful wench who ensnares the innocent Tom in much same way that Cunégonde seduces Candide.[17] The larger-than-life Molly, in fact, has a good deal in common with Voltaire's Cunégonde, whose character she also influenced.

Still, before considering how *Margot la Ravaudeuse* may have influenced Paquette, there is one further instance where Molly and Paquette's stories converge in a revealing way. In *L'Enfant trouvé*'s final chapter, all of the novel's virtuous protagonists are resettled in the country paradise of their birth. The now vindicated Tom marries the beautiful Sophia, and, mirroring Tom and Sophia, Molly takes up with Partridge. Tom grants Partridge an annual income of £50, and he settles an important sum of money on Molly. The two, we are told will soon marry, and thanks to Tom's munificence their happiness and prosperity are assured:

> M. Jones a distribué les 500 livres sterling à sa famille (de George Seagrim), et Moly (comme de raison) en a eu *double part*. Partridge avec *50 livres sterling* de rente créées par M. Jones a levé une nouvelle école, où il fait des merveilles. On parle même d'un mariage entre lui et Moly Seagrim. C'est Sophie, dit-on qui s'en mêle et tout fait croire que cette alliance aura lieu.[18]
>
> (Mr Jones distributed the £500 among George Seagrim's family and, as one might expect, Molly received a double share. Partridge with annual income of £50 granted by Mr Jones has established a new school where he is working miracles. There is even talk of marriage between him and Molly orchestrated by Sophia.)

A very similar motif in Chapter 24 shows how *Candide* challenges Fielding's original intention and reveals Voltaire's profound cynicism. Having become reacquainted with Paquette in Venice, Candide – taking his lead from Tom

Jones – gives Paquette 2,000 piastres and a further 1,000 to Frère Giroflée. Still optimistic, Candide persists in believing that his largesse will make the couple happy. The pessimistic Martin warns, however, that they will end up more miserable than they were when they were penniless.

> Candide donna deux mille piastres à Paquette, et mille piastres à frère Giroflée. 'Je vous réponds, dit-il, qu'avec cela ils seront heureux. – Je n'en crois rien du tout, dit Martin; vous les rendrez peut-être avec ces piastres beaucoup plus malheureux encore.[19]
>
> (Candide gave 2,000 piastres to Paquette, and 1,000 to Frère Giroflée. 'I'll answer for it that this will make them happy.' – 'I don't believe a word of it,' said Martin. 'You will perhaps make them unhappier still.')

Martin's warning is naturally borne out in Chapter 30. Meantime, we learn that Paquette and Giroflée readily accepted Candide's money, and that that they callously failed to thank him for it.[20]

Paquette and Margot

Tom Jones's Molly Seagrim may have influenced *Candide*'s Paquette in a revealing way, but her sufferings as a lowly prostitute were almost certainly inspired by Monbron's Margot. *Margot la Ravaudeuse* is the story of a Parisian stocking darner who eventually becomes a high-class lady of pleasure. In the novel's first segment she seduces a neighbourhood boy and is consequently forced to leave her unhappy home. With no family and nowhere to go, La Ravaudeuse falls easy prey to a certain Madame Florence, a bawd who cajoles her into embracing life as a 'catin' in a 'maison close'.

> Pendant environ quatre mois que je demeurai chez Madame Florence, je puis me vanter d'avoir fait un cours complet dans la profession de fille du monde; et lorsque je sortis de cette école, j'avais assez d'acquis pour le disputer à tous les luxurieux anciens et modernes, dans l'art profond de varier les plaisirs, et dans la pratique de toutes les possibilités physiques en matière de paillardise.[21]
>
> (For about four months I lived under the care of Madame Florence; I can lay claim to having successfully completed a course in the world's oldest profession. When I left the school, I could rival the lustful, both ancient and modern, in the art of gratifying every desire as well as in the physical expression of bawdiness.)

Margot learns the profession with great tribulation, and it is during this early segment of her story that she gives voice to feelings of anger and resentment similar to those voiced by Paquette in Chapter 24 of *Candide*.

Despite the novel's stated aim to portray the life of a prostitute under 'les couleurs les plus odieuses',[22] Margot's career turns into a great success. Having left Madame Florence's brothel on friendly terms, Margot makes her own way. Thanks to her good looks, cunning and aptitude to please her clients, she succeeds as a 'demoiselle de l'opéra', amassing a fortune in the process. The downside is that, discovering that her health has been seriously compromised by venereal infection, she is forced to retire to the country with her old mother to recover. She does recover and, at the novel's happy conclusion, her time is spent in domestic pursuits between town and country.

A first-person narrative, the novel is a piece of erotica, which, while it appears to stigmatize the low-class 'métier', lends considerable glamour the life of the high-class prostitute. Its influence on *Candide* can be shown through a number of previously unnoticed idiosyncratic expressions common to both novels. For instance, in the first few pages of the tale, Margot describes herself as 'la perle des ravaudeuses'.[23] The expression 'la perle des ...' in reference to a woman is not unknown in the writing of the period; Voltaire himself used it in his *Lettres Philosophiques*.[24] It is nonetheless remarkable that Cunégonde, whose affinity with Margot has already been noted, is ironically twice described in *Candide* as 'la perle des filles'.[25] In addition, *Margot la Ravaudeuse* twice employs the expression 'tout va au mieux'[26] anticipating Candide's famous variations on a very similar phrase ('tout est au mieux', 'tout va au mieux', 'tout allait le mieux du monde'). The expression 'prendre la chose en patience' is also common to both works. Narrating how she was raped by thirty musketeers, Margot exclaims: 'Quant à moi, chétive pécheresse, j'avoue que loin d'avoir *pris la chose en patience* ... je ne cessai de vomir contre eux toutes les imprécations imaginables'[27] ('As for me, poor sinner that I was, far from taking their assault lying down, I hurled every imaginable insult at them'). Precisely the same expression is used in reference to *Candide*'s pessimistic philosopher Martin. Faced with life's vicissitudes, his attitude is somewhat more resigned than Margot's: 'Pour Martin, il était fermement persuadé qu'on est également mal partout; il *prenait les choses en patience*.'[28] ('As for Martin, he was persuaded that a person is equally unhappy everywhere. He took things in stride.') Revealingly, the novel also prefigures *Candide*'s 'baron allemand'. La Ravaudeuse herself counts two separate German barons among her many lovers.[29] Yet another lover wears a superb diamond ring that Margot hankers after, similar to the enormous diamonds la marquise de Parolignac admires on Candide's fingers and with which she manages to abscond.[30] In Margot's case the diamond turns out to be paste. And lastly, at the end of Monbron's novel, Margot learns that just like like Pangloss and Cunégonde's brother in Chapter 27, her father is a galley slave,[31] while her mother, (foreshadowing the Old Woman's role in *Candide*'s final chapter), having been previously released from confinement in a prison-hôpital, becomes her daughter's housekeeper.[32]

As previously suggested, it seems highly likely that Margot's character may have helped shape Voltaire's overtly sexual Cunégonde. Margot admits that at a very young age she had, 'un ... grand penchant pour les plaisirs libidineux'[33] ('a strong penchant for libidinal pleasures'). Her sexual awareness is in fact stirred by overhearing her parents' lovemaking. She begins masturbating at the age of 14, and then turns her attention to the young stable-boy, mentioned earlier. Margot's predatory attitude toward Pierrot is not unlike Molly Seagrim's determination to ensnare Tom. Her sexual awakening meanwhile, anticipates Cunégonde's who is aroused not by hearing, but by watching Pangloss and Paquette in the underbrush.[34] Immediately thereafter she seduces the innocent Candide. As for Margot, her first sexual encounter with Pierrot takes place in a dingy unfurnished room, where, like Pangloss and Paquette, the pair copulate standing up.[35] Then as Pierrot prepares to deflower her, Margot remarks: 'Ah! Puissant dieu des jardins! Je fus effrayé à l'aspect qu'il me montra.'[36] ('By the powerful god of gardens, I was frightened to death by what he then revealed!') The 'god of gardens' invoked here is a euphemism for Priapus whose presence points to Pangloss's outdoor lesson, where Cunégonde rather than Paquette, ogles the philospher's 'raison suffisante'. Voltaire's description of Paquette, as 'très docile' nevertheless echoes the advice offered by Madame Florence to the newly discovered Margot: 'tout ce que je vous demande à présent, c'est de la docilité et de vous laisser conduire'[37] ('All that I ask for is obedience. Don't resist. Relax and let yourself be guided'). Later, when she has learned the profession and has come to know men from every conceivable walk of life, Margot's utterance on the different sorts of men she has encountered clearly announces Cunégonde's 'désir d'être savante':

> Est-il quelque profession, quelque métier dans la vie dont nous n'ayons incessamment occasion d'entendre discourir ? Le guerrier, le robin, le financier, le philosophe, l'homme d'Église, tous ces êtres divers recherchent également notre commerce. Chacun d'eux parle le jargon de son état. Comment avec tant de moyens de devenir *savantes*, serait-il possible que nous ne le devinssions pas?[38]
>
> (Is there any profession that we do not soon learn about? The soldier, the lawyer, the financier, the philosopher, the clergyman, men from all these walks of life seek our company. And each speaks the jargon of his own profession. How, I ask, with so many ways to become 'learned', could we manage not to?)

I have argued elsewhere in my published work that Cunégonde's aptitude for 'learning' might be traced to Tom's putative mother, Jenny Jones, presented in *L'Enfant trouvé* under the chapter heading: 'Combien il est dangereux pour les jeunes filles de vouloir devenir trop *savantes*' ('The Danger of a Young Girl Wanting to Become Too Learned'].[39] What now seems likely is that Cunégonde's appetite for learning results from Voltaire's merging of two almost identical verbal images, one relating to Jenny Jones and the other to Margot. In neither case is the term 'savante' an obvious euphemism for carnal knowledge; but then neither Jenny nor Margot is what we would call unknowing. Thus when Paquette then takes up the idea of Margot's list of clients she condenses it, and focuses on the professions rather than the jargon specific to each:

Ah! monsieur, si vous pouviez vous imaginer ce que c'est que d'être obligée de caresser indifféremment un vieux marchand, un avocat, un moine, un gondolier, un abbé ...[40]

(Ah sir, if you could only imagine what it is like to have to caress without any inclination whatsoever an old merchant, a lawyer, a monk, a gondolier, an abbot ...)

Broome argued that Margot's impact on Paquette's lament in Chapter 24 derives from the first segment of *La Ravaudeuse* where Margot prepares to leave Madame Florence's bawdy house. In another commentary on this remarkable soliloquy, Vivienne Mylne has observed that 'at the close of her (Paquette's) [recitation], Voltaire abandons the crisp style which is characteristic of most of *Candide*, and [that he] launch[es] into a long periodic sentence ... built up of successive clauses filled with humiliating details concerning the miseries of [Paquette's] present way of life and her expectations for the future'.[41] Mylne rightly notes that, unlike much of the satire in *Candide*, Paquette's life-story is not a parody of a conventional genre. It is rather a 'straightforward tale ... reminiscent of a kind of novel published in France around the middle of the eighteenth-century'.[42] Mylne is of course referring to the fictionalized autobiographies of prostitutes such as *La Belle Allemande ou les galanteries de Thérèse* (1745), *Les dégoûts du plaisir* (1752), *Les Égarements de Julie* (1755) or Paul Baret's *Mademoiselle Javotte* (1757), all of which appeared before *Candide*, and which may have had some impact on it. Written by men (but in decent language) these short narratives are all highly erotic; viewed together, they present a mid-eighteenth century anatomy of prostitution-as-narrative, a conceit providing a plausible pretext for erotica. Not surprisingly, the stories are animated by a rogue's gallery of stereotypical characters, some few of which appear in *Candide*. The prostitute-heroine is a pretty girl turned out of doors, sometimes pimped by her own mother, often seduced by an unscrupulous older man. In line with contemporary anti-clerical satire, this older man may be monk or a priest. The novels' episodic structure presents a series of debauchees and grotesques (obese women, impotent old men, aristocratic sodomites, castrati, fantastically endowed clerics, etc.) all of whom indulge in a predicable catalogue of sexual fantasies: anal penetration, flagellation, sadism, voyeurism, cross-dressing and so forth. Of interest to students of *Candide* is the comic transmission of venereal infection. In *La belle Allemande*, for example, Thérèse passes it deliberately to a miserly money lender. Mylne suggests that the four contemporary texts mentioned share *Candide*'s flair for obscene innuendo; yet in truth, none presents as many inter-textual echoes with *Candide* as *Margot la Ravaudeuse*. Broome has identified eight verbal images in Margot's rant on the evils of prostitution alone that appear to have their counterpart in *Candide*. Read alongside a condensed version of Margot's much longer diatribe, *Candide*'s verbal and thematic debt to *Margot la Ravaudeuse* is unmistakable. There is, however, one final reference to *L'Enfant trouvé* in the following passage that shows how Paquette proceeds from two distinct works, and three different characters: Molly Seagrim, Margot la Ravaudeuse and Jenny Jones. The phrase 'j'ai été hier volée et battue par un officier' is an explicit reminder of Jenny Jones's treatment at the hands of the vicious Ensign Northerton in Book 9 of *L'Enfant trouvé*.

Margot la Ravaudeuse

Quand je fais réflexion aux épreuves cruelles et bizarres où se trouvent réduite une fille du monde, je ne saurais m'imaginer qu'il y ait de *condition plus rebutante et plus misérable* ... En effet, qu'y a-t-il de plus insupportable que *d'être obligée d'essuyer* les caprices du premier venu ; que de sourire à un faquin que nous méprisons dans l'âme ; *de caresser l'objet de l'aversion universelle*; de nous prêter à des goûts aussi singuliers que monstrueux ; en un mot, d'être éternellement couvertes du masque de l'artifice et de la dissimulation, de rire, de chanter, de boire, de nous livrer à toute sorte d'excès et de débauche, le plus souvent à contrecœur et avec une répugnance extrême? *Que ceux qui se figurent notre vie un tissu de plaisirs et d'agréments nous connaissent mal*! ... Comme un vil intérêt est le mobile et la fin de notre prostitution, aussi les mépris les plus accablants, *les avanies*, les outrages en sont presque toujours le juste salaire. Il faut avoir été catin pour concevoir toutes *les horreurs du métier*.[43]

(When I think about the bizarre and cruel conditions that a whore has to put up with, I can scarce imagine a viler condition. Is there anything more disgusting than having to satisfying the fantasies of any Tom, Dick or Harry? To smile at a detestable old fart, to caress somebody that everyone finds hideous, in a word, to hide one's true feelings behind an impenetrable mask, in order to laugh, sing and drink, in order to give oneself over to the wildest excesses, nay, to the most degrading and humiliating acts of debauchery. Those who imagine that the life of a whore consists only in pleasure don't know the half of it. ... Depraved self-interest oils the wheels of our trade; the whore can expect as her just reward public scorn and brutality. Only a whore knows the horror of it.)

Candide

Je fus bientôt supplantée par une rivale, chassée sans récompense, et obligée de continuer ce *métier abominable qui vous paraît si plaisant à vous autres hommes*, et qui n'est pour nous qu'un *abîme de misère*. J'allai exercer la profession à Venise. Ah! monsieur, si vous pouviez vous imaginer ce que c'est que d'être *obligée de caresser* indifféremment un vieux marchand, un avocat, un moine, un gondolier, un abbé; *d'être exposée à toutes les insultes, à toutes les avanies*; d'être souvent réduite à emprunter une jupe pour aller se la faire lever par *un homme dégoûtant*; d'être volée par l'un de ce qu'on a gagné avec l'autre; d'être rançonnée par les officiers de justice, et de n'avoir en perspective qu'une vieillesse affreuse, un hôpital, et un fumier, vous concluriez que je suis une des plus malheureuses créatures du monde ...

– Ah! monsieur, répondit Paquette, c'est encore là une des *misères du métier*. J'ai été hier volée et battue par un officier, et il faut aujourd'hui que je paraisse de bonne humeur pour plaire à un moine.[44]

(I was soon replaced by a rival, turned out of doors, destitute and had to carry on with this abominable trade, which appears so pleasant to you men, and which to us women is an abyss of misery. Needless to say, I have come to Venice to exercise the profession. Ah! sir, if you could only imagine what it is to be obliged to caress without any inclination whatsoever an old merchant, a lawyer, a monk, a gondolier, an abbot, to be exposed to abuse and insults; to be reduced to borrowing a petticoat only to have it pulled off by a vile old man; to be robbed by one of what you've earned from another; to be subject to the extortions of the police; and to contemplate the prospect of a ghastly old age, a hospital, and finally a pauper's grave; you would conclude that I am one of the unhappiest creatures in the world ... – Ah! sir, answered Paquette, this is one of the miseries of the trade. Yesterday I was robbed and beaten by an officer; yet today I must put on good humor to please a friar.)

Consistent with his adaptation of the source material behind *Candide*, Voltaire condenses some aspects of Monbron's eight-page denunciation of prostitution and expands others. Paquette's lament recapitulates the extreme physical and moral humiliation expressed by Margot except in its startling conclusion. For unlike La Ravaudeuse, the still youthful Paquette contemplates with horror the life of the ageing prostitute, 'une vieillesse affreuse, un hôpital, et un fumier': a miserable old age, illness and a pauper's grave. Paquette's account takes Margot's tale to its logical, one might even say inevitable conclusion, rather than to the sentimental one favoured by the lesser writer Monbron. The moral of Monbron's novel appears to vindicate Margot's chosen profession. Voltaire, on the other hand, pushes Paquette to the brink of ruin, before re-establishing her in *Candide*'s famous garden. Voltaire bends the source material borrowed from Monbron to his own will so completely that it is seamlessly woven into a narrative and moral scheme that effectively absorbs it. When Paquette and Giroflée reappear in the tale in a state of extreme misery, they produce a 'final burst of philosophizing' before Candide and Martin conclude that happiness lies in work rather than in metaphysical speculation.[45]

> Une chose acheva de confirmer Martin dans ses détestables principes, de faire hésiter plus que jamais Candide, et d'embarrasser Pangloss. C'est qu'ils virent un jour aborder dans leur métairie Paquette et le frère Giroflée, qui étaient dans la plus extrême misère; ils avaient bien vite mangé leurs trois mille piastres, s'étaient quittés, s'étaient raccommodés, s'étaient brouillés, avaient été mis en prison; s'étaient enfuis, et enfin frère Giroflée s'était fait turc. Paquette continuait son métier partout, et n'y gagnait plus rien. – Je l'avais bien prévu, dit Martin à Candide, que vos présents seraient bientôt dissipés et ne les rendraient que plus misérables.[46]
>
> (What helped to confirm Martin's detestable principles, what stumped Candide more than ever and what puzzled Pangloss, was that Paquette and Frère Giroflée landed at the farm completely destitute. They had soon squandered the three thousand piastres Candide had given them, parted, were reconciled, quarreled again, were thrown into gaol, had escaped. Frère Giroflée then converted to Islam. Paquette plied her trade wherever she went, but she no longer could make any money. – I foresaw, said Martin to Candide, that your presents would soon be wasted and would make them more miserable than they were before.)

Paquette is a cameo figure whose life-story nevertheless is central to *Candide*'s moral purpose; her reappearance in the novel's final chapter is almost certainly an echo of Molly Seagrim's rehabilitation at the end of *Tom Jones*, and it is instructive to consider that episode which serves to underscore the double theme of forgiveness and redemption Fielding clearly wished to emphasize. *Candide*'s final chapter drives home a similar theme, and it seems fair to suggest that the tale's conclusion, as exemplified by Paquette's salvation, owes something to Fielding's famous happy ending, reviewed and corrected, as it were, by Voltaire.

What I have demonstrated here is the emergence of Paquette as a composite character inspired by Fielding's Molly Seagrim and Jenny Jones as well as Monbron's Margot la Ravaudeuse. In eighteenth-century usage (in English and French respectively) the names Molly and Margot were both evocative of prostitution.[47] Unlike Margot, Molly Seagrim is not a prostitute *per se,* but she is a 'hussy', and her character is symmetrically aligned with that of Fielding's virginal heroine, the well-born Sophia Western. Voltaire was certainly alert to Fielding's portrayal of Molly and Jenny as highly sexed women. His deconstruction of these two fictional types merged with Monbron's overtly sexual Margot and influenced his portrait of the lubricious Cunégonde in revealing ways. What is also apparent is that the same three characters also gave rise to Voltaire's portrayal of Paquette. Thus it seems that the high-born Cunégonde, and the low-born Paquette proceed from the same three fictional models: Molly, Jenny and Margot. There is one noteworthy difference, however. Whatever other fictional models impacted Voltaire at the time he was writing *Candide*, Cunégonde's character was primarily written in response to Fielding's paean to aristocratic womanhood: the unforgettable Sophia Western.

9 THE PROSTITUTE AS NEO-MANAGER: SADE'S *JULIETTE* AND THE NEW SPIRIT OF CAPITALISM

Olivier Delers

The heroine of *Histoire de Juliette* (1797) is Sade's fantasized version of a violent, cruel and perverted female libertine. Drawn from a young age to sexual experimentation, Juliette routinely participates in rapes and murders and becomes an advocate for the necessity of evil in the world. But there is another version of the character, which appears briefly in two earlier texts dedicated to her innocent and virtuous sister Justine: *Les Infortunes de la vertu* (1787) and *Justine, ou les Malheurs de la vertu* (1791). Both texts stage the life of Juliette, the orphaned daughter of a bankrupt *financier* who decides to make a career selling herself to rich Parisian aristocrats.[1] These two texts portray her rapid ascent through the social strata of Ancien Régime France, from a young girl in a convent to a common prostitute, and eventually to a respected – if still promiscuous – noblewoman. What is particularly striking about this early Juliette is her concern for economic calculation: she is first concerned with survival and carefully accumulates cash, property and titles in an attempt to gain ever greater economic power and social prestige. If each venal transaction brings new acts of *libertinage*, it also reaffirms Juliette's keen understanding of what drives the production, multiplication and preservation of wealth. In fact, Juliette's actions reveal a fundamental truth about the underlying social and economic structures of Sade's universe: the existence of two different groups, one composed of exploiters who are mobile, adaptable and connected, and the other formed by the exploited, who are condemned to a life of suffering and vagabondage. This division is also characteristic of what theorists have called 'modern network economies' and my analysis will explore the continuities between prostitution in Sade's fictional society and the nature of the post-industrial world as described by the French sociologists Luc Boltanski and Eve Chiapello in a recent study, *The New Spirit of Capitalism*. I will draw on their description of 'neo-managers' and 'connectionist spaces' as two crucial components of modern capitalism to show how Juliette's identity as a venal body is a function of the social connections that she chooses to pursue.[2]

Sade's heroine, in her successive attempts to attract new potential clients and to extract everything she can from them, is depicted as a deft manager of her body and of her relations with other economic actors. Not only does she seem to possess an instinctive knowledge of what drives success in Sade's social world, she also has an uncanny ability to avoid being punished for her crimes. This essay suggests that Juliette's successful negotiation of her adventures shares characteristics with Boltanski and Chiapello's account of those who succeed in advanced capitalist societies, and that libertine modes of behaviour prefigure a number of features of what they designate as network societies.

Boltanski and Chiapello's *New Spirit of Capitalism* is first and foremost a sociological project whose aim is to make sense of the various motivations of social actors for believing and participating in the capitalist system at different periods in history. In their analysis, the third spirit of capitalism, the age of 'neo-managers' and network economies, succeeds the first spirit of capitalism centered around the figure of the bourgeois entrepreneur in the nineteenth century, and the second spirit of capitalism articulated around large industrial firms run by expert managers in the twentieth century.[3] But it is also an epistemological project: by looking at the different strategies used by social actors to justify their engagement in capitalism, Boltanski and Chiapello interrogate the ways in which sociology, as a discipline, has traditionally codified the position of individuals in relation to social structures. The theoretical implications of their analyses are not only valid in the context of post-industrial societies but also apply to earlier stages of capitalism and pre-capitalist societies. By juxtaposing Sade's early works of fiction and *The New Spirit of Capitalism*, I will suggest ways that these texts depict individuals who affirm a certain independence of action even when their bodies are entrapped in systems of industrial production.

Even though the intensity of her sexual appetite is kept in check by her desire for social elevation in *Les Infortunes de la vertu* and *Justine, ou les malheurs de la vertu*, Juliette is still a paradigmatic example of what Kathryn Norberg has called 'the libertine whore'. As a type in early-modern pornographic fiction, she conforms to a series of characteristics that highlight both her specific skills and multiple identities:

> the 'libertine whore' ... is independent, sensual, sensible and skilled. She is healthy and possessed of a very healthy – that is, normal – sexual appetite. She is a businesswoman and an artist who provides 'varied' sex for men who can afford it. She is a courtesan who lives in luxury and abides by 'philosophy', usually materialist philosophy. Intelligent, independent, proud and reasonable, she is *not* diseased or monstrous; she is not humiliated or victimized either by life or her clients. She may have come from working-class roots, but she overcomes them through her education and intelligence. An *arriviste*, she can scoff at social distinctions and hoodwink the rich and powerful.[4]

Juliette's journey, as we will see, is not unlike that of the generic libertine whore sketched out by Norberg. She stands out as a subversive female character who challenges the traditional gender stereotypes of eighteenth-century literature and who, in doing so, 'reveals a great deal about attitudes towards women, female sexuality and women's social role'.[5] Or, to put it differently, Juliette's transgressions and her performance as a prostitute 'offer alternative narratives of female sexuality and experience'.[6] Sade, the 'terrorist pornographer', as Angela Carter calls him, who 'reinstitute[s] sexuality as a primary mode of being' creates a space for female sexual agency by depicting a successful prostitute at the end of the eighteenth century.[7] He also creates a space where identities are not predetermined and essentialized, but rather fluid and relational. If the representation of this kind of venal body necessarily brings up gender issues, it also offers new possibilities to think of Sade's philosophy of action as a 'radical empiricism', to use Boltanski and Chiapello's terms, in which relational ontologies underpin a series of loosely connected networks.[8]

Juliette as 'Neo-Manager'

Before our heroine Juliette can escape the fate of the submissive and silenced prostitute and become a case study for new social practices, she must learn her trade and experience the inner workings of the prostitution industry. Sade's description of Juliette's journey is as intense as it is condensed: only four pages are devoted to her in *Les Infortunes de la vertu* and five pages in *Justine, ou les Malheurs de la vertu*. Juliette's story begins in the safety of the domestic sphere, where young girls are supposed to be protected from the economic transactions of the outside world. The sudden bankruptcy and subsequent death of their parents force Juliette and Justine, her sister, to find means of supporting themselves. Juliette, already drawn to vice and physical pleasures, leaves her fate in the hands of La Duvergier, a brothel owner who promises her that with hard work and dedication, she will be able to retire after a few years as a financially independent woman.[9] But prostitution, for La Duvergier, follows the logic of industrial production: Juliette's body is temporarily turned into a commodity available for purchase on the sex market:

> dès le lendemain, ses prémices furent en vente; en quatre mois de temps, la même marchandise fut successivement vendue à quatre-vingt personnes qui toutes la payèrent comme neuve[10]
>
> (the very next day her virginity was up for sale. Within a space of four months, the same merchandise was sold in turn to eighty persons, who each paid as though for unused goods)[11]

In *Justine, ou les malheurs de la vertu*, Juliette becomes even more productive and the narrator is more specific about what gives the commodity/body its intrinsic value:

> En quatre mois, la marchandise est successivement vendue à près de cent personnes ... Chaque fois, la Duvergier rétrécit, rajuste, et pendant quatre mois ce sont toujours des prémices que la friponne offre au public.
>
> (In four months, the same merchandise is sold in turn to about a hundred persons ... Each time, La Duvergier takes in and reshapes, and for four months, it is the same unspoiled goods that the rascal offers the public.)[12]

Beyond the high number of clients, La Duvergier focuses here on the efficiency and mechanization of production, as the procurer repeatedly alters Juliette's body to increase her profits by selling her as a virgin over and over again. Still, her industrial scheme is based on a sham, on reselling the same good – Juliette's virginity – for what it is not. Sade also suggests that Juliette's activities are not limited to consuming and exploiting the body: her 'prémices' are not marketed to individual buyers but to the 'public' at large, as if 'la friponne', as Sade calls her, were engaged in a four-month long performance that was in itself remarkable. In other words, prostitution is not simply an illicit and mechanized transaction taking place in the relative anonymity of the brothel, but the sale of an unique product, advertised as such and paradoxically available to all.

But what is of particular interest is what comes after the heroine's brothel experience. After moving from traditional family relationships that protect women from the forces of the open sexual market to a form of industrial prostitution that subjects the prostitute's body to its sustained rhythm and yield requirements, Juliette finally gains her independence, 'working' as a courtesan whose sexual skills coupled with a talent for cunning and anticipation make her highly successful in expanding her personal wealth and her circle of influence:

> elle devint en quinze ans femme titrée, possédant plus de trente mille livres de rente, de très beaux bijoux, deux ou trois maisons tant à la campagne qu'à Paris, et pour l'instant, le cœur, la richesse et la confiance de M. de Corville, conseiller d'état, homme dans le plus grand crédit et à la veille d'entrer dans le ministère ...[13]
>
> (she became within the space of fifteen years a lady possessing a title, an income of 30,000 livres, gorgeous jewels, two or three houses in Paris, and in the country, plus, for the time being, the heart, purse, and confidence of Monsieur de Corville, a Councillor of State, a man enjoying the highest credit and poised to become a Minister of the Crown ...)[14]

Fifteen years after starting her career as a prostitute, Juliette possesses economic, social and cultural capital: not only has she secured the long-term financial stability of the *rentière*, she has also adapted to the lifestyle of the nobility, and she has managed to develop important connections with the inner circle of political power. The narrator explains that she has done so through a series of 'conquêtes':

> Jusqu'à vingt-six ans elle fit encore de brillantes conquêtes, ruina trois ambassadeurs, quatre fermiers généraux, deux évêques et trois chevaliers des ordres du roi ...[15]
> (Until she was 26, she continued to make brilliant conquests, ruined three ambassadors, four tax-farmers, two bishops, and three Knights of Royal Orders ...)[16]

The number of ruined clients is impressive, but prostitution, in this case, differs from sex being sold as a commodity and from the logic of industrial production. The verb 'ruiner' implies a process, as if each lover were considered a separate project requiring a combination of her skills of seduction and of her ability to drain those men of their possessions. Interestingly, the categories of men mentioned here cover the spectrum of the rich and powerful in Ancien Régime France: foreign dignitaries, tax collectors, clergymen and nobles of high rank. They also attest to Juliette's capacity to adapt and to her knowledge and understanding of how to be successful in a specific social context. In fact, the narrator describes her as a 'créature adroite et ambitieuse de trouver journellement de nouvelles dupes et de grossir à tout moment sa fortune tout en accumulant ses crimes'[17] ('a scheming and ambitious woman who could find new dupes daily and swell her fortune at every turn as her crimes accumulated')[18] mixing the language of gain ('ambitieux', 'grossir', 'accumulant') with the language of skills ('adroite') and deception ('dupes'). The courtesan-prostitute develops her prowess as a con artist with the necessary skills and knowledge to come out on top of the projects (or 'conquêtes') in which she is engaged.

The character of Juliette, in the way that she navigates Sade's social world, resembles the figure of the neo-manager, a term coined by Luc Boltanski and Eve Chiapello to describe the type of economic actors who understand the nature and the rules of success in post-industrial network societies. Just like our courtesan, who spends more than fifteen years recruiting rich prospects from various backgrounds, neo-managers 'are at ease in *fluid* situations', and 'prefer the exploration of new networks to the stability of established relations'. Like Juliette, they possess a form of knowledge and skills that are 'highly specialized, creative, and personalized'.[19] What differentiates Sade's heroine from the common prostitute is her ability to design new forms of *libertinage* for each of her new lovers, but also to imagine ways of getting rid of them without endangering her social rise. Prostitution, for Juliette, is not serial but adaptive. In short, Sade's heroine is what Boltanski and Chiapello would call 'un créatif' ('a creative figure'), 'a person of intuition, invention, contacts and chance encounters'.[20] She combines her artistic abilities with a keen understanding of the social world and of the dominant network, which is what allows her to be at the right place at the right time making the right connections.

So like other 'libertine whores', Juliette is more than a body meant to be consumed by male clients. 'She has her art and her equipment', as Kathryn Norberg puts it, and she knows when and how to use them.[21] Sade uses the word 'art' repeatedly to characterize his heroine but always qualifies any claims to aesthetic perfection by reminding the reader that Juliette's 'talents' have a practical purpose. In both novels, art is linked to 'finesse'[22] and denotes a means to an end: 'l'art de s'en faire entretenir'.[23] Furetière himself, in his *Dictionnaire universel,* gives a rather polysemous definition of the word 'art': it means, among other definitions, 'les manières et inventions dont on se sert pour déguiser les choses' ('the ways and inventions one uses to conceal things'), but also 'pour embellir' ('to embellish') and finally 'réussir dans les desseins' ('to succeed in one's schemes').[24] Deceit, beauty, and successful scheming: Juliette's peculiar form of artistry makes it difficult to limit the prostitute-turned-courtesan to neatly defined categories. Juliette can be seen as a performance artist: she thinks of her actions as a specific creative moment that will be publicized as such and identified with her. Like the neo-manager, her goal is to 'create a *happening* and to *put [her] name* to it'.[25] The performance becomes part of her body of work only to the extent that it helps her build her reputation and thus to move on to new projects. In other words, it is an expression of the character's selfishness. Feminist critics have noted the discursive slip between the body of the whore and the body of the actress and Sade's Juliette certainly illustrates this phenomenon.[26] The more Juliette takes on the role of performer and escapes the mechanical rhythm of industrial production, the more she is endowed with a creative potential and insider knowledge. Yet, at the same time, her artistic abilities only seem to make her a more efficient sexual worker: the more she performs and imposes her 'signature' on her style of *libertinage*, the more astute she becomes at using her body in expert ways to extract advantages out of prostituting herself. What matters to her are the new connections that she is able to establish, and not so much the substance of these connections. Even when she has secured an enviable social and financial position, she continues to make herself available for venal performances: 'c'était une riche veuve qui donnait de jolis soupers, chez laquelle la ville et la cour étaient trop heureuses d'être admises, et qui néanmoins couchait pour deux cent louis et se donnait pour cinq cent par mois'[27] ('She was a rich widow who gave gay supper-parties to which the ornaments of town and court were only too happy to be admitted – yet she could be bedded for 200 louis and bought for 500 a month').[28] The randomness and anonymity of the relationships in which she engages complement the selfish individualism of the character and underline a desire to form bonds outside of the rules of traditional economic or interpersonal relationships.

The narrator pinpoints the moment when the young prostitute makes her first connection and begins her social ascent:

Elle plut à un vieux seigneur fort débauché qui d'abord ne l'avait fait venir que pour l'aventure d'un quart d'heure, elle eut l'art de s'en faire magnifiquement entretenir et parut enfin aux spectacles, aux promenades aux côtés des cordons bleus de l'ordre de Cythère ...[29]

(She took the fancy of an old, thoroughly depraved nobleman who at first had singled her out for a mere quarter of an hour's amusement. She managed to beguile him into keeping her in the most opulent manner and at last began to be seen in theatres and in the fashionable walks on an equal footing with the luminaries of the Order of Cythera ...)[30]

Juliette turns a fifteen-minute trick into a valuable relationship which brings her both a steady income ('entretenir') and a chance to make contact with Parisian aristocratic circles. But Juliette, like the neo-manager, is 'always on the move, passing from one project to the next, from one world to the other'.[31] Both are 'faiseurs de réseaux' (networkers) who 'connect, profit and disconnect in order to find a more lucrative project', without paying too much attention to relations of friendship or to loyalty.[32] Even marriage, with its suggestion of a return to the safety of the domestic sphere, is just another node along the network for the heroine. The conte de Lorsange, whom she marries,

lui reconnut douze mille livres de rente, lui assura le reste de sa fortune qui allait à huit, s'il venait à mourir avant elle, lui donna une maison, des gens, une livrée, et une sorte de considération dans le monde qui parvint en deux ou trois ans à faire oublier ses débuts.[33]

(made over an income of 12,000 livres to her, and arranged that the remainder of his fortune, a further 8,000, would be hers should he die before she did; he gave her a house, servants, and a retinue and conferred on her a degree of respectability in society which ensured that within two or three years her beginnings were forgotten.)[34]

But Juliette prefers to continue her successful career as a courtesan, even if she has to kill her husband: 'pressée de jouir seule, d'avoir un nom, et point de chaînes, [elle] osa se livrer à la coupable pensée d'abréger les jours de son mari'[35] ('impatient to enjoy her advantages alone, to have a name and to get rid of all chains, she dared yield to the culpable notion of abridging her husband's life').[36] The goal of this particular project is clear: 'avoir un nom', that is gaining a new, more respectable outside identity. But the narrator also insists on two important features of Juliette's character: freedom of movement ('point de chaînes') and selfish individualism. In fact, the expression 'jouir seule' seems to indicate a refusal to acknowledge the bonds created by interpersonal relationships (whether it is of love, friendship, or more venal relationships). It is about a form of success – and by semantic extension, a form of sexual pleasure – that can never be bilateral, that simply cannot be shared.

As a character who constantly searches for new connections but who defends a unilateral conception of relationships, Juliette embodies one of the central contradictions of the neo-manager. On the one hand, Sade's description of her journey clearly underlines her 'desire to *connect* with others, *to make contact*, to make *connections*, so as not to remain *isolated*' and her ability of '*adjusting* to other people and situations, depending on what the latter demands of them, without being held back by timidity, rigidity or mistrust'.[37] On the other hand, the heroine needs to be '*adaptable*, physically and intellectually *mobile*' because 'the ability to disengage from a project in order to be *available* for new connections counts as much as the capacity for engagement'.[38] Connection and mobility are both critical to Juliette, yet they do not preclude egotistic self-interest. In fact, Juliette's venal relations in Les Infortunes de la vertu and Les Malheurs de la vertu paint the picture of a social world dominated by connections and dominant networks where selfish behavior is not discouraged and where the moral and political structures that could guard against such behavior are non-existent. Sade's version of prostitution becomes a case study for a dystopic network society ruled by anomie, where, as Boltanski and Chiapello predict, 'opportunist behavior, even if it were adopted only by a few people to start off with, would tend to spread rapidly'.[39]

The disappearance of traditional forms of policing and the development of opportunistic behavior point to another central characteristic of the network economy in which neo-managers strive: the apparent immunity of those who commit crimes. Sade makes it clear that Juliette is particularly talented at hiding her evil deeds and that she feels free to commit crimes in order to carry her projects through. She murders her husband 'avec assez de secret ... pour se mettre à l'abri des poursuites, et pour ensevelir avec cet époux qui la gênait toutes les traces de son abominable forfait'[40] ('with such stealth ... that she was able both to elude the arm of the law and to bury all traces of her abominable crime along with her hindrance of a husband').[41] Later on,

> Juliette se noircit de deux nouveaux crimes semblables au premier; l'un pour voler un de ses amants qui lui avait confié une somme considérable que toute la famille de cet homme ignorait et que Mme de Lorsange [Juliette] put mettre à l'abri par ce crime odieux; l'autre pour avoir plut tôt un legs de cent mille francs qu'un de ses adorateurs lui faisait sur son testament en sa faveur au nom d'un tiers qui devait rendre la somme au moyen d'une légère rétribution.[42]
>
> (Juliette sank even deeper into the mire with two more crimes of the same kind as the first; one, that she might rob one of her lovers of a sum of money put into her keeping by him without his family's knowing which she sequestered to her own profit by means of her odious crime, the other, that she might the sooner receive a bequest of 100,000 livres which one of her admirers had written into his will in the name of a third party who was appointed to hand the money over to her against a small consideration.)[43]

In either case, Juliette is not punished for her criminal actions, and her ability to go on killing unsuspected is even more pronounced in *Histoire de Juliette*. This kind of immunity, for Boltanski and Chiapello, is the direct consequence of the increased mobility of powerful economic actors. It shows the growing irrelevance of the domestic world in relation to the connectionist world of network societies:

> In a domestic world, honoring debts that have been contracted is based upon the coexistence of the same persons in the same space, and the reciprocal control they exercise over one another. Now, in a connectionist world, mobility, which constitutes a fundamental requirement, makes it largely possible to elude the collective reprisals entailed in the former domestic world by defaulting and displaying ingratitude towards those whose support one enjoyed.[44]

In both novels, *Les Infortunes de la vertu* and *Justine, ou les Malheurs de la vertu*, the domestic world no longer affords the protection it traditionally provided, and Justine's attempts to seek the protection of trusted friends and figures of moral authority after her parents' death prove useless.[45] On the contrary, Juliette's first instinct – choosing prostitution as a career – puts her on the right track to reclaim a privileged position in society. Her natural understanding of space allows her to remain relevant on the network and to keep doing what she does best: connecting, exploiting, destroying, and eventually disconnecting – destruction and murder being perhaps the feature that distinguishes Sade's character most from Boltanski and Chiapello's neo-manager.

Sade, Venality and the Network Society

My reading of Juliette indicates that some elements that dominate later phases of capitalism can already be prefigured at the end of the eighteenth century, at a time when French society is still governed by the pre-capitalist political and economic structures of the Ancien Régime. Sade, in his master-narrative that opposes vice and virtue, paints a social environment that is already ripe for dominant networks and neo-managers. Juliette's journey as a prostitute and courtesan provides a privileged vantage point to observe these phenomena because she lays bare the exchanges that occur between economic actors, but also because she manages her body in a way that combines the logic of business transactions with a certain aesthetic idealism. This is a trait that she shares with other Sadean 'neo-managers' like M. de Bressac, La Dubois or the monks of Saint-Marie des Bois – to name only a few other characters who appear in *Les Infortunes de la vertu* and *Justine, ou les malheurs de la vertu*. I now want to explore the usefulness of the concepts I have been using – the connectionist world of network societies in which neo-managers thrive – to think about both the nature of Sade's fictionalized social world and prostitution in eighteenth-century France.

Needless to say, networks do not suddenly become relevant in the second half of the twentieth century when they provide the operative metaphor for what Boltanski and Chiapello call the 'third spirit of capitalism'.[46] If networks act as an interpretive framework to analyse how the capitalist system has transformed itself and has supported its ideology in comparison with earlier stages of capitalist development, they can also offer ways of thinking about the internal rules, patterns of exchange and modes of recruitment of pre-capitalist economic systems. Juliette's particular way of approaching venality, for instance, is closely related to managing her body in efficient ways, continually forming new ties and preserving her mobility. Of course, Juliette's story is highly idiosyncratic and Sade constantly pushes his lead character to the limits of verisimilitude. But that feature of the two early Justine novels actually allows Sade to sketch out a unique set of social structures and to tackle broad sociological questions that also underlie the analysis of network economies that Boltanksi and Chiapello engage in: to what extent do systemic impositions cripple any claims to free action? Is success generally reserved to those who have internalized the rules of the system, or is there room for outsiders to subvert established hierarchies? What happens to a society when social identity ceases to be linked to birth or occupation and becomes dependent on the relations that individuals are able to build and maintain? Juliette's trajectory as a prostitute and a courtesan who is endowed with creative agency provides unexpected answers to these questions by presenting identity as being primarily relational rather than essential, and by questioning the power of fate to constrain personal ambitions.

Sade begins the two novels with an ironic attack against 'la Providence': the ultimate achievement of philosophy, he tells us, would be to decipher 'les caprices bizarres de cette fatalité à laquelle on donne vingt noms différents' ('the bizarre caprices of the Fate to which a score of different names are given') and thus to help man understand 'la manière dont il faut qu'il marche dans la carrière épineuse de la vie'[47] ('the ways in which he is supposed to tread in the thorny career of life').[48] Justine's story as a whole reads as an ironic parable against the discourse of fate, which tends to reduce complex social phenomena and individual volition to suspiciously simplistic answers. If it is Justine's destiny to be systematically abused and victimized, then it might be mere chance that gives Juliette wealth and titles. The forms of exploitation created in societies where networks operate are often naturalized as being produced by fate, as being the logical consequence of a person's innate nature. Boltanski and Chiapello notice a tendency to de-emphasize structural inequalities in network economies and to resort to the language of destiny to explain the inability of some to form connections: 'Exclusion is thus presented as someone's misfortune [*destin*] (to be struggled against), not as the result of a social asymmetry from which some people profit to the detriment of others'.[49] Justine, while at times wondering why an innocent and honest young woman like herself would be subjected to a long streak of misfortunes, never seeks to identify specific causes and instead keeps 'struggling' to find safety and employment. Likewise, Juliette just goes on accumulating lovers and wealth without a moment of introspection to question the source of her success. Sade plays with these two characters who seem hard-wired for a certain kind of life and who, often in preposterous ways, seem to have no say in the decisions that affect them directly.

Of course, the two sisters Justine and Juliette should theoretically share the same type of social and cultural capital and respond in similar ways to the constraints imposed by the society in which they live.[50] Instead, we are confronted by a paradoxical situation: one sister is subjected to entrenched hierarchies and privileges while the other has seemingly internalized the social rules that allow her to succeed in different social positions, as a prostitute, a courtesan or a noblewoman. As Sade stages characters in a space where making new connections is essential, he also delineates a theory of action that distances itself from – and in fact clearly mocks – predetermined outcomes and that credits social actors with agency, creativity and originality.[51] In doing so, Sade again prefigures a similar process that accompanies the deployment of network economies in post-industrial societies:

> In a network world, where the more unpredictable and remote connections are, the more likely they are to prove profitable, the class *habitus*, on which the spontaneous convergence of taste relies in predominantly domestic social orders, is no longer a sufficient support for intuition or flair. On the contrary, the great man is he who establishes links between beings who are not only removed from one another, located in different universes, but also distant from his social background and the circle of his immediate relations.[52]

Juliette and Justine correspond perfectly to the dichotomy between the strong and the weak in a connectionist world. One sets out to explore a new world and subsequently moves unencumbered from one social group to another, while the other relies on domestic allies who reject her. The original opposition between vice and virtue unfolds into an opposition between prostitution and sexual restraint, between the world of global exchanges and movement and the local world of stagnation.

As we have seen, what separates one life from the other is Juliette's affinity for a new economy of venality, one that supersedes the traditional economy of prostitution in which the bodies of women of lower birth are consumed by well-off men. This new economy requires full engagement – body and soul – from its participants, but in return the sexual marketplace is no longer kept separate from other sites of social exchange. There is now a natural continuity between the world of prostitution and the world of the noble elite: in fact, venality seems to characterize a whole set of relationships and connections that are more open and fluid. The economy of venality, as it is portrayed by Juliette, subverts and redefines gender and social expectations: the rich and powerful are willing to sell themselves as a way to preserve their mobility; women take advantage of men – to gain wealth and prestige – at least as much as men take advantage of them sexually; and finally, status is no longer solely dependent on birth or wealth. For characters like Juliette, venality offers the possibility to take on new identities when needed, depending on the connections that seem most profitable.

The story of Juliette's transformation into a shrewd manager of her body and of her interests in *Les Infortunes de la vertu* and *Justine, ou les Malheurs de la vertu* provides an alternative narrative of feminine success and liberation, a narrative that will be revised, refined and complicated in *Histoire de Juliette*. Sade's new economy of venality retools the traditional sexual contracts of patriarchy into new forms of exploitation in which gender roles are interchangeable and in which women are not systematically subjected to the position of the exploited.[53] In reimagining venal relations through the character of Juliette, Sade also makes an interesting hypothesis about the nature of social identity in the late eighteenth century, one that Boltanski and Chiapello's analysis of the new spirit of capitalism helps us uncover. Throughout her social rise, Juliette takes on several identities, but she remains a character with little substance: the few narratorial comments explaining how the heroine chooses perversion and vice over virtue hardly conceal the fact that she is almost entirely defined by what she does and who she associates with. Boltanski and Chiapello suggests that in a connectionist world, existence itself is a relational attribute: 'every entity, and human persons by the same token as the rest, exists to a greater or lesser extent depending upon the number and value of the connections that pass via it', or, to put it differently, 'they are themselves only because they are the links that constitute them'.[54] Juliette's journey points to ontological possibilities that go beyond a critique of patriarchal contracts and traditional forms of prostitution. And even if, in the end, this form of liberation from systemic constraints is not limited to female characters in *Les infortunes de la vertu* or *Justine, ou les malheurs de la vertu*, it is first introduced through a new economy of venality in which identities cannot be essentialized according to birth, levels of wealth, occupation or gender expectations. In short, the 'libertine whore' is not alienated from her body and reduced to the substantial identity of the common prostitute with the social and moral stigmas attached to it.

Relational ontologies are a central characteristic of Sade's fictional depiction of prostitution in the last years of the Ancien Régime. If they help us rethink the nature of prostitution in relation to old hierarchies and new networks, they also provide new ways of sketching a Sadean theory of action that anticipates not only the social structures of network economies but also a new sociological paradigm which would

> replac[e] essentialist ontologies with open spaces, without borders, centres or fixed points, where entities are constituted by the relations they enter into and alter in line with the flows, transfers, exchanges, permutations, and displacements that are the relevant events in this space.[55]

Sade's political economy in the shorter and earlier novels that I have focused on in this article is that of a radical empiricist who conceives of action and identities not as absolutes but as flows. As I have suggested elsewhere, longer novels like *La Nouvelle Justine* or *Histoire de Juliette* have a very different narrative structure and simply alternate between long philosophical tirades on the necessity of evil in the world and pornographic tableaux.[56] We often forget, however, that before becoming a structuralist with a repetitive view of how economic structures limit individual possibilities, Sade outlines an original and daring vision of the social world, a 'new spirit of capitalism' of sorts that can be brought to light through the insights of the sociology of post-industrial network societies.

10 FIGURING THE LONDON MAGDALEN HOUSE: MERCANTILIST HOSPITAL, SENTIMENTAL ASYLUM OR PROTO-EVANGELICAL PENITENTIARY?

Mary Peace

When the London Magdalen Hospital for Penitent Prostitutes first opened its doors in August 1758, the institution was a striking novelty. Jonas Hanway, founding father and well-known social reformer, spoke for the more general public response to the project when he stated that 'no subject, has come before us, for a long time, so *new* as this, and yet so *interesting*'.[1] The institution's distinctiveness lay in its commitment to the idea that prostitutes were victims of their situation, and were reformable. The novelty of this reform agenda was evident from William Dodd's inaugural sermon in the Magdalen Hospital chapel, where he described how the charity had met with ridicule on the grounds that reforming prostitutes was a 'scheme to wash Aethiopians white'.[2] The founders of the London Magdalen Hospital, drawing on the continental Catholic tradition of Magdalen homes for reformed prostitutes, instituted a signal transformation of the figure of the prostitute in British culture. From vilified agent of moral and social contamination, the prostitute had become a virtuous and recuperable victim of circumstance.

The new representation of the prostitute had been gaining currency in sentimental and charitable literature over the previous decades, but it is clear that the practical commitment to the idea which the establishment of a Magdalen Hospital represented and the great support which it went on to enjoy from the polite public in the following decades marked a radical cultural shift. What is not quite so clear is how to interpret this shift. The literary critics and cultural historians who have focused on this moment over the past thirty years have been far from unanimous in their understanding of how to read this institution. Should the Magdalen be read as part of a radical Enlightenment programme of social amelioration or as a conservative chapter in women's history; as a mercantilist hospital or a sentimental asylum or a proto-Evangelical penitentiary? This essay surveys the critical territory to tease out the ideological complexities that make these conflicting interpretations possible.

Mercantilism, Sentimentalism and Evangelicalism

The Magdalen institution figures variously in the literature of the mid-century as a 'Place', a 'House', a 'Hospital', a 'Charity' and an 'Asylum'. These terms are often used apparently interchangeably, even in the same passage.[3] Yet they bring with them distinct ideological beliefs about the nature of prostitutes and mark out the contours of the critically disputed territory. The terms 'hospital' and 'asylum' are most significant here. At the mid-eighteenth century, hospital is predominantly a place of physical recuperation: the Lock Hospital and the Foundling Hospital – the most obvious precedents for the Magdalen – were, respectively, a place for the treatment of venereal disease and a place where orphans were offered physical support and training. The emergence of such hospitals has been understood by historians as a mercantilist response to the general sense that the population of Britain was static and perhaps even declining. The economist Adam Smith coined the term 'mercantile' in *The Wealth of Nations* (1776) to describe the dominant economic thinking of the preceding century: the belief that 'a great nation' should enrich itself 'rather by trade and manufactures than by the improvement and cultivation of land'.[4] And to this end, Smith argued, 'a great empire' had been 'established for the sole purpose of raising up a nation of customers who should be obliged to buy from the shops of our different producers'.[5] The forging and maintaining of this empire took manpower, but contemporary political economists argued that the population of Britain was falling. Mercantilist thinking was therefore deeply concerned with questions of how to stimulate population growth and to recover industry from idleness. These problems were perceived to be particularly acute in the middle of the century, around the outbreak the Seven Years' War in 1756. The Magdalen institution, like the Lock and the Foundling, can be read as a hospital because, as Jennie Batchelor and Megan Hiatt have argued, it promised to return 'un (re) productive' bodies to a life of virtuous industry. It would transform barren prostitutes into industrious workers and productive mothers. The rehabilitation of prostitutes became 'a vital part of the war effort, as vital even in Hanway's words, as "the *arduous* affairs of war"'.[6]

An asylum, on the other hand, is more a place of retreat from a vicious or dangerous world; it is not transformative and will not necessarily facilitate a move back out into the world. The idea of an asylum can be traced to contemporary sentimental discourse. Eighteenth-century sentimental thought was predicated on the idea that men and women are naturally in possession of a delicate moral sense, and that this might be either cultivated or stifled by experience of the world. In this discourse, prostitutes are imagined as victims of a corrupt world and their own naturally refined sensibilities. The Magdalen institution, in sentimental discourse, was figured as an asylum for women who had been tricked into prostitution (loosely defined) and become social outcasts. In the words of William Dodd, the notoriously sentimental preacher at the Magdalen House chapel:

> the nobleness of virtue, and the delicacy of sentiment, have been rather canker'd over, than blotted out: and upon the first remove of the filth, have shewn themselves in particulars, which would do honour to the most exalted state and ideas.[7]

The question of what kind of institution the Magdalen House was is further complicated by the general concensus that by the 1790s the institution had fallen into the hands of the Evangelicals. In stark contrast to the sentimental commitment to the idea of human nature as essentially good, the Evangelicals viewed human nature as essentially depraved and believed all social improvement should be predicated on 'individual moral reform and conversion'.[8] Under Evangelical management the Magdalen became, to all intents and purposes, a penitentiary. Indeed one of the definitions offered by the *Oxford English Dictionary* for the term 'penitentiary' from 1806 is specifically 'a refuge for "fallen women"'. Of course the Magdalen had always been concerned with 'penitent' prostitutes, but a 'penitentiary', as the *OED* suggests, was not just about penitence but about punishment, and this marks a clear difference from the mid-century talk of reforming prostitutes and/or removing the filth, 'by which these women had been "canker'd"'. For the Evangelicals, as Hannah More's 1796 tale 'The Story of Sinful Sally' demonstrates, once fallen, the prostitute's virtue was deemed irretrievable in this world: prostitutes could not be recuperated for earthly productivity, nor did they deserve an asylum from a corrupt world, rather they had to be quarantined from it and look only to heaven. The full title of Hannah More's story is indicative of this argument: *The Story of Sinful Sally Told by Herself. Shewing how from being Sally of the Green she was first led to become Sinful Sally, and afterwards Drunken Sal, and how at last she came to a most melancholy end; being therein a warning to all young women both in town and country.* This Evangelical view is reflected in the changes in institutional practice at the Magdalen at the end of the century. The 1790s saw the appointment, for the first time, of a full-time Chaplain at the Magdalen and the abandonment of the vocational skills training for the women. From then on the inmates were employed instead in laundry-work.[9] In the words of the historian Joseph Bristow, by the 1790s it had become a 'sanctimonious sweatshop'.[10] The question then arises as to how far the seeds of this later Evangelical institution were present in the ideological formation of the charity when it was established in the mid-eighteenth century.

In light of the recent critical debate this essay will reconsider the institution at the mid-century as it figured both in the plan which provided the blueprint for its foundation in 1758 and in the anonymous *The Histories of Some of the Penitents in the Magdalen House* (1759); a novel published a year after the establishment of the institution in order to promote the cause of the charity. I will argue that it is not possible to separate out these discourses, or indeed these genres, as cleanly as some historians and literary critics have been keen to do, and that there is, in particular, a far more complicated relationship between the radical sentimental professions of the mid-century and the Evangelical strictures of the 1790s than has been acknowledged. In practical terms the sentimentality of the mid-century institution can be seen to have paved the way for its Evangelical future and indeed, as I will discuss later on, there is a whole strand of feminist literary critical writing which has assumed a definite affiliation between sentimental ideas and Evangelical ideas. But my contention here is that the process by which Magdalen Hospital became more Evangelical proceeded not from ideological continuity between two sets of ideas, but from ideological discontinuity; from the impossibility of aligning the increasingly utopian radicalism of sentimental ideas with any kind of practical reality. Indeed, far from representing an incipient movement towards the Evangelicals, I would suggest that the sentimental literature in which the Magdalen was embedded left a far clearer legacy to the radical novelists of the 1790s such as the Marys Wollstonecraft and Mary Hays.

The Critical Debate

Recent historical and literary debates on the Magdalen Hospital start out with different concerns and come to different conclusions. In the debate among historians the Magdalen is predominantly understood as a hospital. Historians such as Roy Porter, James Taylor and Donna Andrew look at the Magdalen Hospital in the context of the mercantilist charities that emerged in the middle part of the eighteenth century. Their argument hinges upon the extent to which the hospital can be read as a measure of the progress of Enlightenment secularism. Sentimental ideas here are associated with a proto-Victorian religiosity and often the more sentimental aspects of the institution are dismissed as public relations and not fundamentally constitutive of the character of the institution. The literary debate, on the other hand, engages much more closely with the politics of the sentimental literature which surrounded the institution and considers the extent to which the institution represents either a radical or a repressive force in women's history.

Roy Porter typifies the historical debate in his recent cultural history of the British Enlightenment. Here he argues that the establishment of foundation hospitals in the first half of the eighteenth century is a striking illustration of the increased secularization of society. Medieval hospitals had been hospices, 'holy places of "hospitality" for the needy, setting the good death and salvation above surgery'. By contrast, 'the new foundations were centres of care and treatment for the sick and poor'.[11] The Magdalen charity, as one of the 'new foundations', is for Porter a place predominantly of bodily care and not spiritual salvation. This view is corroborated by the historian James Taylor in his study of Jonas Hanway, a philanthropist who helped establish the Magdalen charity. Taylor acknowledges the 'puritan piety' and 'benevolence' in Hanway's philanthropy, but insists that his prime motive was mercantilist. Hanway was, Taylor argues, more than anything interested in '[h]ow lives could be saved and trained to the national good': 'No question in Hanway's writings was more consistently raised or pursued than this, for on the answer, he believed, depended England's well-being in relation to mercantile and military dangers from without'. The Magdalen Hospital project spoke to Hanway's concerns because it would transform prostitutes – in mercantilist terms both economically and reproductively barren – into industrious workers and productive mothers. Indeed, Taylor argues, Hanway was so focused on this political end in his charitable work that he found it preferable, on balance, to see a high birth rate, than to see all births take place within wedlock.[12] Individual moral virtue, Taylor argues, was ultimately less important to Hanway than general economic prosperity and military success. Taylor thus distances Hanway and his projects from the rise of sentimental ideas that excited the interest of the charitable in the middle of the eighteenth century. He concedes that the rhetoric surrounding Hanway's first major project, the Foundling Hospital, may have been sentimental, but suggests that it was 'the businesslike approach' that Hanway employed, rather than 'a more sentimental or religious approach' that was the foundation on which he built the success of the charities.[13] For Taylor, Hanway was a full-blooded mercantilist with the thinnest coating of humanitarianism and piety, and he follows other historians in characterizing the Magdalen as predominantly a mercantilist hospital.

In the literary debate, on the other hand, the Magdalen charity has been read as a profoundly sentimental institution and there has been a focus on the extent to which this represents a conservative chapter in women's history. Initial feminist literary interest in sentimental discourse and the Magdalen institution saw the institution as shaped predominantly by sentimental narratives and identified these narratives as fundamentally conservative. For Vivien Jones, in her influential 1995 essay 'Scandalous Femininity', these sentimental narratives are part of a 'middle-class programme of sexual regulation'.[14] She argues they should be read in contrast to more radical visions of femininity such as those found in the scandalous memoirs of mid-eighteenth-century figures such as Teresia Contantia Phillips. Jennie Batchelor broadly agrees with this analysis in her 2004 essay '"Industry in Distress"'. Here she distinguishes between the enlightened mercantilist emphasis of some of the original plans for the institution and the more conservative sentimental form that the institution eventually took. In the more mercantilist plans Batchelor traces 'the emergence of the female labourer as a vital and active agent in the nation's moral and political economy'.[15] Yet this radical mercantilist vision has, she acknowledges, a much weaker presence in Dingley's more sentimental plan, which provided the final blueprint for the institution. And she argues that those elements of this celebration of female labour which did find their way into the Magdalen institution were ultimately destroyed by an increasing emphasis, in the sentimental narratives which powered the institution, on the 'virtuous working woman' as an 'object of pity'.[16] For Batchelor, the mercantilist narrative is progressive in terms of its representation of women, but it is the sentimental narrative which predominantly dictates the shape of the Magdalen charity, and which proves ultimately regressive by placing women firmly in the private sphere.

Katherine Binhammer also accepts the profoundly sentimental nature of the Magdalen institution in *The Seduction Narrative* (2009), but she takes issue with the idea that the sentimental narratives that pervaded and surrounded the charity were a conservative force. These '[s]tories of virtuous young women who are seduced, abandoned and ruined by evil, libertine men', Binhammer states, have been read as reflecting 'the growing fetishization of female virtue and … [the disciplining] of female readers not to have desires, not to go out in public, not to marry without familial consent'.[17] However although Binhammer accepts that this narrative emerged in the nineteenth century as a fully-fledged 'domestic woman narrative', in its mid-eighteenth-century incarnation, she argues, it showed some very different potential. The Victorian 'Angel-in-the-House' was not 'always already the inevitable outcome of a gender ideology in flux during the eighteenth century'.[18] Rather she argues, the sentimental seduction narrative staged a 'historical contestation over what it might mean for women to have a right to feel love and erotic desire for their conjugal mate'.[19]

In her contribution to this collection Jennie Batchelor explores further the more radical proto-feminist implications of the sentimental narrative that surrounds the charity at the mid-century. Batchelor is still wary of characterizing the institution itself as anything other than oppressive in its practical operation, but she identifies a much more radical sentimental narrative in the novel which was written to promote the institution in 1759: *The Histories of Some of the Penitents in the Magdalen House*. Here she argues, there is an insistence not only that fallen woman can still be virtuous, but in particular that fallen women can still be good mothers: an insistence that clearly destabilizes the reductive 'virgin/mother/whore' triad, which Vivien Jones has argued 'defines femininity within modernity'.[20] Batchelor and Binhammer represent an attempt in recent years to wrest the sentimental narratives that surrounded and facilitated the Magdalen institution at the mid-century from the clutches of the 'domestic woman thesis', which characterizes sentimental narrative at the end of the century.

My own work to date has been hesitant about characterizing the Magdalen at the mid-century as predominantly either a mercantilist or a sentimental institution, but has attempted to explore the relationship between these competing discourses both in terms of social policy and literature. In particular I have been concerned to tease out the ideological knot of mid-century sentimentalism by looking at this discourse as a spectrum characterized at each extreme by apparently opposing ideas. At one extreme is the Humean idea that all individuals are born with a moral sense that is refined by social and cultural commerce and which, in its refined state, provides a bulwark against the excesses that an increasingly luxurious society is imagined to bring in its wake. This version shares with mercantilism a commitment to the transformative power of education. At the other extreme, sentimental discourse is characterized by the more Rousseauian idea that sensibility is a delicate plant that is not refined by commerce with the world and can survive only in asylum from it. The period from the 1740s to 1770s I have argued, sees the centre of gravity shift very decidedly from one end of the spectrum to the other.[21] And in relation to the Magdalen institution, this shift can be seen in an ever-diminishing overlap between sentimental discourse and the mercantilist discourse with which it coexisted at its foundation; between the asylum and the hospital.

My work follows Binhammer and Batchelor in identifying a rupture between the sentimental character of the Magdalen Hospital at the mid-century and the Evangelical reformation of the institution in the 1790s as a penitentiary. Indeed, it would seem perverse not to see a rupture between an institution that insisted on the essentially virtuous nature of its objects and one which insisted that their objects were irremediably sullied. Yet, I have also always been exercised by the obvious links between the mid-century supporters of the institution and the Evangelical governors of the 1790. Take, for example, the Evangelical father and son, John and Henry Thornton, where John was a founding member of the charity and Henry a governor in the 1790s. And the case of *The Histories of Some of the Penitents* (1759) is similarly intriguing. Though the exact authorship is unknown, it is clear that the novel emerged in a loose sense out of the Bluestocking circle; a society renowned at the mid-century at least as much for its radical vision as for its piety and philanthropy, but which could produce from its ranks that key Evangelical figure of the late century, Hannah More.[22] I do not want to argue that the sentimentalism of the mid-century facilitated its late century Evangelical incarnation. But I do want to think about how the increasingly radical and utopian trajectory of the sentimental narrative at the mid-century left the charity vulnerable to an Evangelical agenda.

Mercantilist Hospital vs Sentimental Asylum

The key question to be addressed, then, is the extent to which the Magdalen institution, as envisioned and established in the 1750s, was either a mercantilist hospital or a sentimental asylum? At one level, the answer to this question is clear: the Magdalen institution was established as a result of a competition, and there was one winning plan.[23] Roughly speaking, the plans submitted to the competition divide into two camps: those which are distinguished above all by their sentimental approach to the issue of prostitution, and those which are distinguished predominantly by mercantilist ideas. Those of John Fielding (Henry Fielding's magistrate half-brother), Saunders Welch (a London magistrate), and Joseph Massie (a political economist) broadly fall into the mercantilist category. They are not predominantly interested in the moral qualities of the individual prostitute but are concerned to 'manage' the problem of prostitution, and to reform the behaviour of prostitutes in order to turn social miscreants into productive citizens. Other plans, such as those advocated by the merchants Robert Dingley and Jonas Hanway, were predominantly sentimental. They proceed from the conviction that men and women are naturally in possession of a delicate moral sense, but that this may have been either cultivated or stifled depending on their experience in the world. In his plan Dingley imagined that by 'far the greater part of them [prostitutes], having taken to this dreadful way of life ... not of choice, but through fatal necessity' would readily embrace the opportunity of a new life. Dingley represents prostitutes as the greatest 'Objects of Compassion', and he imagines them typically as 'thoughtless Females, plunged into ruin by those temp[t]ations, to which their very youth and personal advantages exposes them'.[24] The Magdalen Hospital, Dingley imagined, would offer these 'unfortunate' women a sanctuary and alternative to an otherwise inevitable descent into prostitution.

The competing plans do in places overlap. Hanway's plan, for example, though predominantly sentimental, refers to his hopes that his scheme for the reformation of prostitutes will encourage the growth of population through marriage, while Saunders Welch, though predominantly mercantilist, refers in a sentimental moment to how he had 'often wished with an aching heart that there was among the noble charities, which distinguish this age ... one instituted by the legislature ... for these true objects of compassion'.[25] It is clear, however, that the authors of these plans believed themselves to have distinctly different approaches, to such an extent that Hanway attempted to veto the committee's initial decision to award the prize to the mercantilist Saunders Welch. Hanway prevailed on the fifty-one strong committee, which included many well-known names including David Garrick, Samuel Johnson, and John Wilkes, not to award the prize to Welch. It was, therefore, Dingley's more sentimental proposal that formed the practical and ideological ground-plan for the first London Magdalen Hospital.[26] The sentimental aspects of the institution were intrinsic to its foundation.

Dingley's sentimental approach to prostitution clearly emphasized the spiritual needs of the prostitute in a way which marks the Magdalen out from some of the other mid-century charities. The project was structured around a moral idealism about the nature of women, which is a far cry from the political pragmatism that is the defining feature of the mid-century hospitals, and of Hanway himself in Taylor's account. Indeed, Hanway explicitly states that he abhors the cynical pragmatism of the Welch's more mercantilist plan, even if, as he half acknowledges, it may represent a better knowledge of the world. In a direct challenge to Welch he states: 'A close adherence to some political principles, however well grounded in observation, not only *depreciates* human nature, but betrays us into an opinion, that our *efforts* to obey the laws of God, in certain instances, are *romantic* and ridiculous'.[27] The Magdalen, as I have argued elsewhere, is a distinctly idealistic enterprise.[28]

This is not to argue, however, that the Magdalen institute as it was established in 1758 was merely a sanctuary or an asylum. Batchelor and Hiatt are right to insist that both in its plan and in its physical incarnation it functioned as a mercantilist hospital intended to render its inmates both suitable both for the world but also to restore them to virtue. It was both hospital and asylum. 'The women', as Batchelor and Hiatt have described:

> were subjected to strictly regulated sixteen-hour daily routine of work and prayer, during which they were instructed in the skills needed to qualify them for service or to fit them for an apprenticeship in one of the dress-making trades. Once they had been in the Magdalen House for three years, the penitents were either released to friends or sent into service, to 'any housekeeper of sufficient credit' who would take them.[29]

One can attribute the hybrid representations of the Hospital at the mid-century to the competing ideologies of mercantilism and sentimentality from which it emerged, but one can also, as I suggested earlier, read this very tension in the discourse of sentimentality itself: in the contradictory nature of a discourse which in the 1750s looks both to the Humean idea that the moral sense might be refined and improved by an engagement with the world, and to the Rousseauian idea that a refined sensibility somehow precedes the world and cannot survive uncorrupted. This is a distinction that Roy Porter identifies in his chapter on sentimental ideas, between 'good sense' and 'sensibility', and which John Mullan has persuasively mapped onto the trajectory of Richardson's fiction in the course of the 1740s.[30] In *Pamela*, sensibility, though always native, can be improved by the world, and can in turn improve the world; in *Clarissa,* sensibility cannot survive uncorrupted in the world and is not an effective agent of reform. Broadly speaking the discourse of sentiment finds Enlightenment optimism and Romantic pessimism yoked together in the same harness, but pulling in different directions. This ambiguity characterizes the Magdalen Hospital at the mid-century. And if the Humean aspects of sentimental discourse pull backwards towards the mercantilist projects of the Enlightenment, the Rousseauian Romantic aspects pull not exactly towards an Evangelical future but in the direction of an impossibly radical idealism which cannot support a practical institution without the supplement of Evangelicalism. In other words, the sentimental story is increasingly one in which 'the natural delicacy of sentiment' will need to be protected from the world, and which is increasingly pessimistic about the possibility that it will ever thrive back in the world.

Asylum to Penitentiary: *The Histories of Some of the Penitents in the Magdalen House*

The dual character of the Magdalen as mercantilist hospital and sentimental asylum, and the ultimate irreconcilability of these two aspects, is demonstrated particularly clearly in *The Histories of Some of the Penitents in the Magdalen House*. The novel was published in 1759 to promote the Magdalen charity. Batchelor and Hiatt have argued in their recent introduction to *The Histories of the Penitents* that it is 'strikingly different to other meditations on prostitution produced by reformers'.[31] They have suggested, in particular, that it does not treat the individuals as 'objects' but listens at length to their stories and that it places much more of an emphasis on female community.[32] *The Histories of the Penitents* is, I agree, strikingly different to the mercantilist accounts of prostitution which dominated the rejected plans for the Magdalen Hospital, but what becomes clear when one takes into consideration the different emphases inevitably produced by genres as distinct as the novel and the charitable proposal is that the *The Histories of the Penitents* is written across the same ideological faultline as that of Dingley's *Proposals*: that it dramatizes the tensions between the mercantilist hospital and the sentimental asylum aspects of the Magdalen.

Like Dingley's *Proposals*, the novel proceeds from the sentimental premise that prostitutes are victims of society. Dingley's description of prostitutes as 'Objects of Compassion' finds a distinct echo in the preface to the *The Histories of the Penitents* where the author asks if there can be any 'objects so miserable, consequently so deserving of compassion, as those for whose relief this institution is designed'.[33] And both texts subscribe to the idea that prostitutes are victims of circumstance, although where the novel explicitly asserts the sentimental belief that everyone, including prostitutes 'esteems virtue, tho' temptations may lead them to neglect the practice of it', the *Proposals* is a little less sanguine. The Magdalens are 'poor, young, thoughtless Females, plunged into ruin by those temp[t]ations, to which their very youth and personal advantages exposes them'. In both texts they are victims but where the novel stresses the essential virtue of these women, the *Proposals* suggests only their inexperience. The implication in *The Histories of the Penitents* that the Magdalens will be in some sense more essentially virtuous and full of sensibility than their respectable sisters.[34] This implication is not present in the *Proposals*. The charitable proposal suggests a more Humean sentimental model than the novel; a model in which innocence, betrayed by the world, can be restored through education, rather than a Rousseauian model in which virtue, misunderstood, must be protected from the world.

Yet both texts do to some extent invoke the Humean version of sentimentality that shares common ground with mercantilism. In both, the reader is invited to understand the institution as a tribute to the compassion that commerce and refinement have generated in the modern age. Dingley insists in his *Proposals*, for example, that 'Numbers ... amongst my Countrymen, famed through every nation for their extreme Humanity, will readily and gladly bear a part in so benevolent a Design, and rejoice to promote an undertaking that will be a Blessing to the Commonwealth, and an Honour to human nature'.[35] And these sentiments are clearly echoed in the preface to the *The Histories of the Penitents* where the Magdalen is described as 'an institution which does so much honour to the present age; [and] which will reflect never-fading glory on those who instituted it'.[36] Indeed, taking, as it does, the form of a novel, *The Histories of the Penitents*, like the plan for the institution itself, clearly subscribes to the idea that individuals can be refined and implicitly reformed by their engagement with cultural institutions, and that through reading the histories of these women our compassion for their plight will be awakened. The intention is made explicit in the anonymous narrator's assertion that she will esteem herself 'peculiarly happy if [she] can have any share in preventing one person from standing in need of penitence'.[37]

The landscape of Dingley's plan and *The Histories of the Penitents* is therefore not, I think, as significantly different as Batchelor has suggested, although the demands of the novel do lead to a distinct difference of emphasis in the representation of the Magdalens. The 'thoughtless' reformable girls of the plan become, in the novel, girls with acute natural sensibility who have been corrupted and require asylum from the world. The argument of the novel lies much closer to the Rousseauian end of the sentimental spectrum. There is a more acute emphasis on exceptionally refined sensibilities of the fallen women whose stories it relates, and a more radical emphasis on their essential virtue, despite their unfortunate circumstances. But in parallel with this, there is a greater sense of their unsuitability for the world, of their absolute need for an asylum. The Magdalens in this novel are quixotic and idealized romantic heroines. The novel tempts the reader to identify with these figures and even to read these figures as more virtuous, in their reliance on their refined sensibilities, than their more dutiful contemporaries. In this it prefigures Rousseau's *La Nouvelle Héloïse* and the 1790s novels by disaffected radicals created in its wake, such as Wollstonecraft's *Maria, and the Wrongs of Women* and Hays's *The Memoirs of Emma Courtney*. *The Histories of the Penitents* has a radical heart that, as Jennie Batchelor argues in this collection, argues not only that a fallen woman may be virtuous, but that, in an ideal sense, she has even more virtue than a chaste woman.

Delicacy of sensibility is the supreme characteristic of the four Magdalens in the *The Histories of the Penitents*. Of the first penitent, Emily, the reader is told from the outset that her 'nature is superior' to any offences against 'honesty, or sincerity' but that she has 'tenderness of heart' which may make her susceptible to the snares of the world.[38] The second penitent has a delicacy of sentiment which makes her an outsider and a victim in the worldly aristocratic household in which she finds herself. She has a 'delicate conscience' and it is this, rather than her sexual fall that lays her open to being unprovided for in the world, and which forces her into prostitution and then the Magdalen Hospital. The third penitent, like Emily, has a sensibility that naturally leads her to shy away from the moral laxity of the brothel she is staying in, even though she believes the Madam to be her real mother and wants to follow her advice dutifully. The fourth is a thoroughly Romantic soul whose sensibility shudders at the mercenary marriage proposed to her by her father. All three of the penitents who bear children are shown to have an acute maternal sensibility; and all display a delicacy of taste that prefers elegant simplicity to decadent display.

Sensibility is undoubtedly a highly prized moral attribute in this text, but it is also very clear that we are not to understand it as a sufficient virtue in itself, at least in terms of this world. Indeed, in the case of these penitents, it is most frequently a contributing factor in their fall. For the three mothers it is the extent of their maternal sensibility which forces them into prostitution; moreover the refined sensibilities of these women leave them a prey to the machinations of selfish plotters. When Emily, for example, is spontaneously lent money to pay off her debts by an old woman who turns out then to be a bawd, she says 'I thought that, in the same situation, I should have done like her; and therefore was grateful, but not surprised'.[39] Emily's sister turns out to have been right in predicting that Emily will be as much in danger 'from the tenderness of ... [her] heart' as from 'the snares that will be laid in her way'.[40] Moreover sensibility is shown in itself to be very little different to amorous love. When, the third penitent, Fanny, goes to live with the Lafew family she is inspired, by love for the husband, to the most extravagant acts of benevolence to the family, risking her life to save one of his children. Here the tender sensibilities of both parties lead them very swiftly into the bedroom. Sensibility, the novel suggests, is an exquisite moral attribute, and one can certainly not be esteemed, in this novel, without it, but it is not sufficient, in its own right as an instrument for guiding one through the world. For this one needs religion. When Emily is forced to choose between becoming a prostitute in a brothel or having her child taken away from her, her moral 'delicacy' does not, as it should, lead her to the correct decision in religious terms. Emily prefers prostitution to losing her child, and the reader is very clearly made aware that this is because Emily's actions are dictated by sentimental 'delicacy', and not as she calls it 'the sacred one of virtue'.[41]

The Rousseauian sentimental narrative, in which sensibility has become an inadequate moral compass in the world, provided an opening for Evangelical religious ideas. Alongside the mercantilist statement in the Preface about the importance of restoring these women 'to industry and order [to] render them useful members of society', there are statements that prefigure the institution's Evangelical future.[42] The Preface explains that 'No person will dispute the use of Hospitals which are instituted for the relief of corporal distempers; but of much higher benefit is that intended to heal the soul; and not only to abate temporary pains, but to save from eternal torments'.[43] The sentimental emphasis on morality over practicality, on asylum over hospital, paradoxically, paves the way for the Evangelicalization of the Magdalen Charity in the 1790s.

Nonetheless, *The Histories of the Penitents,* like Rousseau's *La Nouvelle Héloïse*, offers some very persuasive images of a more radical way of living, which the religious frame of the novel largely fails to contain, and which point much more to the writings of Wollstonecraft and Mary Hays, than to Hannah More. The description, for example, of the relationship between the second penitent and Mr. Senwill, is highly seductive. She says:

> I lived with Mr. Senwill in great tranquility, full of confidence in his love, his generosity, and his honour. He possessed a delicacy of mind, and a gentleness of manners, which rendered him peculiarly amiable. He suffered for every mortification that I received, and was delighted with every incident that gave me pleasure. I had, I believe, less passion for him than I felt for Mr Monkerton, but much more tenderness. The one had captivated my fancy, and amused my mind ... But my judgement applauded all my sentiments for Mr. Senwill; without intoxicating my fancy, he gained my whole soul[44]

The reader cannot then help being bruised when this happy but unconsecrated relationship is severed by the marriage of Mr Senwill to a respectable woman, brokered by his father. The Magdalens of *The Histories of the Penitents* are quixotic heroines. They make mistakes and fall from innocence but, like Arabella in Lennox's *Female Quixote,* the reader is left as much with the impression that in an ideal world their virtues would be the truest ones, as one is left with the sense that they need to reform themselves for the world. Indeed the novel is threaded through with references to romance and quixotism. Significantly, those who complain of the romantic notions of the penitents are often the most vicious characters. It is the despicable brothelkeeper who says to Emily when she invokes the law, 'Dost thou take lawyers for knights errant, who have nothing to do but to deliver distressed damsels? Know, that money only can obtain justice; those who cannot buy must go without it'.[45] The novel, implicitly, has a great deal of time for romance and idealism.

Moreover the narrative offers scant rewards and even in places sympathy for those who dutifully submit to conventional morality and pragmatism. Emily's older sister is a clear example. She submits to reason and duty, and makes a conventional marriage. But the marriage allows her very little autonomy, she is entirely dependent on her husband for money, she has to manage his moods, and she is prevented from following her heartfelt impulse to succour her sister in her hour of need.[46] There may, it is true, be a strong implication that the sister's rewards will be in heaven, and yet the reader is left not so much with a sense of the rightness of religion, but of the greater beauty of sentiment. And the second penitent's dutiful and disfigured sister seems to merit neither rewards nor sympathy on this earth. The ugly sister warns her that 'one leg, which hobbled constantly in the road of oeconomy and notability, was preferable to any two that were ever gadding abroad to places where flattery abounded'.[47] Yet even when the ugly sister has been proved right, and the second penitent has fallen, the heart of the novel still beats for her. It is the second penitent who finds herself in a relationship with Mr Senwill. The narrative is very unforgiving to the dutiful but disabled daughter. When the two sisters meet at the theatre it turns out that the only reward the sister has reaped for her dutiful behaviour is a marriage with her father's apprentice. But the reader is not asked to feel sympathy for her, but rather disdain, as she first acts ungenerously to her fallen sister, and then is spitefully jealous when it seems that she is married.

Indeed, although the frame of the novel contains a discussion about how one should read the moral argument of the novel, and not be carried away by the sentiment, the presence of the latter prompts the reader to much more radical conclusions about the world. The author of the Preface concludes by stating that

> Many have given directions to the world how to read history ... If I may be permitted to be so methodical, upon that species of writing which seems generally to owe its rise to the wild wanderings of that wildest of things, the imagination; I will venture to give direction for the reading of Novels ...
>
> The method, therefore that I would recommend to those who apply themselves to this sort of reading, is, to attend to the Moral as much as to the Story.[48]

Sentimental narrative, generally in this period, and particularly in this least worldly, most Rousseauian guise, implies the need for a moral framework which might provide an effective compass for navigating the world. It is here that one can see how sentimentalism overlaps with proto-Evangelical religion. However, this sentimentalism also leaves a radical legacy, demonstrating that it is the world that is wrong and not the heroines who fall foul of it: this form of sentimentalism leads both to Mary Wollstonecraft and Hannah More.

In conclusion, I want to suggest that the Magdalen is both hospital and asylum at the mid-century, and that these two apparently incompatible facets are for a time almost contained by the Janus-like nature of the sentimental discourse through which it was conceived, imagined and marketed. I want to suggest, further, that the gradual shift in emphasis in sentimental discourse during the course of the century ultimately fractured this precarious alliance. The cultural shift that saw sentimentalism migrate from being an attribute predominantly understood as something which might be polished and improved by the things of the world, to being an attribute which needs protecting from the corruption of the world, creates an unbridgeable rift between the hospital and the asylum.

11 MOTHERS AND OTHERS: SEXUALITY AND MATERNITY IN *THE HISTORIES OF SOME OF THE PENITENTS IN THE MAGDALEN-HOUSE* (1760)[1]

Jennie Batchelor

The crucial role that the prostitute played in the construction of bourgeois femininity in the second half of the eighteenth century has received considerable scholarly attention. Accounts of this uneasy relationship have traditionally focused upon the prostitute's symbolic function as the domestic woman's degraded other: a figure against which virtuous femininity and sexuality were defined and upon whose abjection the middle-ranking woman's respectability was parasitically dependent.[2] More recent studies, such as those by Katherine Binhammer, Ruth Perry and Laura J. Rosenthal, have painted a more complex picture that emphasizes the disquieting similarities that eighteenth-century commentators observed between whore and wife and between sex for money and the legalized prostitution that was, in Binhammer's words, 'mercenary marriage'.[3] If, as Perry suggests, it became increasingly difficult by the mid-eighteenth century 'to mention wives without mentioning prostitutes or prostitutes without mentioning wives', then it was, in part, because the prostitute spoke to readers' fears about themselves as much as to their fears of others.[4] Although, as Rosenthal argues, prostitutes were, in many ways, 'set apart from other women' throughout the period, 'in other ways, however, they came to seem more and more like everyone else'.[5] Testifying to the pressures under which virtue and selfhood were put by a modern, commercial society, the prostitute was not only subject to anxious displacement, but also a provocation to uncomfortable self-recognition.

Discussions of the prostitute's dual function as other and double of bourgeois domesticity have elaborated how 'shifting economic structures' – that is, structures that blurred the lines between 'the private and the public, the personal and the economic' – produced this ambiguity.[6] In its concern with contemporary debates about *re*productivity, rather than those surrounding capitalism, labour and productivity, this essay pursues a different, if parallel, track. Its focus is the mother-prostitute, a rare yet disquieting and significant presence in eighteenth-century literature, who has much to contribute to our understanding of the prostitute's cultural functions and the challenge she posed to emerging constructions of gender and sexuality. Much of the attention that has been directed towards this literary type has been devoted to the sexually transgressive and socially ambitious Moll Flanders and Roxana, although these women's status as prostitutes is not clear cut.[7] The heroines of Daniel Defoe's novels notoriously display an aberrant lack of attachment to their children, a character flaw that has been variously read by scholars as evidence of the naturalization of maternal affect in the period (in the form of the punishments exacted upon the heroines for violating these norms); of the fallacy of the universality of maternal affect; or of the unavailability of the new maternal ideal to low-ranking women.[8] Where consensus lies is in the certainty of the novels' illustration of the perceived incompatibility of women's motherly and libidinal lives.

In this respect, Defoe's novels seem consistent with a wealth of eighteenth-century texts in which, as Felicity Nussbaum argues, 'the maternal seems to function in contention with the sexual' and 'women's reproductive and nonreproductive labour' is divided into 'two often incommensurable categories'.[9] Such narratives persisted with remarkable resilience throughout the century. Even Mary Wollstonecraft's *The Wrongs of Woman; or, Maria* (1798), a novel that opens with the literal pangs of a maternal bosom 'bursting with ... nutriment' for a lost child and that reaches its dramatic climax with its heroine's radical claims for women's right to defend their political and sexual 'feelings', is unable to unite women's parental and erotic desires.[10] As Susan C. Greenfield has observed, the intensity of the novel's 'preoccupation with maternity' is matched only by its 'pessimistic account of heterosexuality'.[11] Maria embarks upon her doomed relationship with Darnford only after her daughter has been torn from her, while the couple's relationship develops further only when she believes the daughter is dead. When her child returns in the novel's putative conclusion with her second 'mother', the former prostitute Jemima, it is to a community in which heterosexual love has been abandoned for the more enduring solace of female companionship.[12]

Despite the apparent consistency of accounts of the (non-)relationship between the maternal and the sexual across the eighteenth century, cultural historians and literary scholars have commonly identified the mid-century as a landmark moment in the creation of the 'newly elaborated social and sexual identity' for women that Defoe's heroines imply through their failures and that Wollstonecraft attempted to co-opt for the radical cause.[13] As Perry has influentially asserted, the creation of the 'contradiction in terms' that was 'the asexual mother' was a 'highly complex social phenomenon' that emerged in the context of the Seven Years' War (1756–63) and in response to the need to stock the military, the nation and the empire with healthy citizens. Subsequently naturalized in novels, poetry, plays, medical treatises, conduct books and breastfeeding manuals, and firmly relocated within the private sphere of bourgeois home, the ideal of the pure, self-sacrificing mother that emerged 'succeeded, supplanted, and repressed the sexual definition of women'. 'Non-reproductive' sexuality, including prostitution, became the focus of an intensified cultural anxiety, and reproductive (hetero)sexuality, as a consequence, became the norm. The result, as Nussbaum argues, was 'to pit the sex against itself' as concerns about women's sexuality were displaced onto foreign and labouring-class female others.[14] Read in this context, the anonymous *The Histories of Some of the Penitents in the Magdalen-House* (1760) is something of a puzzle. Through the construction of a series of sentimentalized portraits of mother-prostitutes – three of the four 'Penitents' whose 'cause' the novel 'plead[s]' have children whom they love with as much zeal as they love their seducers – the novel posits a model of acceptably sexual maternity that was as unthinkable in Defoe's fiction as it would be in Wollstonecraft's polemical works.[15]

The novel's departure from literary conventions of the maternal is signalled in its opening chapter, in which the reader is introduced to Emily, an orphaned clergyman's daughter who has been seduced by her master, lived as his mistress, borne his child, and been summarily abandoned to a life of penury, including time in a brothel. In the Magdalen House, the former whore becomes a penitential paragon, 'awakened to repentance' and 'taught to apply for pardon to Him who came on earth to save sinners'.[16] This overlaying of the penitent's biography with the story of Mary Magdalen would have been familiar to readers of sentimentalized prostitution narratives and, moreover, would have been recognized as an extension of a well-known disciplinary mechanism of the Magdalen House itself, which as Ann Van Sant explains, aimed to separate its female charges from their past and rewrite their futures through the fictionalization and universalization of their plight as generic 'Magdalens'.[17] Funded by subscription and precariously dependent upon goodwill, the charity set out to transform its inmates into benign yet spectacular objects of sympathy, whose modestly adorned bodies and decorously retold stories would pull on the public's heart and purse strings. The superimposition of the redeemed penitent Mary Magdalen's story upon the women's own was a powerful and rhetorically effective strategy that underscored the centrality of narrative and 'models of reading', to borrow Martha J. Koehler's phrase, to the charity's mission.[18] It is, therefore, curious that when Emily is first introduced to the reader, it is not as the familiar penitential Madgalen, but as a latter-day Madonna:

> her person was extremely elegant, her hands and arms finely turned, her neck white as alabaster, and exquisitely formed. Her face expressed all the humble modesty of a Madona [sic], with a countenance languishingly sweet.[19]

The novel's rewriting of the penitential, fallen Magdalen as her antithesis – the chaste Madonna – might be read as further evidence of the cultural imperative to erase maternal sexuality: to be redeemed, Emily's sexual past (her seduction and the birth of her illegitimate child) must be overwritten by a narrative of penitence before it is erased entirely when she is recast as the 'contradiction in terms' that is the virgin mother.[20] As this essay will demonstrate, however, when read in the context of the novel as a whole, it is clear that there is something more complex at work in this provocative and unsettling description. Emily's figuring as the Magdalen-Madonna destabilizes the virgin/mother/whore triad, which, as Vivien Jones argues, 'defines femininity within modernity' and in which the 'whore' plays a particularly important role in ensuring the respectability of the other two categories.[21] In this novel, the prostitute Emily – a whore of necessity but an exemplary mother by instinct – offers no such guarantees. Indeed her story, like that of each of the penitents, proves the speciousness of equating sexual and moral rectitude: as this novel proves time and again, whores can be virtuous, while the chaste can be, and usually are, morally bankrupt. Most radically of all, the sexually ambiguous figure of the Magdalen-Madonna, worked through in slightly different forms in each of the novel's inset narratives, carves out a new kind of eroticized femininity that is compatible with, rather than supplanted by, the exemplary maternal virtue the Madonna represents. As such, *The Histories of the Penitents* gives cause to reconsider the dominance of the normative and supposedly monolithic constructions of the maternal, the sexual and the feminine outlined above, and attests further to the prostitute's power to disturb the cultural fictions her abjection supposedly upheld.

Like *Moll Flanders* (1722) and *Roxana* (1724), *The Histories of the Penitents* exposes the harsh realities faced by women lacking the social, educational or familial support necessary to their survival within the labour and marital marketplaces. But if the later novel recalls Defoe's works in its revelation of a split 'between the unforgiving marketplace and maternal desire', as Rosenthal observes, then it rewrites these works in its demonstration of maternal affection's resilience.[22] The penitents' love for their children is a moral touchstone in a novel in which affect is otherwise superseded by the economic pressures attendant upon the emergence of capitalism.[23] The devastating consequences of the subordination of feelings to financial motivation – particularly in the form of 'mercenary marriage' – are writ large throughout the inset narratives. Indeed, as much as the novel is a self-declared warning against the vices of 'vanity' and 'indiscretion', it is also a cautionary tale that elucidates the personal tragedies and social problems occasioned by young men and women being forced to follow money rather than their hearts.[24] The unwilling marriage of the beautiful fourth penitent to the wealthy, elderly and infirm Mr Merton, rather than the dashing young redcoat with whom she is in love, is only the most graphic of the novel's illustrations of the grotesqueness of modern marriage. Equally grotesque, are the predatory instincts of the various maternal surrogates who populate this text. In common with numerous novels from the period, biological mothers are absent or otherwise remote in *The Histories of the Penitents*: Emily's mother, we learn, died when her daughter was thirteen; the mother of the second (childless and unnamed) penitent is not mentioned at all; the mother of Fanny, the third penitent, is forced to give up her infant daughter to a family of spinners; while the fourth penitent is one of many children born to a woman who is so 'extremely prolific' in her childbearing that she can barely satisfy her children's bodily needs let alone pay attention to 'the cultivation of [their] minds'.[25]

The women who offer themselves, or who are called upon to act, as surrogate mothers are no better placed to serve their charges. When Emily's unnamed older sister – an industrious and happily married milliner whom Emily describes as her 'only parent' after their father's death – learns of her situation following her abandonment by Markland and descent into prostitution, she is powerless to aid her sibling despite her relative economic comfort.[26] Having been forced to sacrifice 'all her stock in trade' to her husband and to suppress 'her inclinations' as a wife and sister in order to satisfy those of her husband, the sister is unable to use the fruits of her own hard work to prevent Emily's further degeneration. The marital 'harmony' the sister has hitherto experienced is thus exposed as a sham: a trap she 'knew not how to break through'.[27] The plight of the virtuous, industrious sister and that of the fallen Emily are revealed to be painfully similar despite the very different worlds the women inhabit. In highlighting how both siblings are precariously dependent upon the goodwill of a man, women's economic dependence upon men is exposed as the common denominator of female experience within the novel.[28]

Non-blood relatives who assume the role of surrogate mother are little better placed to offer the emotional or financial support their female charges require, sometimes through no fault of their own. Fanny Tent's foster mother, for example, a poor spinner with a 'great number' of children of her own, raises the young girl with 'distinction' and kindness, but is beleaguered by poverty and dies when Fanny is just thirteen. More troubling are the greater number of other mother-substitutes in the text who feign interest in their charges because they consider them ripe for economic and sexual exploitation. The erosion of familial affection by the economics of modern life – one of the novel's recurrent refrains – is perhaps nowhere better demonstrated than by the novel's dwelling on the long-standing mother-madam-bawd analogy, which is central to Fanny's story.[29] Fanny's birth is obscure; all her foster family can tell her is that her biological mother was 'very young and melancholy', of superior rank, and 'went by the name of Tent'. The first (in chronological terms) of the exemplary yet non-conventional mothers in the novel, Miss Tent parts with her presumably illegitimate daughter 'with the greatest agonies of grief and despair' and provides financially for her daughter until her premature death four years later.[30] The maternal 'fondness' Miss Tent feels for the daughter from whom she is cruelly parted is grimly parodied later in the narrative, when Fanny travels, at the age of fourteen, to London in an attempt to find the mother she refuses to believe is dead and where she persists in 'inquiring', much to everyone's amusement, 'where Madam Tent lived'.[31] It is no surprise to the reader, alert to the suggestiveness of Fanny's name – 'tent' was a vulgar term for a speculum – as well as to the similarities between the description of Fanny's journey to London and Plate 1 of *A Harlot's Progress* (1732, see p. 101) and the opening chapter of *Memoirs of a Woman of Pleasure* (1748–9), that Fanny's journey will lead her to a brothel.[32] What distinguishes her journey from that of her infamous predecessors, however, is that its course is intricately plotted by a series of misunderstandings generated by the unstable meanings of, and slippage between, the terms 'mother' and 'madam'. In an exchange that marks the beginning of the penitent's downfall, a man tells Fanny that he thinks he knows 'such an one' as she inquires after, but asks 'what Madam Tent [she] meant?' Fanny replies:

> 'My mother, an't please your Honour', replied I, who took him for such a very fine gentleman, never having seen even the 'Squire of our parish with so much lace on his waistcoat'.
> 'Oh!' answered he, 'then it is the same: she lives in the next street: it must be her; for she is mother to a great many'.
> 'If she has so many children', said I, 'it may be she will not be glad to have any more'.
> 'Never fear', answered the man; 'she will hardly refuse such a daughter as you are: no, if there were an hundred like you, they would be all welcome: she is mighty good-humoured; an excellent kind mother you will find her'.[33]

All too keen to exploit the economic potential of Fanny's deep-seated sense of filial 'oblig[ation]', the bawd (Mother/Madam Tent) passes herself off as Fanny's biological '*mother*' (a term frequently used and italicized in this section of the novel) and tricks her into prostitution by erroneously persuading her that she is married to a potential client, Mr Mastin. When Fanny expresses doubt about the legitimacy of a union that has not been sanctified by the church, Madam Tent retorts: "I desire you will learn to respect your mother more: your duty is to believe every thing I say, and do every thing I bid you, or I shall disclaim you for my child: I will harbour no undutiful children".[34] When Mastin learns of Fanny's story, he cannot bring himself to subject her to Madam Tent's deception and removes her from the brothel. Fanny's gratitude to Mastin is matched only by the profound sense of loss she experiences when she realizes that her quest for family has concluded with the discovery that she has 'neither husband nor mother'.[35]

Fanny's innocent confusion of Mother/Madam for mother draws on the longstanding mother-madam-bawd analogy. Although the analogy has its origins in a pornographic fantasy about the erotic lives of women in convents ('abbesses' and 'nuns' being common terms for bawds and prostitutes from the sixteenth century onwards), its functions extended well beyond the localized religious prejudice and sexual wishful thinking it implies. As Jennifer Panek observes, the mother-as-bawd 'motif' was an important locus of early modern anxiety about the maternal body and maternal authority.[36] Moreover, it could serve as a form of social commentary: when 'motherhood fails' in so spectacular a fashion that the mother becomes synonymous with (or actually becomes) the bawd, as Richard A. Levin writes, society is revealed to be 'hollow and hence doomed'.[37] Fanny's narrative mobilizes all of these established discourses. By painfully elaborating how the language of filial devotion ('duty', 'oblig[ation]', 'respect' and 'love') is exploited for the bawd's financial gain, however, the text channels these discourses the more explicitly to underscore the extent to which the economic imperatives of an emerging capitalist marketplace pervert or destroy domestic relationships.[38] Fanny's conflation of mother, madam and bawd, thus, does double work: on the one hand, the infiltration of the language of the maternal into the brothel reveals the bawdy house's illegitimacy; on the other, the parodic association of the familial household and the brothel through the mother/bawd analogy destabilizes the domestic sphere by revealing the unsentimental economics that characterize both whorehouse and home in the novel. Madam Tent's masking of economic motives beneath the language of familial responsibility is re-enacted in various different ways in the nominally legitimate world of heterosexual domesticity the novel exposes. The world *The Histories of the Penitents* conjures is one in which children must 'sacrifice' their 'inclination' to their parents' 'will' (read: interest) and a mother and sister will drag a young woman 'more dead than alive' to an altar to marry an aged 'battered rake' simply to get her 'off [her parents'] hands'.[39]

Familial affection rarely withstands economic pressure in this novel, except in the case of the penitents' relationships with their children. The fact that all of these children are sons is both significant and consistent with the majority of narratives of illegitimate birth in the period, which, as Lisa Zunshine documents, tend to focus upon male children. Zunshine explains this phenomenon as, in part at least, a consequence of the male child's greater 'dramatic potential' as the potential inheritor of estates, titles and power commonly denied to female offspring.[40] In *The Histories of the Penitents*, however, sons are valued not because of the heights they might scale, but because they are less likely than daughters to plunge into the depths of economic and emotional despair the penitents experience. As the fourth penitent observes: 'I rejoiced in the sex of my children, as it saved me from all fears of their becoming as forlorn and wretched beings as their mother'.[41] As the mothers' wretchedness increases, so their love for their 'dear Innocent' sons is heightened. And in the cases of the first and fourth penitents, maternal affection redeems the women despite the drastic measures they take to support themselves, with prostitution being cast as a form of self-sacrifice that signals the depths of motherly love.[42] Emily, for instance, can withstand the vicious abuse to which she is subjected by a bawd who imprisons her for debt when she refuses to sell sex for money, but is powerless to refuse the bawd's demands that she become one of her 'girls' when the brothelkeeper threatens to 'send [her] brat away'. Emily allows herself momentarily to believe that 'the law' might offer some 'redress' against such action, but is disabused of this fanciful notion with the realization that 'money only can obtain justice'. Prepared to part with her 'own life' but not with her son, Emily's 'Delicacy' gives 'way to maternal love'.[43] The 'delicacy' that Emily overcomes was, as Perry has suggested in a different context, a mid-century innovation, most famously naturalized in fictional form by *Clarissa* (1748–9).[44] *The Histories of the Penitents* exposes such delicacy as a middle-class luxury, one that mothers who were forced to rely upon their bodily labour to support themselves and their families could ill afford. That in the relentlessly brutalizing economy of this novel such 'squeamishness' is mere indulgence, incompatible with 'true maternal love', is brought home in the final narrative, in which the heroine supports her three sons, following their father's death, through prostitution.[45] Unable to earn enough to support her family by taking in needlework, the penitent turns to whoredom, which renders her 'miserable', but proves so 'profitable', that it enables her to pay for her two eldest sons to attend school where their 'tender minds' are 'instilled with religious principles'.[46] This investment in her sons' education – made possible by her descent into prostitution – facilitates the penitent's redemption. The exemplary piety her eldest son demonstrates as a direct consequence of his schooling when forced to confront his early death 'awaken[s]' his mother's 'conscience' and leads her to the Magdalen charity's door.[47] The maternal martyrdom the penitent performs when she sacrifices her 'will' to the demands of '[n]ecessity' by becoming a prostitute is, paradoxically, the means to moral salvation.[48]

To the extent that *The Histories of the Penitents* presents the maternal love exemplified by the penitents as instinctive and overwhelming, it seems consistent with more conventional and conservative fictional representations of motherhood. What distinguishes its treatment of maternity, however, is its refusal to deny its maternal heroines sexual desire. The centrality of erotic desire to the novel has been persuasively foregrounded by Binhammer, who argues that its valorization of 'the whore's love' (all four penitents, she notes, fall first for love not money) posits a radically unconventional model of affective relations, which lays bare the unfeeling economics of bourgeois marriage and, in the process, imagines alternative affective agencies.[49] Binhammer's focus is primarily upon the radical potential of the 'erotic agency' the novel imagines for women, with maternity figuring, incidentally, as that which justifies the women's recourse to prostitution and renders them worthy of sympathy.[50] Maternity and sexuality are, I would suggest, more complexly and politically intertwined in *The Histories of the Penitents* than this argument implies; indeed, the novel's construction of an eroticized *maternal* agency is one of its principal innovations.

Bearing children explicitly intensifies the penitents' love for their sexual partners. Emily and Markland find that 'instead of [their] affection's being lessened, by having a third to share it with us', the birth of their 'fine boy' leads to 'an increase of fondness' between them.[51] Although this heightened passion wanes for Markland (it often does for men in this novel), Emily's persists even after her lover abandons her, when her desire is displaced onto the body of the child whose uncanny resemblance to his father reminds Emily of those characteristics which 'charmed her soul' and led to her seduction.[52] In such moments, the novel challenges the cultural idealization of maternal virtue as 'the absence of sexual desire', which as Toni Bowers observes, was becoming entrenched as one of the 'exclusive markers of motherhood ... imposed on women of all social positions' from mid-century. At precisely the moment when cultural historians and literary scholars claim that motherhood was being transformed into 'a more easily controlled social *institution*, an institution defined according to a limited set of supposedly timeless behaviours and sentiments', *The Histories of the Penitents* presents a series of compelling counter-narratives that collectively argue for the interdependence and complexity of women's erotic and maternal lives.[53] When the fourth penitent seems momentarily to accede to the dictates of contemporary conduct books, breastfeeding and midwifery manuals, and novels with the claim that 'This tie [i.e. the maternal bond] I fansied was all', she is forced quickly to qualify her statement: 'My love for them was accompanied with no alloy ... but I have since learned, that my affection for Captain Turnham was still so great, that tho' beheld by him with indifference, his absence would have appeared still a heavier misfortune.'[54] Here, as in Emily's narrative, the novel conceives of a maternal subjectivity that reveals parental affection to be a natural extension of women's passion for their lovers, and casts the maternal 'tie' as a consequence of the male child's resemblance to, and biological connection with, the object of the woman's sexual desire.

Motherhood without passion, by contrast, is a lonely and unsatisfactory experience in this novel, as Mrs Lafew, the virtuous, pious wife of the man with whom Fanny falls in love, finds to her cost. As Binhammer explains, Fanny's relationship with Mr Lafew, which inspires 'warmer passions' than the Lafews' marriage, forces an acknowledgement that 'sentimental marriage erases erotic desire'; thus, even while the novel seems partly to idealize the Lafews' relationship, it also shows Fanny to be the 'better wife because her love includes sexual desire'.[55] Moreover, as the better (more loving and loved) 'wife', Fanny also has the potential to be the better mother, as Mrs Lafew painfully realizes. Fanny's 'little boy' eventually falls into the care of Mrs Lafew who treats him exactly like her own children. Indeed, Mrs Lafew cannot help but feel maternal 'tenderness' towards the boy, not least because he, like Markland's son, 'resembled [his father] extremely'.[56] But this striking resemblance is also a source of disquiet for Mrs Lafew because it speaks of her 'husband's attachment to another', an attachment so strong that after Fanny's separation from Lafew, he begs his wife not to tell him 'what place [his former lover] had retired to' for fear he would prove so 'weak … he might endeavour to see [her]' and reconstitute his relationship with her and his son.[57] The 'offspring of [Fanny's] crime' is the offspring of a mutual desire that eludes Mrs Lafew, who, in the narrative's conclusion, experiences the sincere but platonic 'veneration and respect' of a husband she had once 'tenderly', but not passionately 'loved', only with 'pain'.[58] Fanny's son, perhaps even more than his mother's affair, unsettles the model sentimental marriage the Lafews seem to represent and reveals the emptiness at the heart of the bourgeois maternal ideal.

In its assertion of the interconnectedness of erotic desire and maternal love, *The Histories of the Penitents* flouts earlier novelistic representations of mother-whores as monstrously unfeminine – mothers in name only – at the same time that it runs counter to emergent sentimental models of chaste femininity. Equally, it challenges a number of the contemporary cultural discourses about prostitution, perhaps most significantly the belief that prostitutes were either barren or, if not, incapable of harbouring affection for children they might bear, the latter supposition evident in the widespread assumption that unmarried women accused of infanticide were prostitutes.[59] Significantly, the novel also stands as a critique of the official rhetoric of the Magdalen House itself, which persistently described the Magdalens as neglected children and presented the charity's governors as surrogate fathers, who would provide the parental guidance that would guarantee the women's return to virtue. The charity's mission, according to William Dodd, was guided by 'the most noble and commendable of human affections, the parental': 'By restoring, then and recovering such children … not only the child, but the parent too shares in the generous mercy'.[60] When the Magdalens are imagined as mothers in the charity's official, non-imaginative publications, it is in the future tense. Numerous supporters of the charity echoed Jonas Hanway's belief that its inmates might become 'joyful mothers of children', but only once their idle and misused bodies had been made fit for productive and reproductive labour through the charity's educational programme, and only then within the context of heterosexual marriage.[61] By allowing all but one of its heroines to be mothers before their entry into the Magdalen House, the novel can tell a different narrative about virtue, maternity and female sexuality than that countenanced by the charity's spokesmen; a narrative that resists the charity's tendency to infantilize and objectify its inmates, and articulates a virtuous, sexualized maternal subjectivity that forces readers to rethink their attitudes towards the whore and her chaste (but in this novel often morally, emotionally or economically flawed) counterpart, the domestic woman.

This is not to say that the maternal subjectivity imagined in *The Histories of the Penitents* is uncompromised. After all, all three mothers are heartbreakingly forced to part with their children in order to gain entry into the Magdalen House. In this respect, we might see the novel as replicating, even as it rewrites, *Moll Flanders* and *Roxana* by revealing the socioeconomic conditions that, in Bowers's words, render maternal love 'impossible, inadequate or inappropriate'.[62] Yet once again, in this nod to narrative conventions of the maternal, the novel takes a surprising turn. Both Emily and the fourth penitent register concern that their maternity militates against their applications to the charity: Emily refers to her son being 'a bar to her admission', having heard that 'no provision' was made 'for children'; the fourth penitent similarly notes that she fears her sons are 'an insurmountable obstruction' to her gaining admittance to the charity.[63] In using this vocabulary, the women deploy an institutionalized rhetoric of maternal distress familiar from the petitions to the Foundling Hospital in which, as Tanya Evans notes, women 'commonly described their children as "inconveniences", "incumbrances", "burdens" and "insurmountable obstacles"'.[64] But these terms have different implications for the penitents than they do for the foundling petitioners. When Penelope Hones, for example, referred to her child, like the fourth penitent, as an 'unsurmountable Obstacle' in her petition to the Foundling Hospital on 20 November 1763, she did so in the context of her attempts to find work. Left in 'Debt' and with an infant by her barber husband, Hones had no choice but to plead with the General Committee to take her child if she was to have any chance of 'Gett[ing] her bread in an honest Service'.[65] In *The Histories of the Penitents*, the difficulties women faced in trying to secure work in a labour market in which a 'character' was everything are vividly explored, but it is significant that the women explicitly refer to their children as burdens or impediments only when they are seeking entrance into the charity, not when they are attempting to secure employment.

As it transpires, the women's belief that their children will prevent them gaining access to the Magdalen House proves erroneous: Emily is assured her son will be 'taken care of', 'educated and provided for'; the fourth penitent learns that the charity runs a separate institution for the children of Magdalen inmates, through which its 'humane Institutors ... doubled the benefit they conferred'.[66] Unfortunately, this appears to be a novelistic fantasy. The Magdalen House did not make automatic, or at least official, provision for the inmates' children, preferring to focus upon the wayward children that were the Magdalens themselves. Indeed, the possibility that prospective inmates might have borne children does not seem to have occurred to the authors of the proposals written for the charity in 1758, although, as Ruth McClure has discovered, Robert Dingley was forced to face this reality in 1766 when he applied to the Foundling Hospital for the admission of three children born to women in the House.[67] Dingley's action seems to have been the exception rather than the rule, and it is likely that women who had children would have had to conceal this fact and dispose of them before seeking entry into the institution. How then are we to read the lavish praise bestowed in the novel's conclusion upon the 'Beneficent Institutors of this charity' for an initiative that did not exist?[68] The text offers no definitive answer to this question, but a clue lies in its preface. Here, in the novel's first sentence, the author reminds readers that the text, although based on a real organization, is a work of 'fiction' designed to prick the consciences of those whose 'affectation of too overstrained a chastity' leaves them impervious to the plight of women in whose downfall they are complicit.[69] Fiction is the medium of *The Histories of the Penitents* because only fiction can reveal the truths of female experience – of love, sex, abandonment and motherhood. Only in a work of imagination – not the labour or marriage markets, not even in the Magdalen House itself – can women find justice, compassion and redemption. In this context, the sleight of hand the novel performs when it fabricates provision for the children of Magdalen inmates in order to expose the lack of such an organization reveals the charity's failure to engage with the reality of some prostitutes' lives and respond to their needs. This is fiction as social criticism. But *The Histories of the Penitents* is also a work of *cultural* criticism that reveals the failure of the vast array of written texts discussed by Bowers, Nussbaum and Perry to countenance the model of sexualized maternity it articulates and to admit that sexuality and the 'true maternal love' Emily demonstrates when she reluctantly parts with her son could, and might naturally, coexist.

If, as Bowers argues, 'Augustan writing on motherhood ... participated in recasting the multiple, contingent *experience* of motherhood as a more easily controlled social *institution*', defined by an 'absence of sexual desire', then *The Histories of the Penitents* finds in its fictional reimagining of a real-life institution a pretext for denaturalizing monolithic constructions of the maternal to imagine plural and, crucially, eroticized 'maternal agencies and subjectivities' that have gone largely unrecognized in eighteenth-century scholarship because they seem to buck the dominant representational trend.[70] The textual spectacle that the novel's mother-prostitutes constitute is significantly different from that offered in the charity's official publications, where, as we have seen, the women are usually infantilized and their reproductive capacity can be imagined only as a future social benefit and principal goal of the charity's reform agenda. It also departs from that conceived in well-known fictional works of the period, from Defoe to Wollstonecraft, in which sexuality seemingly erases or fatally conflicts with maternal feeling. As importantly, and as part of the *The Histories of the Penitents*' broader project to collapse any presumed moral distinctions between the novel's reader and its heroines, the text's detailed explorations of the penitents' love for their sexual partners and sons works to deconstruct the oppositional and mutually constitutive categories of woman (virgin/mother/whore) through which femininity was conventionally defined and understood. By exposing the common moral ground of maternal devotion than unites the Madonna and the Magdalens, *The Histories of the Penitents* can better highlight the divergent economic realities that determine the respective plights of virtuous and fallen women. In the process, it reveals some unpalatable truths about the relationship between affect and economics, which so often trumps or entirely obliterates feeling in this novel, and of the psychic costs paid by ideal maternal figures such as Mrs Lafew when they live up the sentimental ideal of virtuous, chaste femininity and effectively lose their husbands and fathers to their children as a consequence. In thus closing the gap between the Madonna and the Magdalen (other, but not so different after all), the author of *The Histories of the Penitents* could only hope that her readers' 'squeamishness' in relation to sex, money and maternity would, like Emily's '[d]elicacy', give way to the more meaningful 'love' the penitents demonstrate in their relationships with their lovers and offspring. For it is this, ultimately, which offers an oasis of hope in an otherwise mercenary world.

12 MAKING A LIVING BY 'INDECENCY': LIFE STORIES OF PROSTITUTES IN CHRISTIANIA, NORWAY

Johanne Bergkvist

Almost without fear, both inside and outside the city, and often in a disgraceful state of intoxication, they ran into people's arms, and, known to all, shamelessly offered themselves for sale.
(Verdict from the Christiania House of Correction Court sentencing Elen Trulsdatter to the house of correction, 1796)[1]

The two sisters Elen and Anne Magrethe Trulsdatter were publicly visible prostitutes in Christiania in the 1790s. Between 1792 and 1799 they were each incarcerated in the correctional institution *Christiania tukthus* four times, sentenced for vagrancy and indecency, as well as theft. In addition, they were arrested and interrogated at the police station on several occasions, and were repeatedly observed and arrested by the city's watchmen or police officers on street corners in the city, in cemeteries, in enclosures and hills in the poor suburbs of the city, as well as at the quay and on ships anchored in the harbour. The main charge brought against them was vagrancy, but underlying these accusations were assumptions that the women were making a living by 'indecency', which suggested street prostitution. The repeated interrogations of the two sisters make it possible to paint a social portrait of prostitutes within a microhistoric scope. Historical accounts of prostitution in Norway have largely focused on the controlled and de facto legalized prostitution in the nineteenth century. These accounts have been based on the presumption that Norwegian laws against prostitution were not implemented in the eighteenth century, while studies of illicit sexuality and children born out of wedlock in the eighteenth century have dominated the understanding of prostitution. The present study of police interrogations of women accused of vagrancy changes this picture by giving new insight into the regulation of prostitution in Norway. The police records, which are based on the women's own explanations, preserve to some extent the prostitutes' own voices and provide a thorough, and in a Norwegian context, unique source for an historical analysis of prostitution. Who were the arrested women, and how was prostitution regulated in Norway in the late eighteenth century?

A Legislative Shift

Indecency ('løsaktighet') was, according to the Norwegian Law of 1687, a serious offence. Men caught in the act of fornication in a whorehouse were to be sentenced to prison, and women were to be whipped or put to hard labour in a house of correction.[2] Similarly, procurers, whether male or female, were either punished by whipping and ordered to leave the region, or sentenced to imprisonment.[3] But according to a report from the Board of Health in 1880, the police had turned a blind eye to prostitution in the preceding century despite the law's amendments. The report stated that in the eighteenth century there were many brothels and that prostitutes openly conducted 'their nuisance uninterrupted by the police' in the poorer suburbs of the city.[4] In fact, the board claimed that this lack of enforcement encouraged the toleration of prostitution. Later Norwegian studies on the semi-legal public prostitution of the nineteenth century agree with this interpretation.[5]

A thorough look at legal sources from the turn of the eighteenth century makes it clear that the penal code passed in the seventeenth century was not reflected in administrative practice in the eighteenth century, as the police and prison records show that the law's specific statutes against whorehouses, pimps, clients and 'notorious women' ('Beryktede Qvindfolk') were rarely used. The authorities however certainly did not turn a blind eye to prostitution. Rather, prostitutes were accused of vagrancy, sometimes in combination with accusations of leading an 'indecent' ('løsaktig') or 'lecherous' ('lidderlig') life. The transaction of money was only explicitly invoked by the police when the women admitted to making a living by indecency. During the twelve-year period from 1790 to 1802, 163 women were accused of vagrancy by the Christiania police, comprising 74 per cent of the total number of arrests for vagrancy. A quarter of the women were sentenced to the house of correction to be disciplined by hard and monotonous labour. Although the house of correction received a decreasing number of people convicted of vagrancy from 1790, the police continued to sentence a relatively large number of young girls accused of the crime, a situation that needs further explanation.

The Norwegian regional poor laws and the national labour legislation of the eighteenth century defined lack of steady work as vagrancy. According to this mercantilist regulation, prohibiting casual labour and binding both men and unmarried women to serve one master for at least six months without permission to leave, 'vagrancy' ('løsgjengeri') was a broad charge brought against people who lacked such mandatory work. The duty to take whatever work was offered was made clear by stating that any man or woman out of work, who refused any employment offered, was to be considered a vagrant and punished as such. Vagrancy was dealt with in the regional poor laws as well as the national labour legislation, all initiated in the eighteenth century.[6] The vagrancy cases make it evident that the accusations of indecency were of secondary importance relative to the lack of legal employment. This represented a marked judicial shift from a pietistic legislation against illicit sexual activity in the seventeenth century, to a mercantilistic emphasis on the well-being of the national economy and a repressive form of labour legislation in the eighteenth century. Prostitutes were to be found at the core of the ideological change this represented.

'Notorious Houses' and Streetwalking

The fact that the categories used by the police to label detainees were often vague and ambiguous presents a methodological challenge. The words prostitute and prostitution were hardly in use before the early nineteenth century, and only sporadically did the vagrancy interrogations touch on whether acts of indecency or lechery in fact described the women's source of income. Consequently the pitfall for the historian is the tendency to categorize all instances of illicit sexual activity as prostitution. On the other hand, there has been a tendency among Norwegian historians to overlook vagrancy cases as a point of entry to the study of prostitution. Despite these methodological problems, the vagrancy cases provide a rich source for reconstructing the lives of prostitutes. Whereas an examination of a single interrogation might not show with certainty whether or not the arrested woman was a prostitute, several interrogations over a larger time span and at several levels of the judicial system give a broader overview of the cases. This allows for a more diverse analysis and the nature of the accusations becomes clear.

Granted, these sources do not provide us with an exhaustive picture of Christiania's prostitution, as the quantitative data is quite unreliable. In practice, however, this is not an insurmountable problem. Christiania was a moderate-size city with only about 11,000 inhabitants at the time of the census of 1801. In comparison, the capital of the Danish-Norwegian kingdom, Copenhagen, had approximately 100,000 inhabitants, and London at the time had 1 million inhabitants. The size of the city of Christiania therefore makes an extensive and varied underworld of prostitution and brothels unlikely, and there are no contemporary literary accounts, such as memoirs or novels, that describe it thus. Still, police records give the impression of small brothel-like inns, called 'notorious houses' ('Beryktede Huus'), where only a couple of girls lodged. Presumably the retailing of liquor was as important as the activity of prostitution. These brothels were found in the poorer suburbs by the main roads into the city, Fjerdingen, Vaterland and Pipervika in particular. These 'notorious houses' were subject to only minor control, and only exceptionally were the owners brought in to the police station for questioning, either concerning their female lodgers, or to be accused of pimping. Furthermore, the testimonies of the city's watchmen give us an idea of streetwalking in certain areas and places. Streetwalkers circulated mainly in the suburbs where the brothels were found and especially in the two streets Ruseløkkveien and Møllergata, as well as in the city's cemeteries and at the quay. Prostitution in these areas seems to have been persistent, and they were indeed the core areas of prostitution up to the beginning of the twentieth century. Still, the accounts give the impression that street prostitution in Christiania was not large-scale. The descriptions given in the police records are of at the most a handful of women seen in the streets. In years with more extensive sweeps for vagrants, the number of yearly arrests did not exceed fifteen different women. The story of the two sisters Elen and Anne provide an insight into the mechanisms that brought women to prostitution.

'She Herself Was Not to Blame'

Elen Trulsdatter was accused of vagrancy and indecency for the first time in 1793. She was apprehended by a watchman a Friday night in July together with another woman by the hills nearby the poor suburb of Ruseløkka (Ruseløkkbakken). She gave her age as nineteen years, and said that she had taken up a post as a servant in a huckster's house in the suburb of Pipervika seven years earlier, due to her mother catching consumption. After two years, she said, she returned to her parents in Christiania's neighbouring parish Aker, when it was time for her confirmation, where she had stayed ever since.[7] She admitted that she had been imprisoned for committing theft from the chamberlain Anker at the prominent Bogstad mansion, but that another girl, whose parents were Anker's cottars (tenant farmers), had framed her. The two women claimed that their difficult circumstances had forced them into vagrancy and Elen

> complained that she was taken into custody, as she herself was not to blame that she had not obtained a post as a servant girl, as her mother's illness required that she care for her, though she promised that if she were forgiven this time, she would never more be found in any unlawfulness.[8]

The police released the two girls, instructing them to lead a more proper life and to report immediately to the women in charge of brokering servant's posts ('festekoner'), and to accept the very first post they were offered. If not, they would be arrested again and sentenced to the house of correction. Despite this warning, Elen was soon taken up and interrogated again.

In November 1793 Elen was arrested with four other girls at night for vagrancy, and what the watchman assumed was indecency, as they were known to him to walk the streets. Among the girls were Lisbeth Jensdatter, the girl Elen had previously been sentenced to the house of correction with, and Karen Sophie Olsdatter, whose name reappears with that of Elen over the years. Lisbeth had unlawfully left her last post at an inn because 'she found it a bad place to be'.[9] Both Elen and Lisbeth claimed that they tried to obtain a proper servant's post, but that they had been turned down by the intermediary, shoemaker Halle's wife, who claimed that she could not provide them with employment since they were former inmates of the house of correction. None of the girls were sentenced, but only a month later Elen was arrested again, this time together with her younger sister Anne. Both were accused of being found on the streets at ten o'clock in the evening with the intent of frivolity ('letfærdighed'). They were still not sentenced, but this time they were ordered not to roam the streets and to seek employment at the city's public spinning mill for poor women and children.[10] When Elen was arrested again the following year, in March 1794, together with the two girls known from previous arrests, Lisbeth and Karen, and a fourth woman, they had still not obtained any legal employment as servants or been to the public spinning mill. Elen repeated her previous explanation, but added that 'she couldn't deny that she for some time has led an indecent life'.[11] Lisbet explained that since her last arrest she had resided with Elen's parents and had earned her living helping Elen's mother with spinning. Karen explained that she had maintained herself partly by labour, partly by cleaning for people. The watchmen and the police officers all declared that 'they knew all these four women to be indulging in indecency and lecherous lives'. Whereas the fourth woman was sentenced for petty theft, Elen, Lisbeth and Karen were despite the accusations of indecency each sentenced to four months in the house of correction for their lack of service according to the regional labour legislation of 1766, which stated that:

> Young and able-bodied women, who are able to make a living, shall not be idle and without service, neither shall they walk about selling fruit and such. Should any woman, between the ages of 12 and 40, act against this ... then she shall be punished with a period of work in the house of correction.[12]

The sentence reflects police practice at the end of the eighteenth century, where a large number of the young women accused of vagrancy were sentenced for their lack of service even though indecency was part of the accusation. Public indecency may have been the reason the women were arrested in the first place, but to the police this was of secondary importance as their main goal was to regulate the lack of mandatory work. Because the sentenced women complained, however, the punishment at the house of correction was not carried out on this occasion. Even for the women living on the margins a complaint could be heard.

This leniency was in line with a reform ideology that was prominent at the turn of the century. The legislation was rooted in the mercantilist view that vagrancy was a threat to the prosperity of the state, and to control the working population, vagrants were to be punished by hard and monotonous labour in the house of correction. An ideological shift at the end of the century substantially affected this use of correctional institutions. Due to a legal change in 1789, a larger number of people were sentenced to the house of correction for theft, and consequently there was from 1790 a marked decline in vagrancy sentences. This decline reflected the growing concern that vagrancy was caused by unemployment, and as a result of the increased mix of prisoners after 1789 critiques of the correctional institutions intensified.[13] For example, the head of the regional administration, *Stiftamtmann* Frederik Moltke, complained in 1791 that the house of correction was a disproportionally harsh sentence, and that one could hardly expect improvement from those whose vagrancy, idleness or indecency was the result of a lack of upbringing and schooling, when they were put together in prison with 'criminals, not expected to be brought back to honesty'.[14] This reluctance to convict people of vagrancy explains why the young girls, at the previous arrests, were first ordered to obtain a proper post, and when they failed to do so, were ordered to seek employment at the public spinning mill for the poor. Only after continually not doing so were they convicted of vagrancy.

Several authorities expressed their concern about the difficulties of obtaining work when released from the house of correction. The inspector of the house of correction claimed at the turn of the century that it was difficult for the inmates to find work due to the stigma of being convicts, and released prisoners were reportedly begging in the streets with the characteristic yellow skin called 'the house of correction colour', which bore witness to the ill health and hardship the sentence caused.[15] While the intention of a sentence might have been not only to punish, but also to correct errant behaviour and teach willingness to work, the result was that prisoners found it almost impossible to maintain themselves by legal employment upon their release, which meant an ongoing marginalization process for convicts. The commission at the house of correction expressed in the 1790s a concern that the lower classes for the most part lived in poverty and that employment was difficult to obtain. The situation for those who had formerly been sentenced to the house of correction was especially severe, and for women in particular.[16] Having been incarcerated for theft meant that Elen's ability to obtain mandatory work was seriously limited. Furthermore, there were few legal sources of income, other than being a servant, for an unmarried woman of the lower classes. Moreover, several of the arrested girls admitted they had left their former service before the terms of their contracts allowed them to do so. The younger sister Anne did find work, but on several occasions she left the households where she was a servant girl. She gave no explanation for this when questioned, but it is indicative of the difficult conditions for the poorest group of servants.

The sisters Elen and Anne fit into the pattern of women accused of vagrancy; they were young, poor, unmarried and from the outskirts of the city. When first sentenced to the house of correction the sisters were in their late teens or early twenties, and as was the case for most other women accused of vagrancy, they were able-bodied but found it difficult to earn a legal livelihood. The dilemma of the chief of police was how to sentence people for vagrancy when they claimed that they were not capable of obtaining any employment. Where the legislation had categorized all idleness as self-inflicted, in the 1790s the poor authorities were more eager to find out whether or not vagrants were involuntarily out of work. To the commission at the house of correction, moral virtues were now important criteria used to distinguish the deserving poor from the undeserving, or the depraved from those who might still be reformed into obedience and industriousness. But to do so, the commission implied that the authorities would be required to offer work.

'The Most Indecent and Scandalous Night-Running'

Elen and Karen were arrested again the following year, in November 1795, after being brought to the police station by a man who apparently approached Elen while she was in the company of men in the streets late at night.[17] This time the interrogation continued over two days, and witnesses were called. The watchman claimed that he had known these women for nine years and had in particular encountered Elen in the streets, early and late at night, and that the women's moral character was very wicked. The police officers added that when the women were apprehended in the street, on street corners, and in the city cemetery, they had no legitimate errand to speak of. Though the chief of police alone possessed the authority to sentence vagrants and beggars in the police station court, the case was taken on to an extra court of Christiania's Magistrate's Court, the House of Correction Court. Here, Elen and Karen were sentenced to the house of correction in January 1796 not solely for vagrancy, but in addition 'the most indecent and scandalous night-running'.[18] In the register of the prisoners of the house of correction their offence was noted as lechery.[19] This represented a shift from the first arrests; now, the verdict seems to have been based more on their disorderly behaviour and illicit sexual conduct than on the accusations of idleness. This suggested a reluctance to sentence the arrested women to the house of correction for their lack of employment alone, but both the police and courts emphasized instead their assumed bad moral conduct and repeated arrests.

Elen still claimed that she had obtained no employment due to taking care of her ill mother. The man who brought them in claimed that Elen and Karen were known vagrants who indulged in a suspicious ('mistænkelig') lifestyle. Further, 'the common man knows very well how they are to be found, almost every evening and night, in the streets and suspicious places to great annoyance and the seduction of youth'.[20] Elen's behaviour in particular was provoking, and according to one witness, 'if everything about her suspicious character were to be thoroughly described, it would take up several pages'.[21] The women denied these accusations of indecent behaviour, but according to the verdict, 'Almost without fear, both inside and outside the city, and often in a disgraceful state of intoxication, they ran into people's arms, and, known to all, shamelessly offered themselves for sale'.[22] The women were not only publicly visible prostitutes, but also offered their services aggressively. The court felt that the reason for Elen's rude behaviour was her mother, who was 'from many years back the notorious Karen Sollie who so many times have been accused and some times sentenced for pimping and theft'.[23] The description of Elen and Anne's mother now differed from that of the previous interrogations. A collocation of the different source material confirms that the mother, as well as acting as a procuress, had been accused of prostitution herself. According to the record of prisoners of the house of correction she had been sentenced for 'night-running' in 1781, indicating that she too had been a prostitute.[24] Due to her upbringing, Elen had, according to the witnesses, been taught theft and gross indecency ('utukt') from her youth by her mother, and had thus become a 'notorious woman' herself, and 'such a Master of denying and hiding' that it was almost impossible to catch her in the act.[25] This court would have found her upbringing to be an extenuating circumstance if this had been the first time she had been arrested, and if she had not been 'such a scandalous being beyond all limits of virtue'.[26] This time Elen was sentenced to one year in the house of correction, and Karen to two years. In the house of correction they were met by a welcoming whip just inside the gates, before being put to hard and monotonous labour. While Elen was imprisoned, her younger sister Anne was sentenced to the house of correction as well, for leaving her servant post unlawfully while bound by contract. Surprisingly, the sheriff of Christiania's surrounding county, Aker, posted bail for Anne the very day she arrived. Both sisters and their mother were accused of activity connected to prostitution, which indicates that prostitution had been a means of living for the family for at least two generations.

Generational Poverty

The police interrogations of these women give the impression of severe poverty, which is an obvious factor causing prostitution. The sisters were noticeably poor. The records of the house of correction even reveal that Elen and Anne lacked basic clothing such as shoes and stockings.[27] Because the police did not understand indecency as being a source of income, they did not describe the women's poverty in the way they openly discussed lack of food and clothing for arrested beggars during the same period. Poverty alone however does not explain recruitment into prostitution according to the historian Robert Jütte, as that would have resulted in a much larger number of prostitutes in early-modern times. European studies have generally focused on the fact that the women recruited into prostitution were servant girls between jobs or those who could not obtain employment, workers in the textile industry or unmarried mothers.[28]

In the interrogations that we find in the archives of the Christiania police and in the verdicts of the house of correction court many of the women explained that their difficulties in obtaining a position were due either to a former sentence at the house of correction or to the fact that they were unmarried mothers. For the former detainees, the resulting stigma and the degrading lack of clothing kept them out of work; for the unmarried mothers it was impossible to combine a full-time live-in service position with raising a child alone. Neither the interrogations nor verdicts give any impression that Elen or Anne had children, in contrast to many of the other arrested young women. Despite this, both sisters obviously had problems obtaining and keeping mandatory work. Elen claimed that she had not been able to obtain work as a servant because she had been incarcerated in the house of correction. Prior to her first sentence she had worked for two years as a servant, and then lived for several years at home with her parents, a situation that was prohibited for a girl older than 16. The penalty for theft was thus not the only explanation for her lack of steady service. The main reason, Elen claimed, was that her mother needed her care because of suffering from tuberculosis. Her mother had been sentenced to the house of correction in 1781, when Elen was about nine years old and Anne only six. The mother's sentence and coincident illness would have meant the loss of the household's bread winner, and been catastrophic for a family already on the brink of financial disaster. The stigma this may have imposed on the daughters might have resulted in few prospects for a proper servant post. Under these circumstances, the choice of prostitution was not unthinkable.

The social backgrounds of the arrested women bear witness to severe problems of maintenance that persisted over generations. None of the arrested women were daughters of farmers, and where the father was a skilled artisan, in each case one of the parents was deceased or supported by poor relief. The women belonged to the undifferentiated working classes of cottars, seasonal and casual labourers, peddlars, miners, servants and soldiers. Elen and Anne's father was a soldier, and in addition he died the very year Elen was sentenced to the house of correction for the first time. Structural poverty thus combined with an immediate crisis such as the death or illness of a breadwinner, or children born out of wedlock, and this seems to have been an important factor as to why these women ended up in prostitution. In addition, being sentenced to the house of correction contributed significantly to a process of further marginalization. A first sentence of theft could easily lead to severe problems in gaining employment and thus to a new sentence of vagrancy or a related accusation of indecency.

In the case of Elen and Anne, however, the household was not dissolved even though the family was in crisis. Most of the time the sisters were under police scrutiny they lived with their mother, either to nurse her or simply to reside in her home. The two other girls, Lisbeth and Karen, lived with Elen's mother at times, helping out with spinning, during the same period they were accused of leading indecent lives. This may be connected to the accusations that the mother was a procuress, as it is likely that – formerly being a prostitute herself – she was helping out her daughters and other girls.

The police focused on the violation of the labour legislation though the arrests were often triggered by the women's visibility. Only occasionally were the men connected with the women mentioned and the police were even less interested in the organization of prostitution. Clients for the most part fled when the watchmen approached them. But in the case of Elen a glimpse of a larger milieu is given. The watchmen claimed that when approaching the girls and accusing them of 'improper circulation and conduct' not only had the girls 'answered with impudent words' but the men accompanying them, seemingly attracted to them, had gone as far as to attack the watchmen.[29] The men in the company of Elen and other girls are seemingly distinct from their clients, but their presence is described with a certain ambiguity. The impression given is either that we are dealing with a broader group of disorderly young people or with the presence of procurers, pimps or some other types of protector.

Unwilling to Improve

Elen was arrested again in July 1797, only months after her release from the house of correction. This arrest occurred as part of a general sweep for vagrants initiated by the regional authorities.[30] Ten women and one man were arrested, including Elen and her younger sister Anne. The two sisters explained that their mother was still alive, and that 'they admitted that they had had no regular work for a long time, but were maintaining themselves as best as they could'.[31] At this point, the police emphasized the arrested women's unwillingness to improve. Elen had been warned and punished several times already, and her sister had followed in her footsteps. They were seen as 'vagrants and in addition they had led a dissolute life, which could not be excused by either age nor weakness'.[32] The chief of police, Fleischer, sentenced the two sisters and one of the other women, stating: 'Nothing is more inexcusable, than a young, able-bodied person indulging in idleness and vagrancy; and nothing is more certain than that the result of such a conduct is a lecherous life, which in the end becomes a burden to the public'.[33] In other words, the police stated that the women had no legitimate reason to be out of work. According to the police, prostitution was a moral vice that resulted from idleness, rather than a problem related to poverty. The punishment was, according to the police, for their own good. By contrast, the commission at the house of correction complained several times in the early 1790s that former inmates were unable to obtain work, and that especially women were unable to maintain a living after such a sentence. A decisive factor in the rather harsh sentence was the police case that the women's repeated arrests implied their unwillingness to reform. In this way, by the 1790s, moral failings such as 'callousness' and 'unwillingness' had been added to the vagrancy accusation, whereby vagrancy in the legislation merely implied the lack of legitimate work.

Only seven weeks after her release, and after spending two years in the house of correction, Elen was again arrested on a street corner in the city on a September night in 1799.[34] This time, the watchman and the police officers explained that they had encountered Elen several times during the autumn very drunk in the streets at night, and that 'this Elen Trulsdatter is the most lecherous woman, and they all wished for the good of the city, that she should be condemned to the house of correction for life'.[35] Even at this stage, though, Elen does not appear to be a totally marginalized person without support or network. She explained that since her release from the house of correction she had resided with her mother, now living in the early-industrialized area of Sagene along the city's river, and that she had lodged for a time with a potter in Vaterland. To earn a living, she explained that she tended the garden of the inspector at the house of correction, Hartwig. Still, this did not prevent her from being accused and convicted of idleness. An elderly woman appeared at the interrogation claiming that she had promised Elen work as a servant. This widow, Berthe Rasmusdatter, was presumably an acquaintance of Elen's mother. The chief of police claimed this was a ruse to prevent Elen from being sentenced as a vagrant, and that Elen never intended to seek steady service but rather walked the streets to maintain herself illegally.[36] The widow maintained that she spoke the truth, but Elen was still sentenced to the house of correction, this time for lechery.[37] The accusations of vagrancy of earlier arrests had gradually become pure accusations of disorderly conduct and sexual deviance. Furthermore, now indecency was described as the women's source of income and the categorizing of prostitution became explicit in cases where women were accused of making a living by 'indecency'.

While Elen was sentenced, five other girls in this regional sweep for vagrants were released. The police officers feared that one girl had a contagious disease and called for an internal examination by the military surgeon, who stated that the girl was severely infected with venereal disease. Increased control of prostitutes from the early nineteenth century was initiated for reasons of public health.[38] The fear of contagious disease is evident also in the vagrancy interrogations at the turn of the eighteenth to nineteenth century, and several of the women involved were subject to an internal examination at the police station, performed by the city doctor or even the military surgeon.

The very same month, September 1799, the younger sister Anne was convicted of indecency.[39] Since her last sentence for vagrancy she had been incarcerated in the house of correction for theft.[40] Now she was arrested with another girl on a ship in the roadstead, after the shipmaster complained that they were fraternizing with his men. The watchmen explained that 'both these women ... are well-known night misses, who are for the most part found outside the city at night, where according to rumour they even attack people'.[41] The watchmen found no excuse for their behaviour, and the court sentenced them to the house of correction stating that it was commonly known that the girls were not only vagrants, but even indulged in 'naughty indecency' and were thus deserving of punishment in the house of correction.[42]

A One-Way Ticket?

In a more general context, the historian Olwen Hufton claims that prostitution as a means of making a living was a one-way ticket into poverty. She states that prostitution was not only a source of income resulting from poverty, but also a cause of poverty.[43] This view is confirmed by the fact that Norwegian prostitutes in the nineteenth century had a shorter lifespan than the average population due to tuberculosis and syphilis, and that many had to be supported by poor relief when they had become 'physically useless' as prostitutes due to age or disease.[44] How does this compare to the case studies we have looked at, in our tracing of Elen and Anne's lifespans? They had obtained almost no regular employment while in their twenties, and they were reported as being disorderly and rude. When arrested for the last time, Elen was accused of alcoholic excess. The tuberculosis of their mother fits into this pattern, as she herself had been sentenced for 'night-running'. But while other girls were reported to be affected by venereal disease, there were no internal examinations of Elen and Anne at the time of their arrests. Whether or not prostitution meant a one-way ticket into increased poverty for the two sisters we do not know, but the effects of prostitution were not the lone cause of their sustained poverty and hardship. The sisters were already in a state of severe poverty to start with, but a major factor in their degradation and marginalization arose from their repeated sentences to the house of correction. These must have been physically exhausting as well as stigmatizing.

A comparison of the interrogations of the women accused of prostitution with the other vagrancy cases and the arrests of beggars in 1790s, suggests that there is no rigid demarcation between the arrested women and the poor in general. While there is certainly no reason to romanticize the prostitution of apparently very poor women there are thus some grounds for modifying Hufton's claim that prostitution was a one-way ticket into poverty. For many women, prostitution seems to have been merely a temporary or part-time source of income. The police interrogations suggest that for many women, prostitution was one of many ways of maintaining themselves in addition to casual labour, spinning, handicraft and petty theft, though to what extent is an unresolved question.

Thus the stigma of prostitution might have been minimal among the poor themselves, even though being sentenced to the correctional house was an undoubted stigma to employers. Studies of nineteenth-century prostitution show that many women married within the lower classes after ending their careers in prostitution, which was also the case for Elen and Anne's mother. The extent to which prostitution was stigmatizing was thus dependent on the community to which the women belonged. Despite several arrests and sentences, the two sisters Elen and Anne were not totally socially excluded. The women's life stories reveal a process of marginalization, but also of social interaction that demonstrates no clear demarcation between the poor underclass at large and women in prostitution. The sisters were part of a larger network of family, friends and neighbours, and were even defended by persons of authority. The stigma from the house of correction made it difficult for them to obtain proper work, but it may not have excluded them from their community, which consisted of the broadly poor, and partly disorderly, lower classes.

In the interrogations dating from the 1790s the prostitute was not seen by the police as a specific or separate category of criminal. Only at the turn of the century was there a marked increase in this form of categorization when more girls were accused of making a living by indecency, and not only of leading an indecent life. These references to prostitution were restricted to the charges made against prostituted women, while the broader organization of prostitution was barely mentioned at all in the interrogations. For the most part, police targeted streetwalking, though not systematically. This leaves us with the questions of whether the prostitution targeted in this way was full-time or merely one of many sources of income, and whether or not there were brothelkeepers, pimps or other forms of organization.

The social portrait of the two sisters Elen and Anne, known for making a living by indecency and part of a larger community of poor, sheds new light on prostitution and its regulation in the eighteenth century. Tracing their lives during the 1790s, significant changes are seen in the police interrogations and verdicts. While there was a prominent decline in the number of persons sentenced for vagrancy in the 1790s, the two sisters' former sentences were increasingly used against them and they were subsequently sentenced four times each. While the poor laws and labour legislation defined vagrancy merely as lack of legitimate employment, the courts in the 1790s, and especially from the mid-1790s, focused increasingly on the women's moral vices and their reluctance to improve. Vagrancy was now not merely seen as a state of unemployment, but also connected to indecency, lechery and unwillingness to reform. By the turn of the century the category of prostitution was increasingly visible in cases where the accusations of indecency was not only described as a moral vice, but a way of making a living. The eighteenth century represents a transitional period where the prostitute was found at the core of a range of ideological changes. While the pietistic legislation of the seventeenth century, with statutes against whorehouses, prostitution and procuring, was hardly in use in the eighteenth century, prostitutes were nonetheless targeted by the mercantilist legislation implemented in this period directed at the poor and labour regulation. But in addition the 1790s represented a second shift, where vagrancy was turning from being a broad accusation criminalizing all unemployment, to a narrower accusation of unwillingness to maintain a proper life.

In 1799 the sisters were incarcerated simultaneously at the house of correction, both serving their fourth sentences. Elen was now approximately 27 years and Anne 24 years old. In December of that year they escaped together, with help from the porter's daughter, who let them out. After this escape there is no trace of the sisters in the records of the house of correction or in the national census of 1801. They had been arrested each year during the previous seven-year period; now, they had apparently escaped the authorities' control. Whether prostitution was a one-way ticket into enduring poverty or a stage in their lives, and whether their escape gave them the opportunity to create another life, the sources do not tell. How the two sisters ended their lives is yet unknown.

13 MALE PROSTITUTION AND THE EMERGENCE OF THE MODERN SEXUAL SYSTEM: EIGHTEENTH-CENTURY LONDON

Randolph Trumbach

Most historians of prostitution have concentrated on the lives of female prostitutes. Alain Corbin's *Women for Hire* (1978; trans. 1990) and my own *Sex and the Gender Revolution*, vol. 1 (1998) are exceptional in attempting to study the male clients as well as the women themselves. The history of male prostitution before the twentieth century has similarly gone unstudied. There are two pioneering books on the Cleveland Street male brothel in the late nineteenth century and an essay by Jeffrey Weeks; more recently Rafael Carrasco published an exceptional study of boy prostitutes drawn from the records of the Inquisition; and in 2010 Barry Reay published a book on twentieth-century hustlers in New York City.[1] The present article argues that the forms and changes in the organization of male prostitution provide one of the most revealing guides as to whether a particular society has moved from a traditional to a modern sexual system. This essay therefore contrasts male prostitution in eighteenth-century London with what had preceded it before 1700. The essay argues that in the traditional sexual system, all adult males were attracted both to women and to adolescent males. But in a modern sexual system adult males were divided into a heterosexual majority attracted only to women, and a homosexual minority attracted only to males, either adults or adolescents. That is, at any rate, the theory. In actual practice, as will be shown, a considerable number of heterosexual men (perhaps as many as a third), in the early stages of a modern sexual system, occasionally had sex with men from the homosexual minority, some of whom were adult transvestite prostitutes.[2]

I. Male Prostitution in the Traditional Sexual System

Before the eighteenth century in western Europe, the evidence suggests that most if not all adult men were sexually attracted to both women and adolescent boys, with puberty beginning at 14 or 15 years of age.[3] Men went either to female prostitutes or to male prostitutes who were mostly adolescent boys but among whom there were a few adult males. Some men used both male and female prostitutes. Female prostitutes often dressed as boys to attract men, and some boys and most adult male prostitutes dressed as girls or women. Male prostitution can be documented in England from literary sources, biographical anecdotes and a few legal cases, whereas for Italy, Spain and Portugal there is extensive legal evidence for these two kinds of male prostitution. In fifteenth-century Florence, at least two-thirds of all adult men were charged with sodomy with adolescent males; most of this behavior was voluntary between the partners but some of it took the form of prostitution. The category of the young male prostitute, for example, was recognized by the use of the term '*bardassa*'. In Venice in 1585, Captain Annibale Contucci's landlady complained that having installed over his bed a painting of a naked woman in an obscene pose, he then brought home female prostitutes and boys. The records of the Spanish Inquisition from the sixteenth to the eighteenth centuries document the prostitution of young males: some boys were paid occasionally for sex, and some made prostitution their means of living. In Valencia in 1629 Francisco de Lindo said that he had 'nothing left to pawn but my arse'; and when in 1712 a fourteen-year-old surgeon's apprentice agreed to let a man 'stick it up his arse' for one *real*, he knew where in the town they could go to do it safely. The Portuguese Inquisition records give evidence of boy prostitutes and the occasional adult transvestite.[4]

In the London sources documenting the traditional sexual system before the eighteenth century, two kinds of male prostitute are evident: the adult male transvestite, and adolescent boys, some of whom might be transvestite. Before the turn of the eighteenth century, the world of male prostitution was mostly populated by adolescent male prostitutes, who might sometimes be transvestite, but whose clients were usually men who also desired women (alongside some adult male transvestites). After the turn of the eighteenth century, the transvestite male prostitute conceived of himself as a 'molly' who desired only men, but many of his unsuspecting clients would have been men who desired only women. These clients could therefore be blackmailed with the threat that sodomy would be sworn against them. After 1700 it was also the case that clients of most male prostitutes would have been mollies or men who desired only men even though they might be married to women. These clients would often have had as their prostitutes soldiers in their early twenties (that is, in late adolescence) whose attraction for the molly was partly that they could be thought of as men who desired only women. Male transvestite prostitution in the traditional sexual system had one meaning because it occurred in a world in which most men desired both women and boys. It had an entirely different meaning in the modern sexual system when it occurred in a world in which most men desired only women and the minority who desired males might pursue either adults or adolescents and might wish to be penetrated as well as to penetrate.

A good example of male prostitution at the end of the seventeenth century comes from the life of the libertine lawyer John Hoyle, who had once been the lover of Aphra Behn. At the end of January 1687 Benjamin Bourne, an apprentice of a poulterer in Gracechurch Street, told the magistrate that Hoyle in December had buggered him in Leadenhall Market and given him five shillings. Hoyle had then invited the seventeen-year-old boy several times to his chambers in the Inner Temple where they had had sex again, but the boy complained that for these subsequent acts he got no more money. Instead Hoyle gave him a pair of turtledoves. This looks as though Hoyle had tried to turn a prostituted affair into a love relationship, but the boy does not seem to have been interested. Hoyle admitted that he had been with the boy several times in his master's shop and had invited him to his chambers in the Temple. Hoyle confessed to 'several indecent acts' between himself and the boy, but he denied that penetration had occurred, as he had to if he was to avoid being hanged for sodomy. Hoyle also said that he had attempted an indecent act with Thomas Archer who worked as an apprentice in the same poulterer's shop. Roger Morrice commented of the first boy, that when 'there was a difference between' Hoyle and Aphra Behn, 'this boy used to carry messages between them'. The case came to trial, but Hoyle was discharged for reasons that are not clear: perhaps the boy had retracted his claim to have been buggered several times. Lord Sackville in a poem on the trial called the boy Hoyle's 'he-mistress' and ironically praised the jurors for allowing Hoyle to show that a man a 'greater hazard runs who f[uck]s one daughter than a hundred sons'.[5]

Hoyle had had previous affairs with males. Behn, for instance, had written of his love affair with the actor Edward Bedford, and there is a supposed letter of hers warning him that his 'too close familiarity with young f[ello]ws' was ruining his reputation. But Behn in plays like *The Town Fop* or *The Amorous Prince*, easily introduced the idea that a character like Bellmour might be 'Italianiz'd, and lovest thy own sex' and has Lorenzo look at the boy Philbert (who is a girl in disguise) and think 'Tis a fine lad, how plump and white he is; would I could meet him somewhere i'th' dark, I'd have a fling at him, and try whether I were right Florentine'. Lorenzo also tells the boy to avoid sex with women since "twill spoil a good face, and mar your better market on the two'. Hoyle was killed by George Pitt in 1692 in a quarrel over politics. Whitelocke Bulstrode at Hoyle's death described him as having been 'an atheist, a sodomite professed, a corrupter of youth, and a blasphemer of Christ'. Bulstrode did not say but Hoyle's blasphemy had probably taken the form of claiming that Jesus and St John had been lovers, as Christopher Marlowe, King James I, and Captain Edward Rigby had all done.[6]

II. Male Prostitution in Eighteenth-Century London: The Transition to the Modern Sexual System

In the early eighteenth century, as female prostitution in London became more widespread, it also gained greater importance for the 'heterosexual' majority of men (as it was later called), who felt impelled to demonstrate that they had not been contaminated by the effeminate minority of sodomites or mollies, and that their sexual desire was exclusively for women. This early eighteenth-century transformation in sexuality and gender roles also changed the nature of male prostitution, as the following case studies indicate. Before providing detailed examples of each of various types of male prostitution, variously organized in this essay as soldiers, boys, molly house clients and transvestites, it is useful to given an overview of these different types. Men most likely to prostitute themselves were soldiers in their late teens and early twenties, whose uniforms made them conspicuous sexual objects throughout the city. The following evidence shows that they sometimes engaged in sodomy, especially those who stood sentry in the London parks. Soldiers were as a consequence knowledgeable about the sodomites' world, making use of that knowledge to blackmail them. Evidence suggests that approximately half of the men who were sodomites preferred boys who were just entering puberty in their middle teens, some of whom became prostitutes. Some of these boys also engaged in blackmail. Both the boys and the soldiers who were prostitutes were probably in most cases not sodomites themselves. The effeminate mollies who operated as prostitutes out of the molly houses were also sometimes coerced into betraying their world to the magistrates. The most effeminate prostitutes were transvestites who sometimes had sex with men who did not realize that their partners were biological males. This could make these transvestites into yet another category of blackmailer.[7] All these types of prostitutes were poor. Among the well off, there were instances of patronage between older and younger males, which can be seen as a kind of more polite prostitution (the equivalent perhaps of a man who kept a mistress).

Soldiers

Soldiers were the group of males in London most likely to prostitute themselves. They were also the men most likely to blackmail sodomites, and it is probable that prostitution often turned into blackmail. When a soldier was apprehended it would seem that he was more prepared to admit to blackmail than prostitution since blackmail was less threatening to the honor of a young male than engaging in sodomy. These issues arise at the very beginning of the century in the case in 1709 of George Skelthorp, a twenty-five-year-old man born in Bury St Edmunds, Suffolk. He first worked as a servant in the families of gentlemen in the country and in London. Seven years before his trial and execution, he joined the army, served in two different companies in Ireland and in Flanders, and was in five campaigns. When he was arrested in London, he was serving in the First Regiment of Foot Guards. He told the chaplain of Newgate prison that 'he had been a wild young man' who 'would be rambling abroad instead of going to church' and that he had been 'easily induced to a loose life of drinking, whoring, and breaking the Sabbath-day'.

On February 18, 1709 in the neighborhood of Covent Garden, William Hills asked Skelthorp the way to King Street. Skelthorp led Hills into a byway, and taking out his bayonet, held it at Hills's breast. He demanded 'satisfaction' from Hills because 'he was a sodomite'. He took 4s 6d from Hills, forced Hills's great coat off his back and tried to get his rings from off his fingers. Hills was rescued by passers-by who heard him begging for his life. They seized Skelthorp and took him to the magistrate. Skelthorp must have secured his release since nine days later he threatened James Booker that he would swear sodomy against him and took from him a golden ring, a muslin neckcloth and ten shillings. Two days later Skelthorp was brought to trial, found guilty and hanged on March 23 for these robberies.

Skelthorp explained what had happened by telling the chaplain that knowing the time and place 'where some sodomites were resorting about Covent Garden', he would 'stand in their way' to be picked up, but that when they took him into a by-place for sex, he would take hold of them and threaten them with a justice of the peace. By these means '(he said) he got a great deal of money at several times'. Skelthorp said that he could identify these men as sodomites because 'there was a certain public house about Covent Garden, where he knew these sodomites used frequently to meet, and [he] had seen some of them there several times'. This may have been the molly house that Ned Ward described in his account of molly houses in 1709. But Skelthorp seems to have described several houses to the justices, possibly in the mistaken hope that this would save him from the gallows. Certainly a little later a brandy shop near German Street was raided and nine men were taken up. The brandyman and a duke's foot-boy were committed to the Gatehouse prison. Skelthorp had clearly been inside these molly houses and had presumably been approached for sex by the men present in the houses. He denied to the chaplain that he had ever had sex with any of them, but he added that 'he could not tell whether if he had gone on in that trade, it would not at last have brought him to yield to their lewd and foul practices'. It is hard to believe that the sodomites in the molly houses had not viewed the visiting soldier in his foot-guards uniform as a prostitute available for hire. If Skelthorp had always only threatened and blackmailed and never given sex, one presumes that his reputation would have become known soon enough and that this would have put a stop to his lucrative trade. It is also difficult to say what had happened with the two men who brought him to trial. Had he misidentified these men as sodomites? Skelthorp denied that he was guilty 'of any crime that should have brought him before any justice'. Did he mean that demanding 'satisfaction' from sodomites was not a crime? At his execution as he stood on the cart (which when driven away would leave him hanging by his neck), he began to argue as to what had actually occurred with one of the men who had charged him and had come to see him hang. He then complained that six others who had been condemned to hang had been pardoned but not him. The chaplain silenced him. Skelthorp then warned other young men to avoid his sins and returned to his prayers until the cart was driven away.[8]

Two generations after Skelthorp, in 1776, Anthony Loame, a soldier in a guards regiment stationed in London, claimed to have knowledge of male prostitution for gentlemen organized out of a house in Nag's Head Court, Drury Lane. This courtyard in 1777 was cited as having a nest of six bawdy houses for female prostitutes run by Catherine French, Sarah Broxden, Jonathan Buckley and his wife Catherine, Sarah Williams and Joseph Stanhope and his wife. Loame gave his evidence in the sodomy trial of Joseph Burrows. Loame at first claimed to be a cabinet and chair-maker living in Hart Street, Covent Garden, but he admitted to being a soldier after Burrows said that he was. Burrows, on the other hand, said that by trade he himself was a watchcase-maker but Loame described Burrows as washing and cooking 'for these sodomites; and picks up young fellows for them'. Loame said that Burrows had picked him up in the Harlequin, a public house in Drury Lane. Burrows plied Loame with beer and gin and then asked him to come home with him to Nag's Head Court to share some turkey and goose. The house in Nag's Head was kept by a gentleman who kept a carriage. There were five other gentlemen present for supper and they sent for a couple of bottles of wine. At the end of the meal Loame went home. In Burrows's account, he and another young fellow were drinking at a public house, where they had a pound of buttock of beef, which they had asked Loame to share. Burrows did not see Loame again until walking through the Park he met Loame who was on sentry duty. Loame said he had longed to see Burrows and asked him where he lived. Loame had quarrelled with his wife, 'had dashed her through the windows and cut her arm almost off'. Loame insisted that Burrows go with him to visit his wife in hospital, then made him drunk and took Burrows 'home to sleep with him'. Burrows had a pair of silk stockings in his pocket which Loame took. Afraid that Burrows would charge him with stealing them, Loame first had him impressed as a soldier and then brought sodomy charges against him, at which point he told a quite different story to Sir John Fielding than he did later in court. Burrows said that the sodomy accusation was 'as false as God is true' and that he had 'been harassed about so, that I have not had time', presumably to assemble an adequate defense.

But the jury believed Loame and condemned Burrows to death for sodomy. In Loame's account, Burrows came to fetch Loame to take him to the house in Nag's Head Court, saying that there was 'a gentleman would be glad to speak to me concerning some business out of the country'. This house apparently did exist and Burrows had been there, but he said that Loame had 'sent for me to Mr. Robertson's; I did not send for him'. At Mr Robertson's, Loame found fourteen men who were 'gentlemen and gentlemen's servants together'. A rug taken from a bed in the room had been hung up over a corner. Burrows took William Brooks, a gentleman's servant, behind the rug. (Brooks had not been arrested by the time of Burrows's trial.) Loame, sitting by the fireplace, saw Brooks lean his head against the wall. After both men had taken down their breeches and tucked up their shirts, Burrows took out his penis and entered Brooks's backside. This took about ten minutes. Loame saw Burrows's 'nastiness about the room' after he withdrew from Brooks. Brooks and Burrows now came over to Loame and said they 'wanted to do the same' to him as they 'began kissing and slavering' over him. A gentleman offered Loame three guineas if 'I would go and lie with him at an inn; and afterwards he offered to make it up to ten'. This house of prostitution probably existed, and it may well have catered to gentlemen and their servants. But it is likely that poor Burrows told the truth, and that it was the guardsman Loame who was the active prostitute who recruited young fellows for gentlemen.[9]

A soldier could have a relation over a number of years with a man who occasionally paid him: this is what the evidence seems to suggest about Charles Butts and Paul Hill. Butts was a married man. He and his wife were both servants, but they lived and served in different households. In February 1794 another soldier, Thomas Steward, appeared late at night at the door of the house in which Butts worked as a footman. Steward told Butts that he was going abroad with a draft of soldiers and asked if Butts had anything to send to Paul Hill who had already left with his regiment. Butts simply asked Steward to say that he was well if Steward found Hill alive. Steward said that if Butts had nothing to send Hill, he wanted a guinea for himself, and stuck his foot in the door when Butts tried to close it. Steward told Butts that he was 'a bloody b[u]gg[e]r' and that he 'understood that there were connections between Hill' and Butts. A woman now appeared who turned out to be Hill's landlady but claimed to be his wife. She said that Butts 'had given her husband many pounds' and 'had been intimate with her husband, and slept along with him'. Butts said he had known both soldiers for four and a half years and that the soldiers frequently drank together at the Bunch of Grapes in Queen Square Westminster. Butts, of course, denied any sodomy with Hill. If there had been a relationship, it seems that Steward and the other acquaintances of Hill's had known and tolerated it. The relationship only became problematical when Hill's friends in his absence tried to blackmail Butts. Butts prevailed and Steward was sentenced to two years in prison.[10]

The clearest evidence for soldiers as prostitutes comes from the sodomy trial in 1727 of Charles Hitchen, the under-marshal of the City of London. In 1726 and 1727, as in 1709, there had been raids on molly houses in which a number of sodomites were arrested, some of whom were condemned to death and hanged. The crucial evidence against these men was given by two young male prostitutes who had worked in the molly houses, and to their story we will return. The men in the molly houses were often effeminate: they took women's names, spoke and moved like women, and sometimes wore women's clothes. This kind of sodomy was not to Charles Hitchen's taste. Hitchen in 1727 was in his early forties and like a number of men taken from the molly houses he was married, in his case for twenty-four years. With his wife's fortune in 1711 Hitchen had purchased the office of under-marshal. He used this office to extort money from the keepers of brothels and taverns and forced young pickpockets to bring their stolen goods to him so that for a fee he could negotiate with the owners of the goods for their return. He engaged Jonathan Wild as his assistant, but Wild took over the protection racket. When the two men fell out, they attacked each other in pamphlets. Wild described a tour of a molly house that Hitchen gave him. Hitchen had described the men as 'a company of he-whores', which when Wild asked 'if they were hermaphrodites', Hitchen answered, 'No ye fool ... they are sodomites such as deal with their own sex instead of females'. When Hitchen was embarrassed by the appearance of some people he had not expected at the molly house, he stormed out with threats. His revenge was to have the men arrested when they came to dance dressed as women. The Lord Mayor ordered them to the workhouse and had them paraded through the streets in their costumes. They remained in the workhouse until one of them threatened that he would reveal Hitchen's own sodomy unless he secured their release.[11]

Hitchen's taste was less for men and more for early adolescent soldiers. Christopher Finch who was a servant at the Talbot Inn testified that because of Hitchen's 'frequent coming there with soldiers, and calling for a private room, he suspected him to be guilty of sodomitical practices'. On the evening of March 29, Hitchen met Richard Williamson who was a drummer in the army. Sometimes adult men served as drummers, but often drummers were adolescents between fourteen and eighteen. Hitchens invited the youth to drink and took him to the Royal Oak in the Strand where they had two pints of beer. Hitchen now began 'to show some little sodomitical civilities'. This did not please the boy, who said he had business at the Savoy, a military headquarters. Hitchen made him promise to return and took the boy's hat as pledge that he would. Hitchen also gave Williamson 'a little money and a great many fair promises'. When the boy returned, they went to the Rummer Tavern and had two pints of wine. Hitchen now also kissed and caressed him sexually. Then the boy was persuaded to go to the Talbot Inn, which seems to have been Hitchen's usual locale for the climax of his evening. At the Talbot, there was another pint of wine and Hitchen ordered a room and two nightcaps. He had sex with the young drummer but did not anally penetrate him. Some of this was observed through the keyhole by Christopher Finch who had realized for some time what Hitchen did with his young soldiers in the private rooms he took. The next morning Williamson was full of 'frightful apprehensions' and revealed the whole story to his relative Joseph Cockrost. Cockrost came to the Inn (he had arranged to be called) when Hitchen next brought a soldier and also observed the sex through the keyhole. He knocked on the door and confronted Hitchen when he opened it. Sodomitical penetration could not be proven, and so Hitchen was convicted of attempting sodomy. He was sentenced to stand in the pillory, fined £20, imprisoned six months, and required to find security for his good behavior for three years. In the pillory his clothes were torn off his back, his breeches pulled down, and his bare skin whipped with canes. Hitchen died in poverty shortly thereafter.[12]

Thomas White, a drummer in the 3rd Regiment of Guards, aged sixteen in 1810, was an experienced prostitute. He was observed by John Newball Hepburn, an ensign, who spoke to another drummer boy, James Mann, on the parade in St James's Park, and told him that he would reward Mann if he brought the boy who was beating the big drum to his lodgings in St Martin's Churchyard. The two boys arrived that evening and Hepburn invited them to dine with him in his lodgings on the coming Sunday. White said that it 'was not a good place and proposed that they should meet at the Swan in Vere Street'. The Swan was a notorious molly house whose upper part 'was appropriated to wretches who were constantly in waiting for casual customers'. It was raided shortly afterwards. When the two boys arrived on Sunday at the Swan, they were shown into a private room. Before and after dinner, Hepburn and White had sex as the other boy looked on. Since they were both condemned to death, this must have involved anal penetration. After the Swan was raided, Mann told his drum-major what he had seen and Hepburn and White were arrested. Hepburn seems to have known that White was sexually available and White knew a safe place to take a customer.[13] But not every drummer was available. In December 1776 when a man tried to pick up a boy named Smith who was a drummer in the guards, Smith was 'resolute, he seized the villain, and took him to St Martin's watchouse'.[14]

Boys

Boys who were not in the army could be drawn into prostitution, if only until their bad conscience or physical injury made them draw back. This was the case in the seduction of twelve-year-old Frances Henry Hay by Captain Robert Jones in 1772. Hay lived and worked with his uncle who was a jeweller in Parliament Street. Walking in St Martin's Lane, Jones would run into the boy, who said that Jones 'always used to look at me and give me a halfpence when he met me'. Eventually Jones told the boy that he had a buckle he wished to have mended. He took him into St Martin's Court and upstairs into the dining room of his lodgings where he had lived for eight years when he was in England. Jones locked the door and took down both their breeches. The boy said he was a little frightened. Jones put the boy into an elbow chair, kissed him a little, and then 'made me lay down with my face on the chair, and so he came behind me; he put his c[oc]k into my b[acksid]e'. Hay said he 'submitted to it quietly'. When this was over, Jones kissed the boy again and gave him some halfpence, 'about a groat' or four pence. This all took half an hour. Jones asked the boy to return the next morning when he stayed ten minutes and masturbated Jones until he ejaculated. (Hay himself at twelve was just on the verge of puberty and probably could not ejaculate). Jones gave the boy the buckle to repair and some halfpence. He asked him to return the next morning at the same time. The boy duly came and masturbated Jones a second time. There were no more visits. The penetration had left the boy sore: he said that he 'straddled as I walked' and 'had a pain in my thighs and legs that I could not stand'. A few weeks later Jones came looking for the boy in the shop. Hay was serving another customer, so Jones ordered from the uncle a shirt buckle that was to be delivered to his lodgings. When the boy's uncle ordered him to take the buckle to Jones, he declined, and in this way the story of the three encounters came out. The boy said that he was 'ashamed' of what had happened, but that he had returned the second and third times because he 'thought my uncle might get business by it' and 'because he always used to give me money'. Jones was found guilty and condemned to death but was pardoned by the king. The pardon sparked an extensive debate in the newspapers as to whether this encouraged sodomy. But in none of the discussion was it mentioned that the boy's age had made Jones' actions especially reprehensible.[15]

A boy was capable of pursuing a man. In 1762 a 'well dressed gentleman-like man' of about fifty was taken as he tried to sodomize a boy in St George's Fields. The boy was apprenticed to Thomas Cross, a woolcomber in Shoreditch. The man was examined for three hours during all of which time he maintained 'that the boy run after him, not him after the boy, which was the case, from Westminster Abbey to St George's Fields'. How the boy had identified the man as a potential customer and what their financial arrangements were was not mentioned, but presumably they had met as they had sauntered over the Abbey. The two magistrates held the man responsible and bound him over to be tried at the next Southwark sessions.[16]

A boy who presented himself as an available prostitute could be used in a blackmail scheme. After spending an evening in 1772 visiting a relation in St Martin's Lane, 'a considerable and reputable trader in Cheapside', with a wife and children, made his way home through Covent Garden. There a boy came up to him and bowed, smiled and claimed to know the man. The man denied this, and when the boy audaciously continued to follow him, he seized him and called out for the watch. At this two men immediately stepped up, took the man by the collar, and charged him with attempting an unnatural crime on the boy. The man demanded that they all go to the magistrate who was Sir John Fielding. The two blackmailers now became alarmed, tried to 'soothe and pacify' the man, saying 'what an odious affair it was', how much it would damage his reputation, and that it would be better for them all to go to a public house and work out an accommodation. But the man instead continued to call for the watch who had evidently still not appeared. One of the blackmailers, determined to have some prize, snatched the man's cane out of his hand, and all three ran away across the garden.[17] When the 'reputable tradesman' had decided to make his way through Covent Garden he may, of course, have been taking the quickest way home. But Covent Garden was notoriously full of female prostitutes, and it had an area that a newspaper in 1779 described as the 'Sodomitical Walk'. On a July Sunday that year the constables of the parish arrested four men who were part of a set who 'assembled and paraded nightly within the rails of Covent-Garden market' especially along the Sodomitical Walk. The newspaper explained that 'the speeches, faces, behavior, deportment and dress of those wretches' indicated the kind of men they were. Sir John Fielding sent them to Savoy to serve as soldiers.[18] Had the boy approached the reputable tradesman because he had caught a glint of interest in his eye?

Molly Houses

Four male prostitutes who were familiar with the molly houses and found clients through them gave crucial evidence in the cases the government brought in the seven years between 1726 and 1732 in its campaigns against the molly houses and the men who used them: Mark Partridge, Thomas Newton, Edward Courtney and Edward Curtis. One of these men, Mark Partridge, never actually appeared in court but something of his afterlife can be found in the newspapers. Thomas Newton must have seemed convincing to the juries since they convicted all the men he testified against. Edward Courtney, a wild young man, had a more mixed reception. No one believed Edward Curtis in any of the several trials in which he appeared in 1732, and the failure of all these cases may have persuaded the government to end its campaign against the mollies and their houses.

Thomas Newton was sodomized by Thomas Wright at his house in Christopher's Alley, Moorfields. Mollies came to this house and Wright went out to fetch ale for them: he had the same arrangement when he moved to Beech Lane. Wright acted as a bawd for some of his customers: Newton recalled that 'he has often fetched me to oblige company that way, and especially to one Gregory Turner, whom commonly chose me for his sweetheart'. This was also the practice in houses for female prostitutes: the bawd sent for a woman after a customer had arrived. After Newton was arrested for sodomy himself, he agreed to give evidence against others. Edward Courtney, who was eighteen, after he was 'turned out of' his job met George Kedger with whom he had previously had sex. At that moment Courtney was in 'a very poor and ragged condition'. He told Kedger that 'he had nothing to subsist upon' but what he got from the men he slept with. Kedger advised him to give it up but Courtney said 'he wanted money, and money he would have, by hook or by crook; and if I did not help him to some, he would swear my life away'. According to Courtney, George Whittle kept an alehouse for mollies that had a bed for sex. In this house Whittle 'has brought me to several husbands as we used to call them'. Whittle once told Courtney that 'there's a country gentleman of my acquaintance that's just come to town, and if you'll give him a wedding night, he'll pay you handsomely'. The gentleman did not come, and instead Whittle persuaded Courtney to go to bed with him. He said that he would pay him but in the morning Whittle gave Courtney only sixpence. Courtney thought that Whittle had 'put the bite on me'. The jury believed Courtney about Kedger, but they acquitted Whittle.[19]

William Curtis came to London when he was about sixteen, and went to work for Mr Nutt, a printer in the Old Bailey. There he was befriended by John Ashford, a bookseller in Westminster Hall, who was also one of Nutt's lodgers. Curtis and Ashford shared a bed. After a month Curtis claimed that Ashford began to kiss him, 'call me his dear Billy, and to meddle with my privy parts'. Ashford gave the boy money, three shillings a week, paid his bills at two toyshops, and made a suit of clothes for him at Easter. Eventually, Curtis said, Ashford 'over-persuaded me to let him bugger me', which Ashford did frequently. Other lodgers knew that the man and the boy had their difficulties. Nicholls said that when Ashford came home drunk, the boy complained that he was 'a nasty toad' with whom he would not share a bed. But Ashford also lectured the boy when he failed to do his master's work. Curtis said that Ashford was 'always preaching Presbyterian sermons to him'. But everyone in the house agreed that Curtis was a liar and for this reason Thomas Hambleton did not believe him when Curtis told him that Ashford was 'a molly and a sodomite' who had sodomized him. Curtis had in any case found a livelier set of friends, especially William Bishop, George Cadogan and Henry Catten, who Curtis said were sodomites. The boy began not to come home at night and for this he was eventually fired. In July 1732 Curtis was arrested for sodomitical practices. He persuaded Sir John Gonson, the chairman of the Westminster justices bench, and Justice Thomas De Veil, that he could deliver to them a network of sodomites: 'a club or society of sodomites who meet together weekly in several parts of the town in masquerade habits, many of them in women's apparel, the better to carry on their vile and detestable practices'. He eventually named Bishop, Cadogan and Catten, but he did not initially charge Ashford. All four men were put on trial in early September, Ashford at the Old Bailey, the other three at Hick's Hall, the Middlesex sessions house. All four were acquitted because no one would believe the boy's stories. It looks as though Gonson and De Veil had convinced themselves that they had found another young prostitute who would give them the chance to repeat the successful trials of 1726, but Curtis was too obviously unreliable, a boy who would say anything to get himself out of a tight spot.[20]

Mark Partridge guided Joseph Sellers into the molly houses, passing Sellers off as his husband so that the other mollies would leave him alone. Sellers was able to observe events he was subsequently to report at the trials. Poor Gabriel Lawrence was indicted for sodomizing Partridge who he suspected had betrayed his fellows, but Partridge never had to appear in court since Lawrence was also condemned for sodomizing Thomas Newton, another prostitute. In 1724 it was probably this Mark Partridge who was fined £5, imprisoned six months, and forced to find sureties for his good behavior for three years, all for keeping a disorderly house. It was certainly our Partridge who in October 1735 was fined, imprisoned, and forced to find sureties again. He had entered the house of Edward Dogan with a warrant, pretending to be a constable, and had taken Dogan to a tavern where he had tried to extort money by threatening to charge him with sodomitical practices. The newspaper called Partridge 'Small-Coal Moll', and in 1726, a recognizance he had been identified as a coal seller. The newspaper also identified Partridge as having been 'formerly an evidence against Lawrence the milkman, one Wright, and another who were hanged some years ago at Tyburn for sodomy'. Partridge also tried to cash a promissory note that George Hart had extorted from Josiah Pack by threatening to swear sodomy against Pack. Partridge had gone from betraying his fellow sodomites to the constables to blackmailing them for his own profit, evidently as part of a gang. Partridge also continued to be an active sodomite and was probably still a prostitute: in early September he had been committed to Newgate after being indicted for 'sodomitical practices'.[21]

Transvestites

Men dressed in women's clothes appear throughout the eighteenth century and are the final category of male prostitutes in this discussion. Thomas (or Charles) Jones was such a man. Known as Miss Jenny Jones, he was arrested in the Park in 1778 for trying to pick up a young man. The *London Evening Post* wrote that 'this *wretched lady* is fifty years of age, and grey-headed, and as audacious in his infamy as that paragon of male practices, D[rybutte]r'. (Stories of Samuel Drybutter's sodomitical adventures had been a feature of the newspapers earlier in the 1770s.) The *Post* described Jones as 'a male prostitute', a revealing linguistic usage. At the beginning of the century when the role of the effeminate molly was first discussed, John Dunton in 1710 called all sodomites 'he-whores'. Jonathan Wild in 1718 had claimed that Charles Hitchen had offered to introduce him to 'a company of he-whores'. Wild had not understood the phrase and had asked whether they were 'hermaphrodites', to which Hitchen had replied, 'no ... they are sodomites'. As Wild suggests, the way sodomites behaved among men gave them the status that female prostitutes had among women.[22]

Some sodomites seemed to have presumed that any male could be bought. In 1731, in a public room of the Sun Alehouse in Hungerford Market, a dealer in chinaware tried to pick up one of a group of six gentlemen drinking together, who was entirely unknown to him, by offering him some money. But even in 1731, the presence in the molly houses of younger male prostitutes who could betray their fellows to the authorities shows that there always was a distinction between sodomites who had sex freely with others, and those who expected to be paid. The newspapers seem occasionally to understand that there was an economic basis to male prostitution. In 1752, *Read's Weekly* reported of two men who had been caught in a dark alley, that 'those who are guilty of this bestial crime are seldom cautious enough to choose a privacy to prevent a discovery', although it was common for men to have a female prostitute in a dark place in the street. One of the men was a 'well dressed genteel fellow and had the appearance of a gentleman'. The other man was 'in a ragged condition', and this one, the newspaper noted, 'seems to have been hired for that purpose'. None of the sources recovered describe as prostitutes the many young soldiers who were paid for sex by other men. This may have been because most of those soldiers did not think of themselves as sodomites. But a man who went about in women's clothes probably had a sodomite's identity even though he might be married to a woman. When the *Post* described Jones as a 'male prostitute' it was therefore distinguishing among types of sodomites, and no longer describing all sodomites as he-whores. The men who picked up soldiers, on the other hand, may not have wanted them to be sodomites, and this may explain why they inquired whether a soldier was married. Sex with a man from (to use the nineteenth-century term) the 'heterosexual' majority may have been more thrilling than sex with a fellow sodomite.[23]

In some cases, transvestite prostitutes blackmailed their sometimes-unwitting clients by pointing out to them that they had had sex with a man. James Dalton in 1728 told the tale of Susannah or Sukey Haws. Some of the detail can be corroborated from other sources. Haws took Dalton to visit a number of molly houses including one run by 'Aunt Wittles', who was the George Whittle that the prostitute Edward Courtney had unsuccessfully given evidence against. Dalton described Haws as 'a man who was what they call a bug to the mollies, and sometimes acting in that capacity with those that were not established in clubs, picking 'em up, as if to commit that damnable crime of sodomy; and when they had got an handle... they would extort money from them'. In 1757 a man wrote a letter to Lord Tankerville offering to meet him for an assignation. When he was arrested he was found to be carrying a number of letters which might 'either pass for a begging letter of a man in distress or to offer his person for the basest purposes'. When his neighbors were questioned, they said that 'he lay in bed every day till after twelve; that he constantly breakfasted in bed, wore a bedgown, and a woman's cap and knot: his paint patch boxes [for makeup] were found in his toilet'. Charles Vaughan in 1790 was a well-known character who attended all the masquerades in women's clothes and went similarly dressed to other places of entertainment. He was known as Fat Phillis. Vaughan in the past had made his advances to several noblemen and gentlemen using various names and characters and was well known in the magistrate's office. In April 1790 Vaughan tried to extort money from the Hon. and Rev. Mr Cuff. Vaughan's accomplice was George Smith, a gentleman's servant who had met Vaughan six months before at the races at Newmarket when he was out of work. Vaughan and Smith charged Cuff with taking liberties with one of their friends at the playhouse on a Wednesday night. The theatres were common enough places of sexual encounter for both female prostitutes and male sodomites. Vaughan seems to have had some knowledge of the world in which fashionable and aristocratic sodomites moved, and he probably had successfully blackmailed some of them in the past. But in this case he judged wrongly. Instead of paying up, Cuff took Vaughan to the magistrates and was congratulated by the bench for his public spirit in bringing an old offender to justice.[24]

The men who went to male transvestite prostitutes may or may not have known that their partners were biological males. It is also not clear whether a transvestite's clients were themselves sodomites or men who were not sodomites. It is possible that some 'heterosexual' clients knew that the transvestite was a biological male, and that this was part of the excitement, which would parallel the desire of sodomites that a soldier prostitute should be married, and therefore interested in women. In 1764 John Gill was arrested at 11pm on a Tuesday as he was having sex with a man in a coach. (Sex in a coach was a standard locale for female prostitution.) Gill was known in his neighborhood as Miss Beasly and was dressed in earrings and a bracelet, women's satin shoes and white silk stockings, and an outside petticoat trimmed with silver lace. Later in the same year the constables on a Monday night cleared the streets around Covent Garden of twenty-two female prostitutes, as they thought. But it turned out that two of the prostitutes were men dressed in women's clothes. It would be intriguing to know whether the women with whom they walked the streets, knew the anatomical identity of these men beneath their women's clothes.[25]

All the various types of male prostitution that have been discussed – soldiers in late adolescence, which is to say their early twenties; drummer boys just entering puberty at fifteen or sixteen, as well as boys of similar age without a military connection; the boys and men who operated in the molly houses; the transvestite men who could range into their forties and have grey hair – all of these individuals came from the world of the poor. But there were boys and men with ties to the gentry, who in exchange for giving sex and companionship, were promoted in their professions. This could be called patronage but it could also be seen as a species of polite prostitution. There is no room in this essay to discuss these relations extensively, but it is appropriate to end by giving some examples of what is meant.

Patronage

The most famous of these relations was fictionalized in the epistolary novel of 1723, *Love-Letters between a Certain Late Nobleman and the Famous Mr Wilson: Discovering the True History of the Rise and Surprising Grandeur of That Celebrated Beau*. In this novel, a nobleman keeps a male beau and makes sexual assignations in which the young man is asked to visit dressed in women's clothes. The novel is based on the case of Beau Wilson, who became inexplicably rich before his death in 1694. Charles Spencer, Earl of Sunderland (who had been first minister) died in 1722 and is often presumed to have been the great nobleman of the novel, but Sunderland would have been only twenty when Beau Wilson died. It was the case, however, that a week after Sunderland had kissed hands for his office, he brought a successful action at the Kingston assizes against the Rev. Thomas Kinnersly and William Moore for conspiring to charge Sunderland with attempting sodomy on Moore. The case became well known but it is difficult to say what had occurred. A printed trial was advertised in the newspapers but it does not seem to have ever been published. Thomas Salmon in his *Chronological Historian* (1723) treated the case as one of three famous sodomy trials, Lord Castlehaven and Titus Oates being the others. Stories about Sunderland continued to circulate after his death. Robert Wodrow in 1727 recorded that Lord Ross had told him that 'the Earl of Sunderland was the first to set up houses for that vile sin' of sodomy. But no one has tried to construct a network of Sunderland's young men.[26]

Lord Stanhope, Sunderland's predecessor as First Lord, more certainly liked young men and his patronage network can be reconstructed to some degree. Stanhope and his 'bosom friend' Lord Huntingdon (Huntingdon left Stanhope £400 a year at his death in 1705), had pursued young men together: in 1703 Huntingdon wrote that he wished they could be together in Paris 'with two or three pretty smiling unthinking fellows that know nothing and do everything' but instead he moved on to Venice where he procured catamites for himself. When Stanhope stood for Parliament in 1710 he was called a sodomite and as late as 1787 Alexander Cunningham remembered this episode in his history of Great Britain. Stanhope does seem to have promoted the military and later careers of pretty young men like John Cope and William Cosby.[27]

Archbishop Stone, the Primate of Ireland, in the 1750s was notorious for liking young men and promoting their careers. Horace Walpole told Sir Horace Mann, his sodomite friend in Florence, that Lord George Sackville had taken to Ireland 'a Scotch lad, one Cunningham, who was made aide-de-camp to the Primate ... and by him brought into Parliament'. Pasquinades and pamphlets excoriated the Primate:

> Religion is now become a mere farce
> Since the head of the church is in Cunningham's arse.

A pamphlet published 'Some Love-Letters which passed between Caiaphas [i.e. Stone] and his favourite Ganymede', possibly modelled on the Beau Wilson *Letters*. Caiaphas tells Ganymede that while sodomy had become 'scandalous, but certainly it is a more rational entertainment than women; Lord – one rides so wide with them, that the pleasure of fruition is dissipated; but the tight stricture of the natical foramen is love's great coadjutor'. Walpole said that Stone 'found the means of surmounting the most grievous prejudices, and of gaining popularity' by drinking to excess, which brought on his death. A politically powerful sodomite had surmounted a bad reputation by socializing with his enemies but he had ruined his health at the same time.[28] These three sets of stories taken together with others would make it possible to write a history of polite prostitution passing as patronage.

This essay has described a transition in early eighteenth-century London from a traditional to a modern system of male prostitution. In the traditional system, which was characteristic of the period before the eighteenth century, men sought sexual encounters with women and adolescent boys. In the modern system, sexual activity between men was increasingly confined to a minority of effeminate sodomites; the majority of men were considered 'heterosexual'; but a considerable minority of these 'heterosexual' men occasionally had sex with sodomites, sometimes in the role of prostitutes. The forms of male prostitution present in a society can in this way be used to test whether that society has moved from a traditional to a modern sexual system. Although it is a question beyond the scope of this essay, there is evidence that a similar transition in the forms of male prostitution to that which has been described for London could be found in Paris and Amsterdam in the same period, since the other indicators of the emergence of an effeminate minority of sodomites and a 'heterosexual' majority composed of most other men have been discovered by the recent historians of sodomy in those cities.

NOTES

Ellis and Lewis, 'Introduction'

1. 'J' [William Dodd], *Public Ledger*, (1760?), reprinted in W. Dodd, *The Visitor. By Several Hands*, 2 vols (London: Edward and Charles Dilly, 1764), vol. 2, pp. 104–9, p. 105.
2. P. J. Grosley, *A Tour to London; or, New Observations on England, and Its Inhabitants*, translated by T. Nugent, 2 vols (London: Lockyer Davis, 1772), vol. 1, p. 55.
3. 'Mais le scandale des filles publiques est poussé trop loin dans la capitale. Il ne faudrait pas que le mépris des mœurs fût si visible, si affiché. Il faudrait respecter davantage la pudeur et l'honnêteté publique. Comment un père de famille, pauvre et honnête, se flattera-t-il de conserver sa fille innocente et intacte dans l'âge des passions, lorsque celle-ci verra une prostituée, mise élégamment, attaquer les hommes, faire parade du vice, briller au sein de la débauche, et jouir, sous la protection des lois même, de sa licence effrénée? ... Et ce qui inspire un profond effroi, c'est que si la prostitution venait à cesser tout à coup, vingt-mille filles périraient de misère, les travaux de ce sexe malheureux ne pouvant pas suffire ici à son entretien, ni à sa nourriture'. (L.-S. Mercier, *Tableau de Paris* (1781–8), ed. J.-C. Bonnet, 2 vols (Paris: Mercure de France, 1994), ch. 238: 'Filles publiques' (vol. 1, pp. 596 and 600–1), Ann Lewis's translation).
4. See E.-M. Benabou, *La Prostitution et la police des mœurs au XVIIIe siècle* (Paris: Perrin, 1987).
5. T. Henderson, *Disorderly Women in Eighteenth-Century London: Prostitution and Control in the Metropolis, 1730–1830* (London: Longman, 1999), p. 194.
6. This paragraph reflects on A. Extavasia and T. D. Addison, 'Fucking (with Theory) for Money: Toward an Interrogation of Escort Prostitution', *Postmodern Culture*, 2:3 (1999).
7. See V. Jones, 'Eighteenth-Century Prostitution: Feminist Debates and the Writing of Histories', in A. Horner and A. Keane (eds), *Body Matters: Feminism, Textuality, Corporeality* (Manchester and New York: Manchester University Press, 2000), pp. 127–42.
8. W. Byrd, *The London Diary 1717–1721 and Other Writings*, ed. L. B. Wright and M. Tinling (New York: Oxford University Press, 1958); J. Boswell, *Boswell's London Journal, 1762–1763*, ed. F. A. Pottle (London: William Heinemann, 1950).
9. See for example J. Richetti, *Popular Fiction before Richardson: Narrative Patterns 1700–1739* (Oxford: Clarendon Press, 1992); Julie Peakman (ed.), *Whore Biographies, 1700–1825*, 8 vols (London: Pickering and Chatto, 2006–2007).
10. M. Cortey, *L'Invention de la courtisane au XVIIIe siècle dans les romans-mémoires des 'filles du monde' de Mme de Meheust à Sade (1732–1797)* (Paris: Éditions Arguments, 2001).
11. L. J. Rosenthal, *Infamous Commerce: Prostitution in Eighteenth-Century British Literature and Culture* (Ithaca, NY: Cornell University Press, 2006); K. Binhammer, *The Seduction Narrative in Britain, 1747–1800* (Cambridge: Cambridge University Press, 2009).

12. See for example, K. Norberg, 'The Libertine Whore: Prostitution in French Pornography from Margot to Juliette', in L. Hunt (ed.), *The Invention of Pornography* (New York: Zone Press, 1993), pp. 225–52; and V. van Crugten-André, *Le Roman du Libertinage: 1782–1815: Rédecouverte et rehabilitation* (Paris: Champion, 1997).
13. See Benabou, *La Prostitution*, chapters 9 'Les attitudes envers la prostitution' (pp. 430–81) and 10 'Projets et systèmes utopiques' (pp. 482–99) and D. A. Coward, 'Eighteenth-Century Attitudes to Prostitution', *SVEC*, 189 (1980), pp. 363–99.
14. A. Smith, *An Inquiry into the Nature and Causes of the Wealth of Nations*, 2 vols (1776), vol. 1, book 1, ch. 10, part 1, para. 28, in R. H. Campbell and A. S. Skinner (eds), *The Glasgow Edition of the Works and Correspondence of Adam Smith*, 7 vols (Indianapolis: Liberty Fund, 1981), vol. 2.
15. M. Nussbaum, '"Whether from Reason or Prejudice": Taking Money for Bodily Services', *Journal of Legal Studies*, 27 (1998), pp. 693–724.
16. S. Kingston and T. Sanders, 'Introduction', in K. Hardy, S. Kingston and T. Sanders (eds), *New Sociologies of Sex Work* (Farnham: Ashgate, 2010), pp. 2–3.
17. S. Johnson, *A Dictionary of the English Language*, 2 vols (London, 1755).
18. D. Diderot and J. le R. d'Alembert (eds), *Encyclopédie ou Dictionnaire raisonné des sciences, des arts et des métiers, par une société de gens de lettres*, 17 vols and 11 vols of plates [1751–72], vol. 13, p. 502.
19. P. W. Lasowski, *Dictionnaire libertin: la langue du plaisir au siècledes Lumières* (Paris: Gallimard, 2011), p. 412
20. M. Wollstonecraft, *A Vindication of the Rights of Woman: With Strictures on Political and Moral Subjects* (London: 1792), ch. 9.
21. C. Durston, 'Puritan Rule and the Failure of Cultural Revolution, 1645–1660', in C. Durston and J. Eales (eds), *The Culture of English Puritanism, 1560–1700* (Basingstoke: Macmillan, 1996), pp. 210–33 (esp. pp. 217–20).
22. R. B. Shoemaker, 'Reforming the City: The Reformation of Manners Campaign in London, 1690–1738', in L. Davison, T. Hitchcock, T. Keirn and R. B. Shoemaker (eds), *Stilling the Grumbling Hive: The Response to Social and Economic Problems in England, 1689–1750* (Stroud: Alan Sutton, 1992), pp. 103–10 (pp. 104–6); J. Hurl-Eamon, 'Policing Male Heterosexuality: The Reformation of Manners Societies' Campaign against the Brothels in Westminster, 1690–1720', *Journal of Social History*, 37:4 (Summer, 2004), pp. 1017–35; Henderson, *Disorderly Women*; F. Dabhoiwala, 'Sex and Societies for Moral Reform, 1688–1800', *The Journal of British Studies*, 46:2 (April 2007), pp. 290–319.
23. 'An Abstract of the Penal-Laws against Immorality and Prophaneness', in J. Woodward, 1660–1712, *An Account of the Societies for Reformation of Manners, in England and Ireland. With a Persuasive to Persons of All Ranks, to Be Zealous and Diligent in Promoting the Execution of the Laws against Prophaneness and Debauchery, for the Effecting a National Reformation* (London: 1699), pp. [165]–[172] (p. [171]).
24. *A Help to a National Reformation. An Abstract of the Penal-Laws against Prophaneness and Vice. A Form of the Warrants Issued out upon Offenders against the Said Laws. A Blank Register of Such Warrants. Prudential Rules for the Giving of Informations to the Magistrates in These Cases...* (London, 1700).
25. 'The Six and Twentieth Account of the Progress Made in the Cities of London & Westminster, and Places Adjacent, by the Societies for Promoting a Reformation of Manners', in J. Heylyn, *A Sermon Preached to the Societies for Reformation of Manners; at St. Mary-le-Bow, on Monday, December the 26th, MDCCXX* (London, 1721), p. 1, 3.
26. Dabhoiwala, 'Sex and Societies for Moral Reform', p. 291.
27. B. Mandeville, *A Modest Defence of Publick Stews: Or, an Essay upon Whoring, as It Is Now Practis'd in These Kingdoms. Written by a Layman* (London, 1724).

28. J. G. Turner, *Libertines and Radicals in Early Modern London: Sexuality, Politics, and Literary Culture, 1630–1685* (Cambridge: Cambridge University Press, 2002).
29. Anon., *The London-Bawd: With Her Character and Life. Discovering the Various and Subtle Intrigues of Lewd Women*, 4th edn (London, John Gwillim, 1711); Anon., *The Wandering Whore. Dialogue between* Magdalena, *a Crafty Bawd;* Julietta, *an Exquisite Whore,* Francion, *a Lascivious Gallant, and* Gusman, *a Pimping Hector. Discovering Their Diabolical Practices at the Chuck-Office. With a List of All the Crafty Bawds, Common Whores, Decoys, Hectors, and Trappaners, and Their Usual Meetings* (London: 1660); Anon., *Satan's Harvest Home: Or the Present State of Whorecraft, Adultery, Fornication, Procuring, Pimping, Sodomy and the Game of Flatts* (London, 1749).
30. On libertine literature see B. K. Mudge, *The Whore's Story: Women, Pornography, and the British Novel, 1684–1830* (Oxford: Oxford University Press, 2000).
31. See Rosenthal, *Infamous Commerce*, p. 123.
32. N. Armstrong, *Desire and Domestic Fiction: A Political History of the Novel* (New York, NY: Oxford University Press, 1987); G. J. Barker-Benfield, *The Culture of Sensibility: Sex and Society in Eighteenth-Century Britain* (London: University of Chicago Press, 1992); R. Trumbach, *Sex and the Gender Revolution: Volume One, Heterosexuality and the Third Gender in Enlightenment London* (Chicago, IL University of Chicago Press, 1998).
33. E. J. Clery, *The Feminization Debate in Eighteenth-Century England: Literature, Commerce and Luxury* (Basingstoke: Palgrave Macmillan, 2004).
34. The emergence of the sentimental construction of the prostitute can be traced in M. Ellis, *The Politics of Sensibility: Race, Gender and Commerce in the Sentimental Novel* (Cambridge: Cambridge University Press, 1996), esp. ch. 5; M. Ogborn, *Spaces of Modernity: London's Geographies 1680–1780* (London: Guildford, 1998), esp. ch. 2; T. Henderson, *Disorderly Women* (London: Longman, 1999), esp. 179–90; Rosenthal, *Infamous Commerce*, esp. chap. 4; and Binhammer, esp. ch. 2.
35. Anon. *The Histories of Some of the Penitents in the Magdalen-House, as Supposed to Be Related by Themselves*, 2 vols (London, 1760), vol. 1, p. v.
36. Benabou, *La Prostitution*; A. Corbin, *Women for Hire: Prostitution and Sexuality in France after 1850* (Cambridge, MA: Harvard University Press, 1990). See also J. Merrick, 'Sexual Politics and Public Order in Late Eighteenth-Century France: The *Mémoires secrets* and the *Correspondance secrète*', *Journal of the History of Sexuality*, 1 (1990), pp. 68–84.
37. C. Jones, 'Prostitution and the Ruling Class in Eighteenth-Century Montpellier', *History Workshop*, 6 (Autumn, 1978), pp. 7–28.
38. Ibid., p. 9.
39. Ibid., p. 11.
40. For an account of attitudes to prostitution after the revolution, see S. P. Conner, 'Public Virtue and Public Women: Prostitution in Revolutionary Paris, 1793–1794', *Eighteenth-Century Studies*, 28:2 (1994–5), pp. 221–40.
41. Jones, 'Prostitution', p. 13.
42. See also Norberg, 'The Libertine Whore', pp. 225–52; P. Cheek, 'Prostitutes of "Political Institution"', *Eighteenth-Century Studies*, 28:2 (1994–5), pp. 193–219.
43. For a more focused study on the revolutionary period, see: S. Conner, 'Politics, Prostitution, and the Pox in Revolutionary Paris, 1789–1799', *Journal of Social History*, 22:4 (1989), pp. 713–34, and 'Public Virtue and Public Women: Prostitution in Revolutionary Paris, 1793–94', *Eighteenth-Century Studies*, 28:2 (1994-5), pp. 221–40.
44. S. Maza, *Private Lives and Public Affairs: The Causes Célèbres of Prerevolutionary France* (Berkeley and Los Angeles, CA: University of California Press, 1993); P. Cheek, *Sexual Antipodes: Enlightenment Globalization and the Placing of Sex* (Stanford, CA: Stanford University Press, 2003); R. Darnton, *The Forbidden Best-sellers of Pre-Revolutionary*

France (London: Fontana Press, 1997); C. Thomas, *The Wicked Queen: The Origins of the Myth of Marie-Antoinette*, trans. J. Rose (New York: Zone Books, 2001). See also a series of suggestive articles in *Marie-Antoinette: Writings on the Body of a Queen*, ed. D. Goodman (New York and London: Routledge, 2003).

45. See, for example, Klaus Sasse's study of the emergence of the figure of the 'courtisane vertueuse' in a literary context, with especially reference to Rétif de la Bretonne, in *Die Entdeckung der 'courtisane vertueuse' in der französischen Literatur des 18. Jahrhunderts: Rétif de la Bretonne und seine Vorgänger* (Hamburg, 1967).

46. T. Hitchcock, *English Sexualities, 1700–1800* (Basingstoke: Macmillan, 1997), p. 98.

1 Lewis, 'Classifying the Prostitute in Eighteenth-Century France'

1. *The Myth of the French Bourgeoisie: An Essay on the Social Imaginary 1750–1850* (Cambridge, MA and London: Harvard University Press, 2003). On the historiographical debate surrounding the 'rise of the bourgeoisie' and its relation to the French Revolution, but providing a different argument, see C. Jones, 'Bourgeois Revolution Revivified', in P. Jones (ed.), *The French Revolution in Social and Political Perspective* (London and New York: Arnold, 1996), pp. 71–99.

2. E.-M. Benabou, *La Prostitution et la police de mœurs au dix-huitième siècle* (Paris: Perrin, 1987), p. 32. All translations of quotations are my own unless otherwise indicated.

3. D. Diderot and J. le R. d'Alembert (eds), *Encyclopédie ou Dictionnaire raisonné des sciences, des arts et des métiers, par une société de gens de lettres*, 17 vols and 11 vols of plates [1751–72], vol. 4, p. 400.

4. M. Cortey, *L'Invention de la courtisane au XVIIIe siècle dans les romans-mémoires des 'filles du monde' de Mme de Meheust à Sade (1732–1797)* (Paris: Éditions Arguments, 2001).

5. Rétif's *Le Pornographe* uses the phrase 'un projet de règlement pour les prostituées' in its subtitle, and the terms 'prostituée' and 'prostitution' occur frequently in this text (see note 23 below).

6. For a historical survey which does attempt to establish a range of different types as they actually existed (age, occupation, marital status, etc.) using examples based on archival investigation, especially police and prison reports, see Benabou, *La Prostitution*, chapters 5 'Les filles', and 6 'Femmes galantes et entretenues'.

7. L. Olsson notes such a taxonomy in *A Congratulatory Epistle from a Reformed Rake to John F[ieldin]g, Esq.; Upon the New Scheme of Reclaiming Prostitutes* (London: G. Burnet, [1758]) in her article in the present volume.

8. A useful list of such novels is provided in Cortey, *L'Invention de la courtisane*.

9. Recent editions of such texts include, for example, H. Rubenhold (ed.), *Harris's List of Covent-Garden Ladies: Sex in the City in Georgian Britain* (London: Tempus, 2005 [1793]), E. Pierrat (ed.), *Almanach des Demoiselles de Paris, suivi du Dictionnaire des Nymphes du Palais-Royal* (Paris: Arléa, 1999 [1791]); P. W. Lasowski (ed.), *L'Espion libertin, ou le calendrier du plaisir: histoires, adresses, tarifs et spécialités des courtisanes de Paris* (Paris: Editions Philippe Picquier, 2000) – this also includes extracts from the following texts of a similar genre: *Les Bordels de Paris, avec les noms, demeures et prix*; *Liste complète des plus belles femmes publiques et des plus saines du Palais de Paris. Leurs goûts et caprices, le prix de leurs charmes, et les rôles que remplissaient quelques-unes dans plusieurs théâtres*; and *Nouvelle liste des plus jolies femmes publiques de Paris. Leurs demeures, qualités et savoir-faire*.

10. For a useful account of the dating of the twelve volumes of Mercier's *Tableau de Paris*, see the excellent critical edition by Jean-Claude Bonnet in two volumes, *Louis-Sébastien Mercier: Tableau de Paris* (Paris: Mercure de France, 1994), pp. xiii–xiv and pp. lxix–lxxi.

11. See among others F. Le Borgne, *Rétif de la Bretonne et la crise des genres littéraires (1767–1797)* (Paris: Champion, 2011); J.-C. Bonnet, *Louis-Sébastien Mercier: un hérétique en littérature* (Paris: Mercure de France, 1995), and his substantial introduction to the Mercure de France edition of *Tableau de Paris*; and M. Delon's introductions to *Paris le jour, Paris la nuit* (Paris: Laffont, 1990). More general accounts of each of these writer's attitudes toward women and gender include: C. Berkowe, 'Louis-Sébastien Mercier et les femmes', *Romanic Review*, 55:1 (1964), pp. 16–29; D. Fletcher, 'Restif de la Bretonne and Woman's Estate' and J. Lough, 'Women in Mercier's *Tableau de Paris*', in E. Jacobs, W. H. Barber, J. H. Bloch, F. W Leakey and E. Le Breton (eds), *Woman and Society in Eighteenth-Century France* (London: Athlone, 1979), pp. 96–109, pp. 110–22; and the article by L. Malle cited in note 15 below.
12. He refers to Rétif's proposed reform of prostitution at various points in the *Tableau de Paris*, and mentions *Le Paysan perverti* in 'Filles publiques' (238), p. 595, as well as devoting a whole chapter to it (241).
13. The comment is from Fréron's 1769 review of *Le Pornographe*, quoted by David Coward, 'Restif de la Bretonne and the Reform of Prostitution', *SVEC*, 176 (1979), pp. 349–83 (p. 357).
14. All French quotations from Mercier's *Tableau de Paris* are from the edition by J.-C. Bonnet. All translations are my own unless otherwise indicated.
15. On this point, see also L. Malle, '*Eros et Labor*. Le beau sexe, le travail et le travail du sexe dans le *Tableau de Paris* de Louis-Sébastien Mercier', *Clio, Histoire, Femmes et Sociétés*, 25 (2007), pp. 227–57.
16. *Tableau de Paris* (Bonnet edition), vol. 2, pp. 15–16. The translation is taken from *Panorama of Paris: Selections from the Tableau de Paris*, ed. J. D. Popkin (State College, PN: Pennsylvania State University Press, 1999), pp. 144–5.
17. Popkin, *Panorama*, p. 144.
18. Even these entries are far from a comprehensive list of Mercier's descriptive references to prostitutes, which are frequently evoked throughout the *Tableau*. I have created a table to represent the relationship between the categories listed in the 'gradin symbolique' of Chapter 242, and the definitions provided in other chapters, using a series of extracts. This material, intended to be read in conjunction with the present article, can be viewed at the following web address: http://www.bbk.ac.uk/european/downloads/al_classifying_the_prostitute_appendix.
19. Mercier, *Tableau*, vol. 1, pp. 13–14.
20. Popkin, *Panorama*, p. 23.
21. Ibid., p. 145.
22. I am grateful to Claude Klein for pointing out the existence of the two versions of the taxonomy, when we met at the ISECS conference in Montpellier. On Rétif's attitudes toward prostitution more generally, and his project for reform, see D. Coward, 'Restif de la Bretonne and the Reform of Prostitution', and 'Eighteenth-Century Attitudes to Prostitution', *SVEC*, 189 (1980), pp. 363–99; J. A. Steintrager, 'What Happened to the Porn in Pornography? Rétif, Regulating Prostitution, and the History of Dirty Books', *Symposium: A Quarterly Journal in Modern Literatures*, 60:3 (2006), pp. 189–204; K. Sasse, *Die Entdeckung der 'courtisane vertueuse' in der französischen Literatur des 18. Jahrhunderts: Rétif de la Bretonne und seine Vorgänger* (Hamburg, 1967); and A. Lewis '*Une tâche ineffaçable*? Rétif's Representation of the Prostitute in *Le Pornographe* and *La Paysanne pervertie*', in S. Arnaud and H. Jordheim (eds), *The Body and Its Images: Health, Humours, Illness* (Paris: Champion, forthcoming).

23. The first edition of 1769 is available in a modern edition: in *Œuvres érotiques de Rétif de la Bretonne* (Paris: Libraire Arthème Fayard, 1985), and all references will be to that edition, except where noted. The list of types of prostitutes is within Note A 'État de la prostitution' (II) 'État actuel de la prostitution', pp. 171–7. The second version of the taxonomy can be found in Note B (pp. 313–21) in *Le Pornographe ou idées d'un honnête homme sur le projet de réglement pour les prostituéees, propre à prévenir les malheurs qu'occasionne le Publicisme des femmes: avec des notes historiques et justificatives* (Londres [i.e. Paris?]: chés Jean Nourse. A la Haie. Chés Gosse junior, & Pinet, 1770 [1775]). This edition is available on ECCO, which notes that this is the second edition of the text, written in 1774 and published between June and November 1775 despite the date on the title page. For further details of the various editions of *Le Pornographe* and their publication dates, see J. Rives Childs, *Restif de la Bretonne: témoignages et jugements, bibliographie* (Paris: Briffault, 1949).
24. Rétif also mentions (p. 321) that further to the sixteen categories of 'active prostitutes', he can add three more classes (which are parasitical on the others): 'Les maquarelles ou mamans' (procuresses or bawds); 'Les marcheuses' (old bawds – ruined old prostitutes with no savings, who solicit clients on behalf of one or more brothels); 'Les maquereux, greluchons, gueux, espions, etc.' (pimps, lovers, spies, etc.).
25. See for example the different attributions of Greek and Latin terms to 'les raccrocheuses' in versions 1 and 2 (where the main description of the categories in fact remains the same).
26. Rétif, *Le Pornographe* (1775), p. 313.
27. Ibid.
28. Ibid.
29. On the special place of the 'grisette' in Mercier's survey of working women, see Mall, '*Eros et Labor*', pp. 237–43.
30. Rétif, *Le Pornographe* (1775), p. 313.
31. F. de Montbron, *La Capitale des Gaules ou la Nouvelle Babylone* (The Hague, 1759).
32. Examples of this instability written into the taxonomy itself include remarks relating to 'les filles entretenues par un seul' (version 2), quoted earlier, in which Rétif sketches out her downward trajectory; his evocation of the frequent transformation of 'les concubines' into high-flying 'demoiselles du bon-ton' (p. 315); and the constantly fluctuating state of the 'chauvesouris de Vénus' – between being a kept mistress and available to the 'public at large'.

2 Norberg, 'In Her Own Words'

1. Many different spellings exist of Marie-Madeleine's last name. Even she wrote her name differently at different times. On most official documents she signed her name d'Ossement. But her father signed Dossement and the police authorities described her has Dhosmont, D'Osmont, Ozmont and Ozment. In this paper, I opt for her father's spelling since she herself always adopted a variation on it when she was not using her alias Marie Salle.
2. Dossement is quoted occasionally in the most complete study of prostitution in eighteenth-century Paris, E.-M. Bénabou, *La Prostitution et police des moeurs aux XVIIIe siècle* (Paris: Perrin, 1987).
3. G. Capon, *Les Maisons closes au XVIIIe siècle* (Paris: H. Daragon, 1903), pp. 56–7.
4. I am thinking of the poetry of Veronica Franco which is quite accomplished but which never deals even remotely with prostitution. (See M. Rosenthal, *The Honest Courtesan: Veronica Franco Citizen and Writer in Sixteenth-Century Venice* (Chicago: University of Chicago Press, 1992)). On the achievements of courtesans in a range of the arts see M.

Feldman and B. Gordon, (eds), *The Courtesan's Arts: Cross-Cultural Perspectives* (New York: Oxford University Press, 2006).
5. K. Norberg, 'Prostitution in Eighteenth-Century Paris: Pages from Madam's Notebook', in J. Elias, V. Bullough, V. Elias and G. Brewer (eds), *Prostitution: On Whores, Hustlers, and Johns* (New York: Prometheus Book, 1999), pp. 61–80.
6. Apparently the police were very interested in collecting all sorts of numerical data. Dossement provides prices for girls, suppers, loans, coaches, house rent, men's suits and a variety of other items.
7. By 1755, Dossement had proved herself both an accurate and energetic informer to the degree that Inspector Meusnier sometimes used her to ferret out information. On the July 22, 1755, Meusnier sent Dossement a note instructing her to monitor a garden to determine if it served as the site of romantic trysts. (Bibliothèque de l'Arsenal, Archives de la Bastille, 'Madame Dossement's Journal', Ms A.B. 10,253, (hereafter A.B. 10,253), f. 344 – see note 15 below on this source).
8. In the eighteenth century, police records – including the papers of the Bureau des Moeurs or Morals Bureau – were stored in the Bastille. When the fortress was stormed on 14 July 1789, the papers were burned or thrown into the trenches in and outside the building. There they remained until rescued by the National Assembly. Today they can be found primarily in the Archives de la Bastille which are preserved in the Bibliotheque de l'Arsenal which is itself a part of the Bibliotheque nationale de France. The process by which the Bastille archives were formed is described by Franck Funck-Bretano in the introduction to the index of the documents, Funck-Bretano, *Les Archives de la Bastille*, 2 vols (Paris: Plon, 1892) vol. 1, pp. ii–lxxiv.
9. An example of the police using information to coerce appears in Dossement's journal. One of her clients, a monk, tells her that Berryer had approached him and insinuated that he knew he had been in a brothel on the rue Beaurepaire at a particular time. The monk was terrified: the police arrested clerics found in brothels and reported them to the ecclesiastical authorities. Ironically, the monk did not suspect Dossement, who had reported his activities in her brothel (A.B. 10,253, 2 February 1754, f. 303).
10. On Berryer, see Bibliothèque nationale, Ms Fr NAL 11, 643, ff. 455–7.
11. See J. Peuchet, *Mémoires tirés des archives de la police de Paris*, 8 vols (Paris: A Levasseur, 1838) vol. 2, pp 122–39; M. B. Saint-Edme, *Biographie des Lieutenans-généraux, Ministres, Directeurs-généreux et Préfets de la Police en France* (Paris: 1829), pp. 38–52; A. Farge and J. Revel, *Logiques de la foule: L'affaire des enlèvements d'enfants, Paris, 1750* (Paris: Hachette, 1988).
12. See Berryer's correspondence in Francois Ravaisson, *Archives de la Bastillle: Documents inédits*, 19 vols (Paris: A. Durand et Pedone-Lauriel, 1884) vol. 16, pp. 1–450.
13. A. D. Aisne, GG.7 registres paroissiales de Charly.
14. Brief biographical notices outlining the lives of madams and prostitutes were regularly written by the police inspectors, especially Meusnier. But only Madame Dossement penned her own autobiography and included details of her childhood and early adult life.
15. 'On luy vouloit donner un Marchand ou un Chirugien, mais elle préfera le Petit Maitre ou du moins ce qui en avoit l'air' (A.B. 10,253, 25 October 1750, f. 126). All citations in this text are drawn from Dossement's journal which is preserved in the Archives de la Bastille in the Bibliotheque de l'Arsenal in Paris. Throughout I will refer to the document as A.B. 10,253 and include both the date and page number. Dossement's autobiography was written in October 1750 and occupies pages 124–9. All translations are my own.
16. On Charly, see P. A. Corlieu, *Histoire de Charly-sur-Marne* (Paris: Editions Champollion, 1881).
17. On *huissiers à cheval* see M. Guyot, *Repertoire universel et raisonné de jurisprudence civile criminelle canonique et beneficiale* (Paris: chez Visse, 1784), vol. 8, p. 603.

18. The near total destruction of the Chateau-Thierry archives in World War I has made it impossible to place the Dossements in the city's social life. The parish registers which survive again give little evidence of the Dossements, and I know almost nothing about them save that they lived in the St Crespin parish. Judicial records which escaped the archive fire have, as yet, provided no information.
19. I.E 185/5, état civil de Chateau Thierry (1734).
20. A.B. 10,253, 10 October 1750, f. 128.
21. Dossement has clearly read some fiction for her retelling of her early life closely resembles a plot from Marivaux or a libertine tale.
22. Archives nationals, Y 15186.
23. A.B. 102553, 10 October 1750, f. 124.
24. A.B. 10, 253, 16 April 1753, f. 279.
25. A.B. 10,253, 4 December 1751, f. 203.
26. A.B. 10,253, 21 September 1752, f. 252.
27. A.B. 10,253, 6 July 1754, f. 318.
28. A.B. 10,253, 22 August 1756, f. 372.
29. 'J'ai dans l'idée de passer plus à mon aise que je le suis en effet par ce que ces Messieurs marchandent les filles comme des oranges chez une fruitière, et le moins on parait pauvre, le plus qu'ils offrent' (A.B. 10, 253, 30 June 1752, f. 245).
30. 'Ce n'est pas mon destin de m'enrichir dans la vie' (A.B. 10,253, 20 November 1756, f. 389).
31. 'J'ai été diner chez M. Tarlay qui m'a promis la rente de 2000 livres de fonds pour s'acquiter avec moi de ce qu'il me doit depuis longtemps et qu'il remet à me payer lors qu'il recueil-leroit la succession de Madame Tarlay sa mère. Et comme je le connois pour un homme de probité, je lui fournirai encore la somme de 1500 livres et dudit total il me fera un contract de rente viagère hypothèqué sur ses biens et revenus. Il peut jouir environ de 6 à 7000 de rente. ... Il ne joue plus. Il est devenu rangé et il ne fait pas grande dépense ce qui me persuade que je ne ferais pas une mauvaise affaire.' (A.B 10253, 8 July 1756, f. 371.)
32. P. T. Hoffman, G. Postel-Vinay, J.-L. Rosenthal, *Les Marchés sans prix. Une économie politique du credit à Paris, 1660–1870* (Paris: Editions de l'Ecole des Hautes Etudes en Sciences Sociales, 2001), pp. 208–10.
33. 'Je lui fait replique qu'il ne fallait pas se plaindre des ministres, qu'au contraire il fallait approuver tout ce qui se faisoit dans le gouvernement' (A.B. 10,253, 28 July 1751, f. 185).
34. 'J'ai trouvé que Aubry et Croizet manquoient éssentiellement au respect et la prudence et discretion que l'on doit avoir pour tous les Grands et surtout pour son Prince et pour sa cour' (A.B. 10,253, 1 August 1751, f. 189).
35. 'Je n'aime point les gens d'Eglise et je remarque que ces messieurs font de la Réligion une espèce de métier duquel ils tirent de quoi vivre et se divertir et qu'au fond ils ont moins de dévotion et plus intémperance que les gens du monde' (A.B. 10,253, 26 January 1752, f. 217).
36. 'Si Votre Grandeur vouloit bien réiterer ses charités pour toutes ces pauvres filles, elle ordonnerait qu'il seroit posté en dehors de de l'entrée de chambre une personne sure et d'un age raisonnable ...' (A.B. 10,253, 1 January 1754, ff. 297–8).
37. 'Si vous saviez, Monseigneur, quelle rumeur ces sortes de scènes font dans le quartier, Vôtre Grandeur reprendroit une nouvelle pitié pour toutes ces pauvres malheureuses. Il se peut qu'il y a des personnes présentes qui voudroient prendre l'intêret de la personne offensées et cela peut occasionné la mort d'hommes. Si les jeunes gens se comporteroient différement, l'on pourroit presque ignorer le nombre des femmes galantes dans le public sans quoi il faut donc ordonner par sentence de justice et sous telle peine, qu'il n'y ait plus de femmes ni de filles suspectes de galanterie connues dans Paris.' (A.B. 10,253, 14 June 1751, f. 169.)

38. On the inspector's writing see P. Cheek, 'Prostitutes of Political Origins', *Eighteenth-Century Studies*, 28:2 (1994–5), pp. 193–219.
39. 'Une fille avec une conscience, c'est aussi rare qu'un phénix' (A.B. 10,253, 16 March 1756, f. 354).
40. 'Le trois quarts des hommes sont fourbes' (A.B. 10,253, 10 October 1750, f. 129).
41. 'S'il etait vrai que je fusse riche ... Je m'éloigné toute de meme du mariage parceque j'aime ma liberté' (A.B. 10,253, 7 October 1756, f. 389).
42. J. Rossiaud, *Medieval Prostitution*, trans. by L. Cochrane (New York: Blackwell, 1988), p. 333.
43. Both positions are explored in the essays in J. Spector (ed), *Prostitution and Pornography: Philosophical Debates about Sex* (Palo Alto, CA: Stanford University Press, 2006).
44. Y. Guyot, *Repertoire universel et raisonné de jurisprudence civile criminelle canonique et bénéficiale*, 20 vols (Paris: chez Vissé, 1784) vol. 11, p. 275.
45. Archives nationales, Minutier central, étude LXX, 475, 19 June 1770.

3 Van Hensbergen, '"All the World Knows Her Storie"'

1. F. H. Blackburne Daniell (ed.), *Calendar of State Papers, Domestic Series, March 1st, 1675, to February 29th, 1676* (London: Mackie & Co., 1907), p. 474.
2. S. Wynne, '"The Brightest Glories of the British Sphere": Women at the Court of Charles II', in J. M. Alexander and C. MacLeod (eds), *Painted Ladies: Women at the Court of Charles II* (London: NPG; Yale Centre for British Art, 2001), pp. 36–49 (p. 46).
3. Georgina Masson traces the first use of the word courtesan to late fifteenth-century Rome, with the term adopted into Venetian vocabulary in the 1520s. See G. Masson, *Courtesans of the Italian Renaissance* (London: Secker & Warburg, 1975), pp. 5, 146.
4. Martha Feldman's and Bonnie Gordon's edited collection of essays explore the courtesan's artistic and cultural status; M. Feldman and B. Gordon (eds), *The Courtesan's Arts: Cross-Cultural Perspectives* (Oxford: Oxford University Press, 2006).
5. For a discussion of Mazarin's representation in portraiture of the period, see S. Shifrin, '"Subdued by a Famous Roman Dame": Picturing Foreignness, Notoriety, and Prerogative in the Portraits of Hortense Mancini, Duchess of Mazarin', in C. MacLeod and J. M. Alexander (eds), *Politics, Transgression, and Representation at the Court of Charles II: Studies in British Art* (London; New Haven, CT: Yale Centre for British Art, 2007), pp. 141–74; S. Shifrin, '"At the End of the Walk by Madam Mazarine's Lodgings": Si(gh)ting the Transgressive Woman in Accounts of the Restoration Court', in S. Shifrin (ed.), *Women as Sites of Culture: Women's Roles in Cultural Formation from the Renaissance to the Twentieth Century* (Aldershot: Ashgate, 2002), pp. 195–205.
6. Mazarin is the subject of recent critical interest, with Susan Shifrin editing a collected interdisciplinary essays on the Duchess; S. Shifrin (ed.), *The Wandering Life I Led: Essays on Hortense Mancini, Duchess of Mazarin and Early Modern Women's Border-Crossings* (Newcastle upon Tyne: Cambridge Scholars Publishing, 2009).
7. These works were diverse in their nature, and extend to the visual arts to include portraits Mazarin sat for by artists including Sir Peter Lely, Ferdinand Jacob Voet and Benedetto Gennari.
8. S. Nelson (ed. and trans.), *Memoirs: Hortense Mancini and Marie Mancini* (Chicago, IL London: Chicago University Press, 2008). The first edition of Mazarin's memoirs was printed as *Mémoires D.M.L.D.M. à M. **** (Cologne: chez Pierre du Marteau, 1675).
9. H. Mancini, Duchess of Mazarin, *The Memoires of the Duchess Mazarine. Written in French by Her Own Hand, and Done into English by P. Porter, Esq; Together with the Rea-*

sons of Her Coming into England. Likewise, a Letter Containing a True Character of Her Person and Conversation (London, 1676), p. 2. Hereafter *The Memoires*.
10. Mazarin, *The Memoires*, p. 23.
11. This pension was soon withdrawn, making Mazarin's financial position increasingly difficult. See Mazarin, *The Memoires*, p. 52.
12. Mazarin, *The Memoires*, p. 30.
13. Here I use the term 'client' to describe the patrons, customers and lovers of courtesans, irrespective of whether the exchange that takes place between the courtesan and her client is financial, one of patronage, or unclear.
14. Mazarin, *The Memoires*, p. 109.
15. Ibid., p. 2.
16. M.-C. Desjardins de Villedieu, *Mémoires de la Vie de Henriette-Sylvie de Molière* (1671–4), ed. René Démoris (Paris: Desjonquères, 2003). Hereafter *Mémoires de la Vie*.
17. Nelson, *Memoirs*, p. 17. Elizabeth Goldsmith notes that, '[l]ike her real life counterparts, Henriette-Sylvie makes a credo out of gaity in the face of adversity. Like Marie and Hortense Mancini, she watches her own life become the subject not only of scandal but of fiction, and she works to reconstruct her own image in the public eye by revising other people's published accounts of her life'. See E. Goldsmith, 'Thoroughly Modern Mazarin', in Shifrin (ed.), *The Wandering Life I Led*, pp. 2–30 (p. 18).
18. Mazarin, *The Memoires*, pp. 116–17.
19. A. Behn, 'The History of the Nun', in *Oroonoko and Other Writings*, ed. Paul Salzman (Oxford: Oxford University Press, 1998), pp. 138–90 (p. 138).
20. J. Todd, *The Secret Life of Aphra Behn* (London: Pandora, 2000), p. 394.
21. Ibid., pp. 246–7.
22. M. Duffy, *The Passionate Shepherdess* (London: Phoenix, 1989) pp. 61, 65.
23. Todd, *The Secret Life*, p. 394.
24. Duffy, *Passionate Shepherdess*, p. 285.
25. J. Todd, *The Sign of Angellica: Women, Writing and Fiction, 1660–1800* (London: Virago, 1989); C. Gallagher, *Nobody's Story: The Vanishing Acts of Women Writers in the Marketplace, 1670–1820* (Berkeley, CA: University of California Press, 1994), pp. 1–48; J. Pearson, *The Prostituted Muse: Images of Women and Women Dramatists, 1642–1737* (New York: Harvester, Wheatsheaf, 1988).
26. A. Behn, 'Love-Letters between a Nobleman and His Sister', in J. Todd (ed.), *The Works of Aphra Behn* (London: Pickering & Chatto, 1996), vol. 2, p. 123. Hereafter *Love-Letters*.
27. 'Astrea's Book for Songs & Satyrs', Bodleian Library, MS Oxford, Firth c.16.
28. Behn translated French works by Bonnecourse, Fontenelle, La Rochefoucauld and Tallement. Behn's work as a translator has led Janet Todd to suggest that she would have been a likely choice to translate the English printing of *The Apology: or, the Genuine Memoirs of Madam Maria Manchini, eldest Sister to the Duchess of Mazarin* (1679), by Gabriel de Brémond: 'It is just conceivable that his [Brémond's] usual publishers, whom he shared with Behn, Richard Bentley and James Magnes, asked her to translate the anonymously published work'. See Todd, *The Secret Life*, p. 303.
29. Blackburne, *Calendar of State Papers*, p. 474.
30. J. Dryden, *All For Love* (London, 1678); N. Lee, *The Rival Queens* (London, 1677); C. Sedley, *Antony and Cleopatra* (London, 1677).
31. For further discussion of the Mazarin Cleopatra portrait see, Shifrin, 'Subdued by a Famous Roman Dame', pp. 149–51. Mazarin again invited a direct comparison between

herself and Cleopatra in a poem printed as a two-page pamphlet, 'The Dutchess of Mazarines Farewel to England' (London, 1680), p. 2.
32. E. S. De Beer (ed.), *The Diary of John Evelyn* (Oxford: Clarendon Press, 1955), vol. 4, p. 97.
33. T. Killigrew, 'Thomaso, or The Wanderer', in *Comedies and Tragedies Written by Thomas Killigrew* (London, 1664).
34. A. Behn, 'The Rover', in J. Spencer (ed.), *The Rover and Other Plays* (Oxford: Oxford University Press, 1995), vol. 2, pp. 92–116.
35. Behn, *The Rover*, vol. 2, p. 110.
36. Mazarin, *The Memoires*, pp. 87–8.
37. Other tacit references in *The Memoires* associate Mazarin culturally with the figure of the courtesan, for example, Mazarin's recollection of her visit to an aunt in Rome, during which Mazarin plays 'guitar'; Mazarin, *The Memoires*, p. 87. In Renaissance Venice and Rome the female performance of music carried sexual connotations; it was thus thought a more fitting pursuit for female 'entertainers', such as courtesans, rather than for aristocratic women; see D. E. Davies, 'On Music Fit for a Courtesan: Representations of the Courtesan and Her Music in Sixteenth-Century Italy', in Feldman and Gordon (eds), *The Courtesan's Arts*, pp. 144–58.
38. Vittore Carpaccio's late fifteenth-century painting, 'Two Venetian Gentlewomen' (widely known as 'Two Venetian Courtesans'), housed in the Museo Correr in Venice, further illuminates the associations of Mazarin's stance at the window with the aesthetic figure of the courtesan. Carpaccio's work depicts two courtesans on their balcony waiting for clients: the scene foreshadows that of Angellica Bianca's entrance in *The Rover*, with Carpaccio's courtesans surrounded by the trappings of luxury and exoticism – birds, dogs, pearls – signalling their status as expensive commodities. Carpaccio's painting may be viewed through the Museo Correr's online catalogue, found at http://www.archiviodellacomunicazione.it/.
39. J. Todd, *The Critical Fortunes of Aphra Behn* (Columbia: Camden House, 1998), p. 98.
40. Madame de Villedieu, *The Memoires of the Life, and Rare Adventures of Henrietta Silvia Moliere as They Have Been Very Lately Published in French; with Remarks* (London, 1672–7).
41. Behn, *Love-Letters*, p. 123.
42. Ibid., p. 127 (italics mine).
43. Mazarin, *The Memoires*, pp. 66–8.
44. Duffy, *Passionate Shepherdess*, p. 150.
45. Behn, *History of the Nun*, p. 138.
46. Ibid., p. 139.
47. Ibid., p. 138.
48. Mazarin, *The Memoires*, pp. 115–30.
49. J. Pearson, 'The History of *The History of the Nun*', in H. Hutner (ed.), *Rereading Aphra Behn: History, Theory, and Criticism* (Charlottesville, VA: University Press of Virginia, 1993), p. 244.
50. Mazarin, *The Memoires*, pp. 124–5.
51. Mazarin's case provided the inspiration for Mary Astell's *Some Reflections upon Marriage* (London, 1700). Mazarin was the only woman to be included in Theophile Lucas's *Lives of the Gamesters* (London, 1714).

52. I address this question in depth in my doctoral thesis. See: C. van Hensbergen, 'The Courtesan's Narrative in English Literary Culture, 1660–1730' (DPhil thesis, University of Oxford, 2010).

4 MacDonald, 'Marie Petit's *Persian Adventure* (1705–8)'

1. On the Hôpital du refuge, see G. Cattelona, 'Control and Collaboration: The Role of Women in Regulating Female Sexual Behaviour in Early Modern Marseille', *French Historical Studies*, 18: 1 (1993) p. 13. See also her unpublished PhD thesis, G. Cattelona, 'The Regulation of Female Sexuality: The Hôpital du Refuge in Marseille, 1640–1789' (Indiana University, 1991). On Petit, see R. de Maulde La Clavière, *Les mille et une nuits d'une ambassadrice de Louis XIV* (Paris: Hachette, 1896). Petit has also inspired several works of historical fiction: L. Clarétie, *Marie Petit. Roman d'aventures, 1705* (Paris: Librairie Molière, 1904); L. Aurenche and H. Coquet, *La Brelandière ambassadrice du roi soleil. Roman historique* (Paris: Nouvelles editions latines, 1945); Y. Grès, *La Belle Brelandière: ambassadeur en Perse* (Paris: Société continentale d'éditions modernes illustrées, 1973); G. Schoeller, *Marie d'Ispahan* (Paris: Laffont, 1992).
2. Ferriol was acting on orders from Jérôme Pontchartrain, secretary of state for the navy, who had jurisdiction over the Levant. Pontchartrain's letters to Ferriol regarding Petit are in Archives des affaires étrangères, Correspondance politique (hereafter AAE, corr. pol.), Turquie, vol. 9, ff. 82–9, 110–15, 121–3. On Ferriol, see A. de Saint-Priest, *Mémoire sur l'ambassade de France en Turquie*, ed. Charles Schefer (Paris: Leroux, 1877); and E. Boka, 'Le marquis Charles de Ferriol ambassadeur de France à Constantinople (1699–1703)', *Acta Historica*, 31:1–2 (1985), pp. 87–112.
3. For details of the treaty and its importance, see 'France. ii. Relations with Persia to 1789', in *Encyclopædia Iranica*, <http://iranica.com/articles/france-ii> [accessed 22 July 2010].
4. On Michel's expectation of remuneration, see his letters to Pontchartrain 8.11.1709, 26.11.1709 and 7.2.1710. AAE, corr. pol., Perse, vol. 2, ff. 108–11, 115–16, 169–71.
5. Petit's letters, as well as Ferriol's and Michel's, are in AAE corr. pol., Perse, vol. 2. Pontchartrain's correspondence with Ferriol is in AAE, corr. pol., Turquie, vol. 9. P. V. Michel, *Mémoire du sieur Michel sur son voyage de Perse*, Bibliothèque nationale de France, ms. fr. 7200.
6. AAE, corr. pol., Perse, vol. 2, ff. 235–94. Petit claimed she lent the bankrupt Fabre the money to equip himself for the journey to Persia; Michel argued that this debt was for her company on the voyage, in other words, that she was a venal woman who had contracted her body to Fabre.
7. There is a reference to Petit's manuscript in a letter by the novelist Alain-René Lesage to Pontchartrain. The letter is reproduced in L. Clarétie, *Le Roman en France au début du XVIIIe siècle, Lesage romancier* (Paris: Colin, 1890), pp. 53–5. On Petit's attempt to commission Lesage to write up a more polished version of her adventure, see below.
8. *Mémoire d'instruction au proces de Demoiselle Marie Petit* (1710), AAE, corr. pol., Perse, vol. 2, f. 255, pp. 4–6; *Mémoire d'instruction au proces du Sieur Pierre Victor Michel*, AAE, corr. pol., Perse, vol. 2, ff. 279–94, pp. 8–10; *Mémoire du sieur Michel*, pp. 1–12.
9. 'elle commença alors de se prostituer plus honteusement que jamais, la lubricité avec les Persans étoit son occupation ordinaire', *Mémoire d'instruction du Sieur Michel*, p. 6. ('she then began to prostitute herself more shamelessly than ever; she was constantly engaged in lubricious behaviour with the Persians').
10. *Mémoire d'instruction de Marie Petit*, p. 5.

11. *Mémoire du sieur Michel*, p. 12.
12. 'on peut dire que le Pere Mosnier revint de quelque maniere de mort à la vie, [the governor] lui representa que c'estoit à la seule consideration de la Demoiselle Petit qu'il avoit revoqué son Arrest de mort, & qu'il devoit la regarder comme sa bienfactrice', *Mémoire d'instruction de Marie Petit*, p. 5 ('One could say in a sense that Father Mosnier came back from death to life; the governor made clear to him that it was only out of consideration for Mlle Petit that he had revoked his death sentence, and that he should consider her as his benefactor').
13. 'cette malheureuse avoit entierement gagné le Khan [the governor]', *Mémoire du sieur Michel*, p. 10, ('that wretched woman had entirely won over the Khan').
14. *Mémoire d'instruction de Marie Petit*, p. 7.
15. On 'lettres de cachet', see C. Quétel, *De par le roy. Essai sur les lettres de cachet* (Toulouse: Privat, 1981) and B. E. Strayer, *Lettres de Cachet and Social Control in the Ancien Regime, 1659–1789* (New York, Bern, Frankfurt: Peter Lang, 1992).
16. For such warrants to be issued following the lodging of a *placet*, there was normally a strict legal procedure involving interviews of witnesses. As secretary of state, Pontchartrain adjudicated whether to grant the warrant. See Strayer, *Lettres de cachet*, p. 21. This procedure was not followed in Petit's case, however, as she was imprisoned prior to any formal gathering of evidence against her.
17. Cattelona, *The Regulation of Female Sexuality*, p. 3.
18. AAE, corr. pol., Perse, vol. 2, f. 124.
19. Archives départementales des Bouches-du-Rhône (AD des BdR), 8 HD 1–46. Petit's entry and exit from the Refuge (8.2.1709–26.1.1713) are recorded in 8 HD F 3, pp. 60–61. The Rectors' meetings minutes are in AD des BdR, 8 HD E 4.
20. AD des BdR, H8 E 2, Meeting of 7.05.1688. Cattelona, *Regulation of Female Sexuality*, p. 187.
21. AD des BdR, H8 E 3, Cattelona, *The Regulation of Female Sexuality*, p. 210.
22. P. Goubert, *Louis XIV and Twenty Million Frenchmen*, trans. Anne Carter (London: Allan Lane, 1970), p. 258.
23. E. Baratier (ed), *Histoire de Marseille* (Toulouse: Privat, 1973).
24. AD des BdR, H8 E4. Meeting of 7.04.1709. Cited in Cattelona, *The Regulation of Female Sexuality*, p. 175.
25. 1.04.1709. AAE, corr. pol., Perse, vol. 2, f. 52.
26. For example, Ferriol wrote to Pontchartrain about Petit's stay with him at Constantinople on her return journey to France: 'Le sejour de sept mois qu'elle a fait dans le palais de France a été une des plus grandes mortifications de mon ambassade', AAE, corr. pol., Turquie, vol. 46, f. 52 ('The seven months she spent in the French embassy were one of the greatest humiliations of my diplomatic mission').
27. She refers, for example, to: 'mes robes qui ne sont propre que pour une femme comme moy', AAE, corr. pol., Perse, vol. 2, f. 52 ('my dresses which are only suitable for a woman like me' (that is, of my humble status)).
28. AN des BdR, H 8 E4 (7.7.1709), ff. 51–2. Cattelona (*The Regulation of Female Sexuality*, pp. 207–8) discusses the riot without reference to Petit's biography.
29. Cattelona, *Regulation of Female Sexuality*, p. 204.
30. AN des BdR, H 8 E4 (15.9.1709), f. 60.
31. In fact, Michel's lawyer makes precisely this argument: 'on a bien connu son caractere, en luy destinant une semblable retraite', (*Mémoire d'instruction du Sieur Michel*, p.13) ('by sending her to such a prison, her character had been well-judged').

32. AAE, corr. pol., Perse, vol. 2, ff. 92–4.
33. AAE, corr. pol., Perse, vol. 2, ff. 121–2.
34. AAE, corr. pol., Perse, vol. 2, f. 124.
35. AAE, corr. pol., Perse, vol. 2, f. 100.
36. AAE, corr. pol., Perse, vol. 2, ff. 120–5.
37. It is not clear who Petit referred to when she claimed to have relatives and friends who could intercede for her with Louis XIV. She may have had some connections from her time as manager of a gambling house on the rue Mazarine. As for family, her baptismal certificate shows that her mother was a laundress and her father a cobbler. Reproduced in H. Dussourd, *Histoire de Moulins d'après la chronique de ses habitants* (Clermont-Ferrand: Éditions Volcan, 1975), p. 139. Petit claimed to come from a legal family with a grandfather who was 'petit avocat du roy au parlement de Dijon'. (AAE, corr. pol., Perse, vol. 2, f. 44) Her godfather Jean Fromental was 'procureur' at Moulins.
38. AAE, corr. pol., Perse, vol. 2, ff. 167–8. (24.01.1710).
39. AAE, corr. pol., Perse, vol. 2, f. 167.
40. AAE, corr. pol., Perse, vol. 2, f. 173.
41. Assuming Petit received any replies at all. There is just one reference to a letter from Pontrchartrain to Petit, mentioned above.
42. See for example, AAE, corr. pol., Perse, vol. 2, f. 98. *La Perse et la France: relations diplomatiques et culturelles du XVIIe au XIXe siècle* (Paris: Musée Cernuschi, [1972]).
43. On 23 January 1712. AD des BdR, H8 E4.
44. Full details of the sale are in 'Inventaire des effetz et hardes de la Demoiselle Marie Petit qui ont esté vendus à l'encan à Marseille' (Archives nationales (AN), AE/B/III/137, ff. 304–11).
45. Michel had claimed that he lent Petit money for her return to France. AN, AE/B/III/137, ff. 13–14v.
46. 13.4.1715. AAE, corr. pol., Perse, vol. 4, f. 63.
47. Lesage's greatest success to date was the collection of satirical tales of Parisian society *Le Diable boiteux* (1707). He had written numerous plays, including one with a Persian theme: *Arlequin Mahomet* (1714). The first six books of his masterpiece, the *Histoire de Gil Blas de Santillane* were published in 1715.
48. On Riza Beg's embassy, see L. de Fontenay, *Journal historique du voyage de l'ambassadeur de Perse en France. Février 1715* (= *Nouveau mercure galant*) (Paris: D. Jollet and J. Lamesle, 1715); *Mercure galant*, December 1715. Petit appears in the first chapter of the December issue: 'Des evenemens curieux qui ont precede la Mission de Mehemet Riza Beg en France', pp. 48–58. See also M. Herbette, *Une ambassade persane sous Louis XIV* (Paris: Perrin et cie, 1907).
49. D'Argenson to Pontchartrain, 3.5.1715. AAE, corr. pol., Perse, vol. 4, f. 82.
50. The letter in which D'Argenson recounts Lesage's acceptance of the project bears the following annotation from Pontchartrain: 'A la bonne heure ... on luy donnera le contre poison' ('At the right moment ... we'll give him the antidote'). As we shall see, Pontchartrain was alluding to Michel's memoirs, which he hoped would soon make Lesage see how unwise it was to act as Petit's mouthpiece.
51. Clarétie, *Le Roman en France*, pp. 53–5.
52. Maulde la Clavière, *Les mille et une nuits*.
53. For titles, see above.

5 Olsson, "'A First-Rate Whore'"

1. For eighteenth-century accounts of Salisbury's life history, see C. Walker, *Authentick Memoirs of the Life, Intrigues and Adventures of the Celebrated Sally Salisbury*, 2nd edn (London, 1723) – the first edition, without the 'Compleat KEY', is reprinted in *Authentick Memoirs of the Life, Intrigues and Adventures of the Celebrated Sally Salisbury, by Charles Walker [and] The Agreeable Caledonian, by Eliza Haywood*, ed. J. Grieder (New York: Garland, 1973); Anon., *The Genuine History of Mrs. Sarah Prydden, Usually Called, Sally Salisbury, and Her Gallants* (London: Andrew Moor, 1723), reprinted in L. Olsson (ed.), *Eighteenth-Century British Erotica Part II, Vol. 4: The Prostitute's Life: Sally Salisbury and Fanny Hill* (London: Pickering & Chatto, 2004); Anon., *The Effigies, Parentage, Education, Life, Merry-Pranks and Conversation of the Celebrated Mrs. Sally Salisbury* ([London]: J. Wilson, 1722/3), reprinted in J. Peakman (ed.), *Whore Biographies, 1700–1825*, 8 vols, Part I, vol. 1 (London: Pickering & Chatto, 2006); and Anon., *A Compleat History of the Life, Intrigues and Death of that Celebrated Lady of Pleasure, Sally Salisbury* (London: Tho. Norris, 1724). There is very little modern biographical material, but see E. J. Burford, *Wits, Wenchers and Wantons* (London: Robert Hale, 1986), pp. 46–52 and J. Adlard's *The Softer Paths of Pleasure* (Church Stretton: Onny Press, 1980). No scholarly biography of Salisbury's life has yet been produced.
2. For the trial, see Anon., *An Account of the Tryal of Salley Salisbury, at the Sessions-House in the Old Bailey on Wednesday the 24th of April, 1723* (1723), reprinted in Peakman (ed.), *Whore Biographies*, Part I, vol. 1.
3. C. de Saussure, *Letters from London 1725–1730*, trans. P. Scott (Newnham: Adnax Publications, 2006), pp. 114–15.
4. P. Bliss (ed.), *Reliquiae Hearnianae: The Remains of Thomas Hearne, M.A.*, 2nd edn, 3 vols (London: John Russell Smith, 1869), vol. 2, pp. 192–3. According to Adlard, this entry in Hearne's diary is copied from *Mist's Journal*, 15 February 1724 (Adlard, *The Softer Paths*, p. 49).
5. Two epigrams, originally mentioned by Benjamin Martyn (1698–1763) in his correspondence, were published in *Notes and Queries* in 1850; see 'CH', 'Unpublished Epigrams in the British Museum' in *Notes and Queries*, 2:31 (1850), p. 6. The parish record of her burial is quoted in Adlard, *The Softer Paths*, p. 49.
6. Walker, *Authentick Memoirs*, p. 98. All italics in the quotes occur in the original, unless otherwise stated.
7. J. G. Turner, *Libertines and Radicals in Early Modern London: Sexuality, Politics and Literary Culture, 1630–1685* (Cambridge: Cambridge University Press, 2002), p. 5.
8. Turner, *Libertines and Radicals*, pp. 2, 3.
9. Ibid., pp. 5–10.
10. A good example of this is the anonymous *A Congratulatory Epistle from a Reformed Rake to John F[ieldin]g, Esq.; Upon the New Scheme of Reclaiming Prostitutes* (London: G. Burnet, [1758]), where the author presents a hierarchy consisting of eight categories of prostitutes – 'Women of Fashion, who intrigue. Demi-Reps. Good-natured Girls. Kept Mistresses. Ladies of Pleasure. Whores. Park-Walkers. Street-Walkers. Bunters. Bulk-mongers' (p. 8). However, the first four are set off in a class of their own, as not being relevant to his argument, in effect producing both a dichotomy and a more graduated hierarchy. This dichotomy is similar to that which exists between courtesan and whore, the upper category being distinguished from the lower by means of obscured or non-existent financial transactions, not doing business in the street or in brothels, and so on.

11. C. Walker, advertisement in *The Post Boy* on 8–10 January 1723, quoted in L. J. Rosenthal, 'The Whore's Estate: Sally Salisbury, Prostitution, and Property in Eighteenth-Century London', in N. E. Wright, M. W. Ferguson, and A. R. Buck (eds), *Women, Property, and the Letters of the Law in Early Modern England* (Toronto: University of Toronto Press, 2004), p. 101. The second advertisement was published on 15–17 January.
12. Walker, *Authentick Memoirs*, p. 4.
13. Ibid., p. 149.
14. Some correspondents wrote more than one letter each. In total, there are twelve separate signatures appended to the letters, whereof at least two refer to the same man.
15. Walker, *Authentick Memoirs*, p. 29.
16. Anon., *The Genuine History*, p. 2.
17. For instance on p. 8, where a section from p. 10 of *Authentick Memoirs* is quoted.
18. Anon., *The Genuine History*, pp. iii–iv, vii.
19. Ibid., pp. 1–2.
20. Laura Rosenthal arrives at a similar conclusion; see 'The Whore's Estate', p. 97.
21. Rosenthal discusses this aspect of the depiction of Salisbury, suggesting that *Authentick Memoirs* '[tends] to suggest, albeit comically, that prostitution is ... comparable to other ways of making a living in the marketplace' ('The Whore's Estate', pp. 108–9).
22. Walker, *Authentick Memoirs*, pp. 72–3.
23. Ibid., pp. 72 and 73.
24. Anon., *The Genuine History*, p. 49.
25. Walker, *Authentick Memoirs*, p. 51.
26. Ibid., pp. 109–10.
27. Which she also does; when W—x has introduced her to a potential 'cull', and wants to collect his finder's fee, Salisbury rebuffs him in no uncertain terms, not willing to pay up until she knows exactly how much value she can extract from the 'Milch-Cow' (Walker, *Authentick Memoirs*, p. 110) he brought her.
28. B. K. Mudge, *The Whore's Story: Women, Pornography, and the British Novel, 1684–1830* (Oxford: Oxford University Press, 2000), pp. 49–50.
29. Walker, *Authentick Memoirs*, p. 85.
30. Ibid., pp. 85 and 86.
31. Ibid., p. 90.
32. Ibid.
33. Ibid., p. 133.
34. Ibid., p. 121; Anon., *The Genuine History*, p. 28.
35. Anon., *The Genuine History*, pp. 51–2.
36. Ibid., p. 61.
37. Ibid., pp. 60–1.
38. Ibid., p. 61.
39. AIbid., p. 51; L. J. Rosenthal, *Infamous Commerce: Prostitution in Eighteenth-Century British Literature and Culture* (Ithaca: Cornell University Press, 2006), p. 103.
40. Walker, *Authentick Memoirs*, p. 50.
41. Ibid., p. 51.
42. Ibid., p. 138. Salisbury aims high; a colonelcy was the highest rank that could be acquired by purchase, in 1720 estimated to be worth some £9,000; see A. Bruce, *The Purchase System in the British Army, 1660–1871* (London: Royal Historical Society, 1980), p. 25.
43. Interestingly, Salisbury also turns the parent-child relationship on its head by planning and providing for her father's future, even offering to use her own money to further his 'career'.

44. Walker, *Authentick Memoirs*, p. 81.
45. Ibid., p. 70.
46. Cf. Rosenthal, 'The Whore's Estate', p. 113.
47. Walker, *Authentick Memoirs*, pp. 103–4. 'Buttered bun' was slang for 'a woman that has just lain with another man' (F. Grose, *A Classical Dictionary of the Vulgar Tongue* (London: S. Hooper, 1785), unpaginated).
48. Walker, *Authentick Memoirs*, p. 137–8.
49. Anon., *The Genuine History*, p. 46.
50. Rosenthal, 'The Whore's Estate', p. 98.
51. In Rosenthal's reading, this is the main difference between *The Genuine History* and *Authentick Memoirs*: whereas the former 'reconciles the challenges that Salisbury's career posed to both class stability and gendered divisions between the owners and the owned', the latter 'takes full advantage of the destabilizing possibilities that her life and livelihood potentially suggest' ('The Whore's Estate', p. 105). However, when taking narrative polyvocality into consideration, it is clear that something more complex is going on in these texts.
52. Rosenthal, 'The Whore's Estate', p. 107.
53. Walker, *Authentick Memoirs*, p. 149.
54. Ibid., p. 149. Doctors' Commons was a society for ecclesiatical lawyers, on whose premises the proceedings of the church courts were held. One of these courts was the Consistory Court, which dealt with matrimonial and probate matters, as well as defamation and some contracts cases. For women involved in defamation cases during a somewhat earlier period, see L. Gowing, *Domestic Dangers: Women, Words, and Sex in Early Modern London* (Oxford: Clarendon Press, 1998).
55. Walker, *Authentick Memoirs*, Table of Contents.
56. Ibid., pp. 104–5.
57. Walker is more disingenuous in this instance than he lets on; he takes care never to call Salisbury 'whore' in his own narrative voice, limiting his use of the word to reported speech and to proverbial expressions.
58. Walker, *Authentick Memoirs*, p. 144.
59. Ibid., p. 2.
60. Ibid., pp. 76 and 142.
61. Anon., *The Genuine History*, pp. 50–1.
62. Ibid., pp. 8 and 46.
63. Walker, *Authentick Memoirs*, p. 121.
64. Anon., *The Genuine History*, p. 43.
65. Walker, *Authentick Memoirs*, pp. 79–81.

6 Wynn, 'Prostitutes and Erotic Performances in Eighteenth-Century Paris'

1. Voltaire, 'Dissertation sur la tragédie ancienne et moderne', preface to *Sémiramis* (1748), in R. Niklaus (ed.), *Complete Works* (Oxford: Voltaire Foundation, 1968), vol. 30A, p. 164; P.-A. C. de Beaumarchais, *Essai sur le genre dramatique sérieux* (1767), in P. Larthomas (ed.), *Œuvres* (Paris: Gallimard, 1988), p. 134; D. A. F de Sade, *Aline et Valcour*, in M. Delon (ed.), *Œuvres*, 3 vols (Paris: Gallimard, 1990–98), vol. 1, p. 689.

2. J. McManners, *Church and Society in Eighteenth-Century France*, 2 vols (Oxford: Oxford University Press, 1998–1999), vol. 2, p. 329.
3. P. Cheek, *Sexual Antipodes: Enlightenment Globalization and the Placing of Sex* (Palo Alto, CA: Stanford University Press, 2003), p. 47.
4. Anon., *Etrennes aux grisettes pour l'année 1790* (1790), p. 10. All translations from the French are my own.
5. See his introduction to *L'Espion libertin ou le calendrier du plaisir* (Arles: Philippe Picquier, 2000), p. 18.
6. R. Dawson, *Baculard d'Arnaud: Life and Prose Fiction*, SVEC, 141–2 (1976), p. 56.
7. On this figure, see R. Darnton, 'A Police Inspector Sorts His Files: the Anatomy of the Republic of Letters', in *The Great Cat Massacre and Other Episodes in French Cultural History* (London: Penguin, 1984), pp. 141–83.
8. R. Dawson, 'Naughty French Books and Their Imprints During the Long Eighteenth Century', SVEC, 12 (2007), pp. 152–3.
9. R. Dawson, 'The *Mélange de poésies diverses* (1781) and the Diffusion of Manuscript Pornography in Eighteenth-Century France', in R. P. Maccubbin (ed.), *Unauthorized Sexual Behavior During the Enlightenment*, special issue of *Eighteenth-Century Life*, 9 (1985), pp. 229–43.
10. J. Habermas, *The Structural Transformation of the Public Sphere* (London: Polity Press, 1989), p.43. See R. Darnton, 'Reading, Writing, and Publishing', in *The Literary Underground of the Old Regime* (Cambridge, MA: Harvard University Press, 1982), pp. 167–208; R. Darnton, *The Forbidden Best-Sellers of Pre-Revolutionary France* (London: HarperCollins, 1996); R. Dawson, *Confiscations and Customs: Banned Books and the French Booktrade During the Last Years of the Ancien Régime*, SVEC, 7 (2006).
11. See for instance *De la poésie dramatique* (1758), in *Œuvres esthétiques*, ed. P. Vernière (Paris: Garnier, 1968), p. 259, and *Lettre à Mme Riccoboni*, in *Œuvres complètes*, ed. J Assézat, 20 vols (Paris: Garnier Frères, 1875–77), vol. 7, pp. 400–1.
12. Habermas, *The Structural Transformation of the Public Sphere*, p. 51.
13. Dawson explains the matter somewhat differently when he writes with reference to *Le Parnasse libertin*, 'the police did not like people having a good time, so the book was banned' ('Naughty French Books and Their Imprints', p. 157).
14. See G. Maugras, *Les Comédiens hors la loi* (Paris: Calmann Lévy, 1887); and L. Berlanstein, *Daughters of Eve: a Cultural History of French Theater Women from the Old Regime to the Fin de Siècle* (Cambridge, MA: Harvard University Press, 2001).
15. J. McManners, *Abbés and Actresses: The Church and the Theatrical Profession in Eighteenth-Century France* (Oxford: Clarendon Press, 1986), p. 2.
16. Cited in M. Barras, *The Stage Controversy in France from Corneille to Rousseau* (New York: Phaeton Press, 1973), p. 318.
17. J.-J. Rousseau, *Lettre à M. D'Alembert*, in *Du Contrat social et autres œuvres politiques*, ed. J. Ehrard (Paris: Garnier, 1975), p. 186
18. F.-M. Mayeur de Saint-Paul, *Le Vol plus haut ou l'Espion des principaux théâtres de la capitale* ('Memphis': chez Sincère, 1784), p. 71. Erica-Marie Benabou discusses male prostitution only in terms of homosexual sodomy; see *La Prostitution et la police des mœurs au XVIIIe siècle* (Paris: Perrin, 1987), pp. 180–4.
19. On the period's typology of prostitutes, see the chapters 'Le nom que vous voudrez', 'De certaines femmes', 'Des filles publiques' and 'Courtisanes' in L.-S. Mercier, *Tableau de Paris*, 2 vols (London: 1781), vol. 2, pp. 2–12; and Benabou, *La Prostitution et la police*

des mœurs, pp. 362–83. See also Ann Lewis's article 'Classifying the Prostitute' in the present volume.

20. 'Je demande comment un état dont l'unique objet est de se montrer au public, et qui pis est, de se montrer pour de l'argent, conviendrait à d'honnêtes femmes, et pourrait compatir en elles avec la modestie et les bonnes mœurs? ('I ask how a profession whose unique object is to show oneself in public, and what is worse, to show oneself for money, could suit decent women, and could be reconciled with modesty and good morals'); Rousseau, *Lettre à M. D'Alembert*, in *Du Contrat social*, p. 195.
21. L. Bérenger, *De la prostitution. Cahier et doléances d'un ami des mœurs, adressés [sic] spécialement aux Députés de l'ordre du Tiers-État de Paris* ([Paris] : Au Palais Royal, 1789), p. 14. *Azémia ou le nouveau Robinson*, also called *Azémia ou les sauvages*, is an opéra-comique by Dalayrac and Poisson de la Chabeaussire (1786); *L'Héroïne américaine* is a pantomime in three acts by Jean-François Mussot *dit* Arnould (1786).
22. Lauren Clay, 'Provincial Actors, the Comédie-Française, and the Business of Performing in Eighteenth-Century France', *Eighteenth-Century Studies*, 38:4 (2005), pp. 651–69.
23. Benabou, *La Prostitution et la police des mœurs*, p. 110.
24. D. L. Trumeau de la Morandière, *Représentations à M. le lieutenant général de Police* (1764), cited in Benabou, *La Prostitution et la police des mœurs*, p. 367.
25. *Extraits des rapports des inspecteurs de police du roi*, in *L'Espion libertin*, p. 203. See also Benabou, *La Prostitution et la police des mœurs*, pp. 96–112.
26. F.-A. Chévrier, *Le Colporteur*, in *Romans libertins du XVIIIe siècle*, ed. R. Trousson (Paris: Robert Laffont, 1993), pp.741–884 (p. 808).
27. *Projet de cahier pour le tiers-état de la ville de Paris* (Paris: 1789), p. 17. See also V. Scott, 'The Actress and Utopian Theatre Reform in Eighteenth-Century France: Riccoboni, Rousseau, and Restif', *Theatre Research International*, 27 (2002), pp. 118–127.
28. *L'Espion libertin*, pp. 115–16.
29. *Etrennes aux grisettes*, pp. 21, 32 and 33. It is entirely unlikely that Saint-Huberty was involved in prostitution, but the smear against this royalist actress was an effective one.
30. *Les Sérails de Paris ou Vies et portraits des dames Pâris, Gourdan, Montigny et autres appareilleuses*, in *Anthologie érotique: le XVIIIe siècle*, ed. M. Lever (Paris: Robert Laffont, 2003), pp. 861–1025 (p. 911).
31. *Nouvelle liste des jolies femmes de Paris; leurs noms et leur demeure* (Paris: au Palais des Plaisirs, 1808), pp. 54–5.
32. Bérenger, *De la prostitution*, p. 25.
33. *Le Petit-fils d'Hercule*, in *Romanciers libertins du XVIIIe siècle*, ed. P. W. Lasowski, 2 vols (Paris: Gallimard, 2000–5), vol. 2, pp. 1073–132 (p. 1125).
34. See, for instance, D.-L. Turmeau de La Morandière's *Police sur les mendians, les vagabonds, les joueurs de profession, les intrigans, les filles prostituées, les domestiques hors de maison depuis longtemps, et les gens sans aveu* (Paris: Dessain Junior, 1784).
35. Maugras, *Les Comédiens hors la loi*, p. 216.
36. Chévrier, *Le Colporteur*, p. 808. Such immunity could also make the Opéra a haven from prostitution, allowing a woman an alternative career; see *Sérails de Paris*, in *Anthologie érotique*, p. 958.
37. Pidansat de Mairobert, *Confession d'une jeune fille*, in *Romanciers libertins du XVIIIe siècle*, vol. 2, pp. 1141–99 (p. 1143).
38. Bérenger, *De la prostitution*, p. 22.
39. Mercier, 'Filles d'Opéra', *Tableau de Paris*, vol. 1, p. 265.
40. Ibid. Emphasis added.

41. Bérenger, *De la prostitution*, pp. 13–14.
42. Cited in Benabou, *La Prostitution et la police des mœurs*, p. 195.
43. See *L'Espion libertin*, pp. 115–16.
44. M. F. Pidansat de Mairobet, *L'Espion anglais ou correspondance entre deux milords sur les mœurs publiques et privées des Français*, 2 vols (Paris: Léopold Collin, 1809), vol. 2, p. 326.
45. *Correspondance de Madame Gourdan*, in *Anthologie érotique*, pp. 690–1.
46. Diderot, *Paradoxe sur le comédien*, in *Œuvres esthétiques*, pp. 312–13. See also G. Cerruti, 'Le paradoxe sur le comédien et le paradoxe sur le libertin, Diderot et Sade', *Revue des sciences humaines*, 37 (1972), pp. 235–51.
47. *Correspondance de Madame Gourdan*, in *Anthologie érotique*, p. 693.
48. *Nouvelle liste des jolies femmes de Paris*, p. 32.
49. See C. Santini, 'Théâtralité et exhibition dans le théâtre pornographique du XVIIIe siècle', in *De l'obscène et de la pornographie comme objets d'études*, ed. Jean M. Goulemot, *Cahiers d'histoire culturelle*, 5 (1999), pp. 39–48; and T. Wynn, 'Le dialogue dans le théâtre érotique du XVIIIe siècle', *SVEC*, 7 (2005), pp. 223–30.
50. For example see Sade, *Histoire de Juliette*, in *Œuvres*, vol. 3, pp. 320–1; and the anonymous *Les Costumes théâtrales ou scenes secrettes des foyer. Petit recueil de contes, un peu plus que gaillards, orné de couplets analogues. Dédiés aux jeunes gens des deux sexes qui se destinent aux theatres* (À Hélio-foutropolis: de l'Imprimerie de Crispinaille, à la Matricule, 1793), pp. 23–4.
51. Bibliothèque de l'Arsenal, Ms. 9549, p. 3.
52. Benabou, *La Prostitution et la police des mœurs*, p. 231.
53. F.-T.-M. Baculard d'Arnaud, *L'Art de F****, in *Le Bordel, ou le Jean-foutre puni, comédie, à laquelle on a joint un Ballet en trois scenes* (Ancone: chez Jean Chouard, à l'enseigne du morpion couronné, 1747), pp. 119–31 (p. 126).
54. Cushing Library, Texas A&M University, College Station, TX, PQ 1177. M45 1780, pp. 202–13 (p. 205).
55. *Almanach royal* (1741), p. 259. This cannot be the more famous Antoine-Raymond-Jean-Gualbert-Gabriel de Sartine, comte d'Alby, who was the chief of police, because he was born in 1729.
56. Baculard d'Arnaud, *L'Art de F****, p. 122.
57. PQ 1177. M45 1780, p. 205.
58. Baculard d'Arnaud, *L'Art de F****, pp. 124–5. I have been unable to identify in the erotic literature of the period exactly what this first position is.
59. Bibliothèque de l'Arsenal, Archives de la Bastille, Ms 11480, f. 149.
60. G. Capon and R. Yve-Plessis, *Les Théâtres clandestins* (Paris: Plessis, 1905), p.257; Dawson, *Baculard d'Arnaud*, p. 55; Benabou, *La Prostitution et la police des mœurs*, p. 232.
61. This finding challenges Benabou's assertion that women were the prime target of police repression in matters of prostitution; see *La Prostitution et la police des mœurs*, p. 19.
62. Ms 11480, f. 139.
63. Ms 11480, f. 140; this notice is not dated. It is possible that this is the manuscript Maurepas mentioned.
64. Ms 12484, f. 24.v.
65. Ms 11480, f. 151; emphasis added.
66. Ms 11480, f. 152; emphasis added.
67. Ms 11480, f. 206; emphasis added.

68. F. Funck-Brentano, *Les Lettres de cachet à Paris, étude suivie d'une liste des prisonniers de la Bastille* (1659–1789) (Paris: Imprimerie Nationale, 1903), p. 279.
69. Ms 11480, f. 127.
70. The letter is from Dubut to Maurepas; ms 11480, f. 153. See also Ms 11480, ff. 223, 225 and 227.
71. Ms 11480, f. 136, undated.
72. Quoted in Dawson, *Baculard d'Arnaud*, p. 59.
73. See Ms 11480, f. 127.
74. B. de La Villehervé, *François-Thomas Baculard d'Arnaud: son théâtre et ses théories dramatiques* (Paris: Champion, 1920), pp. 13 and 16; Dawson, *Baculard d'Arnaud*, p. 59.
75. Quoted in H. Monod-Cassidy, *Un Voyageur-philosophe au XVIIIe siècle: l'abbé Jean-Bernard Le Blanc* (Cambridge MA: Harvard University Press, 1941), p. 360.
76. Ms 11480, f. 127.
77. Ms 11480, f. 141. See also f. 130, dated March 1731.
78. Dawson, *Baculard d'Arnauld*, p. 56.
79. Ibid., p. 55. At this point, Dawson did not know of the Cushing manuscript.

7 Grant, 'Visible Prostitutes'

1. R. Paulson, *Hogarth: Vol.1, The Modern Moral Subject 1697–1732*, rev. edn (Cambridge: Lutterworth Press, 1992). See also D. Bindman, *Hogarth*, (London: Thames and Hudson, 1981), and M. Godby, 'The First Steps of Hogarth's Harlot's Progress', *Art History*, 10 (1987), pp. 23–37.
2. M. Hallett, *The Spectacle of Difference: Graphic Satire in the Age of Hogarth* (New Haven, CT: Yale University Press, 1999); and S. Carter, *Purchasing Power: Representing Prostitution in Eighteenth-Century English Popular Print Culture* (Aldershot: Ashgate 2004).
3. Carter, *Purchasing Power*, p. 37.
4. Hallett, *Spectacle of Difference*, p.129
5. Tate Britain, Hogarth's Modern Moral Series <http://www.tate.org.uk/britain/exhibitions/hogarth/modernmorals/> (accessed 12 June 2011).
6. Hallett, *Spectacle of Difference,* p. 128. Hallett cites J. Nichols, *Biographical Anecdotes of William Hogarth*, 2nd edn (London: Printed by and for John Nichols, 1782), p. 33.
7. F. Antal, 'The Moral Purpose of Hogarth's Art', *Journal of the Warburg and Courtauld Institutes*, 15: 3/4 (1952), pp. 169–97.
8. H. Fielding, 'Preface', in *The History of the Adventures of Joseph Andrews and of His Friend Mr. Abraham Adams; And, An Apology for the Life of Mrs. Shamela Andrews*, ed. Douglas Brooks-Davies and Tom Keymer (Oxford: Oxford University Press, 1999), p.5.
9. R. Steele, 'The Spectator No. 266, Friday January 4 1712', in D. Bond (ed.), *The Spectator*, 5 vols (Oxford: The Clarendon press, 1965), vol. 2, pp. 536–7.
10. Paulson, *Hogarth*, vol. 1, p.241.
11. *The Life of Colonel Don Francisco. Containing the Whole Series of the Most Remarkable and Unprecedented Actions from His Birth to the Time of His Receiving Sentence of Death for a Rape* (London: printed for the author, and sold by the booksellers, pamphlet-sellers and hawkers, 1730), quoted in Paulson, *Hogarth* 1, p. 242.
12. Paulson, *Hogarth*, vol. 1, pp. 242–6.
13. See Carter, *Purchasing Power*, p. 38ff.

14. W. A. Speck, 'The Harlot's Progress in Eighteenth Century England', *British Journal of Eighteenth-Century Studies*, 3 (1980), pp. 127–39, 131.
15. J. Uglow, *Hogarth: A Life and a World* (London: Faber and Faber, 1997), p. 196.
16. R. Paulson, *Emblem and Expression: Meaning in English Art of the Eighteenth Century* (London: Thames and Hudson, 1975), pp.38ff.
17. J. Barrell, *The Political Theory of Painting from Reynolds to Hazlitt: 'The Body of the Public'* (New Haven, CT: Yale University Press, 1986); and D. H. Solkin, *Painting for Money: The Visual Arts and the Public Sphere in Eighteenth-Century England* (New Haven, CT: Yale University Press, 1992), see also C. Grant, 'The Choice of Hercules: The Polite Arts and "Female Excellence" in Eighteenth-Century London' in E. Eger, C. Grant, C. Ó Gallchoir and P. Warburton (eds), *Women, Writing and the Public Sphere 1700–1830* (Cambridge: Cambridge University Press, 2001), pp.75–103, p.76ff.
18. See M. Berg and E. Eger, 'Introduction', and E. Hundert, 'Mandeville, Rousseau and the Political Economy of Fantasy', in M. Berg and E. Eger (eds), *Luxury in the Eighteenth-Century: Debates, Desires and Delectable Goods* (Basingstoke: Palgrave Macmillan, 2003), pp. 1–27; 28–41.
19. Paulson, *Hogarth,* vol. 1, p. 376, n. 51.
20. B. Mandeville, *The Fable of the Bees* (Harmondsworth: Penguin, 1989), p. 130.
21. I. Primer, *Bernhard Mandeville's 'A Modest Defence of Public Stews' Prostitution and Its Discontents in Early Georgian England* (New York and Basingstoke: Palgrave Macmillan, 2006), pp. 49–50.
22. Paulson, Hogarth, vol. 1, p. 254.
23. Primer, *Mandeville's Modest Defence,* pp. 4–5. Primer cites W. A. Speck, 'Bernhard Mandeville and the Middlesex Grand Jury', *Eighteenth-Century Studies,* 11 (1978), pp. 362–74. Speck's article examines the political context and makeup of the Grand Jury.
24. For an account of the Societies see A. Hunt, *Governing Morals* (Cambridge: Cambridge University Press, 1999).
25. R. B. Shoemaker, *Gender in English Society, 1650–1850: The Emergence of Separate Spheres* (London and New York: Longman, 1988), p. 105.
26. D. Defoe 'Reformation of Manners, A Satyr, Vae Vobis Hypocrite' (1702), in *Poems on Affairs of State,* ed. F.H. Ellis (New Haven: Yale University Press, 1970), vol. 6, p. 404.
27. B. Mandeville, *A Modest Defence of Publick Stews: Or, an Essay upon Whoring, as It Is Now Practis'd in These Kingdoms.* (London, 1724), p. 44.
28. Hunt, *Governing Morals.*
29. Speck, 'The Harlot's Progress in the Eighteenth Century', pp. 127–139.
30. V. Jones, 'Luxury, Satire and Prostitution Narratives', in Berg and Eger (eds), *Luxury in the Eighteenth-Century,* pp.178–89, 282.
31. Jones, 'Luxury', p. 180, p.188, n. 11.
32. Primer, *Mandeville's Modest Defence,* pp. 49–50.
33. Primer, *Mandeville's Modest Defence* p. 137; and W. Redfern, *Puns* (Oxford and New York: Blackwell, 1984) p.91.
34. K. Harvey, *Reading Sex in the Eighteenth Century: Bodies and Gender in English Erotic Culture* (Cambridge: Cambridge University Press, 2004).
35. Jones, *Luxury,* p.180.
36. G. Vertue, *Notebooks, The Walpole Society Journal,* 22 (1933–34), p.58.
37. D. Dabydeen, *Hogarth's Blacks: Images of Blacks in Eighteenth Century English Art* (Manchester: Manchester University Press, 1987), pp. 116–18.
38. Hallett, *Spectacle of Difference,* p. 100.

39. W. Hogarth, *The Analysis of Beauty* (1753), ed. Ronald Paulson (New Haven, CT: Yale University Press, 1997).
40. Hogarth, *The Analysis,* p.115.
41. Hogarth, *The Analysis,* p. 59.
42. Hogarth, *The Analysis,* p.8.
43. Paulson, pp.274–80, 275. See also Hallett, *Spectacle of Difference* p.116–19.
44. See J. Uglow, *Hogarth* (London: Faber, 1997), p. 328.
45. M. Hallet and C. Riding, *Hogarth* (London: Tate Gallery, 2006), p.162.

8 Langille, 'The Narrative Sources of *Candide*'s Paquette'

1. The author wishes to thank T. E. D. Braun and P. M. Urbach for their helpful comments. All translations are my own.
2. Voltaire, *Candide ou l'optimisme* (1759), ed. R. Pomeau, *Complete Works of Voltaire*, vol. 48 (Oxford: Voltaire Foundation, 1980).
3. F. de Monbron, *Margot La Ravaudeuse* (1750), ed. Maurice Saillet (Paris: Jean-Jacques Pauvert, 1965).
4. J. H. Broome, '*Voltaire* and Fougeret de Monbron: a *Candide* Problem Reconsidered', *Modern Language Review*, 55:4 (1960), pp. 509–18.
5. M. Sandmann, 'La Source anglaise de *Candide* (I et II)', *Zeitschrift für fransösiche Sprache und Literatur,* 83 (1973), pp. 255–59.
6. E. M. Langille, 'La Place's *Histoire de Tom Jones, ou l'enfant trouvé* and *Candide*', *Eighteenth-Century Fiction,* 19 (2007), pp. 267–89; E. M. Langille, 'Indebted to Tom', *Times Literary Supplement,* 6 Apr. 2007, p. 15; E. M. Langille, '*L'Histoire de Tom Jones, ou l'enfant trouvé* et la genèse de *Candide*', *Revue d'Histoire Littéraire de la France*, 2 (2008), pp. 269–87.
7. P. A. de La Place, *Histoire de Tom Jones ou l'enfant trouvé, traduction de l'anglais de M. Fielding. Par M.D.L.P.* [i.e. Monsieur de La Place] (London [Paris]: John Nourse, 1750), hereafter *L'enfant trouvé*.
8. V. Mylne, 'A Picara in *Candide*: Paquette', *College Literature,* 6 (1979), pp. 205–10.
9. Votaire, *Candide*, p. 120.
10. Ibid., pp. 130–1.
11. 'On appelle Demoiselle suivante, Une Demoiselle attachée au service d'une grande Dame; & quelquefois on l'appelle absolument Suivante'; 'On appelle Femme de chambre, Une femme ou fille qui sert une Dame à la chambre', *Dictionnaire de l'Académie française*, 4th edn (1762).
12. La Place, *L'enfant trouvé,* vol. 1, p. 189.
13. M. Pavlovich, *Catalogues des livres de la bibliothèque de Voltaire* (Leningrad and Moscow: Academy of Sciences, 1961).
14. Nicolas Claude Thierot to Voltaire, 14 octobre 1758, *Correspondence and Related Documents*, ed. T. Besterman, OCV (Oxford: Voltaire Foundation, 1968–). D7902.
15. La Place, *L'enfant trouvé*, vol. 1, p. 206.
16. Votaire, *Candide*, p. 122.
17. La Place, *L'enfant trouvé,* vol. 1, p. 131.
18. Ibid., vol. 4, p. 334.
19. Votaire, *Candide*, p. 229.
20. Ibid., p. 237.
21. Monbron, *Margot La Ravaudeuse*, p. 37.

22. Ibid., p. 147.
23. Ibid., p. 4.
24. Voltaire, *Lettres philosophiques*, ed. Jacques Van den Heuvel, *Mélanges* (Paris: Gallimard, 1961), p. 86.
25. Votaire, *Candide*, pp. 129 and 140.
26. Monbron, *Margot La Ravaudeuse*, pp. 17 and 118.
27. Ibid., pp. 38–9.
28. Votaire, *Candide*, p. 255.
29. Monbron, *Margot La Ravaudeuse*, pp. 19, 77–95.
30. 'Il y avait longtemps que je convoitais un superbe diamant qu'il portait au doigt' (Monbron, *Margot La Ravaudeuse*, p. 100); 'La belle, ayant aperçu deux énormes diamants aux deux mains de son jeune étranger, les loua de si bonne foi que des doigts de Candide ils passèrent aux doigts de la marquise' (Votaire, *Candide*, p. 218).
31. Monbron, *Margot La Ravaudeuse*, p. 145.
32. Ibid.
33. Ibid., p. 5.
34. Votaire, *Candide*, p. 120.
35. Monbron, *Margot La Ravaudeuse*, p. 8.
36. Ibid.
37. Ibid., pp. 14–15.
38. Ibid., p. 41.
39. La Place, *L'enfant trouvé*, vol. 1, p. 16; E. M. Langille, 'Candide and Tom Jones: Voltaire, Perched on Fielding's Shoulders', in A. W. Lee (ed.) *Mentoring in Eighteenth-Century British Literature and Culture* (Farnham: Ashgate, 2010), p. 85–107.
40. Votaire, *Candide*, p. 228.
41. Mylne, 'A Picara in *Candide*', p. 207.
42. Ibid., p. 208.
43. Monbron, *Margot La Ravaudeuse*.
44. Votaire, *Candide*, pp. 227–32.
45. Mylne, 'A Picara in *Candide*', p. 206.
46. Votaire, *Candide*, p. 256.
47. See J. S. Farmer, *Vocabula Amatoria, French-English Dictionary of Erotica*, s.l. (1896), reprinted: (New York: University Books, 1966).

9 Delers, 'The Prostitute as Neo-Manager'

1. For a study of literary realism in *Les Infortunes de la vertu*, see O. Delers, 'Mais où est le cul? Life and Form in Sade's *Les Infortunes de la vertu* and *La Nouvelle Justine*', *Eighteenth-Century Fiction*, 22:4 (Summer 2010), pp. 657–72.
2. L. Boltanski and E. Chiapello, *Le Nouvel esprit du capitalisme* (Paris: Gallimard, 1999); translated as *The New Spirit of Capitalism*, tr. by Gregory Elliott (London: Verso, 2006). All quotes refer to this edition.
3. Boltanski and Chiapello, *The New Spirit*, pp. 17–18.
4. K. Norberg, 'The Libertine Whore: Prostitution in French Pornography from Margot to Juliette', in L. Hunt (ed.), *The Invention of Pornography: Obscenity and the Origins of Modernity, 1500–1800* (New York: Zone Books, 1993), pp. 225–52 (p. 227).
5. Norberg, 'The Libertine Whore', p. 226.

6. K. Pullen, *Actresses and Whores: On Stage and in Society* (Cambridge: Cambridge University Press, 2005), p. 2.
7. A. Carter, *The Sadeian Woman and the Ideology of Pornography* (New York: Phanteon Books, 1978), p. 3.
8. Boltanski and Chiapello, *The New Spirit*, p. 218 and p. 216.
9. 'Eh bien mon enfant, vous n'avez qu'à rester ici, beaucoup de soumissions à mes conseils, un grand fonds de complaisance et de soumission pour mes pratiques, de la propreté, de l'économie, de la candeur vis-à-vis de moi, de l'urbanité envers vos compagnes et de la fourberie avec les hommes, dans quelques années d'ici je vous mettrai en état de vous retirer dans une chambre avec une commode, un trumeau, une servante, et l'art que vous aurez acquis chez moi vous donnera de quoi vous procurer le reste.' ('Well, child, you may stay here. Follow my advice strictly, be accommodating in observing my rules, be clean and thrifty, behave candidly with me, courteously with your companions and deceitfully with men, and under my direction you shall be in a position a few years hence to withdraw from this place to a room of your own with a chest for your clothes, a pier-glass, and a maid, and the art which you acquire in my house will provide you with the means of procuring the rest.') D. A. F. Sade, *Les Infortunes de la vertu*, in *Œuvres Complètes du Marquis de Sade* (Paris: Pauvert, 1986), vol. 2, p. 262; D.A.F. Sade, *The Misfortunes of Virtue and Other Early Tales*, trans. D. Coward (Oxford: Oxford University Press, 1999), pp. 6–7: all translations are taken from the latter. As Nancy K. Miller rightly notes, Juliette's story rejects the ideals of domesticity and femininity: 'Juliette's *bildung* – her self-development – is achieved by a reversal of the valorization assigned to the cultural and literary conventions encoding femaleness, the positively marked status of daughter, wife, mother. The novel builds upon the stages of emancipation from the familial, or the denegation of bourgeois femininity' (N. K. Miller, 'Juliette and the Posterity of Prosperity', *L'Esprit créateur* (Winter 1975), pp. 413–24 (p. 414)).
10. Sade, *Les Infortunes*, p. 263.
11. Sade, *The Misfortunes*, p. 6.
12. D. A. F. Sade, *Justine, ou les malheurs de la vertu*, in *Œuvres Complètes du Marquis de Sade*, (Paris: Pauvert, 1986), vol. 3, p. 30. The translations are mine unless otherwise indicated.
13. Sade, *Les Infortunes*, pp. 261–2.
14. Sade, *The Misfortunes*, pp. 5–6.
15. Sade, *Les Infortunes*, p. 264.
16. Sade, *The Misfortunes*, p. 9.
17. Sade, *Les Infortunes*, p. 265.
18. Sade, *The Misfortunes*, p. 9. This translation altered slightly from Coward edition.
19. Boltanski and Chiapello, *The New Spirit*, p. 116 (their italics).
20. Ibid., p. 312.
21. Norberg, 'The Libertine Whore', p. 239.
22. Sade, *Les Infortunes*, p. 259 and Sade, *Justine*, p. 25.
23. Sade, *Les Infortunes*, p. 263 and Sade, *Justine*, p. 30.
24. A. Furetière, *Dictionnaire universel*, 3 vols (Paris, 1690).
25. Boltanski and Chiapello, *The New Spirit*, pp. 442–3 (their italics). The two sociologists link the artistic aptitudes of neo-managers to their individualism and make the connection with processes of exclusion and exploitation in network societies.
26. See for instance Kirsten Pullen's analysis: 'At particular moments, the body of the actress (assumed to be an object onto which male desires were projected) and the

body of the prostitute (assumed to be an object onto which male desires were enacted) slipped discursively into one: whore/actress', Pullen, *Actresses and Whores*, p. 2. See also V. Jones, 'Eighteenth-Century Prostitution: Feminist Debates and the Writing of Histories', in A. Horner and A. Keane (eds), *Body Matters: Feminism, Textuality, Corporeality* (Manchester: Manchester University Press, 2000), pp. 127–42 and S. Bell, *Reading, Writing and Rewriting the Prostitute Body* (Bloomington, IN: Indiana University Press, 1994).

27. Sade, *Les Infortunes*, p. 264.
28. Sade, *The Misfortunes*, p. 9.
29. Sade, *Les Infortunes*, p. 263.
30. Sade, *The Misfortunes*, p. 8.
31. Boltanski and Chiapello, *The New Spirit*, p. 312.
32. Ibid., p. 356.
33. Sade, *Les Infortunes*, p. 264.
34. Sade, *The Misfortunes*, p. 8.
35. Sade, *Les Infortunes*, p. 264.
36. Sade, *The Misfortunes*, p. 8.
37. Boltanski and Chiapello, *The New Spirit*, pp. 111–12 (their italics).
38. Ibid., pp. 112 (their italics).
39. Ibid., p. 378.
40. Sade, *Les Infortunes*, p. 264.
41. Sade, *The Misfortunes*, p. 8.
42. Sade, *Les Infortunes*, pp. 264–5.
43. Sade, *The Misfortunes*, p. 9.
44. Boltanski and Chiapello, *The New Spirit*, p. 379.
45. Justine 'fut durement rejetée' ('was sent away with harsh words') by her mother's seamstress and 'le curé de sa paroisse ... lui avait passé la main sous le menton en lui donnant un baiser beaucoup trop mondain pour un homme d'Eglise' ('her parish priest ... had placed his hand beneath her chin and gave her far too worldly a kiss for a man of the cloth'), instead of offering her the advice that she is looking for (Sade, *Les Infortunes*, p. 261; Sade, *The Misfortunes*, p. 4–5).
46. Networks, they explain, become a dominant metaphor in advanced industrial societies as connectivity emerges as a central asset: 'The formation of more or less extensive networks is no more novel than commercial activity was when Adam Smith wrote *The Wealth of Nations*. But it is as if we had to wait until the last third of the twentieth century for the activity of mediating, the art of making and using the most diverse and remote kinds of connection, to be autonomized – separated from the other forms of activity it had hitherto been bound up with – and identified and valued for itself', Boltanski and Chiapello, *The New Spirit*, p. 108.
47. Sade, *Justine*, p. 23.
48. I borrow Coward's translation from *The Misfortunes* for the first part of the quote. The translation for the second part is mine.
49. Boltanski and Chiapello, *The New Spirit*, p. 354.
50. The narrator indicates that '[Juliette] avait reçu néanmoins la plus brillante éducation possible ... elle avait été élevée avec une sœur plus jeune qu'elle de trois ans dans un des meilleurs couvents de Paris, où jusqu'à l'âge de quinze ans, aucun conseil, aucun maitre, aucun bon livre, aucun talent ne lui avait été refusé' (Sade, *Les Infortunes*, p. 259) ('She had nevertheless been given the finest of educations ... she was brought up with her sister

three years her junior in one of the best convents in Paris where, until the age of 15, she was never denied good counsel or teachers nor good books or talents' (Sade, *The Misfortunes*, p. 3)).
51. A careful reading of Justine's actions in the two novels also shows that she is not simply a victim of fate but that she actively and consciously participates in the decisions that lead her from one violent oppressor to another.
52. Boltanski and Chiapello, *The New Spirit*, p. 117.
53. For more on the sexual contract, see C. Pateman, *The Sexual Contract* (Stanford: Stanford University Press, 1988).
54. Boltanski and Chiapello, *The New Spirit*, p. 126 and p. 125.
55. Ibid., p. 145.
56. See my article, O. Delers, 'Mais où est le cul?'.

10 Peace, 'Figuring the London Magdalen House'

1. [J. Hanway], *Thoughts on the Plan for a Magdalen-House for Repentant Prostitutes, with the several Reasons for such an Establishment; the Custom of other Nations with Regard to such penitents and the Great Advantages Which will probably arise from this Institution, upon political and Religious Principles* (London: James Waugh, 1758), p. 5.
2. W. Dodd, *A Sermon on St. Matthew, Chap. IX. Ver. 12, 13. Preach'd at the Parish Church of St. Laurence, Near Guild-Hall, April the 26th, 1759, before the President, Vice-Presidents, Treasurer and Governors of the Magdalen House for the Reception of Penitent Prostitutes* (London: L. Davis and C. Reymers, [1759]), p. ii.
3. Anon., *The Histories of Some of the Penitents in the Magdalen House*, eds. Jennie Batchelor and Megan Hiatt (London: Pickering and Chatto, 2007), p. 182.
4. A. Smith, *An Inquiry into the Nature and Causes of the Wealth of Nations*, 3rd edn, 3 vols (London: printed for W. Strahan; and T. Cadell, [1784]), vol. 2, p. 459.
5. Smith, *Wealth of Nations*, vol. 2, p. 517.
6. Batchelor and Hiatt, 'Introduction', *Histories of the Penitents*, pp. xi–xii.
7. Dodd, *A Sermon on St. Matthew*, p. ii.
8. D. T. Andrew, *Philanthropy and Police: Charity in the Eighteenth Century* (Princeton, NJ: Princeton University Press, 1989), p. 191.
9. Andrew, *Philanthropy and Police*, p. 191.
10. E. J. Bristow, *Vice and Vigilance: Purity Movements in Britain Since 1700* (Totowa, NJ: Rowman and Littlefield, 1977), pp. 54–6.
11. R. Porter, *Enlightenment: Britain and the Creation of the Modern World* (London: Penguin Books, 2006), pp. 206–7.
12. J. S. Taylor, 'Philanthropy and Empire: Jonas Hanway and the Infant Poor of London', *Eighteenth-Century Studies*, 12:3 (1979), pp. 285–305 (pp. 587, 257, 259).
13. Taylor, 'Philanthropy and Empire', pp. 290; 292.
14. V. Jones, 'Scandalous Femininity: Prostitution and Eighteenth-Century Narrative', in D. Castiglione and L. Sharpe (eds), *Shifting the Boundaries, Transformation of the Language of Public and Private in the Eighteenth Century* (Exeter: University of Exeter Press, 1995), p. 58.
15. J. Batchelor, '"Industry in Distress"': Reconfiguring Femininity and Labor in the Magdalen House', *Eighteenth-Century Life*, 28:1 (2004), p. 3.
16. Ibid., p. 17.

17. K. Binhammer, *The Seduction Narrative in Britain, 1747–1800* (Cambridge: Cambridge University Press, 2009), p. 2.
18. Ibid., p. 4.
19. Ibid., p. 1.
20. See Jennie Batchelor's chapter in this collection, 'Mothers and Others', p. 160.
21. M. Peace, 'The Magdalen Hospital and the Fortunes of Whiggish Sentimentality in Mid-Eighteenth-Century Britain: "Well-Grounded" Exemplarity vs. "Romantic" Exceptionality', *The Eighteenth Century*, 48:2 (2007), pp. 125–48.
22. The novel was brokered by Barbara Montagu and is sometimes attributed to Sarah Scott, sister to the Queen of the Bluestockings, Elizabeth Montagu. For a full discussion see M. Peace, '"Epicures in Rural Pleasures": Revolution, Desire and Sentimental Economy in Sarah Scott's Millenium Hall', *Women's Writing*, 9:2 (2002), p. 312 and J. Grossman, '"Sympathetic Visibility", Social Reform and the English Woman Writer: *The Histories of Some of the Penitents in the Magdalen-House*', *Women's Writing*, 7:2 (2000), pp. 255–6.
23. For a more detailed discussion of this competition see J. L. Abbott and D. G. C. Allan, '"Compassion and Horror in Every Humane Mind": Samuel Johnson, the Society of Arts, and Eighteenth-Century Prostitution', *Journal of the Royal Society of the Arts*, 136 (1988), pp. 749–54; 827–32; M. Ellis, *The Politics of Sensibility: Race, Gender and Commerce in the Sentimental Novel* (Cambridge: Cambridge University Press, 1996), pp. 170–7 and M. Peace, 'The Magdalen Hospital', pp. 126–30.
24. Dingley, *Proposals for Establishing a Public Place of Reception for Penitent Prostitutes* (London: W. Faden, 1758), pp. 4, 3–4.
25. [Hanway], *Thoughts*, p. 12; S. Welch, *A Proposal to Render Effectual a Plan, to Remove the Nuisance of Common Prostitutes from the Streets of this Metropolis* (London, 1758), p. 16.
26. Abbott and Allan, '"Compassion and Horror"', p. 36.
27. [Hanway], *Thoughts*, p. 25.
28. Peace, 'The Magdalen Hospital', pp. 125–48.
29. *Histories of the Penitents*, p. xii.
30. See J. Mullan, *Sentiment and Sociability: The Language of Feeling in the Eighteenth Century* (Oxford: Clarendon Press), pp. 57–114 and Porter, *Enlightenment*, pp. 276–95.
31. *Histories of the Penitents*, pp. ix–x.
32. I am not so convinced by the idea that there is an absolute distinction between prostitutes as subjects and prostitutes as objects, in the novel and the charitable proposal respectively. Both the novel and the plan both use the term 'objects' to describe the prostitutes and recourse to the *OED* suggests that in this context at the mid-century the term refers to '[a] person who, or thing which provokes admiration, pity, indignation, sorrow, etc.; a sight, a spectacle'. In other words it does not necessarily carry the modern association of 'objectification' that it would imply today.
33. Dingley, *Proposals*, p. 3; *Histories of the Penitents*, p. 4.
34. Dingley, *Proposals*, pp. 3–4.
35. Ibid., p. 5.
36. *Histories of the Penitents*, p. 4.
37. Ibid., p. 7.
38. Ibid., p. 12.
39. Ibid., p. 37.
40. Ibid., p. 13.
41. Ibid. p. 42
42. Ibid., p. 7.

43. *Histories of the Penitents*, p. 7.
44. Ibid., p. 75.
45. Ibid., p. 42.
46. Ibid., p. 45.
47. Ibid., p. 54.
48. Ibid., pp. 7–8.

11 Batchelor, 'Mothers and Others'

1. I would like to thank Megan Hiatt for her incisive comments on an earlier draft of this essay.
2. S. Bell describes this 'process of othering' by which the prostitute became 'the other within the other: the other within the categorical others, "woman"', in *Reading, Writing and Rewriting the Prostitute Body* (Bloomington, IA: Indiana University Press, 1994). See also J. R. Walkowitz's *Prostitution and Victorian Society: Women, Class, and the State* (Cambridge: Cambridge University Press, 1980), which locates the origins of Victorian representations of, and attitudes towards, prostitution in the mid-eighteenth century. On the domestic woman's relationship with her prostitute antithesis/double, see N. Armstrong, *Desire and Domestic Fiction: A Political History of the Novel* (New York: Oxford University Press, 1987).
3. K. Binhammer, *The Seduction Narrative in Britain, 1747–1800* (Cambridge: Cambridge University Press, 2009); R. Perry, *Novel Relations: The Transformation of Kinship in English Literature and Culture, 1748–1818* (Cambridge: Cambridge University Press, 2004), see particularly, pp. 265–87; and L. J. Rosenthal, *Infamous Commerce: Prostitution in Eighteenth-Century British Literature and Culture* (Ithaca and London: Cornell University Press, 2006).
4. Perry, *Novel Relations*, p. 280.
5. Rosenthal, *Infamous Commerce*, p. 5.
6. Ibid., p. 5. Chapter 6 of Perry, *Novel Relations* is also germane.
7. Notable exceptions (although concerned with sexually transgressive, rather than specifically prostitute, mothers) include M. Francus, 'The Monstrous Mother: Reproductive Anxiety in Swift and Pope', *ELH*, 61 (1994), pp. 829–51; and F. Nussbaum, '"Savage Mothers": Narratives of Maternity in the Mid-Eighteenth Century', *Cultural Critique* (1991–92), pp. 123–51.
8. Toni Bowers has an excellent discussion of these novels and the surrounding scholarship in *The Politics of Motherhood: British Writing and Culture 1680–1760* (Cambridge: Cambridge University Press, 1996).
9. F. A. Nussbaum, *Torrid Zones: Maternity, Sexuality, and Empire in Eighteenth-Century English Narratives* (Baltimore, MD and London: Johns Hopkins University Press, 1995), p. 25.
10. M. Wollstonecraft, *The Wrongs of Woman; or Maria*, reprinted in *Mary and The Wrongs of Woman*, ed. G. Kelly (Oxford: Oxford University Press, 1998), p. 75; p. 199.
11. S. C. Greenfield, *Mothering Daughters: Novels and the Politics of Family Romance, Frances Burney to Jane Austen* (Detroit: Wayne State University Press, 2003), p. 94.
12. Wollstonecraft, *The Wrongs of Woman*, p. 121.
13. R. Perry, 'Colonizing the Breast: Sexuality and Maternity in Eighteenth-Century England', *Journal of the History of Sexuality*, 2:2 (1991), p. 205. See also Bowers, *The Politics of Motherhood*; and Nussbaum, *Torrid Zones.*.

14. Nussbaum, *Torrid Zones*, p. 18.
15. Anon., *The Histories of Some of the Penitents in the Magdalen-House. As Supposed to be Related by Themselves*, ed. J. Batchelor and M. Hiatt (London: Pickering & Chatto, 2007), p. 3.
16. Ibid., p. 52.
17. A. Van Sant, *Eighteenth-Century Sensibility and the Novel: The Senses in Social Context* (Cambridge: Cambridge University Press, 1993), p. 37.
18. M. J. Koehler, *Models of Reading: Paragons and Parasites in Richardson, Burney, and Laclos* (Lewisburg: Bucknell University Press, 2005).
19. *Histories of the Penitents*, p. 10.
20. For a fascinating discussion of the Virgin Mary and her cultural representation in early eighteenth-century literature see C. Harol, *Enlightened Virginity in Eighteenth-Century Literature* (Basingstoke: Palgrave Macmillan, 2006), pp. 111–16.
21. V. Jones, 'Eighteenth-Century Prostitution: Feminist Debates and the Writing of Histories', in *Body Matters: Feminism, Textuality, Corporeality*, ed. A. Horner and A. Keane (Manchester: Manchester University Press, 2000), p. 127.
22. Rosenthal, *Infamous Commerce*, p. 119.
23. As Perry observes in *Novel Relations*, the *Histories of the Penitents'* focus upon the 'spectacle of the deracinated woman, separated from her family of origin, [and] unable to survive alone by waged labour, is an irony of the age of individualism, a necessary corrective to the myth of the socially mobile individual' produced by capitalism (p. 280).
24. *Histories of the Penitents*, p. 8.
25. Ibid., p. 91; pp. 129–30.
26. Ibid., p. 13.
27. Ibid., p. 46.
28. In making this point, there is continuity between *Histories of the Penitents* and the more radical 1790s works of Mary Hays and Mary Wollstonecraft, a point also noted by Binhammer (*The Seduction Narrative*, p. 52). However, in coupling this argument regarding female emotional and economic dependence with the eroticized maternal subjectivity discussed below, *Histories of the Penitents* allows for a kind of female agency that cannot be realized in these later works, as my brief account of Wollstonecraft's *Wrongs of Woman* suggests.
29. The *OED* dates the earliest usage of 'Mother' to signify a brothel-keeper as 1596. In F. Grose, *A Classical Dictionary of the Vulgar Tongue* (London: S. Hooper, 1785), the definition for 'Mother, or the Mother' begins thus: 'a bawd; Mother abbess, the same; Mother Midnight, a midwife'.
30. *Histories of the Penitents*, p. 91.
31. Ibid., p. 98.
32. Fanny is of identical age to her namesake and arrives in London, like Cleland's heroine and Hogarth's Moll Hackabout before her, in a wagon from the north only to be intercepted by a bawd.
33. *Histories of the Penitents*, p. 98.
34. Ibid. p. 102.
35. Ibid., p. 104.
36. J. Panek, 'The Mother as Bawd in *The Revenger's Tragedy* and *A Mad Word, My Masters*', *SEL*, 43:2 (2003), p. 415.
37. R. A. Levin, 'If Women Should Beware Women, Bianca Should Beware Mother', *SEL*, 37 (1997), p. 385.

38. On the effects of capitalism on the family and marriage, see Perry, *Novel Relations*, particularly pp. 129–30 and pp. 222–4.
39. *Histories of the Penitents*, p. 79; p. 135; p. 133; p. 134.
40. L. Zunshine, *Bastards and Foundlings: Illegitimacy in Eighteenth-Century England* (Columbus: Ohio State University Press, 2005), p. 8.
41. *Histories of the Penitents*, p. 167.
42. For a grim twist on this narrative, see *The History of Emma; or, The Victim of Depravity; … To Which Is Added the Life of the Abandoned Kitty Clark* (1800) in which a mother prostitutes herself to feed her starving child but contracts a venereal disease, which she then passes on to the child through breast-milk.
43. *Histories of the Penitents*, p. 42.
44. Perry, *Novel Relations*, p, 257.
45. *Histories of the Penitents*, p. 42; p. 51.
46. Ibid., p. 179.
47. Ibid., p. 181.
48. There is a similar dynamic in M. Madan, *The Magdalen; or Dying Penitent. Exemplified in the Death of F.S., Who Died April, 1763, Aged Twenty-Six Years* (1763). Fanny Sidney falls into poverty, is seduced, falls pregnant and is abandoned by her lover. She tries various employments before turning to prostitution and then seeking admittance into the Magdalen House. Much of the final section of the text is devoted to Fanny's religious reflections prior to her death. Oddly, and in direct contrast to *Histories of the Penitents*, the child is entirely forgotten as the narrative progresses and his fate unknown at its conclusion.
49. Binhammer, *The Seduction Narrative*, p. 68.
50. Ibid., p. 57; p. 194n43.
51. *Histories of the Penitents*, p. 29.
52. Ibid., p. 31.
53. Bowers, *The Politics of Motherhood*, p. 28.
54. *Histories of the Penitents*, p. 171.
55. Binhammer, *The Seduction Narrative*, p. 57.
56. *Histories of the Penitents*, p. 122.
57. Ibid., p. 122; p. 124.
58. Ibid., p. 128.
59. See Bowers, *The Politics of Motherhood*, p. 15.
60. W. Dodd, *A Sermon on St. Luke xix. 10. Preach'd at the Chapel of the Magdalen-House. On Sunday, January 27, 1760. before His Royal Highness Prince Edward* (London: W. Faden, [1760]), p. 12.
61. J. Hanway, *Thoughts on the Plan for a Magdalen-House for Repentant Prostitutes* (London: J. Waugh, 1758), p. 34. On this point see J. Batchelor, '"Industry in Distress": Reconfiguring Labour and Femininity in the Magdalen House', *Eighteenth-Century Life*, 28:1 (2004), pp. 1–20.
62. Bowers, *The Politics of Motherhood*, p. 29.
63. *Histories of the Penitents*, p. 51; p. 182.
64. T. Evans, *'Unfortunate Objects': Lone Mothers in Eighteenth-Century London* (Basingstoke: Palgrave Macmillan, 2005), p. 134.
65. Unfortunately, there is no record of the outcome of Penelope Hones's petition, read on 20 November 1763. It is reprinted in A. Levene (ed.), *Narratives of the Poor in*

Eighteenth-Century Britain. Vol. 3. Initial Responses: The London Foundling Hospital (London: Pickering & Chatto, 2006), p. 185.
66. *Histories of the Penitents*, p. 51; p. 182.
67. R. McClure, *Coram's Children: The London Foundling Hospital in the Eighteenth Century* (New Haven, CT and London: Yale University Press, 1981), p. 140.
68. *Histories of the Penitents*, p. 182.
69. Ibid., p. 3; p. 4.
70. Bowers, *The Politics of Motherhood*, p. 28; p. 4.

12 Bergkvist, 'Making a Living by "Indecency"'

1. Verdict from Christiania tukthusrett, Christiania byfogd, tingbøker (*Christiania House of Correction Court*), Statsarkivet i Oslo, (hereafter Christiania House of Correction Court) 6 January 1796. All quotations from the Norwegian sources are my own, and are supplied in the footnotes: 'de næsten uden Sky have saavel i som udenfor Byen ofte udi skammelig beskienket Tilstand løbet Folk paa Armene, og som saa almindelig bekiendt er, ubluelig have fahlbudne sig'.
2. King Christian V Norwegian Law of 15 April 1687 ('Kong Christian V Norske Lov'), (hereafter NL 1687), Book 6, ch. 13, p. 31. Art. <http://www.hf.uio.no/iakh/forskning/prosjekter/tingbok/kilder/> (accessed 15 April 2010).
3. NL 1687, Book 6, ch. 22.
4. G. E. Benzon 'Historiske Oplysninger om Prostitutionsvæsenet i Christiania', in *Beretning om Folkemængden og Sundhedstilstanden i Christiania i Aaret 1880* (Kristiania: Chr. Schibsteds, 1881), p. 29.
5. For instance A. Schiøtz, 'Prostitusjon og samfunn i 1870- og 1880-åras Kristiania' in J. E.Myhre and S. Østberg (eds), *Mennesker i Kristiania. Sosialhistorisk søkelys på 1800-tallet* (Oslo: Universitetsforlaget, 1979), pp. 71–89.
6. See: the regional 'The House of Correction Act of 2 December 1741' (*'Anordning om Tugthusets Indrettelse i Christiania og de Fattiges Forflegning i Aggershuus Stift'*), at <http://www.hf.uio.no/iakh/forskning/prosjekter/tingbok/kilder/> (accessed 15 April 2010); the national labour legislation 'The Service Act of 9 August 1754' (*'Fr. At alle af Bondestanden i Norge, baade Mands- og Qvinde-Personer, som ei bruge Gaarde eller Husmands-Pladser, Skal være forbundne at fæste sig i aarlig Tieneste, og ei være tilladte at arbeide for Dagløn'*), in J. H. Schou, *Chronologisk Register over de kongelige Forordninger og Aabne Breve, Samt andre Trykte Anordninger som fra Aar 1670 ere udkomne, tilligmed et nøiaktig Udtog af de endnu gjeldende, forsaavidt somme i Almindelighed angaae undersaaterne i Danmark og Norge: forsynet med et alphabetisk Register* (Kiøbenhavn, 1797/1795–1850), pp. 390–7; the regional 'The Servant decree of 26 January 1766' (*'Radstue-Pl. [3 December 1755] Ang. Tienestetyende i Khavn og deres Forhold, samt Omgang imod dem i deres Tieneste; item om Fardag og Opsigelses-Tiden'*), implemented for the cities of Akershus, Norway by amendment decree 26 January 1776, in Schou, J.H. *Chronologisk Register...*, pp. 427–32.
7. Christiania police, minutes (*Christiania politikammer, forhørsprotokoll*), Statsarkivet i Oslo, (hereafter Christiania police, minutes) 9 July 1793, folio page 238A and B.
8. Christiania police, minutes 9 July 1793, f. 238A and B. The original Norwegian quotation is '[Hun] beklaget nu at være paagreben, da hun ikke selv ville være skyld i at hun ingen Tieneste havde bekommet, da hendes moders svaghed udfordrede hendes til-

syn, dog lovede hun, at om hun denne Gang maatte tilgives, hun da aldrig effter skulle befindes i nogen ulovlighed'.
9. Christiania police, minutes 7 November 1793, folio page 256A, B and 257A. The original Norwegian quotation is 'da hun syntes der var slemt at være'.
10. Christiania police, minutes 9 December 1793.
11. Christiania police, minutes 1 March 1794, folio page 272A and B. The original Norwegian quotation is 'hun ikke kunde nægte at hun paa nogen tid har ført et Løsagtig Levnet'.
12. 'The Servant decree of 26 January 1766', §17. The original Norwegian quotation is 'Unge og Friske Qvindfolk, som kan tiene for deres Brød, maae ikke henligge ledige og uden Tieneste, ei heller maae de omgaae og sælge Frugter og deslige. Handler noget Qvindfolk, der er imellem 12 og 40 Aar, imod denne ... da skal hun straffes med nogen Tids Arbeide i Spindehuset.'
13. A. L. Seip, *Sosialhjelpstaten blir til. Norsk sosialpolitikk 1740–1920* (Oslo: Gyldendal norsk forlag, 1984), pp. 48–51.
14. 'A stiftamtmann was the King's appointed legal and administrative representative for a given diocese. 'Letter of Moltke to the Danish authorities (*Det danske kanselliet*)', 4 August 1791, pp. 3 and 4, Riksarkivet, Det danske kanselliet, Skapsaker, Skap 16, pakke 31 'Om Tugt – og Forbedringshuse i Norge' [hereafter Kanselliet].
15. Dunker in A. Daae, *Tugthuset og Arbejdshuse i Kristiania 1733–1814. Særtryk af Nordisk Tidsskrift for Fængselsvæsen og Praktisk Strafferet* (Kjøbenhavn: Nielsen & Lydiche, 1908), p. 154.
16. 'Letter of the commission at Christiania House of Correction (*tukthuskommisjonen*) to the regional authorities (*stiftsdireksjonen*)', 9 November 1791 and 15 February 1792, Kanselliet.
17. Christiania police, minutes 23 November 1795, folio page 330A and 24 November 1795, folio page 330B.
18. The House of Correction Court was an extra-court of Christiania's Magistrate's Court. Christiania House of Correction Court 6 January 1796. The original Norwegian quotation is 'den aller usømmeligste og forargeligste Natteløben paa Gaderne'.
19. Christiania House of Correction, prisoners (*Christiania tukthus, fanger, Rekke II, Fangeprotokoll 3*) 1775–1809, Statsarkivet i Oslo, (hereafter Christiania House of Correction, prisoners) 17.01.1796.
20. The original Norwegian quotation is 'meenige Mand ved vitterlig, hvorledes de, næsten vær Aften og Nat lader sig finde paa Gaderne og andre mistænkelige Stæder til sto forargelse og ungdommens forførelse'.
21. 'om alt hendes mistænkelige Væsen skulle nøyagtig beskrives, ville det medtage mange Ark'.
22. Christiania House of Correction Court 6 January 1796. The original Norwegian quotation is 'de næsten uden Sky have saavel i som udenfor Byen ofte udi skammelig beskienket Tilstand løbet Folk paa Armene, og som saa almindelig bekiendt er, ubluelig have fahlbudne sig'.
23. The original Norwegian quotation is 'den fra mange Aar tilbage berygtede Karen Sollie hvilken saa mange Gange har været anklaget og nogle Gange efter Dom for baade Ruffe- og Tyverier er bleven afstraffet'.
24. Christiania House of Correction, prisoners 19 March 1781.
25. The original quotation in Norwegian is '[en] saadan Mester i at nægte og skiule sig'.
26. The original quotation in Norwegian is '[et] saadant forargelig Væsen over alle Ærbarheds Grændser'.

27. Christiania House of Correction, prisoners (*Christiania tukthus Fanger, Fanger, Rekke VI, Diverse fangeprotokoller 3*) 1796–1803, Statsarkivet i Oslo, 25 July 1797.
28. R. Jütte, *Poverty and Deviance in Early Modern Europe* (Cambridge: Cambridge University Press, 2001), pp. 156–7.
29. Christiania House of Correction Court 6 January 1796. The original quotation in Norwegian is '[Naar de Vidnerne, haver tiltalt dem for] saadan uanstændig omløben og Vandel, have de svart igien uforskammede Ord, og ofte været udsadt for overfald af de Mands-Personer, som de disse have haft i Følge med sig og dels locket til sig'.
30. Christiania police, minutes 24 July 1797, ff. 391B, 392A and B.
31. The original quotation in Norwegian is 'de tilsade at de ikke i Lang Tid har havt stadig Tieneste, men ellers ernærer sig som de kan'.
32. Christiania police, minutes 25 July 1797, f. 393A and B. Christiania House of Correction, prisoners 25 July 1797. Sentenced according the house of Correction Act, ch. 3, 14 §. The original quotation in Norwegian is 'Løsgiengersker og dessuden ført et udsvævende Liv, hvortil verken Alderdom eller Svaghed skulle behøve at drive dem'.
33. The original quotation in Norwegian is 'Intet er meer uundskyldeligt, end at et ungt, arbeidsført Menneske overlader sig til Dovenskab og Løsgiengerie og intet mere vist, end at Følgerne af en saadan Vandel genemlig blive et Liderligt Levnet, som til Slutning paadrager det Almindelige Byrder'.
34. Christiania police, minutes 30 September 1799, folio page 112A. The arrests were ordered by the regional authorities.
35. 'Alle 3 vare Eenige i at denne Elen Trulsdatter er det mest Liderligst Qvinde-Menniske som kan gives, og de ønskede alle til beste for Byen, at hun for Livs Tiid, kunde blive hensadt paa Tugthuuset'.
36. Christiania police, minutes 30 September 1799, folio page 112B and 113A.
37. Christiania House of Correction, prisoners 2 October 1799.
38. Schiøtz, 'Prostitusjon og samfunn i 1870– og 1880–åras Kristiania', p. 72.
39. Christiania House of Correction Court 29 August 1799.
40. Christiania House of Correction, prisoners 9 February 1798.
41. Christiania House of Correction Court 29 August 1799. The original quotation in Norwegian is 'begge disse Qvindemennesker … ere bekiendte Nat-Frøkener, de som offteste ved Nattetide lade sig finde udenfor Byen, hvor de efter Røgte endog skal angribe Folck'.
42. The original Norwegian term is 'fræk løsagtighed'.
43. Hufton in Jütte, *Poverty and Deviance in Early Modern Europe*, p. 157.
44. Schiøtz, 'Prostitusjon og samfunn i 1870– og 1880–åras Kristiania', p. 87.

13 Trumbach, 'Male Prostitution and the Emergence of the Modern Sexual System'

1. A. Corbin, *Women for Hire: Prostitution and Sexuality in France after 1850* (Cambridge, MA: Harvard University Press, 1990; French ed. 1978); R. Trumbach, *Sex and the Gender Revolution. Volume 1: Heterosexuality and the Third Gender in Enlightenment London* (Chicago: University of Chicago Press, 1998); H. M. Hyde, *The Cleveland Street Scandal* (New York: Coward, McCann & Geoghegan, 1976); C. Simpson, L. Chester and D. Leitch, *The Cleveland Street Affair* (Boston: Little Brown, 1976); J. Weeks, 'Inverts, Perverts, and Mary-Annes: Male Prostitution and the Regulation of Homosexuality in England in the Nineteenth and Early Twentieth Centuries', *Against Nature* (London: Rivers Oram, 1992; first in *The Journal of Homosexuality*, VI, 1980/81); R. Carrasco, 'Lazarillo on a Street Corner: What the Picaresque Novel did not Say about Fallen Boys',

in A. Saint-Saëns (ed.) *Sex and Love in Golden Age Spain* (New Orleans, LA: University Press of the South, 1996); B. Reay, *New York Hustlers: Masculinity and Sex in Modern America* (Manchester: Manchester University Press, 2010).

2. R. Trumbach, 'Renaissance Sodomy 1500–1700', 'Modern Sodomy: The Origins of Homosexuality, 1700–1800', in M. Cook (ed.), *A Gay History of Britain* (Oxford: Greenwood Press, 2007), pp. 45–75; pp. 77–105. I cite and briefly discuss the literature on eighteenth-century England, France and the Dutch Republic in: R. Trumbach, 'The Heterosexual Male in Eighteenth-Century London and His Queer Interactions', in K. O'Donnell and M. O'Rourke (eds), *Love, Sex, Intimacy and Friendship between Men 1550–1800* (New York: Palgrave MacMillan, 2003), pp. 99–127 (pp. 122–5).

3. On changes to the onset of puberty see S. F. Daw, 'Age of Boys' Puberty in Leipzig, 1727–49, as Indicated by Voice Breaking in J. S. Bach's Choir Members', *Human Biology*, 42 (1970), pp. 87–9; and the data on 250 boys who sang in the Magdalen College, Oxford choir in the eighteenth century: J. R. Bloxam, *A Register of... Magdalen College ... Vol. 1, The Choristers* (Oxford: William Graham, 1853).

4. M. Rocke, *Forbidden Friendships: Homosexuality and Male Culture in Renaissance Florence* (New York: Oxford University Press, 1996), pp. 37–9, 106–7, 164–5, 175–6; G. Ruggiero, *The Boundaries of Eros: Sex Crime and Sexuality in Renaissance Venice* (New York: Oxford University Press, 1985), p. 136; M. Milani, *Piccole storie di stroggoneria nella Venezia del'500* (Verona: Essedue, 1989), pp. 179–192; Carrasco, 'Lazarillio'; Cristian Berco, *Sexual Hierarchies, Public Status: Men, Sodomy and Society in Spain's Golden Age* (Toronto: University of Toronto Press, 2007), p. 28; L. Mott, 'Pagode portugûes: a subcultura gay em Portugal nos tempos inquisitorais', *Ciência e Cultura*, 40 (1988), pp. 120–139; D. Higgs, 'Lisbon', in D. Higgs (ed.), *Queer Sites: Gay Urban Histories since 1600* (New York: Routledge, 1999); D. Higgs, 'Tales of Two Carmelites: inquisitorial narratives from Portugal and Brazil', in P. Sigal (ed.), *Infamous Desire: Male Homosexuality in Colonial Latin America* (Chicago: University of Chicago Press, 2003); D. Higgs, 'The Historiography of Male-Male Love in Portugal, 1550-1800', in K. O'Donnell and M. O'Rourke (eds), *Queer Masculinities: Siting Same-Sex Desire in the Early Modern World* (New York: Palgrave MacMillan, 2006).

5. Corporation of London Record Office: Sessions Papers 1687, examinations of Benjamin Bourne and John Hoyle, 25 January; T. Harris, ed. *The Entring Book of Roger Morrice 1677–1691, Vol. III The Reign of James II, 1685--1687* (Woodbridge, Suffolk: Boydell Press, 2007), pp. 531, 351–2, 381; G. M. Crump (ed.), *Poems on Affairs of State, Volume 4: 1685-1688* (New Haven: Yale University Press, 1968), pp. 213–14.

6. A. Behn, *Works*, ed. M. Summers (New York: Phaeton Press, 1967, repr. of 1915), vol. 6, pp. 160–2; *Familiar Letters of Love and Gallantry*, 2 vols (London, 1718), vol. 1, pp. 38–9; A. Behn, 'The Town Fop' and 'The Amorous Prince', in *Works*, vol. 3, p. 64; vol. 4, pp. 186, 197, 210–11; Whitelocke Bulstrode: Harry Ransom Research Center, University of Texas, Austin: Pforz, Ms, 2k, bv7, p. [93]: Summers had printed this, *Works*, vol. 1, p. xxxvi, but did not note that Whitelocke had written 'Bug' and crossed it out to write 'Sodomite'; Jesus and St John: Trumbach, 'Renaissance Sodomy', pp. 59, 72–3. Secondary Literature: P. A. Hopkins, 'Aphra Behn and John Hoyle: A Contemporary Mention and Sir Charles Sedley's Poem on his Death', *Notes and Queries*, 41:2 (1994), pp. 176–185; J. Todd, *The Secret Life of Aphra Behn* (New Brunswick: Rutgers University Press, 1997); M. Duffy, *The Passionate Shepherdess* (London: Jonathan Cape, 1977), p. 132: Hoyle misbehaves in church; A. Goreau, *Reconstructing Aphra* (New York: Dial Press, 1980); G. Woodcock, *The Incomparable Aphra* (London: T. V. Boardman, 1948). For Woodcock, Hoyle is a homosexual, but in the more recent works, he becomes a bisexual libertine. Hopkins is the best guide to the legal sources.

7. For a general discussion of blackmail: R. Trumbach, 'Blackmail for Sodomy in Eighteenth-Century London', *Historical Reflections*, 33 (2007), pp. 23–39; Antony Simpson, 'Blackmail as a Crime of Sexual Indiscretion in Eighteenth-Century England', in L. A. Knafla (ed.), *Crime, Gender, and Sexuality in Criminal Prosecutions* (Westport, CT: Greenwood, 2002); A. McLaren, *Sexual Blackmail* (Cambridge, MA: Harvard University Press, 2002). McLaren deals mainly with the nineteenth and twentieth centuries. He shows that men were at first blackmailed for sodomy and only later for breaking their marriage vows. This demonstrates that, under the new sexual system, it was initially more important not to be a sodomite than it was to desire women.
8. G. Skelthorp, alias Skulthorp, *Proceedings ... at the Old Bailey*, 2 March 1709; *Ordinary of Newgate's Account*, March 1709; both reprinted in *The Bloody Register*, 4 vols (London: printed for E. and M. Viney, 1764), vol. 1, 136–9; E. Ward, *The Secret History of Clubs* (London: printed, and sold by the booksellers, 1709); *A Full Account of the Discovery and Apprehending of a Notorious Gang of Sodomites in St James's* (London: printed for T. Bland near Fleetstreet, 1709).
9. *Proceedings ... at the Old Bailey*, 4 December 1776; houses in Nag's Head Court: London Metropolitan Archive: MJ/SR/3271, bond of John Shade, Matthew Sandsteen, John Gates, 27 July 1777; see also, R. Trumbach, *Sex the Gender Revolution Volume 1*, pp. 129–130. At his execution Burrows asserted his innocence again and threw a paper into the crowd on which he had written his case. (*Public Advertiser*, 30 January 1777.) On February 6, the *Morning Chronicle* published a letter asking why Brooks (with whom Burrows supposedly had had sex) had not been found, nor any of the fourteen other men.
10. *Proceedings... at the Old Bailey*, no. 4, part 2 (1794): pp. 783–8, #370.
11. J. M. Beattie, 'Charles Hitchen', *Oxford Dictionary of National Biography*; G. Howson, *Thief-Taker General: The Rise and Fall of Jonathan Wild* (New York: St Martin's Press, 1970); [Jonathan Wild], *An Answer to a Late Insolent Libel* (London: printed for Tho. Warner, at the Black-Boy in Paternoster-Row, 1718), pp. 30–41 (recte 33).
12. Charles Hitchen, *Proceedings... at the Old Bailey*, 12 April 1727; also, *Select Trials at the ... Old Bailey*, 4 vols (London: 1742), vol. 3, pp. 74–5; *Daily Post* (15 April 1727); *Parker's Penny Post* (17 April): identify Williamson as drummer; Hitchens's sentences: *Weekly Journal* (22 April); his treatment in pillory: *Evening Post* (29 April). For drummers: S. M. Baule, 'Drummers in the British army during the American Revolution', *Journal of the Society for Army Historical Research*, 86 (2008), pp. 20–3; J. U. Rees, '"The Music of the Army": An Abbreviated Study of the Ages of Musicians in the Continental Army', *The Brigade Dispatch*, 24 (1993), pp. 2–8; 25 (1994), pp. 2–12.
13. Newspaper clippings, July 20, August 12, 1816, at the beginning [Robert Holloway], *The Phoenix of Sodom, or the Vere Street Coterie* (London: 1813), p. 11 (prostitutes on premises), reprinted in R. Trumbach (ed.), *Sodomy Trials* (New York: Garland, 1986).
14. *London Evening Post* (5 December 1776).
15. *Proceedings ... at the Old Bailey*, no. 6, part 1 (1772), pp. 315–23. R. Norton, *Mother Clap's Molly House: The Gay Subculture in England, 1700-1830*, 2nd edn (Stroud, Gloucestershire: Chalford Press, 2006) has a long discussion of the newspaper controversy.
16. *London Evening Post* (1 June 1762).
17. *Middlesex Journal or Universal Evening Post* (3 November 1772).
18. *Gazetteer and New Daily Advertiser* (16 July 1779).

19. *Proceedings ... at the Old Bailey*: Thomas Wright, 20 April 1726, George Kedger, alias Kegar, alias Kedger, 20 April, George Whytle, alias Whittle, 20 April. The versions in *Select Trials at the Sessions in the Old Bailey*, 4 vols (London, 1742), vol. 2, pp. 366–70, reprinted in 2 vols, ed. R. Trumbach (New York: Garland Press, 1985), are longer but both sets are probably abbreviations or rearrangements of a still longer short-hand version. For female prostitution and bawds, see Trumbach, *Sex and the Gender Revolution*.
20. *Proceedings ... at Old Bailey*, 6 September 1732, trial 85, John Ashford; *Daily Journal* (28 July, 2 August, 7 September, 8 September, 11 September 1732).
21. *Select Trials*, vol. 2, p. 368, vol. 3, p. 36 and pp. 362–64; *Daily Post* (24 October 1728); *Country Journal* (25 October 1735); Corporation of London Record Office: Session Roll, April 1726, Recognizance 19; *Read's Weekly Journal* (25 October 1735); *London Daily Post* (3 September 1735).
22. *London Evening Post* (24 September 1778), *General Advertiser* (28 September, same story); John Dunton, *Atheanism*, 2 vols (London, 1710), vol. 2, pp. 93–9; Wild, *An Answer*, pp. 30–1.
23. *Daily Advertiser* (15 September 1731); *Read's Weekly Journal* (4 January 1752).
24. *A Genuine Narrative of all the street robberies... by James Dalton* (London, 1728), pp. 31–43; *London Chronicle* (4–6 January 1757): Lord Tankerville; *London Chronicle* (29 April – 1 May, 6–8 May 1779): Charles Vaughan.
25. John Gill: *London Evening Post* (17–19 July 1764); two transvestites: *London Chronicle* (11–13 September 1764).
26. *Love-Letters between a certain late nobleman and the famous Mr Wilson* (London, [1723]); there is a modern edition (with an uncertain text), ed. Michael S. Kimmel (New York: Haworth Press, 1990), with essays by G. S. Rousseau, D. F. Greenberg, R. Trumbach; T. Salmon, *The Chronological Historian* (London, 1723), pp. 67, 161, 380; Robert Wodrow, *Analecta* (Edinburgh: The Maitland Club), vol. 3, p. 443.
27. Historical Manuscripts Commission: Portland Manuscripts, vol. 4, p. 168; Aubrey Newman, *The Stanhopes of Chevening* (London: Macmillan, 1969), p. 27; J. Ingamells (ed.), *A Dictionary of British and Irish Travellers in Italy, 1701–1800* (New Haven, CT: Yale University Press, 1997), p. 538; A. Cunningham, *The History of Great Britain*, 2 vols (London, 1787), vol. 2, p. 306; I. F. Burton and A. N. Newman, 'Sir John Cope: promotion in the eighteenth-century army', *English Historical Review*, 78 (1963), pp. 655–68.
28. W. S. Lewis (ed.), *Yale Edition of Horace Walpole's Correspondence* (New Haven, CT: Yale University Press, 1960), vol. 20, pp. 315–16; *An Address from the Ladies of the Provinces of Munster and Leinster* (London, 1754), pp. 13-15; Walpole, *Memoirs of the Reign of King George III*, ed. D. Jarrett, 4 vols (New Haven, CT: Yale University Press, 2000), vol. 2, 73. The 'natical foramen' is a periphrasis for arse (natical) hole (foramen), the text explaining that arseholes are tighter than vaginas and thereby give more pleasure.

INDEX

actress, 87–93
Adultery Act (1650), 8
Andrew, Donna, 144
Argenson, Marc René d', 68
Armstrong, Nancy, 11
Ashford, John, 196

Baculard d'Arnaud, François-Thomas-Marie de, 87–98
Baret, Paul, 123
Barker-Benfield, G. J., 11
Barrell, John, 104
Bastille, Archives de la, 33, 88
Bataille, Gaillard de la, 90
Batchelor, Jenny, 142, 145–7, 151
bawdy house, *see* brothel
Bedoy, Charles Estienne, 37
Behn, Aphra, 46, 49–58, 187
Belle Allemande ou les galanteries de Thérèse, La (1745),
Benabou, Erica-Marie, 2, 5, 12, 18–19
Berkeley, Henrietta, 54
Berryer de Ravenoville, René, 33, 35, 43
Binhammer, Katharine, 146–7, 157, 164–5
Boltanski, Luc, 127
Bon Pasteur, Montpellier, 13
bookseller, low moral status of, 47, 97, 196
Boswell, James, 4
Bowers, Toni, 165, 168
Broome, J.H., 115
brothel, 2, 3, 9, 27, 33–43, 94–5, 98, 190, *see also* molly houses
Butts, Charles, 191
Byrd, William, 4

Calendar of State Papers, Domestic, 45, 51, 55
Campra, André, 94
Capon, Gaston, 33
Carrasco, Rafael, 185
Carter, Angela, 129
Carter, Sophie, 99
Charles II, of England, Scotland and Ireland, 45
Charteris, Francis, 103–4, 110, 113
Chevrier, François-Antoine, 90, 92
Chiapello, Eve, 127
Christiana, Norway, 16, 171–84
Cleland, John, 10, 104
Constantinople, 59
Coram, Thomas, 113
Corbin, Alain, 12, 185
Correspondance de Madame Gourdan (1783), 93
Cortey, Mathilde, 4
Courtesan, *see* prostitution
Curtis, William, 196
Cushing Library, Texas, 88

Dabhoiwala, Faramerz, 9
Dalton, John, 104
Dalton, James, 198–9
Darnton, Robert, 88
Dawson, Robert, 88
Defoe, Daniel, 4, 100, 104, 158, 160, 167
Dégoûts du plaisir, Les (1752),
Delisle de Sales, Jean-Baptiste-Claude, 94
Demoiselles de Paris, Les, 19
Diderot, Denis, 88–9, 93
Dingley, Robert, 146, 148–51, 154, 167–8
Dodd, William, 1, 141, 166

Dossemont, Marie-Madeleine, 4, 33–43
Dryden, John, 52–3
Duffy, Maureen, 55

Égarements de Julie, Les (1755)
Encyclopédie, 19
Etrennes aux grisettes (*Presents to Girls of Easy Virtue*, 1790), 87, 91
Evelyn, John, 53

Ferriol, Charles de, 59–60, 63
Fielding, Henry, 102, 115–26
Fielding, John, 148
Fougeret de Monbron, Louis-Charles, 30, 115–26

Gay, John, 100, 109
George II, of England, Ireland and Scotland, 71
Gould, Philip, 10
Goldsmith, Elizabeth, 48–9
Gonson, John, 110
Greenfield, Susan, 158
Grosley, Pierre Jean, 1
Gwyn, Nell, 45

Habermas, Jürgen, 88
Hallett, Mark, 99–100, 110
Hanway, Jonas, 141, 145, 148–51, 154
Harnoncourt de Morsan, Joseph-Marie-Anne Durey d', 97–8
Harris's List of Covent-Garden Ladies, 19
Haws, Sukey, 198–9
Hays, Mary, 144, 152, 155
Henderson, Tony, 2
Hiatt, Megan, 142
Histories of Some of the Penitents in the Magdalen House (1759), 144, 146–55, 159–69
Hitchcock, Tim, 14
Hitchen, Charles, 192–3
Hogarth, William, 15, 99–113, 162
Hoyle, John, 187
Hufton, Olwyn, 182–3
Hume, David, 147, 149, 150

Istanbul, *see* Constantinople
Johnson, Samuel, 6
Jones, Colin, 12

Jones, Captain Robert, 193–4
Jones, Vivien, 4, 107, 145, 146, 160
Jones, Thomas, 197–8
Jütte, Robert, 179

Keroualle, Louise, Duchess of Portsmouth, 45, 51
Killigrew, Thomas, 53
Koehler, Martha, 159

La Place, Pierre-Antoine de, 116–26
Lennox, Charlotte, 153
Lesage, Alain-René, 68–9
Levin, Richard, 163
libertinism (*libertinage*), 10, 127–39
Liste complète des plus belles femmes publiques et des plus saines du Palais de Paris (1790), 91
Loame, Anthony, 190–1
London, 1–3, 8, 11, 15–16, 45–53, 71, 100–13, 141–55
Louis XIV of France, 59, 63–4
Love-Letters between a Certain Late Nobleman and the Famous Mr Wilson (1723), 200

McClure, Ruth, 167–8
Magdalen Hospital, London, 11–15, 141–55, 166–7
Mandeville, Bernard, 10, 105–9
Maza, Sarah, 17
Marseille, 59
    Marseille Refuge, 60, 62–4
Massie, Joseph, 148
Maurepas, Jean Frédéric Phélypeaux de, 96
Mazarin, Hortense Mancini, Duchess de, 14–15, 45–58
Mercier, Louis-Sébastien, 1, 7, 15, 17–32, 88, 92
Michel, Pierre-Victor, 59–62, 66–9
Moltke, Frederik, 176
mollies, 188–200
molly houses, 195–7
Montmort, Jean-Louis Habert de Fargis de, 65
Montpellier, 12
More, Hannah, 143, 147
Mullan, John, 149
Mylne, Vivienne, 123

Needham, Elizabeth 'Mother', 103–4, 109
Nelson, Sarah, 48–9
Newton, Thomas, 195–7
Norberg, Kathryn, 3, 5, 13, 88, 128–9, 132
Norway, 171–83
Nouvelle liste des jolies femmes de Paris (1808), 91, 94
Nussbaum, Felicity, 158, 168
Nussbaum, Martha, 5

Oslo, *see* Christiana

Panck, Jennifer, 163
Paris, France, 1–2, 4, 12–13, 19, 20–1, 33–43, 87–98
Paulson, Ronald, 99
Perry, Ruth, 157
Persia, 59–70
Petit-fils d'Hercule, Le (*Hercules's Grandson*, 1784), 91–2
Petit, Marie, 14, 59–70
Phillips, Theresa Constantia, 145
Pidansat de Mairobert, Mathieu-François, 92
Pompadour, Madame, 35
Pontchartrain, Jérôme, 60, 63–9
Porter, Roy, 144–5, 149
poverty, 2, 5, 11–15, 21, 176, 182–3
Primer, Irwin, 107–8
prostitution
  courtesan, 14, 45, 72–5, 81–3
  prosecution, 9, 106, 172–3
  definitions, 2–8, 17–32, 173
  historiography, 11–13, 171–2
  madam, 33–43, 71, 103–4, 109, 162
  male, 185–201
  stigma of, 5–8, 16, 121, 138, 183
  street walkers, 2, 10, 1, 12, 16, 18, 21, 24, 27, 46, 72, 107–8, 113, 171–4, 178, 181
  whore, 71–2, 76–77
  see also actress, brothel, libertinism, mollies, soldiers, transvestites
Prydden, Sarah, *see* Sally Salisbury
publisher, *see* bookseller

Reay, Barry, 185
Reformation of Manners, Society for the, 7–10, 106–8

Rétif de la Bretonne, Nicolas-Edme, 7, 15, 17–32, 94
Rochester, John Wilmot, Earl of, 9, 50
Rosenthal, Laura, 5, 11, 157
Rousseau, Jean-Jacques, 30, 89, 147, 151, 153

Sacheverell, Henry, 71, 109
Sade, Donatien Alphonse François, Marquis de, 14, 127–39
Salisbury, Sally, 4, 14, 71–85
Salmon, Thomas, 200
Sandmann, Manfred, 115–16
sex-worker, 5–6
Shoemaker, Robert, 8
Smith, Adam, 5, 8, 142
Skelthorp, George, 188–90
sodomy, 16, 89, 185–201
soldiers, 188–93
Solkin, David, 100, 104
Speck, W. A., 104, 107
Spectator, The, 11, 102–3
Sterne, Laurence, 102, 108
Stone, George, 201

Taylor, James, 144–5
Thornton, John and Henry, 147
Todd, Janet, 49–50
Turner, James Grantham, 10, 72
transvestites, 197–200
Trulsdatter, Elen and Anne, 171–84
Trumbach, Randolph, 11, 15, 185

Uglow, Jenny, 104

vagrancy, 2, 12, 172–3
Van Crugten-André, Valérie, 5
Vertue, George, 103, 109–10
Villiers, Barbara, Countess of Castlemaine, 45
Voet, Jacob-Ferdinand, 52
Voltaire, François-Marie Arouet *dit*, 15, 87, 115–26

Wald Lasowski, Patrick, 5, 87, 89
Walker, Charles, 72–5, 81–5
Waller, Edmund, 51–2
Weeks, Jeffrey, 185
Welch, Saunders, 148–9

White, Thomas, 193
whore, *see* prostitution
Wisebourn, Mother, 71, 78
Wollstonecraft, Mary, 7, 144, 152, 155, 158

Wynne, Sonya, 46

Zunshine, Lisa, 163

CPSIA information can be obtained
at www.ICGtesting.com
Printed in the USA
BVHW072110071218
535054BV00010B/279/P